Florida A&M University, Tallahassee
Florida Atlantic University, Boca Raton
Florida Gulf Coast University, Ft. Myers
Florida International University, Miami
Florida State University, Tallahassee
University of Central Florida, Orlando
University of Florida, Gainesville
University of North Florida, Jacksonville
University of South Florida, Tampa
University of West Florida, Pensacola

Gaitanismo, Left Liberalism, and Popular Mobilization in Colombia

W. John Green

University Press of Florida

Gainesville/Tallahassee/Tampa/Boca Raton

Pensacola/Orlando/Miami/Jacksonville/Ft. Myers

First cloth printing, 2003
First paperback printing, 2004

Library of Congress Cataloging-in-Publication Data
Green, W. John, 1963–
Gaitanismo, left liberalism, and popular mobilization in Colombia / W. John Green.
p. cm.
Includes bibliographical references and index.
ISBN 0-8130-2598-2 (cloth); ISBN 0-8130-2811-6 (pbk.)
1. Colombia—Politics and government—1930–1946. 2. Colombia—Politics and
government—1946–1974. 3. Populism—Colombia. 4. Liberalism—Colombia.
5. Gaitán, Jorge Eliécer, 1898?–1948. I. Title.
F2277 .G74 2003
986.106'31—dc21   2002035275

The University Press of Florida is the scholarly publishing agency for the State
University System of Florida, comprising Florida A&M University, Florida Atlantic
University, Florida Gulf Coast University, Florida International University, Florida
State University, University of Central Florida, University of Florida, University
of North Florida, University of South Florida, and University of West Florida.

University Press of Florida
15 Northwest 15th Street
Gainesville, FL 32611-2079
http://www.upf.com

For Jasper and Pieter
(who have their own notions of agency and resistance)

Contents

List of Illustrations   ix

Preface   xi

Introduction: Populism, Popular Agency, Hegemony, and Gaitanismo   1

1. Popular Mobilization and the Left-Liberal Tradition in Colombia   14

2. Genesis of a Left-Liberal *Caudillo*   46

3. Early Mobilizations: Gaitán, the Liberal Party, and UNIR, 1928–1935   65

4. The Lopista Interlude: *Revolución en Marcha*, Pause, and Crisis, 1934–1946   85

5. The *Pueblo*: Gender, Race, and Class in the Liberal Republic, 1930–1946   111

6. The Moral and Democratic Challenge: Oligarchic Political Practice and Gaitanismo, 1944–1946   159

7. Collective Vibrations: The Ideologies of Gaitanismo   203

8. The Dilemmas of Liberal Integration in the Twilight of Politics, 1946–1948   233

Epilogue and Conclusion: Gaitanismo, *la Violencia*, and Colombia's Enduring Predicament   260

Notes   271

Bibliography   331

Index   349

Illustrations

Figures

1. Rafael Uribe Uribe   144
2. Left-Liberal popular mobilization, armed and electoral, in the nineteenth and twentieth centuries, as seen from late 1946   144
3. Emblem of UNIR   145
4. Alfonso López Pumarejo   145
5. Women breaking their chains and voting   146
6. Demonstrating the obvious race and class overtones of the old Liberal/Conservative divide in 1947, the parties face off as boxers   146
7. Carlos Lozano y Lozano, Alfonso López Pumarejo, and Gabriel Turbay   147
8. Gaitanista rally in the Plaza de Bolívar   148
9. Gaitán broadcasting one of his "Viernes Culturales"   149
10. The famous image of a defiant Gaitán on a campaign poster   149
11. Calle 12, Bogotá, November 12, 1945   150
12. Gaitán with Rafael Uribe Uribe and Benjamin Herrera   151
13. Gaitán arriving in Barranquilla   151
14. Gaitanista support in Barranquilla   152
15. Procession of Mariano Ospina Pérez, August 7, 1946   152
16. Cocktail party for Gaitán at El Embajador, May 7, 1947   153
17. Alberto Lleras Camargo in the Senate, October 22, 1946   153
18. Political cartoon depicting the oligarchic nature of elections as seen by the Liberal pueblo   154
19. Gaitán, Laureano Gómez, and Roberto Urdaneta   154
20. The Manifestación del Silencio in the Plaza de Bolívar, Bogotá, February 7, 1948   155
21. Plinio Mendoza Neira, Roberto García Peña, and Gaitán   156
22. Gaitanistas in the Carrera Séptima, Bogotá   156
23. Pedro Eliseo Cruz holds the head of Gaitán after his death   157

24. Gaitanistas, April 9, 1948   157
25. Darío Echandía, Carlos Lleras Restrepo, Víctor J. Merchán, Alfonso Araújo, Jaime Posada, and other Gaitanistas   158
26. Memorial service for Jorge Eliécer Gaitán, April 20, 1948   158

Maps

Colombia, ca. 1940   xv
Colombia, ca. 1940, with inset details   xvi

Preface

For the last decade or so, I have felt as though I were trailing King Pellinore's "Questing Beast" from T. H. White's *The Once and Future King*. It had the head of a serpent, body of a leopard, haunches of a lion, feet of a red deer buck, and made a noise in its belly like sixty hounds in the noisy and chaotic riot of chase. Gaitanismo proved to be no less intriguing a creature.

Thanks to a Fulbright Fellowship, the hunt began in the archive of the Instituto Colombiano de la Participación "Jorge Eliécer Gaitán" (then called the Centro Gaitán) in late July of 1991. There I came to know the Gaitanistas through their massive correspondence with the *caudillo*. I discovered who many of them were, and learned of their hopes, desires, activities, and demands, as well as their perspective on Colombia's history of armed and political struggle. In the process, I also had the opportunity to speak with several individuals who, after more than forty years, still proudly called themselves "Gaitanista." From there I went to the *hemeroteca* of the Biblioteca Nacional in Bogotá and immersed myself in the press of the period (especially the regional and local press, closer to the ground, where the popular movement played out), while periodically spending long sessions in the Archivo Presidencial of Colombia. I also made significant forays in the archives of the Fundación Patrimonio Fílmico Colombiano, the Centro de Investigación y Educación Popular, and the Biblioteca Luis-Angel Arango, all in Bogotá, the Archivo Histórico of Cartagena, the Biblioteca Departamental of Atlántico in Barranquilla, and the National Archives of the United States. This phase of the pursuit yielded a doctoral dissertation that focused on Gaitanismo on the Atlantic coast and along the Magdalena River.

I returned to my old haunts in 1994 while teaching a semester at the Universidad Nacional, and again in 1996 thanks to a grant from the American Philosophical Society, with the goal of expanding the study back in time and more broadly around the country. I followed the movement out of the northern coast and lower Magdalena River valley into other left-Liberal regions. Gaitanismo ranged throughout the nation, nourished on ideological and social flora firmly planted in Colombia's nineteenth century. I felt, therefore, that the movement deserved the broadest treatment I could give it. Though this bucked the trend toward evermore fine-grained microstudies, it was where the character of the documents took me. To continue to focus exclusively on the northern coast would have meant ignoring a large portion of the remarkable material available.

Of course, I was never really alone in this quest. I was aided and abetted by a host of individuals too numerous to name entirely. I owe a tremendous debt to Aline Helg and Alan Knight, who co-supervised the dissertation. Alan originally encouraged me to pursue the topic of Gaitanismo. He also remained with the project despite the rigors of long-distance supervising and provided invaluable criticism and support. Aline's intimate knowledge of Colombian history and close reading of each draft kept my writing and reasoning focused. And her pointed commentary on both form and content pushed my analysis much further along than I would have been able to propel it by myself. I am also grateful to the other members of my committee, Carolyn Boyd, Jonathan Brown, Henry Dietz, and Richard Graham. Their encouragement along the way ensured that I would finish the dissertation in good time, and their comments upon its completion helped me find my way in the thickets of postdoctoral research.

My debts in Colombia are, if possible, even more profound. Gloria Gaitán facilitated my search in various ways, while members of the Instituto's staff, especially Teresa Galinda Lozano and Maria Ester Rodríguez made sure that I had the widest possible access to its resources. The same thanks are due to the staffs of the Biblioteca Nacional and Archivo Presidencial, places where I spent many a pleasant day. Under the hospitable roof of Hilda Aguilera de Piedrahita, Orlando Fals Borda graciously suggested avenues of research, while Jorge Orlando Melo and Daniel Gacia Peña wrote letters in support of the project. The officers and staff of the Comisión Fulbright, especially Consuelo Valdivieso, Maria Isabel Mendoza, and its director, Agustín Lombana, made my research time a joy to remember, as they have for scores of Colombianistas before and after me. A good number of Colombian scholars suffered my gringo impertinence and gave me essential support and advice, including Guiomar Dueñas, Eduardo Sáenz Rovner, José Antonio Amaya, Ernesto Ramírez P., Mauricio Archila (who allowed unselfish access to his interviews with Colombian workers), Gonzalo Sánchez, Medófilo Medina, César Ayala Diago, Claudia Steiner, Mario Hernández, and Abel Ricardo López. I am also quite thankful that Guillermo González, director of the revista *Número*, scoured the photographic archive of his father Sady González for excellent images of Gaitán and the Gaitanistas. And finally, I owe a very special debt to the familia Segovia, who first introduced a wayward high-school exchange student to Colombia, and who still make him feel like a member of their family.

Along the way from dissertation to book I presented various aspects of the overall project at many different conferences, and myriad comments (and criticisms) found their way into my work, where I can shamelessly take credit for the improvements they generated. In particular I must thank Keith Haynes, Joan Supplee, Michael Conniff, Eduardo Posada-Carbó, David Sowell, Catherine LeGrand, Richard Sharpless, Malcolm Deas, Thomas Klubock, Andy Daitsman, Francisco Iturraspe, Leon Fink, Anne Farnsworth-Alvear, Charles Bergquist, John Tutino, Jim Riley, Barbara Tenenbaum, Vince Peloso, and Barbara Weinstein for giving feedback or commenting on papers I gave.

I have also benefited from conversations with and critiques by Gary Long, Thomas Fischer, and Andy Boeger that began in the early stages of my research and have continued on to the present. In his seminar on regional ethnicity, Greg Knapp opened my eyes to the geography of race in many useful ways. Doug Sofer kindly shared his research on the 9th of April. At various points I was assisted by Michael Jiménez and J. Cordell Robinson, and they are sadly missed. Roxann Prazniak and Arif Dirlik were liberal enough with their time to read and express support for a work outside their normal area of investigations. Thanks to Karen Racine and Ingrid Fey, I looked a little closer at Gaitán's trek to Italy. While teaching at Virginia Tech, I could count on Linda Arnold's enthusiasm, her profound knowledge of the historiography, and her unflinching and direct analyses, as well as John Boyer's conspicuous cartographic abilities. Linda read an earlier version of the manuscript and suggested (demanded) changes that were decisive improvements. John created two very useful maps that demonstrate the geographic extension of the movement. Tico Braun and Jane Rausch both also read different versions of the entire manuscript. Tico, whose own indispensable study of Gaitán and his movement has been a constant presence in my life since the 1980s, proved extremely generous with hospitality, essential advise, praise, useful critique, and strong dissent. Jane brought her decades of experience with Colombian history and historiography to bear, and much to my advantage, though always remaining charitable toward a junior colleague.

Finally, some debts are almost too significant for words. Bill Cooper, one of my cardinal mentors while I was an undergraduate at Baylor, was the prime mover in my doing Latin American history in a focused way and the one who guided my early course toward graduate school at UT Austin. Once there, Mary Helen Quinn, graduate secretary in the history department, showed a special care (or so it seemed to me) for the aspiring Latin Americanists. Though I am sure he occasionally tired of it, Richard Skinner patiently listened to my Gaitán-obsessed musings over many years. D. A. Hamlin's influence, as one of the surest students of politics I have ever met, can be found throughout the work. My parents never lost faith that this project would actually have a conclusion, and my older sister, Kelly Green, provided a thorough and authoritative edit (happily, she has never given up the habit of telling me what is good for me). Of course the same thanks are due to the University Press of Florida, and especially Gillian Hillis and Amy Gorelick, who made the book a reality. And finally, my wife and fellow "Inmarcesible" (as we Colombianistas call ourselves), Jana DeJong, should have a lock on early sainthood, judging by her patience from beginning to end of this adventure.

Though I have all along (and in the most self-interested way) been open to criticism, and have sought it from many informed and thoughtful people, I am also (for good and for bad) the stubborn scion of generations of independent, hardheaded Missouri farmers. The urge to do it "my way, dammit," has at all times been a usefully compelling force and a potential hazard. Any errors of fact or missteps in interpretation are therefore, most assuredly, mine alone.

I cannot really claim to have captured this elusive quarry that was Gaitanismo, and I would agree that no one really can in these sorts of quests. I did, however, get a pretty good look at it, and this book offers a rendering of what I saw.

Colombia, ca. 1940.

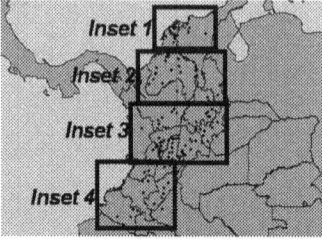

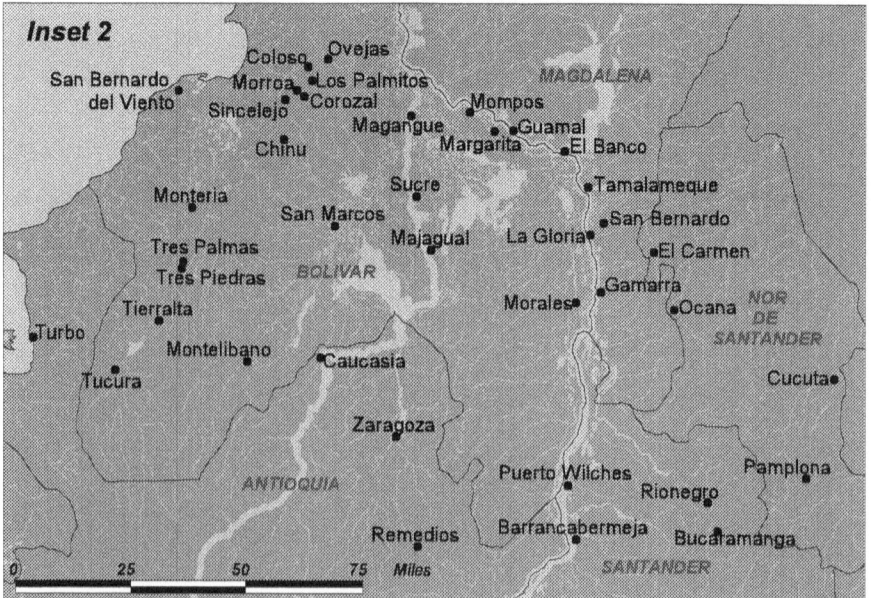

Colombia, ca. 1940, with inset details.

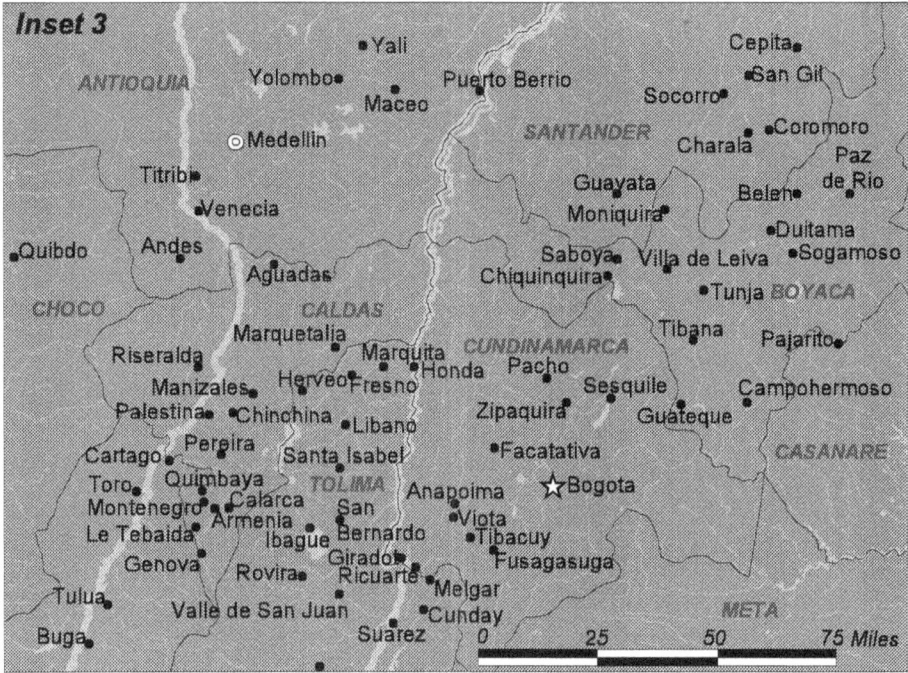

Inset 3

ANTIOQUIA

Yali
Yolombo
Maceo
Puerto Berrio
Cepita
San Gil
Socorro
Medellin
SANTANDER
Charala
Coromoro
Paz de Rio
Titribi
Guayata
Belen
Venecia
Moniquira
Duitama
Quibdo
Andes
Saboya
Villa de Leiva
Sogamoso
Aguadas
Chiquinquira
Tunja
BOYACA
CHOCO
CALDAS
Tibana
Pajarito
Marquetalia
CUNDINAMARCA
Riseralda
Marquita
Pacho
Campohermoso
Manizales
Herveo
Honda
Sesquile
Palestina
Chinchina
Fresno
Zipaquira
Guateque
Pereira
Libano
CASANARE
Cartago
Santa Isabel
Facatativa
Toro
Quimbaya
TOLIMA
Anapoima
Bogota
Montenegro
Calarca
San
Viota
Le Tebaida
Armenia
Bernardo
Tibacuy
Genova
Ibague
Girado
Fusagasuga
Rovira
Ricuarte
Melgar
Tulua
Valle de San Juan
Cunday
META
Buga
Suarez
0   25   50   75 Miles

Inset 4

Buenaventura
Buga
Chaparral
Coyaima
Cali
Palmira
TOLIMA
PACIFIC OCEAN
VALLE DEL CAUCA
HUILA
Caloto
Neiva
Buenos Aires
Yaguara
CAUCA
Gigante
Popayan
Garzon
Pitalito
CAQUETA
Tumaco
NARINO
Florencia
La Union
La Cruz
Ricaurte
Pasto
ECUADOR
Ipiales
PUTUMAYO
0   25   50   75 Miles

Introduction

Populism, Popular Agency, Hegemony, and Gaitanismo

Jorge Eliécer Gaitán has been dead for more than half a century, yet any mention of his name can still rouse powerful emotions in Colombians. Certainly those old enough to remember *el nueve de abril* of 1948, the day he was shot and mortally wounded outside his office in downtown Bogotá, need little prompting to launch into a heartfelt narrative of their experiences of that day and those that followed. And Colombians too young to remember him from personal experience typically know his legacy on a strikingly intimate level. There is little mystery, however, as to why Gaitán continues to haunt the Colombian historical imagination. After 1928, Gaitán came to embody the hopes and demands of such large numbers of Colombians that his assassination produced seismic convulsions at the very foundations of Colombian society. With his death, large portions of Bogotá, as well as other cities, were reduced to rubble, and the nation plunged into seemingly eternal bloody strife.

Known as the "Tribune of the People," when Gaitán rose to address Colombians both his supporters and his adversaries listened with passionate intensity. A speech by Gaitán, whether presented in person or broadcast over the radio, could paralyze a city. A lawyer noted for his defense of the *pueblo*, Gaitán also served as Bogotá city councilman, departmental assembly deputy for Cundinamarca, mayor of Bogotá, congressman, senator, cabinet minister, presidential candidate, and, finally, *jefe único* (sole leader) of the Liberal party in 1947–48. Gaitán led a movement of national scope, generally recognized as a watershed in the Colombian collective experience. *Gaitanismo*, as the movement came to be called, was easily the pivotal political movement in Colombia's raucous twentieth century.

Colombia is rightly known for its "oligarchic democracy," a political system that, while recognized as democratic and legitimate by most Colombians in Gaitán's day, was overshadowed by the elite-dominated Liberal and Conservative parties. Colombia has also been, paradoxically, the seat of widespread and recurring popular mobilizations during the nineteenth and twentieth centuries, many of which grew out of the left-Liberal tradition.[1] In fact, Gaitanismo represented the culmination of a tendency toward popular political movements on the Liberal left, which permeated Colombia's post-independence development. This inclination toward popular mobilization was manifested in Colombia's many civil wars and electoral contests before 1902, in its struggles over land and labor relations, in the reform movement of President Alfonso López Pumarejo in the 1930s, and in Gaitanismo in the 1940s.

Though regional and cultural differences in Colombia created a wide variety of historical experiences, what was interesting and notable about Gaitanismo was its united and coherent character throughout the country, arising as it did from established left-Liberal patterns. In particular Gaitanismo was strong in cities and towns, along the Magdalena River, and in those rural areas noted for concentrated land ownership. Gaitán's assassination marked a dramatic transformation in the left-Liberal tradition and began a new, troubling, and decidedly violent political process that has yet to come to a close. The consequences of Gaitanismo's brutal suppression during the late 1940s and early 1950s continue to reverberate even as Colombians enter a new century.

Populism

While Gaitanismo had deep roots in Colombian history, it can and perhaps must be placed within the general political category known as populism, which flourished in Latin America between 1930 and the 1960s.[2] Populist movements oversaw the "entrance of the masses" into the political life of many Latin nations on a truly unprecedented scale. Any general characterization of populism in Latin America usually includes an urban setting, a multiclass social base, an eclectic, ambiguous ideology with a tinge of nationalism, and a charismatic leader. Populists were different from their nineteenth-century predecessors, the caudillos, in that most were not military men: all could claim a more representative rise to power and, especially important, populism was a mass phenomenon whereas *caudillismo* (in comparative terms) was not.[3] Populist movements appeared as Latin American nations began to move beyond their economic reliance on traditional agricultural commodities and to experiment with import-substitution industrialization in the years after 1930.[4] Under such new conditions most populists shared the conviction that government should take an active interest in, and thereby control through direct state intervention, their nations' growing wage labor sectors.[5] As a result, scholars looked upon Latin American populism as primarily a vehicle through which ruling elites, or portions of them, continued to dominate their respective societies (making comparisons to fascism almost inevitable). Beginning in the 1960s, investigations of populism were generally pursued as studies of leadership. Such interpretations also tended to view populist movements through the lens of modernization theory. In the words of Ernesto Laclau, the modernization theorists defined populism as "an aberrant phenomenon" produced by the "transition from a traditional to an industrial society."[6]

In 1965, Torcuato Di Tella described populism as a political movement that relied upon the support of urban workers, and sometimes rural workers, but did not emanate from any "autonomous organizational power" on their part. While recognizing populism's "anti-status quo ideology" and characterizing it as the best opportunity for meaningful social change during the period, Di Tella denied that the popular masses exercised an active leadership role. In general Di Tella argued that social classes did not function as classes within populism; their natures as classes had been distorted, which resulted in political arrangements that did not further their interests.[7] In a similar vein, Gino Germani stressed two key concepts. The first was "mobilization," whereby formerly "passive" groups entered national political life, sometimes flaring in diffuse movements of protest, but generally channeled through the existing political establishment. Thus Germani's emphasis on the second key concept, "integration," that is, mobilization that recognizes the legitimacy of existing institutions and social relations.[8]

Francisco Weffort made the critique even more explicit in his depiction of the relations between populist leaders and their mass followings. Weffort exemplified the tendency to berate populist movements for their failure to bring about significant reform. Populist leaders, he argued, mouthed progressive rhetoric while actually subverting the interests of the masses, and ultimately strengthened the hand of capitalism.[9] At best, the impact of populist movements altered the trajectory of Latin American societies but did not destroy, or even significantly alter, the various political and economic systems. The consensus position that arose from these interpretations usually contrasted these movements' radical discourses with the moderate behavior of their proponents and portrayed the masses within populist movements as passive followers of Machiavellian leaders.

In one of the most succinct expressions of the elite domination perspective, Steve Stein pointed to populism as "the single institution that best demonstrates the interaction of various elements for social control" in the Latin American context. Though he allowed that populism was perhaps a more "benign" form of social control than other blatantly violent methods, he emphasized its manipulative character. Stein suggested that populism was the primary reason why "the expected buildup of popular pressures for revolutionary change has not occurred." He portrayed populism's "central dynamic" as the "personalistic particularistic ties between powerful leaders and dependent followers." Its "primary impact" was to channel popular mobilization into "forms that have served to bolster an exploitative status quo." Accordingly, populism represented a form of co-optation—and the subversion of "genuine" popular movements—in which gains made by the "masses" are simple "symbolic concessions."[10] Students arguing from this perspective often quote Brazilian Antonio Carlos Ribeiro de Andrada's infamous 1930 statement, "Facamos a revolucâo antes que o povo a faca" ("We will make the revolution before the people do").

Popular Agency and Hegemony

All of this literature on the co-opted and controlled nature of populism did not jibe well before the new prevailing theoretical winds that stormed through the 1970s and 1980s, specifically, the concepts of resistance and popular agency. Historians and social scientists came to focus on questions of power more and more in terms of the capacity and autonomy of common men and women as political actors—as subjects (not objects) engaged in bottom-up struggles for their own interests. The earlier works on populism and the questions they raised had to be reexamined through this new interpretive lens. James Scott, who made a name investigating the "moral economy" of peasant rebellions in Southeast Asia, became one of the high priests of the resistance perspective.[11] He pointed out that though most members of the "subordinate classes" have had few opportunities for open political activity, let alone open rebellion, they nevertheless resist in effective ways. They carry on other, "everyday" forms of class struggle, employing "the ordinary weapons of powerless groups: foot dragging, dissimulation, desertion, false compliance, pilfering, feigned ignorance, slander, arson, sabotage, and so on."[12] Or as Daniel Nugent made clear, the resistance perspective attempts "to deal fully with the human subjects of change" and not treat them as "the passive recipients of the effects of power." It came to see common people as capable of shaping their own destiny.[13] Such emphasis on questions of popular resistance has naturally led to interest among Latin Americanists in the work of Ranajit Guha (and others), who at about the same time were looking to Antonio Gramsci to fathom the "subaltern politics of the people" in India.[14]

Yet, since there is always a danger of romanticizing agency, in the 1990s bottom-up perspectives were accompanied more and more by top-down investigations of the political context and power structures that limit and shape popular responses. Indeed, older interpretations of populist movements were by no means mistaken concerning the ubiquity of elite desires for control. So, another Gramscian concept had to be addressed: hegemony. Looking to Marx's discussion of the material and class bases of elite domination in *The German Ideology*, Gramsci developed a theoretical understanding of the way the ruling classes not only control the means of production but also manipulate the realm of ideas.[15] Not surprisingly, James Scott has led the counteroffensive against the more negative implications of hegemony, and especially its fellow traveler, false consciousness. For Scott, "the critical implication of hegemony is that class rule is effected not so much by sanctions and coercion as by the consent and passive compliance of the subordinate classes." Yet he largely has rejected hegemony and especially false consciousness because they ignore "the extent to which most subordinate classes are able, on the basis of their daily material experience, to penetrate and demystify the prevailing ideology."[16] In particular, Scott stressed the differences between the "public transcript" of conformity and the "hidden transcripts" of resistance.[17] Scott recognized the "thorny relationship between hegemonic processes and resistance," but argued that "we cannot simply take it for granted that state elites *have* a 'hegemonic project' at all." And "although one may occasionally be able to speak of *a* hegemonic project of state elites, one must always speak of popular culture and resistance to such projects in the plural." The strength of such resistance "lies precisely in its plurality. . . . Since it does not speak with one voice, it cannot be silenced with a single blow of force or rhetoric."[18]

Though obviously sympathetic to Scott's views, Alan Knight has argued convincingly that "in certain circumstances hegemony, or something like it, seems to fit the historical pattern, just as the 'moral economy' or the 'weapons of the weak' seem to fit elsewhere." Knight contended that "quiescence" cannot be understood only in terms of coercion or economic factors. Just as "protest and revolt" have an "ideological dimension, so too . . . compliance." Addressing the case of Mexico, Knight could also have been speaking of Colombia when he argued that "the heterogeneity of the political landscape . . . calls for an explanation that goes beyond either coercion or grudging economic compliance. . . . Basically, it requires a partial and cautious resort to the idea of hegemony." Knight stressed what he called "historian predispositions," the "cultural and political attitudes that colored particular communities or regions," and conceded "some autonomous role to 'ideology' or 'culture.'"[19]

And there is more to Gramsci's idea of hegemony than generating consent. William Roseberry has recommended viewing Gramsci's hegemony "not as a finished and monolithic ideological formation but as a problematic, contested, political process of domination and struggle." Roseberry argued that hegemony does not construct "a shared ideology" but rather "a common material and meaningful framework for living through, talking about, and acting upon social orders characterized by domination."[20] Florencia Mallon has also come to see the need to transcend the tendency to equate hegemony "with a belief in, or incorporation of, the dominant ideology." She therefore made the distinction between hegemonic process and hegemonic outcome. The first is useful for making sense of moments when power is "being contested, legitimated, and redefined." The second becomes useful when "leaders partially deliver on their promises and control the terms of political discourse through incorporations as well as repression." Indeed, as Mallon pointed out, the key to successful hegemony is partial incorporation of popular notions and discourse.[21] Even James Scott has recognized that "those rulers who aspire to hegemony in the Gramscian sense" must to some extent legitimize their rule as being in the interests of the people, the nation, the dominated classes themselves.[22] Though necessary for elite domination, such ideological incorporations are often volatile and pose dangers to hegemonic projects.

In light of these debates, it is not surprising that students of Latin American populism have also sought a way beyond the Scylla of elite domination and the Charybdis of popular passivity. Paul Drake posed the question whether populism was simply an elite-led "clamp down on mass participation" or rather a more popularly driven "inclusion of new elements" into the political game.[23] Was populism a brake on the popular will or the result of grassroots pressures that could not be ignored? Many students have come to recognize that "co-optation" was not the only alternative to "revolutionary" change. Populism in Latin America often represented a dramatic increase in political power for the non-elite classes.[24] There were, in fact, two opposite tendencies within the phenomenon of populism: it could be either a form of elite social domination through controlled mobilization of the popular classes, or a mode of popular mobilization and resistance to the existing relations of power. Ernesto Laclau was one of the first to make this observation, identifying a "populism of the dominant classes" and a "populism of the dominated classes."[25] And Robert Dix also identified two populisms, which he called "authoritarian populism" and "democratic populism."[26]

Yet if most movements leaned toward one side or the other of the populist continuum, both of these propensities could, and generally did, exit side by side within the same mobilization, and historians have come to recognize the continuous tug of war between the populist masses and their leaders. Studying the interactions of the Argentine working class and Peronism between 1955 and 1973, Daniel James concluded that while Peronist unions had a hand in controlling workers and their mobilization, it was not a simple case of populist manipulation of the masses. He argued that while Peronism was integrated into Argentine economic and political structures, Peronist workers defiantly retained their concept of social justice and insistently imposed their demands on Argentina's leaders. James clearly addressed populism's split personality, which he called "the dyad resistance/integration."[27] In the case of Brazil, John French disputed the long-dominant interpretation of Brazilian populism as an exercise in demobilization. Analyzing the relationships between industrial workers, labor leaders, and populist politicians like Getúlio Vargas during the first half of the twentieth century in the so-called ABC region of São Paulo, French demonstrated that workers could be vigorous advocates of their own interests. French focused upon the class alliance between workers and populist politicians rather than "utilizing notions of co-optation." In doing so he acknowledged that "each side plays a role, however unequal, in setting the terms of the bargain, and that neither achieves its total demands."[28] And finally, Adrian Bantjes examined Cardenismo in the Mexican state of Sonora during the late 1930s and found that while Lázaro Cárdenas and his representatives surely had a defined central program, much of the movement's radicalism (in particular calls for workers' control of industry and land reform) was driven along from below, in the face of foot-dragging by the Cárdenas administration. Bantjes argued that Sonora's popular groups "were hardly the puppets of a cynical Cárdenas government, but major political players who shaped the future of their nation."[29]

Gaitanismo

In Colombia, Gaitanismo represented a momentous surge of popular participation and influence in the nation's political life. Its character as a mobilization, however, is still a matter of dispute. While Gaitanistas believed that their movement represented a serious challenge to Colombian structures of power, Gaitán's detractors on the left have long claimed that the mobilization he came to lead was never a real threat to the status quo. Important studies continue to emphasize the persistent domination exercised by Colombia's elite over the Liberal and Conservative parties and the resultant weakness of more "class conscious" movements. Most studies concerned with Gaitanismo have focused on Gaitán's life and ideas, the reactions of his political and social adversaries, or on the turbulent days after his assassination in 1948, which in part triggered the confusing period of armed struggle known as "la Violencia," 1946–66.[30] Other works that deal in passing with Gaitanismo tend to portray the movement as merely an ephemeral variation within Colombia's elite-dominated two-party system.[31] While these studies are hardly monolithic in their assessments of Gaitanismo, in large part they share a top-down perspective and examine Gaitán and Gaitanismo within the traditional framework of studies of leadership.

Yet as in the archetypal cases of Argentina, Brazil, and Mexico, emphasizing elements of popular resistance in Colombia, while attempting to understand how they interacted with structures of power, generates a different interpretation of Gaitanismo. Indeed, the interplay between resistance and hegemony in Colombia is at times bewildering. Gaitán had his own agenda and ambitions, and was allied at times with portions of the *oligarquía*. What is more, the hegemonic nature of Colombia's political system is not in question. Though Colombia's rather incomplete process of "state formation" has produced a historically weak central government, Colombia's elites have consistently maintained their control over the nation and its "oligarchic democracy." There has always been a degree of acquiescence in the pueblo's recognition of the legitimacy of the Colombian system, while large numbers of non-elite individuals (and even whole regions) have traditionally been unsympathetic to popularly oriented movements like Gaitanismo. Elite hegemony, however, was mitigated by the historically high degree of popular political participation. Such participation both legitimized the hegemonic nature of the system and threatened it with destruction from within. State power, and elite power beyond the state, has never been highly successful at defining boundaries in Colombia, and significant space for effective resistance has always been present. Gaitán came to shoulder the aspirations of many Colombians traditionally on the periphery of power, and he was never free from these pressures. The fact that Gaitán came to personify the more radical elements of the left-Liberal tradition explains why large numbers of Colombians chose to mobilize as Gaitanistas, within the orbit of the traditional party system, and why they had such strong feelings of national identity.

Consideration of such questions as Gaitanismo's social composition, its popular ideology, and how it confronted the political structures of power within Colombian society (all of which were profoundly influenced by left liberalism) reveals the movement's nature as a mass movement of radical, popular mobilization. Such an understanding of Gaitanismo sets it apart from the type of controlled mobilization often associated with populism, even while allowing for the hegemonic nature of Colombian politics.

Multiclass in configuration, Gaitanismo included members of the capital-owning, commercial, and professional classes, the political elite, and even rural small holders and landless agrarian workers. But it was particularly strong among the organized and unorganized urban and industrial workers and artisans. As an example of cross-class alliance, Gaitanismo does not fit neatly into a dualist vision of struggle between capital and the working class, as sought by more orthodox Marxist interpretations. Many historians have been inclined to place the primary focus on the "working class" very narrowly defined, motivated by a residual belief— often buried—that this class and its struggles against the capital-owning class constitute *the* driving engine of the capitalist world. This inherent Marxist dualism is generally wedded to the related view that more middling social strata are "doomed," "schizophrenic," or just plain reactionary. Subaltern studies approaches that blur these distinctions, therefore, have heartened students of Latin America attempting to understand the problematic social composition of many popular movements by demonstrating that class struggle can happen even in the absence of organized labor unions and well-defined class structure. At the same time, basic research into Latin American reality has produced increasing tension with such Marxian notions of class struggle. Though many historians feel uncomfortable in abandoning or even tampering with these categories, the simplistic and uncritical use of notions developed for the European context has often provided faulty road maps for other parts of the world.

The "doomed" intermediate classes retained considerable strength in Colombia during this period, while the "working class" itself was small and in the process of formation. This observation, however, should not be a temptation to throw out all elements of class struggle with the dualist interpretive framework. The hodgepodge of social strata involved in Gaitanismo, almost all identifiably subaltern, did not negate an identifiable set of cohesive interests. Despite real cultural divisions within the pueblo, the needs and demands of workers and members of the middle sectors proved to be quite similar in practice, and the political barriers between worker, artisan, white-collar employee, and small property owner were illusory to a considerable extent. Indeed, Gaitanistas commonly thought of "working class" and "middle class" as intrinsically related, as two peas in the same social (but especially political) pod. It was not by chance that Gaitán employed the rather more elastic and inclusive dualism of *país político*, the "political nation," and the *país nacional*, meaning the "country of nationhood," the real, or true nation. Gaitanistas also used terminology common to most populist movements in Latin America (and throughout the world), mobilizing the pueblo against the oligarquía. Finally, these mutual connections, as well as their shared separation from the elite, were enhanced by the question of race since most Colombians, whether *indio*, *mestizo*, or *negro*, understood the connection between their skin color and their membership in the pueblo.

These connections were made possible by Gaitanista ideology and the inherent radicalism of the Colombian left-Liberal tradition. Both Liberal reformers of the 1930s and Gaitanistas in the 1940s looked back to turn-of-the-century Liberal caudillo Rafael Uribe Uribe and his concept of "socialism of the state" and to the left-Liberal intellectual currents of the nineteenth century he built upon. Around 1850, many liberals in Colombia (as in other parts of Latin America and the world) began to look beyond the "classical" laissez-faire liberalism of the individual and to create a broader, more inclusive, and more popular version of liberalism. This current manifested itself in the 1920s and 1930s as a "collectivist" brand of Colombian liberalism. Grounded in this "left" interpretation of the Liberal party and its traditions, Gaitán became the symbol of democracy and social justice through state intervention. Gaitanistas sought to create "true democracy," though giving uneasy recognition to the existing state. And while not overtly calling for an end to the capitalist relations of production, Gaitán manifested considerable tension with capitalism. Ultimately, Gaitán embodied the Gaitanistas' desires for real change and represented a vehicle for overcoming frustrations and unfulfilled hopes left in the wake of the Liberal governments during the so-called "Liberal Republic" between 1930 and 1946.

Finally, the political struggles Gaitanistas waged against the mechanisms of oligarchic rule embodied both confrontations and negotiations with power. In these processes, one encounters many complicated issues. The traditional political culture—dominated by the *jefes naturales* ("natural leaders") of the Liberal and Conservative parties and anchored on the local level by boss politics that employed the patron-client relationship and electoral manipulation—enjoyed a significant degree of hegemonic control. This system, however, had always been prone to internal fragmentation and long had to contend with the left-Liberal tradition. Transmitted from the nineteenth century, popular strains of liberalism involved significant popular participation in both armed struggle and electoral politics. The Liberal governments' state reforms of the 1930s affected such political and class struggles, both as agents of social control and as instruments of empowerment. Though seeking to abate popular pressures, the political *oligarquía* found itself more overtly challenged in less controlled urban settings by the more fully enfranchised masses after 1936. And while still without the vote, women entered politics as Gaitanistas in unprecedented ways. Struggles on the left pitted a nationalistic, "homegrown" movement against an internationalist Communist party, which in turn characterized its populist rivals as "fascist."[32] The Liberal party continued to suffer intense intra-Liberal struggles between conflicting visions of the true nature of the party's mission. And not to be forgotten, the familiar cradle-to-grave attachment to the Liberal and Conservative parties, the so-called "hereditary hatreds," provided the general context in which Gaitanismo matured.[33] The degree to which popular allegiance to the traditional parties was and was not overcome helps explain the connections between Gaitanismo and the disjointed Violencia.

There were, however, features of Colombian populism that set it apart from other populist movements in Latin America. As a result of Gaitán's assassination, Gaitanismo never enjoyed national political power. And while most other populist movements were largely urban phenomena (the notable exceptions are Venezuela's Acción Democrática and México's Cardenismo), Gaitanismo embodied an important rural component, especially in the 1930s.

By considering the interacting currents of interpretation regarding resistance, agency, and hegemony and how these apply to Latin American populism, a clearer understanding of Gaitanismo is now possible. The movement offered a radical and popular challenge to the social, economic, and political relations of Colombian society, but these "oligarchic" structures also shaped the process and the outcome. Gaitanismo manifested an essential tension converging on class (and race) conflict. For most Gaitanistas, the dynamic struggle between the pueblo and the oligarquía was between the largely dark-skinned "productive masses" and the "owners" of political and economic power. The pueblo was a political and cultural construct in which the working classes and middling classes, men and women, black, brown, and white, saw themselves united by Colombia's traditions and ideological currents of popular mobilization on the Liberal left. These traditions explain why from the late 1920s to the late 1940s Colombia witnessed an unmistakable popular interest in and agitation for increased democratic rights and more popularly controlled institutions. This movement, in turn, was closely related to widespread demands for social and economic justice. Armed with these principles, Gaitanismo (especially in urban areas) overtly disputed, but did not completely overcome or repudiate, the oligarchic practice and institutions of Colombian politics. Finally, it must be remembered that Gaitán became the symbol of mobilization but was not its cause. The emphasis, therefore, must in large part be shifted away from the caudillo to the pueblo. Doing so underscores the basic continuity that existed throughout the period, while reflecting the currents of left-Liberal popular political mobilization that have imbued Colombian history since the nineteenth century, and of which Gaitanismo was simply the most dramatic example.

Chapter 1 sets the stage by discussing the left-Liberal tradition and Colombia's heritage of popular mobilization. Chapter 2 examines Gaitán and his early development. Chapter 3 locates Gaitán in relation to the Liberal establishment and within the Liberal left, and examines the first phase of his movement between 1928 and 1935. Chapter 4 chronicles the years of the official Liberal interlude, the rise and fall of "populist" Liberal president Alfonso López Pumarejo, and Gaitán's inheritance of the López legacy. Chapter 5 examines questions of gender, race, and class in the left-Liberal pueblo that would swell the ranks of Gaitanismo. Chapter 6 deals with the nature and structure of Colombia's oligarchic political system and with the political impact of the left-Liberal challenge presented by Gaitán's presidential campaign between 1944 and 1946. Chapter 7 explores the ideological nature of Gaitanismo. Chapter 8 follows Gaitanismo's continued popular assault on and problematic conquest of the Liberal establishment, as well as Gaitán's struggles with Colombian Communists, in a context where all Liberals had to confront the Conservative party in power after 1946. Finally, I conclude the study by emphasizing the connections between the fate of Gaitanismo, la Violencia, and Colombia's more recent past.

Latin American populism was more than simply a means of socially controlling the masses. Populism often represented an autonomous popular mobilization. While Latin American ruling elites had hoped to control the newly mobilized masses, "authoritarian populism," it turned out, was decidedly porous. The "dominated classes" maximized the opportunities for popular mobilization presented after 1930 to such an extent that populism in all its varieties gave way throughout Latin America after 1960 to decidedly oppressive forms of government and demobilization. But that is another story.

Colombian politics present an excellent example of an elite-dominated political system, while at the same time, Colombia is home to Latin America's longest surviving insurgent guerrilla movements. This ambivalent situation continues in large part thanks to the legacy of Gaitanismo.

Popular Mobilization and
the Left-Liberal Tradition in Colombia

After Gaitán's assassination in April 1948, Gaitanismo too died a violent death in the years of savage repression that followed. Left-Liberal popular mobilization, however, lived on. To demonstrate the significance of these assertions to Colombian history, this study begins by addressing the social, economic, and political context of the nineteenth century, from which the left-Liberal mobilizations of the twentieth century emerged. Such a foundation is necessary because important interpretations continue to portray Gaitanismo's relationship to the Liberal party as a sign of its weakness.[1] Yet ample evidence exists to suggest that the reverse is true. This chapter will demonstrate that with its firm grounding in Colombian history, the left-Liberal tradition was what gave Gaitán's movement its spectacular mobilizing abilities.

A great deal of popular mobilization took place on the Liberal left in Colombia during the nineteenth and early twentieth centuries, expressed as both military conflict and conventional politics. Much of this mobilization reflected the fact that the intellectual tradition of liberalism presented a broad spectrum of ideas that did not resonate equally with all liberals in Latin America. Elites were drawn to ideas that focused on the individual, property, and free markets, while less affluent liberals emphasized liberalism's more egalitarian strains and implications. From its earliest moments, therefore, the Liberal party in Colombia encompassed opposing elite and popular strains. This division was clear in the critical years between 1848 and 1854 and persisted throughout the rest of the nineteenth century. After 1900, Rafael Uribe Uribe manifested a popular and "left" interpretation of Colombian liberalism that was still quite evident in the intra-Liberal debates over the future of liberalism in the 1920s and 1930s. By then, a clear distinction existed between an elite, "bourgeois," "individualist" liberalism and a popular, "left," "collectivist" liberalism.

Tellingly, many Colombian Liberals in the 1920s and 1930s, Gaitán among them, pointed to the connections they saw between their version of liberalism and socialism.

Many left Liberals in the early twentieth century, therefore, did not interpret the wars and electoral contests of the nineteenth century as meaningless battles for control of government; rather, they remembered them as struggles of resistance whose objectives focused on social and political change. By their lights, popular Liberal participation in these conflicts was not "irrational" (as historians have repeatedly argued). And in their turn, neither would the Gaitanistas later be merely the thralls of elite ideological hegemony because they chose to remain within the Liberal party. In fact, the enduring self-identification of left-leaning Colombians as Liberals demonstrated that the elite "individualist" and popular "collectivist" currents continued to compete for the soul of the Liberal party in the 1940s, when their struggle would explode into the raw and impassioned conflicts concerning Gaitán.

This propensity for popular mobilization in Colombia during the nineteenth and early twentieth centuries, and the fact that it was funneled through the left-Liberal tradition, demonstrates that Colombians had a long-standing vision of what a just world should be, and that popularly oriented movements of change could emerge from within the traditional parties. These general currents of thought and mobilization also show that left-Liberal radicalism had long permeated the political environment, overlapping and shifting from movement to movement. Gaitanismo proved to be one of the definitive popular political mobilizations in twentieth-century Latin American history because it represented the high-water mark of Colombia's left-Liberal tradition.

The Setting: Geography, Economy, Society

Coupled with Colombia's largely subsistence internal economy and tortuous topography, long centuries of relative economic isolation provided few opportunities to integrate the nation's different regions. Such conditions resulted in diverse regional identities and racial compositions. What few links to the world market Colombia enjoyed before the late nineteenth century came from the mining of gold, with short episodes of tobacco and quinine exportation. Only in the 1880s and later did coffee production finally reorient the nation's economy, introducing new questions of land tenure and social relations. Geography and history combined to create Colombia's distinctive society and economy.

Throughout its history, Colombia's population has gravitated toward the Andean slopes and Caribbean coast. By custom, therefore, there have always been two separate Colombias: the coasts (especially the Atlantic), inhabited by *costeños*, and the highlands, whose residents are known as *cachacos*.[2] Higher altitudes proved more comfortable and relatively disease-free while the northern coast became a natural middle ground between the inaccessible Andes and the outside world. This primeval dichotomy between the coast and the highlands remains a fundamental divide on ethnic, cultural, and racial levels.[3] In general the highlands have predominantly white, Indian, and *mestizo* racial elements while the coast and the river valleys are black and mulatto in character, with some indigenous and white influences. In practice, finer climatic distinctions are usually drawn between the "hot country" (such as Cartagena), the milder temperatures of the "temperate country" (Medellín or Cali), and the cool to chilly atmosphere of the "cold country" (Bogotá). And in economic terms, there were four basic regions in Gaitán's day: the western cordilleras, the center-east, the Cauca valley, and the Atlantic coast.[4]

In the 1930s and 1940s Colombia was still an essentially agricultural nation. Nineteenth-century Colombia had entered the world market in sporadic fits. Only during the first decades of the twentieth century did the nation find its niche as a producer of coffee, which quickly surpassed all other exports. Indeed, coffee would dominate the economy until the 1980s. By 1930 Colombia was second only to Brazil in coffee yields while its crop was recognized as the world's highest-quality product. Production for export rose throughout the first half of the century, seemingly regardless of world economic conditions, from 1 million 130-pound bags per year in 1913 to 3 million bags in 1930 and 5 million bags in 1943. Before 1930 the principal coffee-producing regions were found in the Santanders and in Cundinamarca, but later the majority of Colombian production originated in Antioquia, Caldas, and the Quindío region.[5] Coffee, unfortunately, was driven by external demand and proved to be a fickle economic engine for several reasons: such demand was elastic; prices were very unstable; there were no real economies of scale in its production; and it was rather sensitive to competition, especially from Brazil.[6]

Colombia is often characterized as a country of small farmers. This image originated with the spread of "*antioqueño* colonization" in the western cordilleras as landless peasants called *colonos* dispersed over the territory south of Antioquia after 1850 and colonized vacant lands with small farms, called *fincas*. Charles Bergquist has shown that the debate over the "relative concentration of ownership" has revolved around the coffee censuses of 1932 and 1955. The first of these studies seemed to show widespread ownership of coffee production. Over 50 percent of all trees were found on small-size operations, with fewer than 5,000 trees. The 5,000–20,000-tree fincas accounted for only 11 percent of the total, while the biggest fincas (20,000 or more trees) were 2 percent of the total farms. The problem arises when discussing who owned the individual fincas. The census did not clarify how many fincas were owned by the same individual, family, or organization. Yet a less extensive coffee census in 1939 indicated that, since 1932, coffee production had risen 75 percent while the absolute number of farms doubled. This jump in the number of fincas also occurred in the smaller-sized holdings. The 1955 coffee census, Bergquist concluded, demonstrated "continuing diffuseness of coffee production in Colombia" and that "small family farms made up the most numerous and important unit of Colombian coffee production."[7] Yet the interpretation that antioqueño colonization supposedly promoted "an egalitarian society in which the rural poor were converted into small coffee farmers enjoying access to land and a modest prosperity" has suffered considerable revision.[8] The consensus view now holds that "the prevailing pattern of frontier expansion in the first half of the twentieth century allowed regional elites to raise property values and seize control of coffee processing and marketing."[9] Finally, focusing on the class reality behind the myth of a dominant agricultural middle class in the region of antioqueño colonization, Keith Christie concluded that the middle-class dimension has been overdrawn.[10]

And despite relatively widespread access to land in Colombia, older social relationships that involved a disadvantaged agrarian work force were still quite strong in many parts of the country during the 1930s and 1940s. Marco Palacios stressed the critical divide between the center-east, where land ownership was more concentrated, and the west, where small fincas were more frequent.[11] Fincas throughout Colombia's coffee-producing regions continued to rely on landless rural workers, but the east in particular was dominated by sizable *haciendas* that were home to large numbers of resident *campesinos*. This was also true in the valley of the "Gran Cauca" in the southwest, which had been a "theater of war" and laboratory of popular mobilization throughout the nineteenth century. It was a region of racial tension and rural poverty known, like the center-east, for great concentrations of land ownership. Its economy, dominated by cattle and sugar production, was characterized by low productivity and underemployment.[12]

The economy of the northern coast in 1930, which revolved around

agriculture, especially cattle raising, with some limited activity in the mining and oil-production sectors, resembled the center-east and Cauca valley
in many important ways. Though the coast greatly benefited from its role
as an economic intermediary between the outside world and the nation's
interior, a significant feature of coastal development was that arable land
tended to be held in large haciendas (though as late as the 1880s huge
portions of land remained unclaimed jungle). Furthermore, between 1880
and 1930 relatively little public land was distributed among the landless
population of the Atlantic coast, while many of the largest haciendas actually expanded.[13] This fact, combined with the collapse of the banana
trade in Magdalena during the period, assured a steady stream of displaced rural people flowing toward the coastal cities, particularly Barranquilla.[14]

To speak of the economy of the northern coast is also to speak of the
Magdalena river.[15] Running south to north from its headwaters more than
a thousand miles inland, the Magdalena river linked Caribbean Colombia
with Andean Colombia for more than four hundred years and served as
the nation's economic lifeline well into the twentieth century. In Gaitán's
day Colombia still suffered from poor roads and a feeble rail network due
to the high cost of their construction and upkeep. Before the 1950s, neither Bogotá nor Medellín enjoyed a direct rail link to the northern coast,
and paddle-wheeled steamboats on the Magdalena continued to function
as the primary form of transportation of cargo and passengers. The introduction of steamboats in the 1830s and after proved sluggish since the
Magdalena is a river of "inopportune sandbanks and deceptive rapids."[16]
Although the navigable parts of the river stretch over eight hundred miles
from Neiva to Barranquilla, modern flat-bottom steam-boats could not
pass over the rapids near Girardot. Thus, even in the 1930s, keel boats
paddled by human muscle still played an important role in the economic
life of the river, especially on the 170-some miles between Neiva and
Girardot.

Travel on the Magdalena remained slow and dangerous. An uneventful
trip by steamer down river from Girardot to Barranquilla in 1910 took as
long as eight days. Sandbars and unseen snags were a constant threat. Due
to breakdowns and the lack of fuel (previous ships' crews having denuded
the river's banks of trees) passengers and goods could be trapped for weeks
along the mosquito-infested shoreline. And as Colombia had been only
marginally plugged into the world economy in the nineteenth century,
shippers suffered a lack of commodities to transport. Despite such difficulties, however, the average travel time on the Magdalena eventually stabi-

lized.[17] In the 1940s, therefore, the river remained the primary link between many departments, touching Atlántico, Bolívar, Magdalena, Antioquia, the Santanders, Boyacá, Cundinamarca, Tolima, Caldas, and Huila.[18] And the Magdalena served as the means by which the majority of Colombia's coffee found its way to the world market after the turn of the century, via Barranquilla and its port on the Caribbean, Puerto Colombia.[19]

Despite obstacles to its development, by 1930 Colombia had already distinguished itself as Latin America's fourth most industrialized nation. Profits from antioqueño gold production, and later from coffee, were reinvested in Medellín, where basic manufactured goods were produced and sold to small farmers and urban consumers. This pattern was soon repeated in Bogotá, Barranquilla, and Cali. These cities were home to the majority of Colombia's industrial workers and artisans. Manufacturing as a portion of GDP climbed from 7 percent in the mid-1920s to 14 percent by the end of the 1940s. As a result, the process of import-substitution industrialization drove the market share of nondurable imports from 30 percent in 1930 to 3 percent by 1950. Yet, during the 1930s and 1940s, Colombian industry continued to suffer from low productivity, small units of production, and a rudimentary technological base.[20] Ultimately, Colombia's non-agricultural workforce remained in large part artisanal.[21]

In the 1930s and 1940s the population continued to be predominantly rural, since urbanization occurred unhurriedly before the 1940s; in 1951, only 25 percent of the country's inhabitants lived in cities of 10,000 souls or more.[22] As a factor of Colombian regionalism, however, the nation has long enjoyed more balance among its urban areas and economic zones than most Latin America countries. In the 1930s and 1940s, Bogotá, the capital, was the urban center for the eastern and central cordilleras; Medellín oversaw vibrant Antioquia; Cali came to be predominant in the Valle del Cauca; and finally, Barranquilla was the primary city of the Caribbean coast. Not surprisingly, most Colombian towns and cities were never dominated by Bogotá (nor, for that matter, were regions dominated by their principal cities). Yet though still affected by the rhythms, values, and limitations of rural life, cities were places of change during the late nineteenth and twentieth centuries, where social and economic diversification was intensified. Literacy spread, as well as trams, pavement, cars, telephones, and electricity, though after 1890 "polyclass" neighborhoods began to disappear as the poorer sorts were pushed to the periphery.[23] Cities and towns, not surprisingly, were vital to liberalism, and would prove especially so to Gaitanismo.

The Tradition of Popular Mobilization: An Overview

The most notorious element of Colombian development since independence has been its political life, in particular its heritage of civil war and the enduring hegemony of its elite-controlled parties. Inescapable in any discussion of Colombia's political life, the primordial divide between Liberals and Conservatives demands serious attention. Elite domination of politics was a constant, and most students of the subject have legitimately focused on the struggles between the traditional parties and the rise of the "hereditary hatreds." Yet a great deal of autonomous popular mobilization pervaded these encounters, which in large part gave Colombian politics its dynamism. Though Colombian elites dominated the parties, the state and its institutions remained manifestly weak, which provided ample space for the pueblo to maneuver and affect the system in dramatic ways. The Colombian heritage of popular mobilization was already in evidence in the late colonial period and became more pronounced throughout the nineteenth century. The Comuneros rebellion, the wars for independence, and the civil wars after 1839 all testify to the magnitude and prevalence of recurrent grassroots mobilization.[24] Finally, and tellingly, it should not be overlooked that popular political participation was not simply a matter of military engagement. Electoral politics in Colombia also saw energetic and widespread participation and only marginally controlled popular mobilization.

The Comuneros insurrection of 1781 in New Granada (as Colombia was known in the late colonial period), along with the Indian revolt of Túpac Amaru that was derailed that same year in Peru, was one of the most significant rebellions in colonial Latin America. The rebellion began as a protest against tax increases on tobacco and alcohol, which the Spanish crown enacted to finance its imperial adventures. Historians agree that from the beginning the movement found its driving force within the humblest ranks of the colony's inhabitants, the indios, mestizos, and *criollos* of modest means.[25] Members of the upper classes had no more love of the tax increases than did the common pueblo but, nevertheless, reluctantly joined the movement to "lead" it. Beginning in the Socorro region, the uprising massed many thousands of supporters and marched on Bogotá under the traditional slogan of "Long live the king and death to bad government." Thus besieged, the government in the viceregal capital gave in to most of the Comuneros' demands. Though the rebellion's leaders eventually succumbed to their fears of punishment and accepted a short-term reimposition of the taxes, the next viceroy quickly restored the status quo from before the rebellion to soothe the general population.

Such popular participation would be echoed in the wars for independence between 1810 and 1821, though the numbers involved in the fighting were never a large percentage of the population. The armed struggle for independence in New Granada was less arduous in terms of lives lost and property destroyed than in Venezuela, and much less costly than in Mexico, and a large portion of the population avoided direct participation. It is also true that the historiography for New Granada is not as well developed as it is for other regions.[26] Characterizations of the degree of popular participation, therefore, are still rather sketchy, but there is little doubt that in some regions popular mobilization would have important social consequences. In the northern regions of the country and Valle de Cauca where slaveholding was predominant, for example, African slaves won their freedom through military service or took the opportunity to run away. But even if popular participation never reached the levels it did in other parts of Latin America, the wars for independence opened the door to patterns of political mobilization that would endure throughout the century.

Like other Latin American countries in the mid-nineteenth century, Colombia was shaken by the struggles of its Liberal and Conservative parties. (Simón Bolívar, the quintessential military *caudillo*, is recognized as the "first" Conservative, while Francisco de Paula Santander, proponent of constitutional government, is claimed as the "first" Liberal.) It is singular, however, in that its civil wars stretch with a throbbing consistency from the end of the Independence Era through the rest of the century: 1828, 1829, 1830, 1831, 1839–41, 1851, 1854, 1859–62, 1867, 1876–77, 1884–86, 1895, and 1899–1902.[27] The list seems endless, and it does not even include the various local civil wars. Interpretations of these wars have reflected the fact that despite its bellicose history, "Colombian politics have conventionally been described as oligarchic." Within the economic and political oligarchy a consensus has long existed "in favor of civilian rule, semi-representative democracy, and some limited opportunities for entry by talented members of the middle class into the small circle that negotiated major decisions."[28] So despite their ancestral allegiance to either the Liberal or Conservative parties, Colombian elites have historically formed a cohesive grouping—especially in the face of popular threats from below.

The groups that fought these wars have been described as "pre-political" because their differences were supposedly insignificant. Their interaction represented "little more than a contest of 'ins' versus 'outs'" struggling for control of the public coffers.[29] Neither party, it is argued, had strong convictions, while both parties drew adherents from all regions and all social classes. Likewise on the Colombian left, the standard line has long been that both parties were simply different subsections of the same oligarchic regime. To cite a famous example, Gabriel García Márquez characterized the two parties at the outset of the political career of his character Colonel Aureliano Buendía in terms that underline the absence of differences between them beyond the religious question.[30]

There were few unequivocal social and economic divisions between Conservatives and Liberals of the elite. Frank Safford thoroughly undermined the so-called "hacienda/tienda" thesis, according to which Conservatives and Liberals were associated respectively with aristocratic agrarianism and urban bourgeois culture. Abundant evidence demonstrates how the elite of both parties, in fact, owned land and participated in urban, mercantile activities. Safford suggested that "perhaps the Liberals were slightly more numerous in commerce, the Conservatives in landowning. But the division between the two, speaking purely in terms of occupation, was not very great." He proposed, rather, that Conservatives were more numerous in the old colonial core regions while Liberals were strongest in peripheral regions. Areas around Bogotá, Cartagena, and Popayán, which showed early tendencies toward Conservatism, were important to and had strong interests in colonial economic and political structures. Areas like Santander, on the other hand, had reasons to desire a break with traditional distributions of economic and political privilege that promoted centralization. Conservative and Liberal distribution also reflected the type of labor system employed in the various regions. Areas relying on former black slaves had more to fear from Liberal ideology than did regions comprised of small individual holdings. Finally, Safford suggested that frontier regions, by their very nature, are more democratic.[31]

These observations rightly temper earlier emphases on the economic foundations of the Liberal and Conservative parties. There were, however, identifiable differences among the elite. Conservatives identified deeply with Hispanic traditions and the Catholic religion. They pontificated on the glories of the family and the Church, with the latter group having a sizable role in Conservative government and education. They emphasized order and a paternalistic hierarchy, strong central government, and a strong executive. Conservatives evoked the 1886 constitution as the bulwark of political and social stability. Liberals were equally exuberant in their defense of reason over tradition and, in the political realm, were generally anti-clerical though most remained Catholic. Few indeed were Colombia's "free-thinkers"; their aim was simply to keep the Church out of secular affairs. Liberals in government generally espoused (though did not always practice) a decentralized or federal national government and laissez-faire economics.[32] Liberals pointed to their social and economic agenda of the 1860s and 1870s.

The real challenge of interpretation, however, concerns why individuals who were clearly from lower socioeconomic classes (that is, identifiably subaltern) joined in the battles led by their rulers. It is widely argued that personal identification with either the Liberal or Conservative label shifted the lower classes away from creating their own political parties.[33] Continued popular attachment to the traditional parties, so the argument goes, prevented the oppressed of Colombian society from recognizing their collective and mutual interests and, consequently, from creating appropriate political arrangements. Orlando Fals Borda provided an excellent example. He argued that Colombia's two-party system was comprised of organizations "without convictions." These parties used the mass of Colombians as "cannon fodder" in elite power struggles that have endured since the nation's consolidation in 1840 "almost without modification." "The working *pueblo*" consequently remained ignorant "of what a real democracy is."[34] Accordingly, once the elite of a certain area was confirmed as Liberal or Conservative, the common isolation endured by the communities they controlled created the illusion among the lower classes that great differences existed. This experience was compounded by the frequency of Colombia's civil wars. Over the years they arbitrarily bonded these isolated communities to one or the other of the political labels. One of the most enduring elements of the political system Colombia inherited from the nineteenth century, therefore, is the arguably irrational attachment of Colombia's lower classes to one or the other of the traditional parties.

One can argue, however, that a good deal of unbridled popular mobilization has taken place in Colombia. What is more, many students of Colombian politics have been quick to point out that despite elements of elite control, Colombia's system has always exhibited "democratic" facets, in both parties.[35] Florencia Mallon has argued that popular liberalisms in Mexico and Peru were the by-products of popular mobilization stimulated by foreign invasions.[36] In Colombia, Alvaro Tirado Mejía pointed out that it was constant civil war that led to increased social mobility, and angst among the elite.[37] Francisco Gutiérrez Sanín noted that many popular groups appropriated the elite-led movements for their own ends.[38] At many points the elites had to put their partisan squabbles behind them to suppress more popular elements of their parties, and the war of 1854 was one of the prime examples. General José María Melo, the commander of the Bogotá army garrison, rose up to protest military reform and was joined by Bogotá's artisans, who had been hurt by the Liberal government's policies of free trade. The situation clearly threatened the dominant role of the upper classes, both Liberal and Conservative, who quickly forgot their differences. Liberal and Conservative leaders formed an alliance, mobilized their supporters into an army, and eventually defeated the forces of the rebellion. This would become a recurring pattern of elite solidarity in the face of popular mobilization.

The other most blatant example of elite unity in the face of undeniably "popular" mobilization occurred during the War of a Thousand Days (1899–1902), as the final and most traumatic conflict of the century came to be known.[39] Initial appearances indicated that it would be a short struggle as had other civil wars to date. Local leaders rallied their supporters and led them to battle as was the custom. The national government followed the well-worn precedent of forced recruitment; financing was pursued in the normal, moderate manners.[40] Although the first few months of combat were intensive, the leaders of both sides displayed the same "chivalrous concern" for their adversaries as had come to be expected. The character of the war, however, changed considerably after the costly battle of Palonegro in May 1900. After a seeming stalemate, the Liberal army was decimated and forced from the field. It was at this point that the Liberal leadership switched to the guerrilla tactics that would prolong the war for another two and a half years.[41] In this long and bloody stage of the war, characterized more by the machete than the rifle, which intensified the Liberal-Conservative antagonisms in the countryside, the guerrilla leaders (who were for the most part of similar social rank to the men they commanded) became increasingly estranged from the national Liberal politicians and militantly violent.[42] And on the ideological front, a marked division became uncomfortably evident during the later stages of the war between Liberal leaders in Bogotá and the party's left wing. This disruptive guerrilla warfare ultimately came to be seen by the leaders of both parties as a threat to upper-class control and helped bring about peace.[43] Though great frictions continued, the moderates in both parties, as in 1854, averted the development of a situation dangerous to their class interests.

The years between 1902 and 1930, an age of coffee and increasing prosperity, were the most politically stable and peaceful that Colombians had witnessed since before the Comuneros rebellion. Yet throughout the period Colombian history demonstrated considerable continuity with the previous century and its tradition of popular mobilization. Among the elite, both Liberals and Conservatives took less interest in the great dividing issues of the prior century (or in struggling over control of the state) in order to benefit from the booming coffee economy and Colombia's belated entrance into the world market. Coffee profits, as well as those from bananas, petroleum, and some limited manufacturing, in combination with an infusion of capital paid to Colombia by the United States for the loss of Panamá, gave the period after World War I its nickname of "the dance of the millions." Despite their reputation for tranquility, however, the first three decades of the twentieth century can be characterized equally well by labor unrest, strikes, land invasions, and attempted armed uprisings by socialists and left Liberals. It is no coincidence that the Liberal party leadership in these years began to make tentative and hesitant reaches toward a more popular political base.

After their experiences in the War of a Thousand Days, artisans and workers employed such traditional mobilization techniques as creating mutual-aid societies, burial societies, and savings banks. In addition, they mobilized politically. They first created the short-lived Union of Industrials and Workers in 1904 and revived it in 1910. This group competed with another organization, the Worker Union of Colombia, and elements of these groups eventually founded the Socialist party in 1919. This nascent workers' party maneuvered with and against factions of the Liberal party between 1919 and 1924, but in general it never diverged greatly from the Liberal left in its doctrine or base of support. After years of frustration, and following the violent episodes accompanying the elections of 1925, portions of the Liberal left and the socialists created the Partido Socialista Revolucionaria (the Revolutionary Socialist Party, PSR) in 1926.[44]

Though it never participated in national elections, there is good evidence that the PSR had a mass base of support. It was active among peasants, river workers, and banana workers but also enjoyed significant artisan backing. After the 1927 oil and river workers' strike was met by the Conservative government with repression, many PSR members with Liberal backgrounds wanted the party to follow the older tradition of armed resistance and began planning an uprising that would coincide with a labor stoppage. This activity and growing militancy among the left Liberals and Socialists paralleled a steady rise in land conflicts between tenants and large landholders, and between *colonos* who had opened and developed land for coffee planting and others who claimed legal title. It was within this context that the infamous United Fruit Workers' strike and its aftermath took place at the end of 1928 in the department of Magdalena. As thousands of banana workers congregated in the train station of Ciénaga to hear of the strike negotiations, government troops who believed they were planning an attack on Santa Marta opened fire on December 6, killing hundreds of workers and their family members. The banana "massacre" did not discourage those portions of the PSR that planned an armed uprising, though their operation was largely neutralized when their cache of weapons was discovered in early 1929 and many of their leaders were arrested. But ironically, just as the PSR was disintegrating, the Liberal party (with mass support from the Socialists' base) recaptured the Colombian presidency from a divided Conservative party in the elections of 1930 (ending the "Conservative Hegemony," 1885–1930, and beginning the "Liberal Republic," 1930–1946).

This historical experience illustrates the vigor of Colombian popular mobilization before 1930. Yet this mobilization took many forms, including full-blown electoral politics. Concerning the question of whether elections in the nineteenth and early twentieth centuries were "genuine contests" or "mere charades, reinforcing social control," Eduardo Posada-Carbó has argued that "many were indeed significant contests" and, along with David Bushnell and Malcolm Deas, stressed the importance of elections to Colombian political culture. In particular, he noted "the early expansion of Colombian suffrage, the relatively high participation in certain periods, the intensity of competition, and the long-term impact of frequent electioneering." These "electoral traditions" were "strongly rooted in the early republic" and "persisted during the Conservative Hegemony." Colombian politics exhibited "a commitment to suffrage that grew to involve substantial sectors of Colombian society." Posada-Carbó forcefully rejected the contention that elections "were mere theatrical events, in which those in power paraded flocks of unaware and indifferent voters to the polls without much difficulty."[45] In 1886 the triumphant Conservative regime centralized the electoral system and established a two-tier structure to limit the influence of the pueblo. All male citizens could vote for *concejales* (city councilmen) and *diputados* to the departmental assemblies; literacy and property requirements were instated for the lower house of Congress (which elected senators) and for presidential electors. In practice, however, the vote was often more widely enjoyed. Voting was taken very seriously, and failed attempts to guarantee fair elections helped spark the War of a Thousand Days.

This heritage of war and partisan mobilization laid the foundation for a well-defined political geography in Colombia by the 1920s, in particular the geography of left liberalism. Ideological currents in liberal thought also played a role in this geography. (Given liberalism's antagonism to slavery, it was no accident that the heavily Afro-Colombian areas would later be left-Liberal strongholds.) In general terms, the Atlantic coast (and one can also add the Pacific coast), large swaths of the Magdalena river valley, the center-east (especially the Upper Magdalena), and the Cauca valley were given to radical and popular mobilization.[46]

During the nineteenth and early twentieth centuries Colombians of the common pueblo repeatedly showed themselves able and quite willing to mobilize without the blessing or guidance of their rulers. Undoubtedly the elite dominated the Liberal and Conservative parties, while the "hereditary hatreds" divided the pueblo in grotesque ways. But autonomous popular mobilization was ubiquitous, and particularly powerful on the Liberal left.

The Historical Roots of Liberal Division

Liberalism, a term that is seldom well defined, encompasses an extended and somewhat contradictory family of ideas.[47] A product of European and North American intellectual tradition and political experience, liberalism emanates from a belief in the "natural" rights of individuals. Political theorists and philosophers stress that one of the essential elements of liberalism is that it is "individualistic" in its assertion of "the moral primacy of the person against the claims of any social collectivity."[48] Individual rights associated with liberalism include: the freedoms of speech, assembly, and of religion; freedom to own property; the right to due process and guarantees against arbitrary state power; and equality before the law, especially no extraordinary privileges based on birth (all forming the constitutionalist core of liberalism). Liberalism is also widely associated with laissez-faire visions of the economy, where an unfettered market reigns supreme. Taken together, these elements comprise what is often known as "classical liberalism."

At the same time, however, alternative liberal notions and practice of government can be found in Rousseau's collectivist concept of the "general will," in the measures of the revolutionary Jacobin regime in France between 1793 and 1794, and in the radical drift of liberal thought between 1815 and 1848. Liberalism is also, therefore, "egalitarian, inasmuch as it confers on all men" the same moral, political, and legal status, while it affirms the universal nature of the human species, and the improvability of human institutions. Rousseau's concept of "liberty" was not, as Benjamin Constant pointed out, merely the "sphere of non-interference or independence under the rule of law"; rather, reminiscent of ancient Greece, it meant "entitlement to a voice in collective decision making."[49] Yet in the context of Latin American history, discussions of liberalism have habitually ignored the clear division between its individual-oriented strains and what can broadly be called its more socially cooperative varieties. Though often overlooked, these currents did manifest themselves in various countries, in patterns that were strikingly similar.

In Britain, the archetypal example, political liberalism sprang from Lockean concepts of liberty, which stressed individual rights, and evolved in close conjunction with classical, laissez-faire market economics (identified with the "Manchester School" of the Liberal party). Indeed among many Latin Americanists, "liberal," "individual," and "laissez-faire" are unquestioningly linked. Yet late in the nineteenth century, theorists such as Matthew Arnold and T. H. Green began to espouse the idea that under the auspices of the state, people could (collectively) be liberated from ignorance and poverty. Eventually, these two factions of what was the British Liberal party broke apart, with its laissez-faire wing merging with conservative forces and its more radical elements gravitating toward socialism. In Germany also there were two decidedly opposed interpretations of liberalism, which can generally be described as Lockean (concerned with individual rights) and *étatiste* (looking to the state to protect collective rights).

The concept of liberalism in the French tradition, whose impact on Latin America has been most profound, is even more nebulous. To begin with, there are those partisans who divide French political thought into two broad camps, *conservateur*, upholding the Catholic church and the established social order, and *libéral*, opposing the church while endorsing progress and the rights of man (which, by the way, strongly resembles the experience of Spain and large parts of Latin America). For these theorists, liberalism encompasses the entire spectrum of the left. Other political thinkers, however, filter the French legacy with a much finer theoretical sieve. On the right they identify royalism and conservatism; on the left they distinguish between socialism, anarchism, syndicalism, and communism; and in the center they locate liberalism. In this construction, *libéralisme* is placed outside, even in opposition, to the left. But among thinkers who call themselves liberal, as in the other cases mentioned, there are conflicting currents in the French political tradition. On the one hand is the Lockean liberalism of limited state involvement, constitutionalism, laissez-faire, and the individual—that is, the liberalism of Voltaire, Montesquieu, and Benjamin Constant. On the other hand is the Rousseau-esque, democratic, collective, and étatiste liberalism of the radicals of the French Revolution and the upheavals of 1848.

There is now a growing body of literature concerning the phenomenon of "popular liberalism" in nineteenth-century Latin America that recognizes this intra-liberal division. In Chile, Andrew Daitsman has identified a "conservative" liberalism that he juxtaposed with more "radical" artisan-based forms of liberalism. He argued that "popular class ideological discussion occurred within an environment dominated by liberalism, and artisans appropriated key elements of that discourse" to define themselves politically. Such "ideological appropriation" involved "choices" and artisans "made different choices than their elite counterparts when they approached . . . liberalism."[50] The case of Mexico has also received significant attention. Brian Hamnett argued that divisions in Mexican liberalism emerged as splits between the national, provincial, and local levels, and especially as political struggles over the distribution of power and resources. "Provincial Liberalism" (also called "popular Liberalism") attracted "middle and lower socioethnic" (and economic) groups who "believed that the movement would redress grievances, set them free, or enable them to advance socially and materially." The Mexican "popular republican tradition" had a profound impact on local popular political mobilization, in contrast to the national level where (as suggested by Guy Thomson) there was a "marked diminution of the popular content of Liberalism."[51] So while the Revolutions of 1776, 1789, and 1848 had broad influence in Latin America, the "ambiguities inherent in the poorly defined, contested boundaries of European liberalism," as Andrew Daitsman trenchantly noted, "were intensified in the Latin American context."[52]

It is no surprise, therefore, that in nineteenth-century Colombia as well there were different and competing ideas of liberalism that led to divergent liberalisms. Almost from its formation at the midpoint of the nineteenth century, there were already significant splits in the Liberal party. Such divisions have regularly been neglected since some historians continue to stress (as already noted) that "the emerging party system was essentially bipolar, Conservative versus Liberal," with a relatively small ideological component.[53]

Ideological differences among Liberals were, however, a driving force. Elite Liberals understood egalitarian concepts to apply mainly to illustrious and wealthy citizens, "equals among equals," especially given the prevalence of racism among the upper classes. The masses of Indians, blacks, and mestizos "were treated as inferiors . . . who were incapable of deciding their own destinies."[54] But among the pueblo, the ideological and cultural aura of the 1848 revolution in France would powerfully jolt Colombian left liberalism at its formative moment. The currents of thought it generated had profound influence on the middling to lower strata, especially artisans, who read the works of Alphonse de Lamartine, Victor Hugo, Eugène Sue, Louis Blanc, and others. Between 1848 and 1870, there "was almost no periodical in Bogotá or in the provinces that did not publish fragments, essays, or serialized works" by these authors. "Their heroes and heroines were taken from the lower reaches of society," and their themes helped Colombians imagine a new world by emphasizing social progress for the disinherited, equality, and justice.[55] In fact, it has been argued that the "appropriation and semantic reelaboration of the ideals and symbols of the French Revolution by the subaltern classes was a constant from the moment of independence." The concepts of "liberty, equality, fraternity, human rights, and democracy" were appropriated by different sectors of society, foremost among whom were the artisans of the nineteenth century and the workers' movement in the 1930s and 1940s, culminating in the Gaitanista movement between 1944 and 1948.[56]

Certainly there is no disagreement that the 1850s were a watershed for increased political participation in Colombia. Around 1850, a new political generation took over from the generation of the wars of independence, the huge majority of which had been directly influenced by liberal ideas.[57] During the period between 1849 and 1854, which began with the election of Liberal president José Hilario López and ended with the military suppression of artisans and popular elements of the army in Bogotá, a division among Liberals momentarily emerged that would endure beneath the surface and periodically reappear in related forms over the next one hundred years.

After 1849, artisans founded *sociedades democráticas* (democratic societies) to protest tariffs, but these quickly became "vehicles for political action," which included elements of the intelligentsia and even some of the wealthier members of the commercial classes.[58] Gerardo Molina maintained that the "multiplication of the *sociedades democráticas*, once the example of Bogotá was followed in other cities . . . led to the radicalization of Liberalism."[59] These sociedades were especially strong, beyond the capital, in Cali, Neiva, Mompós, Cartagena, Santa Marta, and Buga, areas that would be left-Liberal bastions into the 1940s and beyond.[60]

Equally important, the Constitution of 1853 instituted universal male suffrage and direct elections. Many Liberals had their doubts "about the intrinsic ability of the common man to make an intelligent choice of candidates." They especially worried that campesinos would be "easily manipulated by priests, landowners, or other bosses, rather than voting independently." Yet the "always revered example of France," which embraced the vote for all male citizens after the Revolution of 1848, carried the day.[61]

To be sure, this juncture is a confusing one since both of the primary Liberal factions encompassed popular elements and espoused radical ideas. The "Gólgotas" (so-named because one of their number appealed to Jesus Christ as the "martyr of Golgotha") were radical Liberal reformers, mostly from upper-class origins, "who were anxious to move ahead rapidly with the dismantling of all governmental and corporate restrictions on individual liberty." Early on they were allied with organized artisans in support of president José Hilario López. Their key objective (and that of the Liberal regime) was "to eliminate collective in favor of individual forms of property ownership." The "Draconianos" were Liberals who worried that the move toward individual liberties might weaken social order, yet were generally of more popular origin.[62] A leader of the Draconiano faction, General Melo, gained the allegiance of the artisans and the sociedades in his 1854 coup.

Yet even while the 1854 coup is widely recognized as a moment full of contradiction, many historians have come to see this division among Liberals as a class division. Gerardo Molina maintained that the confrontation between the Gólgotas and the Draconianos was a continuation of the division between what he called "the tendency of liberalism proper and the democratic tendency." Molina argued that the Gólgotas represented "liberalism proper," which championed individual rights, and that the Draconianos were democrats who wanted to open up the political system. The differences between the two groups were "established on the level of economic interests" since the Gólgotas encompassed the bigger merchants, and those "who exaggerated the concept of free trade," while the Draconianos represented a political expression of artisans who advocated a protectionist state. Molina recognized "an incongruity" in that the Gólgotas were the ones most responsible for introducing socialist ideas into Colombia, for which many Draconianos "did not hide their antipathy." "The Gólgotas gave the impression of being intellectuals with principles but no masses, while the Draconiano leaders had popular backing but no principles." But ultimately, and most significantly, the Gólgotas made common cause with the Conservatives to crush the Draconiano/ artisan rebellion.[63] Jaime Jaramillo Uribe argued that within the sociedades, commercial factions of the Liberal party (principally the Gólgotas) came to see their cross-class alliances with the artisans as problematic. Artisans were clearly expressing their own interests, coming uncomfortably close to evoking the specter of class conflict.[64] Tirado Mejía stated flat out that the "events of 1854 and the war of that year were the occasion which presented the clearest case of class confrontation during the nineteenth century." For him, the key to understanding the coalition of the Draconianos and the artisans were the Liberal attacks on the military and its prerogatives, which threatened one of the best avenues for social mobility in Colombian society and led to the popular alliance between soldiers and artisans.[65] And David Sowell (who has argued that the "socialist" tendencies of the sociedades have been overstated and stressed the idea that political violence and electoral manipulation "almost immediately warped any sense of genuine representative government, even while appearances suggest a republican facade") granted that "partisan mobilizations allowed non-elites in some instances to express their class interests, making an alternative character for Colombia's political culture possible." Sowell also noted that "artisan republicanism . . . countered the dominant liberalism of the age."[66]

Finally, in a recent work that focused directly on the 1849–1854 period, Francisco Gutiérrez Sanín stressed the class dynamics involved as evolving partisan identities and Liberal factions surfaced at the same time. In 1851–52 members of the "*plebeyo* movement" were described as the "red Liberals" by both the Conservatives and the remaining Liberals. This divide manifested itself on the cultural level in the antagonism between the "artisans, men of the *ruana* (the Colombian poncho)" and the gentlemen "of cloak and shoes." This was a distinct class division between the "Doctores" and the "dregs *(hez)* of the *pueblo*." Gutiérrez Sanín argued that "between 1849 and 1853 it is clear that the *liberales rojos*, the *ruanas*" were at the "extreme left of the spectrum." Yet they thought of themselves as "authentic Liberals" and classified their "fellow party members of other tendencies as turncoats and collaborators with the Conservative party."[67]

Gutiérrez Sanín recognized the long-established interpretation of the struggles of the nineteenth century as mobilizations that were controlled and manipulated for elite ends. In his research, however, he identified "rich traditions of autonomy and resistance" through which the "*plebeyo* sectors rapidly learned to manipulate the political world even as it turned them into instruments" of elite struggle. Autonomous popular mobilization was "a constant" and only more intense in 1854. He ultimately rejected the simple "cannon fodder" image of early-nineteenth-century popular political participation, arguing that parts of the "popular sectors" were very politically sensitive. Artisans were able to organize; they had economic independence and were extremely conscious of their political rights; they were flexible, adaptable, and capable of making alliances with other groups and classes. In this period at mid-century, the *plebeyos* were busy "creating traditions" of popular mobilization.[68]

In fact, such splits among Liberals would survive throughout the rest of the nineteenth century, even as the struggles raging between Liberals and Conservatives seemed to eclipse them. Focusing on the regional dimensions of early Liberal division, Richard Stoller chronicled how conflicts in the early post-independence period about scarce resources and local rivalries came to be transformed by encounters with liberal ideology in the 1850s. Stoller demonstrated that the subversive potential offered by liberal ideology often split the Liberal party, helped create conservative strains, and stimulated violent conflict after 1860.[69] In the late nineteenth century liberalism was still known to be divided between "patricians" and "plebeians."[70] And Charles Bergquist noted that in the 1890s the "war Liberals" were revolutionary "men of the people" who saw their opponents within the party, the *civilistas* or "peace Liberals" as "faint-hearted merchants" in alliance with the Conservatives.[71] Indeed, García Márquez made a similar case in his fictional portrayal of the civil wars in *One Hundred Years of Solitude.*

Given the ideological splits that divided liberals world-wide, as well as the tumultuous nature of its own development, it was no surprise that the Colombian Liberal party continued to be seriously fractured after 1902.

Intra-party Debates over the Future of Liberalism: Two Liberalisms

In the twentieth century, many Liberals would look back to the struggles of the previous century as the birth process of a democratic vision of society that was evolving to include more popular nuances and even class-based notions. The recurring debates among Liberals over the nature and future of the party, debates that occurred throughout the first half of the century, made it clear that the two different (and long-lived) conceptualizations of liberalism were still very much alive. And what is more, the popularly oriented strain would show considerable overlap with other currents on the left.

During the 1920s, 1930s, and 1940s Liberals of a radical bent traced their lineage to Liberal general of the War of a Thousand Days and turn-of-the-century politician, Rafael Uribe Uribe. Gerardo Molina argued that Uribe Uribe and General Benjamín Herrera (another Liberal hero of the War of a Thousand Days and the Liberal presidential candidate of 1922) were part of the same movement to shift liberalism from an "individualist" party and accept a "collectivist creed." They wanted to create a new political organization in which "Liberalism would supply the masses and socialism the doctrine."[72] In 1935 Liberals in Cartagena claimed that the reform doctrines of the 1930s had been derived from the thought of Uribe Uribe and Herrera.[73] Soon after, a group of Liberals in Toro, Valle, sent a manifesto to president López, supporting his efforts to make Colombia "a truly democratic state, with guarantees for all its citizens." They were ready to battle for the "social, political, and economic" soul of the state, as had their "distinguished chieftains, Benjamín Herrera and Rafael Uribe Uribe."[74]

"Uribe's ideals," as the ideological bases of liberalism were often called, proved to be an ambiguous heritage, but nevertheless provided a base for more critical perspectives. Colombian leftists were much better acquainted with Uribe Uribe and his "doctrines grounded in social justice" than with Marx.[75] Indeed, membership in the Liberal party hardly precluded continued leftist sympathies. Many followers of Uribe Uribe considered themselves to be socialists. And though a celebrated Liberal leader of the War of a Thousand Days, Uribe Uribe was not remembered as a Colombian Napoleon, "crazed" for war. He fought, Liberals would later maintain, for a cause.[76] Uribe Uribe's importance to later Liberals is hard to overstate since his fame transcended "the barriers of myth and legend."[77]

The quintessence of Uribe Uribe's enduring fame among Colombian left Liberals found expression in one widely celebrated phrase, long remembered and often quoted by Gaitanistas. Near the turn of the century he argued, "If liberalism hopes to maintain its presence as a political entity, it has to drink at the fount of socialism."[78] This utterance established a dual heritage for Uribe Uribe, since the historical caudillo's personal notion of socialism was somewhat different from that of his later admirers. But he was nevertheless appropriated by the Liberal left as an important Liberal proponent of "socialism."

Uribe Uribe believed in what can be called preventative socialism. He presented his essential statement in a speech at the Teatro Municipal of

Bogotá in October 1904 entitled "Socialism of the State." He clearly stated that he was

> not a partisan of socialism from the bottom towards the top which negates property, attacks capital, denigrates religion, and subverts the legal regime . . . but I declare for socialism from the top to the bottom, carried out by the state.

Uribe Uribe believed that there was no choice but to institute socialism of the state, thereby resolving social conflicts before they appeared. He broke with the Latin American liberals of the nineteenth century who, he claimed, had been the "victims" of Smith, Mill, Spencer "and the other proponents of . . . the celebrated maxims of laissez faire." Such ideas had greatly benefited Europe at Latin America's expense. Indeed, Uribe Uribe asserted that socialism of the state was already a reality in Europe and the United States and was therefore the way of the future. In Europe, he argued, socialism of the state had produced an abundance of roads, rail, telegraphs, ports, improved public hygiene and education, "almost all the things which constitute the conquests of modern progress." Latin Americans, in contrast, believed in "individualism" and, as a consequence, were "poor, weak, and backward."[79]

So, given the nineteenth-century heritage of intra-Liberal struggle and the intellectual codification of its left wing by Uribe Uribe, it is no surprise that Liberals, both on the verge of power and during their first years of governmental control in the early 1930s, manifested a pronounced uncertainty concerning the character and direction of their party. Liberalism confronted a throng of unresolved questions regarding its connections to socialism: whether it was the party of the left, what were the essentials of its nineteenth-century manifestations, and how the party's platforms and policies should change, to name a few. This attempt to pull the party left was what Gerardo Molina has called the process of "socializing Liberalism."[80] Many scholars have investigated the years before and after the Liberal resurrection, yet the interpretation of the intra-Liberal debates of the late 1920s and 1930s is hardly complete.

Did Liberals flirt with radicalism but never really achieve it? So argued Marco Palacios when he admitted that the Liberals absorbed some socialist currents but then co-opted them. In drawing this conclusion, Palacios downplayed intra-Liberal conflict and disregarded the Liberal left as a significant entity. When Richard Stoller examined the party's debates and changes, he asserted that future president Alfonso López Pumarejo, "uniquely among Liberal figures of the 1920s, clearly saw these processes as they were occurring, and moreover he saw them as salutary, the 'freeing of the serfs from the glebe.'" Although he accurately stressed the partisan nature of López's rise, Stoller nevertheless emphasized the Liberal/Conservative dichotomy to the point that he overlooked the depth of intra-Liberal rivalry; indeed he seemed to ignore the importance of all left-Liberal currents other than López, even as he identified them. For Stoller, Liberal radicalism began and ended with Alfonso López. While J. Cordell Robinson acknowledged that the "ideological debate . . . broke many barriers in the country's political mentality," especially regarding "the relations between man and the state," he focused almost exclusively on elite discourse. Though he did note that in the 1920s there was a movement away from the "pillar principles" of nineteenth-century liberalism—namely "individualism" and laissez-faire—toward a redefinition of the Liberal party, Robinson's analysis precluded an acknowledgment of the long history of this process, portraying it as a new phenomenon among "young intellectuals."[81]

In his nuanced discussion of the ideological debates before and after 1930, Herbert Braun stressed "convivencia," the "politics of civility," between Liberal and Conservative leaders. In his treatment, however, little sense was given of inter-elite conflict, nor of ideological dissension among Liberals. Though he noted differences between Liberal and Conservative leaders, he put more stress on their connections and highlighted the division between paternalistic *convivialista* elites and the pueblo they were intent on civilizing. Richard Sharpless noted the "political ferment" of these years, but his analysis of the question was very much from the top down, focused on intellectuals in Bogotá. He too emphasized the convergence of Liberal and Conservative elites. While acknowledging some ideological differences, he pointed to the fact that when the system was threatened, "the oligarchy rediscovered its common interests." He mentioned the new generation called "los nuevos," many of whom, he noted, wanted to "socialize" liberalism, yet Sharpless gave only a limited sense of the left-Liberal tradition.[82]

Though instructive, each of these interpretations neglected to some degree the richness and longevity of the intra-Liberal debate, both among the elite themselves, and between the elites and the pueblo. The Liberal party verged at times on intra-Liberal class struggle, and radical tendencies spread well beyond the usually identified suspects. The observers cited above have focused on the perspective of the elite Liberals (and Conservatives) during the 1920s and 1930s, overlooking the significant contributions of earlier left-Liberal leaders, especially Uribe Uribe. They have also left out completely the ideas generated by the Liberal rank and file. When such intellectual precursors and popular Liberal voices are acknowledged, it becomes clear that this debate over the purpose and identity of liberalism was an important phenomenon with deep historical roots.

For rhetorical purposes some Liberals of the 1920s and 1930s alleged, rather disingenuously, that only in "recent times" could they speak of Liberals of left or right, or argue whether liberalism was or was not a "popular" party. For example, according to left-Liberal intellectual Armando Solano, in the "heroic age" of nineteenth-century liberalism it was not. By the mid 1930s, however, left Liberals such as Solano, who wanted to take the party in a more radical direction, asserted that liberalism should now stand for the cause of the pueblo, the "dispossessed," and equality before the law; "in a word, democracy."[83] Solano had struggled for some time with this issue. In 1928 he had briefly pulled out of the Liberal party. His statement, in which he publicly mused about the relative merits of remaining a Liberal or becoming a socialist, appeared in the *Diario Nacional* of Bogotá in April, the principle left-Liberal paper of Colombia during the 1920s and 1930s. Solano believed that on the one hand, the Liberal party had realized its historical mission, and on the other, that a "fusion" had taken place between the capitalist elements in liberalism and the reactionary Conservative party. Solano therefore declared himself a socialist.[84] His declaration created a rather instructive commotion in the elite Liberal press that demonstrated where the intra-Liberal battle lines were to be drawn. Solano's very public (though momentary) defection has been duly noted by other historians.[85] It was not, however, an anomaly, but rather only one of the more high-profile examples.[86]

The editors of *El Espectador* of Bogotá, one of the party's most prestigious papers, were not terribly concerned about this supposed "melancholy process of disintegration" of liberalism because they identified a Liberal core that would easily survive. Yet they dealt seriously with Solano, a respected representative of the "intellectual youth," who had declared liberalism defunct and baptized himself a socialist. They differed from his position "only with respect to its practical utility." Rejecting "the traditional nomenclature" would have a debilitating effect on the accomplishment of "the ideals of social justice and economic equity," which they held in common. Given *El Espectador*'s somewhat left-of-center position, they argued that in reality Solano was still a good Liberal. They believed that there were leftist, progressive forces within liberalism. They recognized the existence of a "small" and "capitalist" segment within the Liberal party that is "a friend to all Conservative governments." But they also saw in liberalism "the indispensable instrument of democracy" (with a strong economic role implied, and Uribe Uribe in mind).[87]

El Tiempo, bastion of the right wing of the Liberal party, also commented on Armando Solano's defection, but in a more defensive tone. They summarized the essence of his message as arguing that in practice, the Liberal party had ceased to exist because "capitalist elements" within it were seeking fusion with the Conservatives, "whose reactionary program" was "naturally opposed to social reform." They rejected his assertions by characterizing Solano as "an incurable idealist" who was "completely disconnected from reality," though they too asserted that his program was really the liberalism formulated at the convention of Medellín. Solano, whose head had been turned by "Bolshevik agitators," was destined for a "profound disenchantment." These agitators did not inspire the "rural proletariat" with the ideas of love, peace, culture, progress, respect for family and property that the editors of *El Tiempo* believed Solano advocated, but rather with "vengeance" and "barbarity." As Satan showed the earth to Christ and offered it up, so these agitators showed "the simple rural inhabitant" the "hacienda" saying, "it is yours." They predicted that he and other "superior spirits" would "have no influence" and their efforts would "be condemned to sterility."[88]

El Espectador and *El Tiempo* clearly demonstrated the tension in the Liberal party on the eve of its return to power. In fact, they showed that liberalism was divided into two distinct varieties. Historically there had been many Liberal (and Conservative) subgroups. The so-called two-party system in Colombia, therefore, has always been extremely complicated in practice. Eduardo Posada-Carbó has stressed that any understanding of intra-party competition "needs to be complemented by a picture of the rival factions." He drew on the work of Paul Oquist and Malcolm Deas, who made similar observations. Oquist remarked that calling the Colombian political environment a two-party system is tantamount to a "misnomer . . . given the constant proliferation of factions." Deas argued that "the system can only be labeled bipartisan in a vague sense."[89] Indeed Gerardo Molina maintained, as pointed out earlier, that within the Liberal party there had long coexisted a "bourgeois line" and a "popular line." The first emphasized "a long catalogue of individual and political rights" and the second "went further," having in mind "an egalitarian society."[90] By the early 1930s, the Liberal party was clearly divided into two general camps. These appeared in many different but recognizable manifestations that had diverse names, identified as "individualist," "bourgeois," or "Manchesterian" liberalism, versus "collective," "modern," or "left" liberalism.

Many left Liberals perceived a state of open class warfare within the party. Agustín Gusmán in Cúcuta characterized these Liberal divisions in 1932 as a "war" for "real democracy" in the *concejo* between "aristocrats who traffic with the title of Liberal" and the "humble sons of the *pueblo*."[91] A lawyer in Popayán argued that there were two currents within liberalism. The first, which he characterized as "the bourgeois element" had "no program whatsoever," lest it be to "choke all desires for social betterment." They were "castas políticas" that did not represent "collective interests" but rather fought over the spoils of government. They counted "on the incomprehension and Liberal idolatry of the *pueblo*." In opposition struggled "the youth in their movements of the left" and workers.[92] In Bucaramanga, left Liberals of the Casa Liberal rejected the "rude attacks" of Liberals they labeled "conservative" and "bourgeois." The ideological campaign of "leftist doctrine" carried out by the Casa Liberal "threatened" the bourgeois Liberals' "plans of speculation." "As always," said the left Liberals, they were labeled "communist" because they wanted politics in Santander to "take into account popular desires."[93]

Within the party (on both the national and local levels), the left and the right wings waged a struggle for dominance after gaining control of the presidency in 1930. In Santander the left had "an open revolutionary sensibility regarding what liberalism" was and should be. Yet this "political tendency" had "enemies with influence and money who wanted to maintain a distance from leftist thought." These "derechistas" (right-wingers) within the party would not rest until they had brought about "the extinction of the revolutionary focus."[94] The left Liberals of the "Casa Liberal" wanted to lift politics "from the terrain of personalism . . . and raise it to the plane of doctrine." They noted a "fundamental difference" between the "economic theses" of their "leftist movement" and the "thought of professional politicians" within the Liberal party.[95] Leftist liberalism was in "rebellion against the old prejudices to show [workers] the value of the new ideas."[96]

This fundamental dichotomy between Liberals was habitually characterized as a struggle between "individualist" and "collectivist" currents. "As you should know," a left Liberal in Popayán told Gaitán in 1932, "here there are two Liberal currents in struggle: the declining Liberalism, *individualista* and *manchesteriano*; and the truly leftist Liberalism." In the first current were the Governor and his minions and in the second were the university youth and the pueblo.[97] The next year the editors of *El Crisol* of Cali expounded upon the difference between old "individualistic" liberalism and new "collectivist" liberalism. "Liberal philosophers of the old Manchesterian school," they argued "were rigidly individualistic." Bentham, Gladstone, Mill, and many other thinkers "were justly considered apostles of the old liberal ideas." But even they leaned toward "advanced principles" such as the right to strike, freedom from arbitrary abuse of power, and the rights of workers to participate in the profit of large industrial establishments. This was a movement toward "collectivist liberalism." The "simple appreciation of individual acts does not negate the necessity of collective responsibilities."[98] To *El Crisol* it was not a problem that in Bogotá "leftist politicians," who were "radicals and socialists," searched for ways to advance a common agenda by incorporating "collectivist thought" into the realm of "respectable principles." Liberalism for them was "a living force," and they predicted that the forces of the left would march together.[99] And left Liberals resented the pressure they felt from "los individualistas" in the party establishment. As one lamented in Neiva, "Our *copartidarios*, especially the leftists" were "persecuted by the Conservatives and the individualist Liberals of the worse kind."[100]

Collectivist liberalism was also known as "modern" liberalism. Writing in 1937, Rogerio Gómez Suarez argued that "modern Liberalism . . . should only be concerned with bringing social justice." Since the Liberal party was "an essentially democratic party," and since "its immense majority" was comprised of "the middle class, workers *(obreros)*, and rural workers *(trabajadores del campo)*," it was clear that the party "should pass laws that bring about the redemption of the popular classes, creating for them a more elevated standard of living . . . through more egalitarian distribution."[101] For many, this "new" liberalism required the rejection of the "old." Liberals "of the cutting edge" who proclaimed their "liberalism of the left" rejected the "old . . . Manchesterian ideas."[102] Others felt the need to be "divorced from the Liberalism of Manchester."[103] *El Crisol* of Cali believed that the Liberal party, solidly anchored in "the new canons of modern liberalism," would be a part of the vanguard of reform, at the head of the social revolution.[104] Yet they warned of the "dangers" that confronted "advanced ideas" within the Liberal party. For "enthusiastically" defending the ideas of Rafael Uribe Uribe and his "democratic teachings," they had been attacked by the party's "conservative elements," the enemies of the pueblo and of the interests of the worker.[105]

Reminiscent of Uribe Uribe, left Liberals were very likely to stress connections between the "modern" democratic Liberal tradition and socialism. In 1932 left Liberals in Popayán believed that they must consider, "from the firm ground of Liberal principles," what they called the "modern political theories of social organization." These included, "obtaining control of the means of production, of capital, of the land, of property by the state, (and) repressing all exploitation of the proletariat by the capitalist classes." By examining the fundamentals of socialism, Colombian liberalism could "guarantee that its political causes" would be "inspired by the well-being of the popular classes." They considered liberal doctrine, as expressed in the traditions of France, Great Britain, and the United States, in documents such as the Declaration of the Rights of Man, to have had a very important role in civilization. If at an earlier time capitalism had advanced these liberties, now the advance of these ideals depended on socialism.[106]

In 1937 Marco Tulio Salgado touched on many of the elements involved in the Liberal dichotomy. He considered liberalism to be "a dramatic party which evolves and adapts to the conditions of the period" and not a "static organization." The new Liberals had "learned that it is a revolutionary party" based on a "democratic structure." They argued that "the minorities" of the party were what could be called "the aristocrats of liberalism, those who in the economic realm" were "confused with the Conservatives." The left of the party defended "the politics of equality and social justice, the maximum aspiration of the pueblo." They wanted to create "new institutions . . . free of the hegemony exercised by the aristocratic castes." "The left," he claimed, was "in essence the negation of *manzanillaje* (dirty and rotten politics)."[107]

It is no surprise, therefore, that interconnectedness was the essence of the Colombian left of the 1920s, 1930s, and later.[108] Many individuals would have simultaneously included themselves in such categories as artisan, worker, or pueblo and many simultaneously wore different political labels such as leftist, left Liberal, socialist, communist, Lopista (a follower of President Alfonso López Pumarejo after 1934), and later, Gaitanista.

Left Liberals in Magdalena insisted in 1937 that the Liberal youth of Colombia were "unshakably leftist" and that "liberalism and leftism" were "faultlessly synonymous."[109] Guillermo Hernández Rodríguez, lawyer, leftist activist, and one of the founders of the PSR, maintained years later that the relations between socialism and liberalism were very close. A mix of people inhabited these related movements, he pointed out. Individuals of "a socialist tendency," veterans of the civil wars of the last century, and Liberal leaders all began to "associate organically with the nascent (socialist) movement" and "to make a revolution in the style of the past century."[110] This observation was echoed by local historian and longtime resident of Barrancabermeja, Rafael Núñez, who asserted in 1985 that in the 1920s a certain "confusion" existed in the minds of many people regarding the differences between "socialism" and Colombian liberalism. And in the 1930s "there was an affinity between Liberals, socialists, and communists" because of the party's defense of human liberties and its democratic nature.[111]

For left Liberals in Líbano in 1933 connections on the left were embedded in the Colombian past. They grounded their party affiliation in the Liberals' tradition of popular struggle. They addressed the weight of history, of "our inheritance," which was a drag on Colombia despite the efforts and great works of Liberal heroes of the past. The pueblo, "the great mass of the disinherited," suffered and wept "under the burden of injustice." They spoke of the "spirit of equality . . . that animated the champions of Independence after 1812," that "sense of justice" which energized liberalism's "revolutionary ideals" in its struggle for "the future betterment of the humble classes and the proletariat." Yet the party had been "contaminated" by Conservative and reactionary elements. These "so-called Liberals" employed boss politics and favoritism. These Liberals, like the Conservatives before them, "paralyzed" the party's dynamic. They were "enemies of revolutionary ideology." Now was the moment, they argued, to move at full speed toward the "ORGANIZATION OF A LEFT-IST LIBERALISM" (their emphasis).

Another group, in Cartago in 1937, also defined liberalism and the left in terms of Colombia's history of mobilization, linking political rights and economic rights. Liberalism had to "renew its faith in its own men" to guard against "the reactionary right" and "communist demagoguery." It was "necessary to revive the authentic Liberal doctrine" whose "basic principles" they understood as "science at the service of the community and for the glory of the *patria*." Politics was a "social science" that consisted of more than carrying out pure elections, though this they agreed was "an elevated democratic function." They called for Liberal politics of economic intervention and direction. The "center of gravity of democratic concern" had shifted and the Liberal action of the present was not that of yesterday. In the eighteenth and nineteenth centuries "democratic and revolutionary politics" were rightly concerned with civil and political rights, as these Liberals "found solemnly enshrined in the celebrated formulas of French constitutionalism." Now, they argued, the pueblo had "other chains which humble it." Now it was not the tyranny of a monarch but rather the misery and pain of their lives. Therefore, whereas the goal had previously been political liberty, "now the conquest must be of economic liberty." They called for state intervention and administration, but not for the "decapitation" of the rights of the individual. "It is not the STATE against the INDIVIDUAL, but rather intervention that favors liberty and equality . . . of the material conditions . . . of existence" (their emphasis). Now "modern Liberalism" aimed to "realize in the economic order the postulates of justice inspired by the Revolution of 1789."[112]

In Cali left Liberals underscored leftist interconnections in 1933, maintaining that "all the ideological currents on the left" agreed on one thing: "the collective well-being." Radical thought, they argued, sought "more effective and timely ways to bring about socio-political reforms." This "radical current is not nor needs to be independent of liberalism. Rather it is the true essence of modern Liberal theory which seeks out zones of equilibrium between capital and labor."[113] In 1937 Armando Solano, who quickly had returned to the party, argued that liberalism was "leftist," and had a "brilliant popular tradition." He stressed that it had traditionally been "a popular party, a democratic party, friend of the *campesinos*, of the artisan, of workers of all classes."[114] Self-proclaimed leftists in Santa Marta also defined the left in terms of its connections, asserting that "liberalism, leftists, socialistas, comunistas, and the revolutionary students" were "the forces that have to oppose reaction."[115] The right too noticed the connections. Left Liberals were routinely labeled *comunista*.[116]

Some openly called for socialism on the Liberal left, equating Colombian liberalism and socialism. A twenty-one-year-old socialist wrote to Gaitán in 1933 expressing his thoughts on theory, political strategy, class struggle, and moral feeling. He was most interested in finding ways to support "the *clase trabajadora*" and keeping it from being "strangled by the *burgueses*." He looked to "the dawn . . . of a socialism well understood." He wanted a "regenerative socialism" that would "throw to the ground these ideologies that asphyxiate us" and bring the "social transformation . . . demanded by the *pueblo*." It pained him to see the workers, from sunup to sundown, pouring their sweat into the ground, only to have the "great property owners" steal the fruit. This was "horrible and frightful." What was called for, therefore, was "a disinterested element of society which does not share the speculative goal of the *burgueses*, that can defend (the workers) . . . in the name of JUSTICE" (his emphasis).[117] Another leftist youth, after making reference to Uribe Uribe, spoke of his "leftist ideas" and of breaking with the "pseudo politicians that call themselves Liberals."[118]

The *Diario Nacional* of Bogotá in 1934 saw the Liberal party as the party of the left, though not communist. In the face of hardcore "individualism" and "fashionable leftism," its editors argued, the Liberal party stood firm and secure, "not participating in the dictatorships of Manchester or the revolutionary theories of Moscow." It was "a new Liberal party that would give the Liberal as well as Conservative masses the necessary reforms" in the nation's social, judicial, and economic structures. Even if Colombia was still not "a country where revolutionary and Marxist doctrines could be realized," nonetheless, in the next legislature there would be "a great revolutionary spirit intent on obtaining constitutional reforms of an evidently leftist flavor."[119] Others were more bold. In Santa Marta in 1936 there were those who argued that "left" Liberals were the true Liberals because they had "a program in sync with the economic needs of the republic." They would make the party of "we the workers, we the exploited by the current economic system, we the slaves." They wanted "revolution . . . renovation [and] . . . justice."[120]

Radical left Liberals in Cali in 1933 were confident that justice and progress would ensure the inevitable march of the left. *El Crisol* spoke of "the clamorous failure of the capitalist system" that four years into the Great Depression had "provoked everywhere a movement of open rebellion against all manifestations of worker exploitation by the plutocratic organizations." *El Crisol* claimed this was so clear that, in Cali, even the Catholic press was pilfering Marxist phrases. Such economic problems, "the logical consequence of current economic disequilibrium," showed a "sick organism." They interpreted the nation's "economic-social" crisis from the perspective of "revolutionary ideas" embraced by the Liberal youth. "Socialism of the state is the only solution" they proclaimed; the "integral revolution advances triumphantly."[121] Discussing the exploitation of colonos, *El Crisol* called for "distributive justice," since the time had arrived for new leftist economic struggles to replace the old political ones. The next national Congress, they argued, would be "composed in its great majority of leftist elements," and they believed the moment had arrived to confront "all social problems, finding a human solution." They quoted *Diario Nacional*, which argued that now the country felt a burning desire for reform. The moment was ripe "to change the old banners and the political philosophies they represented, around which the old struggles were fought, for a new banner of economic ideals, the primordial base of moral and material progress." They wanted to substitute the "Byzantine discourse" of the past with ideas of "practical betterment." They wanted to leave the old thinkers, "phrase turners," and "deceivers" and follow "men of action and energy, capable of forging the happiness of the pueblo." They wanted fewer "written laws that are not enforced, fewer liberties and rights ridiculously consigned to the constitution, fewer guarantees and illusory prerogatives, and in their place . . . something real and tangible . . . equitable distribution."[122] These were themes that would appear again and again in Gaitanista discourse.

Though firmly rooted in Colombian history, the left-Liberal tradition offered an alternative path within the traditional party system. Given the divisions within liberalism's intellectual legacy, it was no surprise that after the consolidation of the nation in the 1840s, competing elite and popular currents continued to grapple for the soul of the Liberal party. Consequently, when left Liberals looked back to the civil wars and electoral contests of the nineteenth century, they identified a propensity for popular mobilization among Colombians who had a long-standing vision of justice and democracy. These conflicts were not simple battles for control of government; they were also struggles of resistance for social and political change led by the left Liberals. The intra-Liberal contradiction between the "dos corrientes" (two currents) of liberalism was alive and well in the early decades of the twentieth century, manifesting itself in the intra-party debate over the future of liberalism. Colombians of the pueblo entered the 1930s with a sense of left-Liberal radicalism. This radicalism would not be diminished by the fact that it took shape within a multiclass and elite-dominated party.

2

Genesis of a Left-Liberal *Caudillo*

"Give me a balcony," the Ecuadorian populist leader José María Velasco Ibarra is reported to have said, "and I will be president." As he epitomized, populist movements in Latin America were typically unified by a single dynamic individual. Studies of populism, consequently, all too often begin and end with a fetish-like fixation on such leaders and the charismatic personalism they employ. Yet Perón, Vargas, Cárdenas, and other examples of the breed did not call their movements out of the ether like so many gods. Nor was Gaitán the sire of the Gaitanista impulse, but rather, like a lens that focuses light, he brought together many important elements of Colombia's tradition of popular mobilization. This study, therefore, is more about Gaitanismo and the left-Liberal political culture from which it sprang than about Gaitán per se. He was, however, central to the story as it unfolded, so this chapter provides a portrait of Gaitán up until the flowering of his public career in 1928. It examines his origins and rootedness in Colombia's history of struggle, his thought and its internal contradictions, his professional and political formation, and the nagging question of his supposed connections to fascism. It will demonstrate why Gaitán could legitimately, if grandiloquently, claim that he was not a man, "but a *pueblo*."

Origins

Jorge Eliécer Gaitán Ayala was born on the twenty-third of January 1903 in Las Cruces, a downtown Bogotá neighborhood already past its prime.[1] Soon thereafter financial problems obliged his family to move further out to a working-class barrio aptly named El Egipto. His father Eliécer was an intellectual jack-of-all-trades, a precarious way of life not uncommon for the relatively well educated but property-less members of Latin American societies. A political activist, he founded two small Liberal newspapers in 1903 and 1905, which both—not surprising for the breed—quickly disappeared. Don Eliécer had amassed a large collection of books to write a history of Colombia. These turned out to be his only solid asset. He therefore opened a used book shop.

Though he proved to be a rather hapless provider for his family, Don Eliécer instilled in young Jorge Eliécer a love of books, ideas, and the activist left-Liberal tradition. As a student of Colombian history, Gaitán's father often recounted the "heroic" struggles of the Liberal party during the last century. As was the case with other left Liberals, the importance of Gaitán's understanding of Colombian history is hard to overstate. From early in life he was steeped in the Liberal party's culture of struggle, a historical awareness that would color his entire political career.

Gaitán's mother, Doña Manuela Ayala de Gaitán, also greatly influenced his development. A graduate of the Escuela Normal, Colombia's teacher-training institute, she gained a reputation in Bogotá and the surrounding towns of Cundinamarca as a teacher of progressive and moderately feminist views. Jorge Eliécer, the eldest of six children, was Manuela's favorite, and she spared nothing in providing his initial schooling. Her highest aspiration was for him to obtain a university education.

Gaitán grew up in a stressful family atmosphere. As the oldest child, he often had to look after his brothers and sisters, and his relationship with his father was by and large a contentious one. In particular, he clashed with Eliécer senior concerning his future vocation; his father wanted him to follow a sensible route, such as accounting, and not aspire to higher education and a political career. An intelligent and strong-willed boy who suffered numerous insults because of his dark skin, Jorge Eliécer also fought with his teachers and his lighter-skinned and more affluent classmates. He was expelled from several schools before his parents' political connections helped him get a scholarship to the Colegio Araújo in 1913. The school's founder, the renowned Liberal educator Simón Araújo, made a strong impression on the young Gaitán. Since Araújo's school remained unaccredited by the Conservative educational establishment, the ambitious Jorge Eliécer transferred during his last year to the Colegio of Martín Restrepo Mejía. He graduated with high grades in 1919 and in February 1920 entered the Universidad Nacional to study law.

Self-reliant and pugnacious, Gaitán began his political activities and demonstrated his gift for oratory while still a teenager attending the Colegio Araújo. In 1917 he carried out an independent speaking campaign in the towns around Bogotá in favor of the Conservative poet Guillermo Valencia, who led a coalition of moderate Conservatives and Liberals against the ruling party. Though Gaitán was at first ignored by the coalition's leadership, the Liberal caudillo Benjamín Herrera eventually dispatched him on an even more far-reaching stint through the left-Liberal regions of western Cundinamarca and Tolima. This tour brought him important recognition and laid the foundation for later political support. As a university student Gaitán became one of Herrera's senior aides in the caudillo's unsuccessful 1922 presidential campaign. Herrera once again sent Gaitán on a speaking tour, though this time through the Conservative bastions of northern Cundinamarca and Boyacá where he stirred up considerable excitement. Gaitán developed enough of a following among respectful Liberals impressed by his daring to be elected to the Cundinamarca departmental assembly in 1923 to represent the city of Girardot.

At the university Gaitán split his time between political activity and study. Convinced that education was unjustly restricted to a small portion of Colombian society, he founded the University Center for Cultural Propaganda, which lasted from May of 1920 to January of 1921. With support from the Ministry of Education, the center was responsible for organizing lectures in Bogotá on practical subjects, and even took its show on the road to Tolima, Caldas, and Valle. Yet as the center's project drifted into more overtly political territory, with a message critical of the status quo, it came under criticism in the press. Initiating a pattern that would later earn him the label of opportunist, Gaitán let it die when he felt its usefulness was at an end.

Gaitán endured extreme economic difficulties, living off a diet of bread, cheese, and the mainstay of the poorer classes, *agua de panela* (warm brown-sugar water). And though immersed in politics and lacking an adequate place to work, he still found time for intensive learning, often reading in open plazas and parks, and excelled academically. Slightly smug, self-important, and affecting aloofness, Gaitán was a gifted boy of humble background, resentful of his social betters, and driven to achieve.

Rome: Guilt by Association

The years between his graduation from the university in 1924 and his election to the House of Representatives in 1928 were very busy ones for Gaitán. He aspired to study under Enrico Ferri, perhaps the foremost scholar of penal law in his day. After a short period of law practice in Bogotá he helped his brother Manuel, a medical student, open a pharmacy. Though the business provided meager income, barely sufficient for Gaitán to pursue his dream of European study, he turned down a spot on the Colombian Legation in Italy that his mother had cajoled from the

Conservative government. Ever proud, he was intent on owing nothing to the political establishment.

The outline of Gaitán's experience in Italy and its aftermath are well known.[2] In July 1926 Gaitán enrolled at the Royal University in Rome, and a year later graduated at the top of his class. Gaitán returned to Colombia in 1928 just in time to participate in one of the most important labor crises in Colombian history. Though Gaitán's sojourn in Italy was most important to him personally for the impact it had on his professional development, it was remembered for placing him at the epicenter of fascism.

Not only had Gaitán become a champion of Enrico Ferri's ideas in Colombia, Ferri also represented a model for the young Colombian to follow. Ferri came from a modest lower-middle-class background and went on to become an extremely successful trial lawyer and one of Italy's most famous orators. He was a member of parliament and edited the socialist paper *Avanti*. A republican and a socialist, he nevertheless became a fascist sympathizer in his later years. Ferri's ultimate goal was to enact the penal codes that he believed would improve society and the well-being of all its members, especially the less fortunate. Gaitán would be only the second Colombian lawyer, after his fellow left Liberal and political collaborator Carlos Arango Vélez, to study with Ferri.

Gaitán also wanted the prestige that came with having a degree from a European university. Such a distinction would move the young mestizo lawyer closer to the higher spheres of Colombian society. Members of the Colombian elite were often more familiar with Europe than with large portions of their own country and traveled there as a matter of course. Yet his was not the typical European grand tour made by a son of the Latin American upper classes. For Gaitán professional pride proved a much more powerful source of a motivation than did social climbing. Soon after his return to Colombia Gaitán disdainfully pointed out in an interview that many Colombians abroad only experienced "the vain and superficial life of the cabaret."[3]

Limited resources made his life as a student very difficult, though he was no stranger to studying and excelling under conditions of financial adversity. He stayed in the most humble of pensiones, moving often in an attempt to stay ahead of his creditors. He lived beyond his means, imperfectly emulating the lifestyle of his upper-class associates, but because of his intelligence and their fascination with his dark skin, Gaitán was welcomed into exalted social circles. This was ironic given that later in his career he would be denigrated among the Colombian elite because of his dark skin and mestizo features. (The oligarquía and right-wing political cartoonists of the 1940s, Herbert Braun has shown, would emphasize his dark complexion and fixate on the size of his teeth.)[4] Most significantly, Gaitán became the protégé of Ferri himself, and the two men rapidly formed a deep friendship.

In Italy Gaitán witnessed firsthand Mussolini's exploits, and it is certain that he attended Fascist rallies and heard Il Duce speak on various occasions. Gaitán, a true student of politics, was intrigued by the spectacles. He was already a seasoned public speaker long before he went to Italy, but there can be little doubt that he was influenced by the techniques the Italian caudillo employed. His mature style utilized dramatic gestures and alternating vocal patterns, and like Mussolini's, Gaitán's speeches took on the aspect of a dialogue between himself and his listeners. After his return from Italy, Gaitán acknowledged that he was impressed by Mussolini's power to steer a political rally and by his vigor.

Though Gaitán was always a gregarious fellow, and he certainly cut a memorable figure in Rome, he never lost sight of why he was there. After just one short year of industrious study Gaitán graduated magna cum laude and first in his class, and his technically focused thesis, "Criterio positivo de la premeditación," was awarded the Ferri Prize for criminal law from the hand of Professor Ferri himself. Ferri declared Gaitán to be one of the best students he had ever instructed. As a result, Gaitán became the first Latin America member of the Italian section of the International Society of Penal Law. Gaitán fondly remembered the emotional scene in the presence of King Victor Emanuel, Mussolini, and his ministers in which he received his degree and orally presented his thesis. He retold the story numerous times over the years and perhaps embellished it. Back in Colombia Gaitán's winning of the Ferri Prize was front-page news.[5]

After his graduation, Gaitán used the cash award of the Ferri prize to travel through Europe and ended up in Paris, where he lingered a few months. On the trip he visited the great monuments of European culture and thereby earned an exclusive badge of status that very few Colombians could claim. In Paris Gaitán once again made a lasting impression on the other Latin Americans he met. A mestizo from a humble background who nevertheless possessed elegance, charm, sophistication, and unparalleled professional success seemed peculiar and out of place.

Upon his return to Colombia in 1928 it was clear that Gaitán had crossed a significant threshold and had to be taken seriously as an intellectual and as a jurist. Of course, before he left for Italy he had already received a university degree and joined the ranks of the more important young Liberal politicians. Yet now he had become the prize pupil of a famous old-world scholar and had undeniably received the stamp of European approval. For upper-class Colombians this was especially important, and hard to snub. As the Liberal intellectuals at *El Espectador* noted, he was "an impetuous professional" and "a pleasant case of distropicalization."[6]

At this point a slight detour is necessary. As noted earlier many scholars have looked upon Latin American populism as a close cousin to fascism, and in Gaitán's case there was a concrete connection to fascist Italy. Because of his studies in Rome, he has always suffered from guilt by association. As Eric Hobsbawm argued in a recent book, "It was in Latin America that European fascist influence was to be open and acknowledged, both on individual politicians . . . and on regimes," and he named Gaitán along with the other usual suspects, Juan Perón and Getulio Vargas.[7]

The standard communist practice throughout Latin America in the 1930s and 1940s was to characterize their populist rivals as "fascista" to gain political advantage. Indeed, the verdict among many members of Colombia's left-leaning intelligentsia continues to be that Gaitán was a fascist.[8] In addition to his time in Italy, Gaitán's lively speaking style showcased a dramatic flare for gesticulation, emotion, rhetorical embellishment, and allusions to Colombia's national spirit. What is more, his multiclass movement flourished in an atmosphere of tense inter-class alliance and conflict.

The case against Gaitán, however, is based largely on circumstantial evidence and ignores direct proof that he was personally hostile to fascism. Gaitán, after all, was a prime example of the left-Liberal tradition that spawned both the radical elements of the Liberal party and the Communist party itself. The portrayal of Gaitán as a fascist also does not account for his success in eventually transcending the Communist party and Liberal establishment to become the leader of the Colombian left.[9]

Gaitán's experience begs two fundamental questions: what is fascism? and what are its connections to Latin American populism? Both political phenomena generally manifest a personalistic and charismatic leader making highly emotional appeals based upon notions of the "national spirit" to a "mass" or multiclass following. Both populism and fascism arose during the world economic crises resulting from World War I and the Great Depression, and both frequently receive the contradictory labels of "revolutionary" and "counter-revolutionary." Finally, these similarities have been reinforced by the propensity of the organized left in Latin America to employ the fascist label against populists.

Given the problems involved in merely supplying definitions for fascism and populism, let alone making useful comparisons, some historians are tempted to throw out both terms as vague theoretical constructs and focus instead on individual historical cases. Concepts like "fascism" (another good example is "feudalism") were developed to explain European phenomena and generally do not thrive in the Latin American context. A few meaningful distinctions can be made, however. In spite of the many problematic similarities between populists and fascists, they maintained very different relationships with the working class. And though both were arguably mass movements, fascism exemplified a general attempt to demobilize, control, and, through violence, exclude certain groups from power, while populism often represented a dramatic mobilization and increase in political power for the non-elite classes.

Barrington Moore, echoing the interpretation offered by Marx and Engels of "Bonapartism," argued that some forms of capitalist transition are good for accumulation but bad for "free institutions." While Moore placed his view of fascism in a context very much akin to the rise of populism ("what is sometimes more turgidly called the entrance of the masses onto the historical stage"), he nevertheless viewed fascism as "an attempt to make reaction and conservatism popular and plebeian."[10] This was roughly the assessment of fascism offered by socialists and communists in the interwar years, that fascism rose to power through a "counter-revolution." They also tended "to make fascism and capitalism synonymous." The Comintern's (that is, the Third Communist International's) general line came to characterize fascism "as the agent of monopoly capitalism."[11]

There are, of course, problems with the concept of "counter-revolution." To use this phrase implies that a consensus definition exists for the term "revolutionary," which is hardly the case. Since at least the French Revolution, the word revolution has consistently been associated with "progress," "advancement," and "forward motion," but the obvious question is, advancement toward what? As Eugen Weber argued, "towards the Left, of course."[12] But if revolution is defined in terms of popular participation and a social agenda of change that goes beyond simple restoration of something old, the negative essence of counter-revolutionary movements becomes clouded. In both these senses, Italian Fascism and German National Socialism qualify as "revolutions." As Ian Kershaw demonstrated, historians have viewed Nazism as "genuinely revolutionary in content," as "quintessentially counter-revolutionary," as "revolutionary reaction," and as "plain social reaction."[13] At this point, Weber's suggestion that the question "what is revolution?" be replaced with "what kind of revolution is it?" is most helpful. Fascism in most of its varieties was, however, a "counter" movement in one fundamental sense. In post-1917 Europe, where fascism first arose, it reacted against the "red" revolution and the Comintern's popular fronts. Even Weber admitted that in this way, fascism is "properly counterrevolutionary."[14] One of fascism's primary effects was to reinforce the strained position of the agrarian and industrial elites by smashing organized labor. In the case of National Socialism, the composition of class relations in 1933 "reversed in violent fashion the advances made by the working class not only since 1918, but since Bismarck's era, strengthened the weakened position of capitalism, and upheld the reactionary forces of social order."[15]

In general terms, a tension manifested itself in fascism between the working class and the economically and socially jeopardized, downwardly mobile members of all classes. A rough consensus exists, then, that the main troops of the fascist advance were the uprooted, the threatened, the discontented social products of defeat in war and general economic depression.[16] But whether it was from fear of revolution or simply a desire to control workers, there is little disagreement that fascists came to power through an alliance with the political right. And in this coalition, fascism served to demobilize a large part of the population and exclude them from power.

In Latin American populism, on the other hand, the "petty bourgeoisie" often handled its insecurity differently: by casting its lot with the lower classes, especially the urban working class, instead of the industrial and agrarian elites. While often experiencing substantial political participation for the first time, they were in alliance, not competition, with the working classes. They were not a discontented fringe of society but rather represented a large portion of the population with aspirations toward political involvement. Fascism attempted to exclude the "popular" elements of society, especially the working class, from power while populism (even at the "right" end of the continuum) acknowledged the arrival of broad-based participation in politics and simply sought to direct its course—with varying degrees of success. Populist leaders sought out labor as a source of support, not as an enemy to attack.[17] Fascists and populists were also different in their relations with the industrial and agrarian elites. While fascists were embraced, or at least tolerated for reasons of self-interest, by elites in Europe, Latin American elites fought populism to the very end. In Latin America, neither the workers nor the elites saw the gains made by the working class as token.

In the specific case of Gaitán, to label him a fascist one must ignore what he consistently said about fascism and the moral current of social justice in his thought, as well as his obvious connections to the working class. In one of his first public statements after his return from Europe, Gaitán denigrated fascism and its leader. In February 1928 Gaitán characterized Mussolini as a "sad exhibitionist." That Mussolini's speeches were "picturesque," and that he showed considerable energy, no one could deny. Yet Gaitán called him "ridiculous" and argued that Mussolini was fortunate in that Italians simply had no concept of "the ridiculous." Gaitán noted that Italians were expected to respond in a choreographed way to his speeches.[18] Gaitán also made it clear that he was not seduced by fascist thought. In fact, Gaitán argued that fascism had no discernable ideology. It was born in the original sin of violence and had served to negate human liberties. "Mussolini, taking advantage of the masses in the disarray following the World War, could jump from one doctrine to another without losing authority because he held power through fear and intimidation. He had betrayed his own ideas and his followers once in power, with disastrous results for Italy."[19] Gaitán never publicly changed his mind regarding fascism, and indeed, when he spoke of it in later years, it was to criticize it.[20] Even though Ferri, perhaps for reasons of political opportunism and survival, became a fascist sympathizer, there is no real evidence that his student followed suit.

Parenthetically, it should be noted that in contrast to Gaitán, Juan Perón's personal admiration for the fascist state was never in doubt. He served between 1939 and 1941 as a military observer in one of Italy's alpine divisions near the French border and for a short time with the Argentine embassy in Rome. He was much impressed by the "pageantry" and machine-like nature of the Italian state. This "master impression" would "inspire, and in part, reinforce the distinctly pro-Axis coloration of Perón's views concerning the war and Argentina's relationship to it."[21] Yet even in Perón's case, it is difficult to label him a fascist.[22] His mobilization rested on a solid working-class base, and his pro-Axis position during the war was as much a function of the Italian and German ancestry (and origin) of a large portion of Argentina's population as it was of his personal sympathies.

Gaitán's term of study in Mussolini's Rome occasioned the "fascist" analogy that plagued him throughout his political career and which has endured to the present day. It is true that there were elements of his speaking style and early mobilization methods that were influenced by the fascist dictator. Yet while the connections are seductive, Gaitán was attracted to "Roman" discipline rather than to "fascism" per se. The heritage of

Rome is itself ambivalent given the related yet mutually hostile traditions of the Republic and the Empire. Tellingly, Gaitán would also be known in Colombia throughout his career as "the Tribune of the People" in the best tradition of Tiberius and Gaius Gracchus.

Gaitán's Thought: The Law and Social Change

This study can depict the complexities of Gaitán's thought in no more than outline form. It is possible, however, to identify a moral sensibility that imbued his writings and speeches. This was reflected in his preoccupation with justice and his devotion to equality and democracy, concerns that resonated with the left-Liberal spirit of the age. He also advocated many socialist ideas, in particular those concerning property. Yet Gaitán was not a systematic thinker. He could write well, usually in a baroque style, but his real strength lay in partially improvised public speaking. And complicating matters, a fundamental tension existed within Gaitán's worldview between the lawyer, who loved law, harmony, balance, and organization, and the radical, offended by the injustice of the existing order, eager to change the world.

José Antonio Osorio Lizarazo, a left-Liberal intellectual, novelist, and ardent Gaitanista, argued after Gaitán's death that he chose penal law, not for the order it could bring society, but rather because of his "obsession with justice." Civil law, Osorio Lizarazo maintained, did not embody the same "clamor for the weak" and "dignity" that penal law exhibited in its defense of criminals who were the products of "ignorance and misery." Civil law protected the interests of propertied classes while penal law sought the "restoration of justice."[23] Gaitán's "obsession" with ideas of justice persisted throughout his career.

In 1923 Gaitán wrote a highly revealing letter to a leftist intellectual, Luís Tejada, that placed him in the very thick of the collectivist (and quasi-socialist) left-Liberal vanguard.[24] In it he called for a liberalism inspired by socialism. He insisted, in openly recalling Uribe Uribe, that liberalism "plunge its oars into the waters of proletarian revindication and spread its sails before the invigorating winds of social transformation." This was because in Colombia, "the great majority" of the pueblo "exhausted its energies, atrophied its faculties, stupefied its senses, and uselessly wasted its force so that a slothful minority could fatten its hips and live the easy life of the idler." Gaitán directly challenged the contention that "Liberalism can not be socialist . . . because it is, in its base and essence, individualist." Gaitán insisted that political parties change and that their ideas evolve, arguing that they "are not built from the cúpula down . . . but rather from the base up, since they are social phenomena located in a definite time and place." He admitted that "the liberal school" was founded on "individualist principles that in their time responded to economic and political necessities." Such "natural" principles sought to provide the "maximum freedom to the activities of individuals," since the individual was understood as "the motor of economic activity." "That was liberalism then," he argued, "and it could not have been otherwise." Yet the "negative concept" that he asserted "is characteristic of all individual rights" is "imperfect and transitory," while within the "liberal denomination" there was a current that would "rejuvenate its organism, making it anew, so that it would not stand at the margins of present needs, and would open its heart to the suffering proletariat." It would be "from within these excellent and memorable ranks of liberalism" that "the current generation" would "realize its work against the *burguesía* for the economic liberation of work." Gerardo Molina argued that even though it was written in his youth, the letter to Luís Tejada represented Gaitán's perspective throughout his career. Gaitán was "a man of socialist ideas who believed they could be realized through liberalism."[25]

As a law student Gaitán read extensively in history and social theory. Greatly influenced by legal positivism, as well as the more radical elements of the liberal tradition, his ideological perspective found comprehensive expression for the first time in his law thesis, *Las ideas socialistas en Colombia.*[26] Richard Sharpless, Herbert Braun, and Gerardo Molina have critically examined *Las ideas socialistas* and applied it to the later development of Gaitanista ideology.[27] Though an important presentation of Gaitán's personal perspective, however, it should not be taken as a complete expression of the mature Gaitanista program, since his was not the only influence.

Las ideas socialistas is not a work that can be easily characterized, given the tensions inherent in Gaitán's epistemology. Richard Sharpless argued that "First and foremost, he [Gaitán] was a socialist." Sharpless underscored the collective nature of Gaitán's thought and pointed to elements of struggle within *Las ideas socialistas*. Sharpless argued that among the principal conclusions Gaitán drew from his "scientific" study of social relationships were: "first, that the interests of the dominant class and those of the proletariat were in open conflict, and that the class struggle was inevitable. Second, the interests of the dominant class were maintained by force."[28] Gerardo Molina argued that Gaitán was not a "profound ideologue" yet was clear on the choice between "individualism or socialism," vowing that it was "the socialist option" that best addressed "the interests of justice" and "the needs of progress." Molina also noted that Gaitán believed that socialism was possible in a non-industrialized country.[29] Herbert Braun's revisionist position, on the other hand, stressed the individualistic and meritocratic strains in Gaitán's perspective while downplaying struggle in Gaitán's thought. "In the courtroom he attacked society, but did so from within a prestigious institution; he defended the individual against social injustice, but did so through the very laws of an unjust society." Braun stressed that Gaitán employed the imagery of organic life, stressing harmony and order, which he found in the work of his teacher, Enrico Ferri. "Order and progress were described through the metaphor of health; conflict and destruction were diseases and epidemic." He could "concentrate on the concept of social change based on altering individual behavior and attitudes." Gaitán characterized society as "an organism that tends to a state of equilibrium."[30] In reality, both of these motifs existed in Gaitán's worldview, and he never completely reconciled them. His primary concerns, nevertheless, surfaced in *Las ideas socialistas*.

The first of these were the nature of the law and the role of the state. Gaitán rejected concepts of Colombian law based on the classical school, which grounded ethics in universal principles. Rather, Gaitán argued, the justification for all individual rights originated in human society, and he denied that men were born with "natural" rights. Thus, showing a tension with "classical liberalism," Gaitán believed that when the rights of an individual came into conflict with the rights of society, the former had to yield. Following Uribe Uribe, Gaitán envisioned an "interventionist state" that would provide "equal justice" and guarantee just distribution of the material wealth of society among its members.[31] Herbert Braun demonstrated how Gaitán believed that "social convulsions and change" needed to be addressed through reform. The stress should be shifted from "punishment to prevention . . . from individual rights to defense of society." For Gaitán the state had not only the right but also the obligation to change the legal, political, and economic structures that regulated society in order to correct injustices.[32]

Another of Gaitán's primary concerns involved his tension with capitalism and its repercussions on Colombian society. Gaitán made a distinction between "capital" and "capitalism." Capital was described as "a fact of the natural order," the accumulation ensuing from human labor that makes society possible. Capitalism results when this natural process generates individuals who no longer produce by their own labor but control the labor of others through the concentration of capital. For Gaitán such exploitative relations produce an immoral social order. Though in its most primitive stage, capitalism already existed in Colombia, and the inequalities it engendered were directly responsible for the misery that millions of Colombians endured. Gaitán believed that the capitalist mode of social relations obviously would not lead to social justice. There is undoubtedly a backward-looking character to Gaitán's desire to regain a "lost equilibrium" that Colombian society supposedly possessed before the arrival of capitalism.[33] Gaitán wanted "economic and social improvement" through industrialization but "within a socialized means of production."[34]

Gaitán was no Marxist (unorthodox or otherwise). As Herbert Braun pointed out, Gaitán did not consider capitalism "historically . . . progressive" but rather saw it as "a regression, a false step largely imposed from abroad by the imperialist interest of advanced nations and a tiny local minority."[35] Yet his analysis shared certain moral aspects with Marx's critique. Wage relations disrupted reciprocity in society while workers had no dignity and enjoyed little protection. Also reminiscent of Marx, Gaitán divided society into two groups: a minority of property owners and a property-less majority. Gaitán saw "unearned income" or surplus as socially unproductive if not reinvested for social good. Gaitán did not employ "rigorous Marxist analysis"; as Colombian leftist, Gaitanista, and historian Antonio García argued, Gaitán's approach was "more intuitive than dialectical." Yet Gaitán possessed a "socialist sensibility." He was no "theoretician of class struggle" but advocated a "new order" based on "more just distribution of wealth."[36] Gaitán stopped short of calling for the elimination of "the exploitative relationship between capital and labor," which he seemed to consider an unrealistic option. Instead "he sought to pass laws ensuring a decent level of reciprocity and protection for workers."[37]

But if Gaitán did not pointedly embrace the struggle for a post-capitalist society, he nevertheless had some rather disquieting, ardently unliberal views on property. He did not attack private property as the root cause of all social problems (indeed, he believed that it would always exist).[38] Yet of fundamental importance, Gaitán did not see private property as a sacred absolute either. He believed that with property came social responsibilities and that many social problems could be alleviated through the redistribution of property.[39] Gaitán argued that the capitalist mode predominated in Colombian agriculture where it monopolized the most productive lands. Gaitán's solution was to break up the big land holdings and limit the size of individual holdings. This policy was to be applied not only to unused land but also to the most developed land with access to roads, technological improvements, sanitation, etc.[40] Gaitán observed that land owners in the best locations were much better off than others, and this was unjust, leading him to the judgment that the only way to rectify this injustice was to modify property ownership.

Gerardo Molina maintained that Gaitán's conclusions regarding rent were "really revolutionary." Rent benefited the land owner, who did not work, at the expense of the campesino who made the land produce (and as the population increased, the misery in the countryside would only worsen). In Gaitán's words, "As long as ownership of the land" continued to be "individual," as long as "rent" was extracted, there was "no hope of improvement." "This property is unjust, this rent is improper, this social system that it engenders is a crime."[41] This was not just a theoretical point, since Gaitán made these ideas into political objectives.[42] Gaitán vehemently rejected the easy solution that many proposed, that is, to give the landless unused land or *baldíos*. (This would be unjust since this type of land was not worth as much and put its owners at the disadvantage already mentioned.) Private property had to be redistributed; to change the social structure, the economy had to be altered.

For Molina, the elements that made Gaitán a socialist were his material interpretation of history, his acknowledgment of class struggle, the contradiction he identified between social production and individual appropriation, and the role of the state he identified in the prevailing model as the representative of the favored classes. These were Gaitán's socialist ideas, but Molina argued that Gaitán remained open on the question of their implementation. Gaitán declared himself a "revolutionary" but with many reservations and restrictions. His conception of "revolutionary" was evolutionary. Gaitán's "soul" was "divided between sincere socialist convictions" and knowledge of the "precarious political instruments of their realization."[43]

Finally, justice and democracy were inextricably linked in Gaitán's thought, and one of the best expositions of this relationship can be found in his 1947 policy statement, the Plataforma del Colón.[44] It was a general blueprint for Gaitán's vision of the Liberal party as a democratic and interventionist party of the masses and carried the subtitle, "political democracy cannot exist without economic democracy." In practice, the establishment of "economic" democracy would mean much wider distribution of societal resources through state oversight and broader ownership of Colombia's productive forces. Production, the platform declared, should be for man and not man for production.

Gerardo Molina argued that "Gaitán was always a socialist Liberal." During his twenty-five years of active politics he "changed his tactics" but remained "faithful to the ideals of his youth." Gaitán never ceased his quest to "socialize liberalism."[45]

The Banana Massacre

Five years before Gabriel García Márquez published *One Hundred Years of Solitude* in 1967, Álvaro Cepeda Samudio produced *La Casa Grande*. Both works explored the bloody repression of United Fruit's striking laborers in the department of Magdalena in 1928 and stand as testaments to the fact that the strike became an important turning point in Colombia's political history.[46] Yet García Márquez's fictionalized account in particular gave the impression that Colombians soon forgot the tragic conclusion of the ill-fated strike, an idea that has even been echoed by historians.[47] Indeed, one of García Márquez's main themes in *One Hundred Years of Solitude* was the forgetfulness of the pueblo and its resultant domination by the elite-controlled parties. But in actuality, the banana workers' strike and its subsequent suppression were some of the most talked-about events in Colombian history, a situation in great part due to the efforts of Jorge Eliécer Gaitán. His key role in one of Latin American labor history's most symbolic moments engraved his name onto the collective memory of the Colombian people, and especially the working class, until the end of his life and beyond.

The strike itself was the product of years of tension between the United Fruit Company and its workers within the "banana zone." Also important was a determined organizing drive by anarcho-syndicalists and the soon to be Communist party, the PSR.[48] The U.S.-owned company had grown accustomed to virtual autonomy within its concession in the years after it began operations outside Santa Marta near the turn of the century, controlling transportation, communication, and irrigation within the *zona bananera*. It paid its workers in script redeemable only in company stores, harshly forcing low prices on producers. Most *bananeros* were "independent workers" who sold their crop as rent for the company's land.

Not surprisingly, United had suffered labor problems since 1918, but company policy ruled out any compliance with its workforce's demands. The 1928 strike enjoyed early success, greatly disrupting the company's operations. And an alliance with elements of the local commercial class tired of United's near monopoly gave the strike useful legitimacy. Strikers also enjoyed the organizational support of subsequently famous communists Alberto Castrillón, Ignacio Torres Giraldo, and María Cano. The striking workers' demands included recognition of contract workers (the majority of the workforce because the company could forgo paying any insurance or benefits), wage increases, recognition of unions, and the end to company stores.[49] The Conservative government responded by deploying troops under the command of General Carlos Cortés Vargas, who jailed workers and sympathetic government officials and protected strikebreakers. In the ensuing conflicts the general declared a state of siege and carried out the infamous "massacre" at Ciénaga in the early hours of December 6, 1928.[50]

News of the deadly repression spread quickly, and with it more violence, undoubtedly damaging the Conservative government's position. The atrocities did not, however, automatically translate into a Liberal issue. It is true that Conservatives defended "firing the rifles of order" against the enemies of "life and property" and linked the "cowards of Moscow" to the Liberal party, claiming that "100 deaths are 100 communist arguments at the service" of liberalism.[51] Yet Conservatives themselves called for open investigation.[52] And the initial Liberal position demonstrated a similar discomfort with militant labor movements. In the published defense of his actions, General Cortés Vargas could reprint an editorial from the liberal *El Estado* (Santa Marta) of December 5, which fretted over attacks on property and noted with approval a special session of the cabinet that might impose martial law and suspend individual rights in the banana zone.[53]

The attack on the Conservative government fell most naturally to the left Liberals, whose foremost representative was soon to be Gaitán.[54] Newly elected to the lower house of congress, he personally traveled to Ciénaga for his theatrical "investigation" in July 1929. During his return to Bogotá he stopped in numerous cities and towns to tell of his findings, drawing large crowds. Taking a small boat up the Magdalena river from Puerto Wilches, he arrived late in the evening at the oil production center, Barrancabermeja. Barranca, as it is commonly called, was another foreign controlled economic enclave, traditionally known for its working-class militancy and later to be a Gaitanista stronghold. While still in his boat, he told a gathering there that he came "as a witness to the most miserable slaughter the country has ever seen," in answer to which several people jumped in the river to meet him.[55]

Back in Bogotá Gaitán launched his so-called debate on September 3 before packed congressional galleries and an attentive press, and for fifteen days enthusiastically pelted the government with invective and scorn.

His speeches, which Sharpless called "a mixture of intellectuality, fact, threat, indignation, and sensationalism" served the dual purpose of demonstrating the U.S. company's and the Colombian government's culpability in the killings and drawing attention to himself. Swinging abruptly from calm, reasoned argument to wild, emotional denunciations he staged a lively spectacle, complete in its depiction of grisly detail and often illustrated with props such as the skull of a small child.[56]

Gaitán's exploits were followed not only in Bogotá, where crowds accompanied him home each evening, but throughout the country. Writing from Barranquilla "in support and admiration" for his campaign in Congress, one woman claimed that people cheered him on because of their frustration with "the domination of the *gringos*" and the mockery of justice. And a group of "leftist youth" in Valle expressed enthusiasm for his labors in the Cámara on behalf of their compatriots, "sacrificed" by the villainous agents of the government to the shame of the Colombian pueblo.[57]

Gaitán's dramatic performance, along with the beginning of the Great Depression, high unemployment, and rival Conservative presidential candidates, all contributed to the end of the Conservative Hegemony. At the very birth of the Liberal Republic, therefore, he was already known as "the future Messiah" of the working class.[58]

Gaitán the Labor Lawyer

Before moving on, one of the more important of Gaitán's "multiple occupations" (as they were often called) should be noted. Studies of Gaitán have routinely focused on his political career, and noted his expertise in criminal law, but have generally overlooked his practice in labor law. His activity as the foremost labor advocate of the period, however, was fundamental to his political persona. Indeed, he was already busy establishing himself in this field and building a base of support among the working class even before the 1928 banana workers' strike, both in and beyond Bogotá.[59] In 1932 the Comité Nacional Liberal Obrero of Bogotá gave Gaitán their vote of support and adhesion as an "authentic voice and standard bearer of the ideals and the cause of the Colombian proletariat." In 1933 a representative of the Federación Sindical of Bogotá noted Gaitán's "efficient" work for the "betterment of the working masses," while the Confederación Nacional de Empleados thanked him for his work in the Cámara on the behalf of *empleados* and called him their "true defender." And in 1936 left Liberals in Santa Marta recognized Gaitán as one of the nation's leading jurists, toiling for justice and defending the rights of the working man.[60]

As a matter of course, when there were serious organized labor conflicts in the 1930s and 1940s, Gaitán was most often called in as the unions' legal representative and negotiator.[61] And even more important, Gaitán also routinely represented workers who had no officially recognized unions. In fact, during 1933—a year the number of strikes increased dramatically—the geographical distribution of strike activity actually formed a map of left-Liberal (and later Gaitanista) strongholds: Barranquilla and the Magdalena river, Cali and the west of the country, and Bogotá.[62] Gaitanista strongholds were traditionally organized labor strongholds, and vice versa. Gaitán enjoyed his following in these places because of the mutually reinforcing influences of his labor advocacy, his ideas, and his fame as the hero of the bananeros debate. Some of the more notable instances in which Gaitán represented organized workers were the general strike of Medellín, the Germania Brewery and the Red Taxis strikes in Bogotá, and the Cali railroad workers' strike, all during 1934. This intense activity was certainly not lost on the country's "popular" classes and was closely followed in the Liberal press.[63]

Ignacio Torres Giraldo, apostle of the early Communist party and never an advocate of Gaitán, their most threatening rival on the Liberal left, has emphasized Gaitán's repeated "failures" in strike negotiations in Medellín and Cali.[64] Yet even in failure Gaitán could count on continued support. Adherents in Cali pointed out that Gaitán, "prestigious leader of the revolutionary left," had journeyed there because he had been "insistently called by the city's labor organizations." He originally went to Valle "with the objective of finding the best solution to the problems facing the railroad workers." His "disinterested" work was fully in line with his "democratic convictions." They argued that "if his efforts proved in vain, the fault lies with the treachery of the workers themselves." They noted that a distinguished group of citizens and labor representatives saw him off to show "the strong feelings and loyalty of his *compañeros.*" They bid him a respectful adieu, sure that he would continue to contribute to the resolution "of the great social problems that confront the working classes."[65] And the *Diario Nacional* in Bogotá noted that the strike was a failure because the mechanics were ready to cross the picket line and replace the workers; Gaitán was reportedly angry with the workers for inviting him and leading him to believe that their organization was better than it really was (and perhaps making him look bad).[66]

Torres Giraldo simply ignored the significance of the habit so many unions had of turning to Gaitán to look after their interests. Notably, striking rail workers in Bogotá who openly wanted broad working-class support even called him "the head of our movement."[67] It was not by accident, therefore, that Gaitán enjoyed very significant support from workers and maintained intimate relations with the working class throughout his career.

Gaitán would not be Gaitanismo. Like many other leaders of his era, Gaitán maintained a dramatic and personal relationship with his mass of supporters. His charismatic presence is not in question. Yet the foundation of his enduring popularity lay in what he represented to the left Liberals. Gaitán became the embodiment of the pueblo because his personal history and his political and legal careers reflected the essence of the left-Liberal tradition.

3

Early Mobilizations

Gaitán, the Liberal Party, and UNIR, 1928–1935

The first period of mobilization associated with Gaitán falls neatly between his rise in the collective consciousness as the champion of United Fruit's banana workers in 1928 and his return to the Liberal party in 1935 after momentarily abandoning it two years earlier. Historians dealing with this early "Gaitanismo" have agreed concerning its "radical" nature. Compared to the later "populist" mobilizations of the 1940s, Gaitán's movement of the early 1930s occupied a militant and antagonistic position relative to traditional Colombian liberalism. Providing the most succinct general picture of the movement, Richard Sharpless closely identified Gaitán's Revolutionary Leftist National Union (Unión Nacional Izquierdista Revolucionaria, UNIR) with its founding declaration as an organization dedicated to the "struggle for socialism." And even Herbert Braun, not prone to viewing Gaitanismo in these terms, nevertheless characterized Gaitán on the eve of organizing the UNIR as fitting "as comfortably as he ever would . . . within the left wing of the [Liberal] party."[1]

A rough consensus also exists, however, that this early movement distinguished itself by an intimate, and perhaps oppressive, relationship with its leader. While Medófilo Medina portrayed UNIR as one of the "most vigorous" challenges ever to the two party system in Colombia, with similarities to "utopian socialism," he still emphasized Gaitán's belief that there was little class consciousness among the masses. This conclusion seemingly implied the need for a Gaitanista vanguard, in the words of the "Platform of Action for UNIR," "a minority . . . dedicating its activity . . . to the liberation of the majority."[2] In its most complete exposition, this interpretation of early Gaitanismo emphasized the "dependence" of the pueblo on its leader and the "sacrifice" of its autonomy.[3]

The generally accepted picture of early Gaitanismo, therefore, contains certain consistent elements. Rivaling the Communist party, Gaitán's movement in the 1930s represented a radical and leftist alternative to the traditional parties. The UNIR is largely remembered, however, as Gaitán's vehicle—a fact borne out by the type of analysis employed, which emphasizes Gaitán, his actions, and the official line maintained in the movement's organ, *Unirismo*. The wide geographical influence of UNIR is often mentioned, but developments in the coffee regions of western Cundinamarca and eastern Tolima receive the lion's share of attention. Finally, many scholars would agree with Charles Bergquist that UNIR was "short lived" and that "the results" of its mobilization "were not very impressive."[4]

Yet, with a shift in analysis from Gaitán and the formal organization of UNIR to its social base, popular ideology, and regional manifestations, a different picture emerges in this chapter. Gaitán, it is true, held tightly the reins of his movement. It was not simply his creature, however, nor did it take quietly to harness. Rather Gaitán and UNIR were the focal points of a widespread and recurring popular mobilization that found its roots in the left-Liberal tradition. While the experiment of UNIR abruptly ended in 1935, its evolution established patterns that would beget later mobilizations.

Gaitán and the Left Liberals

In 1930 the Liberal party took control of the institutionally powerful Colombian presidency for the first time since 1885. As a reward for his high profile role in the transition, the Liberals elected Gaitán president of the lower house of Congress for 1931 and president of the Liberal National Directorate. President Olaya Herrera even recognized his leadership status by appointing him second vice-president. Though many within the party leadership seemed to believe that by giving Gaitán important positions they could soften his calls for change, he was in fact at the forefront of the struggle for the very soul of the newly emergent Liberal party.[5]

Gaitán was easily one of the leading young leftists within the Liberal sphere.[6] Gaitán represented a growing company of Liberals—intellectuals, workers, and peasants—for whom he was both symbol and rallying point. Darío Samper, another high-ranking left Liberal, described him in early 1932 as "a solitary proletarian rebel who inspired fear in the rich by his struggle . . . in favor of social justice, a socialist who believed in peaceful, evolutionary change."[7] Samper went on to say that no one else had so penetrated "the hearts of Colombia's masses," that Gaitán spoke to his "comrades, the workers," and that he was "the principal captain of democracy."[8]

Evidence for Samper's contention was provided throughout Colombia during the early 1930s. A tailor from Pasto told Gaitán in 1932 that he and others saw in him "the true leader of the *legiones libertarias* of Colombia" and best hope for their "just aspirations." Gaitán had generated a "renovating wave" that would "transform the silence" in which they had always lived.[9] In Medellín the "sons of the mountains" admired Gaitán "as the pinnacle of republican austerity and . . . as the enlightened leader of the Colombian Liberal party." The Liberal pueblo, "awakened from its lethargy" by his words, now had "consciousness" and sought "substantial renovation of the methods and systems of government." Gaitán had the "heart of an apostle" and understood "the miseries and needs of the pueblo" and its "social problems." He would help usher in the "reign of liberty and justice"; he was the "herald of the cry of justice . . . the redeemer of the oppressed." Gaitán heard the "clamor of a people without agrarian legislation . . . the small colono who in the struggle against hostile nature" was "defrauded and absorbed by the latifundista who robbed him of the fruit of his labor . . . left to vegetate in ignorance and misery." He spoke to "a people tortured by hunger . . . and lack of work," the "masses of urban workers" who lacked "the assistance of a labor code that would guarantee their interests and rights in their relations with capital."[10] Workers in Bucaramanga and Rionegro, more than one thousand strong, followed Gaitán, "not out of simple personal devotion, but rather because of the triumph of the new social doctrines" that he had "definitely fixed into the national consciousness."[11] In Cali Gaitán was called "a leader who offers a program of *labores reivindicadores,*" the very opposite of a "demagogic charlatan."[12] In Cundinamarca he was the leader of "liberal leftism."[13] In Cauca he commanded the "young vanguard" of "the leftist youth."[14] In fact, as early as 1932 left Liberals were calling Gaitán the real *jefe supremo* of the party and repudiating the others.[15]

As would be the case in the 1940s, Gaitán was called an apostle and symbol of mobilization. In Popayán Gaitán received "unconditional support from the leftist youth and from the workers" that heard his voice because they saw in him "a sincere apostle and not a political *traficante.*"[16] They evoked nineteenth-century radicalism as they sent him their "warm salute and frantic applause" for his recent work in the Cámara. Not "since the heroic days of valiant radicalism" had words "so full of promise and language so inflamed with faith" in a revolutionary future been heard.

They called Gaitán "defender of the popular classes that suffer the insolent lash of those powers which still control this medieval country." His ideas were just and would not tarry in bringing redemption.[17] In Cali he was known as the "loyal standard-bearer of radicalism."[18] Liberals in Tolima commended his work in Congress and the Liberal Directorate "in defense of the classes until today forgotten by the state." They were people with "hunger and thirst for justice."[19] For them Gaitán was "the true apostle of Colombian democracy."[20]

Gaitán's leftist ideas resonated with like-minded people throughout the nation. In Popayán Gaitán found ardent supporters of and sympathizers with his ideas and activities in favor of the working class.[21] In La Unión, Nariño, he could find many individuals who identified "with the ideas and aspirations" that he professed, and who offered "irresistible adhesion."[22] Gaitán was "a distinguished exponent" of the "modern socialist doctrines, advocated in civilized nations."[23] Indeed, though still very much a Liberal, he was constantly associated with socialism. He showed the way to "a better society, more in accordance with nature and the sincere practice of the virtues of socialism."[24] In Neiva a supporter commended his "formidable" speeches in the Cámara "on the theme of property." The "group of revolutionary youth in Congress" led by Gaitán had "realized a gigantic labor in defense of our principles" and the "revolutionary youth of Huila" saluted them.[25]

Gaitán, therefore, was not alone. The left-Liberal spirit of mobilization during the first years of the Liberal Republic manifested itself obviously enough through enthusiasm for its favorite son, but also through a readiness for popular organization. From the early hours of June 12, 1932, an "enormous multitude" of "democratic Liberals" in Cartagena waited at the train station to show its "delirium" with "vivas" for democracy and for the "fiery leftist Dr. Jorge Eliécer Gaitán."[26] Such rank-and-file emotion translated into demands for political participation. Speaking of upcoming departmental elections, one of Gaitán's new followers affirmed that if in the past they had "waited with the sainted patience of Job," they would do so no longer. He pledged that more than eight thousand liberals waited to lay down their lives for Gaitán's convictions "without knowing why," trusting his "instinct."[27] And in the river port of Honda, a labor activist insisted that the workers aspired "to be represented by genuine voices of the people," and that "the hour had come . . . to fight for the purification" of the political environment.[28]

Some Liberal adherents formed their own political societies and committees. One in Aracataca, which would carry Gaitán's name, was organized to "proclaim" his "leftist" political initiatives.[29] In Barranquilla, the "Liberal Youth Labor Committee," committed to ideas of "social betterment," called him one of their principal influences and named him honorary president.[30] Also in Barranquilla the "Centro Revolucionario Socialista," called a product of the "absurd" politics of "exploitation," reputedly represented one "of the new powerful political currents" capable of transforming the "ideological panorama."[31] In Santa Marta, the "leftist youth" advocating "popular assertions of legal rights" met to form a political group to promote Gaitán's ideas "in favor of the proletariat and humanity."[32] Finally, new to the Colombian political scene, the "Comité Femenino" made its appearance early on and would later be a common feature of Gaitanismo.[33]

In addition to political organization, many future Gaitanistas (as pointed out earlier) sought active participation in the creation of a new leftist identity for the Liberal party. As one group from Cartagena put it, Gaitán's activity in Congress attracted new men with "socialist attitudes." "When we lash out at property abuse, they call us communists; when we speak of agrarian reform, utopians; when we criticize inert political leaders, undisciplined. . . . The Liberal socialist youth support your just cause. Private property ends where collective hunger begins, collectivism over individualism." Also writing from Cartagena, J. M. Conde Ribón (who would be an important Gaitanista in the 1940s) spoke of a "political agenda, broadly Liberal, encompassing a new, robust ideology . . . based on an unblemished ethic" that would defend "the people's" security and existence through popularly oriented reform. And one of Gaitán's key supporters in Santa Marta, a self-styled member of Colombia's leftist forces, Dionisio Rincones Ponce, published a series of articles in which he presented, and perhaps expanded upon, Gaitán's ideas; works that he admitted were less than popular with many Liberal leaders. He shared with Gaitán a "social romanticism" that resulted from having personally felt "social injustices."[34]

Exercising what would be a routine prerogative among left Liberals throughout the 1930s and 1940s, many of the rank and file offered sophisticated discussions on political theory and practice. In his update for the "maximum leader of the Colombian Left," Eduardo Arango Córdoba echoed Uribe Uribe in maintaining that "our leftist liberalism . . . is the genuine liberalism." Because of this stance, he had been "excommunicated from the church of liberalism" and called a communist, but nevertheless wrote a piece entitled "Profession of the Liberal Faith." In it he argued that while *gamonalismo* (boss politics) was stronger in Bolívar

than anywhere else and that unfortunately Liberals were the ones impeding change, he still considered the Liberal party evolutionary. Despite local
setbacks, they would continue with their campaign of "leftist conversion
of the masses."[35] And in a curiously prophetic discussion of many topics,
a Barranquilla postal worker captured the essence of Gaitán's appeal and
of many challenges facing the movement. After hearing Gaitán speak, he
asked the question, would Gaitán put an end to traditional liberalism or
would it put an end to him? In his opinion, Gaitán would soon have to
choose between casting his lot with the Liberal "notables" or openly
breaking with them and throwing himself into "the class struggle."
Though some believed that the monopolistic dictatorship of *El Tiempo* of
Bogotá, "united with the latifundists and notables," would ignore Gaitán,
he did not believe it would be so easy to nullify a voice that spoke directly
to the "proletarian consciousness."[36]

In the early 1930s, therefore, Gaitán marched at the head of a campaign
to reconstruct Colombian liberalism upon more popular foundations.
Though many of those he represented considered themselves "definitively
Liberal" and followers of the party "founded by Santander and advanced
by the ideas . . . of Uribe Uribe, that is . . . genuine Liberals," they nevertheless advocated a "democracy well understood." The spirit of their
movement exhibited a new rebelliousness that would not allow them to
serve "bad causes" even if they were proclaimed by the anointed leader of
liberalism.[37]

Gaitán and the Liberal Party

In the short span of years between his swift rise in the party ranks in 1930
and his frustrated rejection of official liberalism in 1933, Gaitán attempted many ideological and policy-related innovations. While many
young Liberals believed that a new age had dawned, the administration of
Enrique Olaya Herrera, former ambassador to Washington, was anything
but fertile ground for the liberalism Gaitán and his followers sought to
foster. His government of National Concentration reserved positions of
considerable influence for Conservatives, whose party still controlled
both houses of Congress, the judiciary, and most departmental administrations. The 1930–34 Liberal government, therefore, provided no significant rupture with earlier Conservative governments.[38] Though some
feeble attempts were made at land reform, investment in public health and
housing, and financial assistance, most left Liberals came to see it as a
prelude to better times.

Focusing largely on Gaitán's activities in Congress during this period, some interpretations have stressed his relationship to "the salaried middle class and . . . rural *colonos*" rather than the "urban proletariat."[39] This is hardly surprising given Gaitán's statement that the "middle sectors" were in the process of developing a social consciousness and would "form the vanguard" of Colombia's socialist forces.[40] Such understandings of early Gaitanismo also stem from Gaitán's conflicting positions on private property. At any rate, in 1930 he advocated the recognition of property rights for productive squatters and their protection by the state against often violent title holders.

Furthermore, during the early 1930s Gaitán was active in areas other than the legislature. His role as the most prominent labor lawyer of the period, as discussed earlier, qualifies the view of Gaitanismo as merely a "middle-class" movement.[41] Also, as a member of the Liberal Directorate, Gaitán "wanted the party to organize itself with special reference to the masses and orient its platforms to what he called the 'new social and economic realities,'" thereby making the party more beholden to the electorate. In another of his overt paraphrases of Uribe Uribe, he declared that liberalism had "to become socialist" or be "condemned to perish ideologically."[42] And during the opening session of Congress in 1932 he issued his "Manifesto to the Leftists" calling for a constitutional amendment to allow land redistribution. These and his other initiatives were mostly subverted by his detractors within the party or disregarded by the leadership. Stymied by the Liberal "notables," he resigned from the Directorate in July 1932. Finally, while out of the country on an official visit to Mexico, Chile, and Argentina concerning the Colombian-Peruvian conflict over the Amazonian town of Leticia, his name was removed from the Liberal list and he lost his seat in Congress.

In 1932, a year of intense domestic turmoil, Gaitán and his followers came under increasingly heavy attack from the Liberal establishment. As propagators of his ideas and advocates of his "moderately socialist" views, many Liberals were persecuted by local leaders and repeatedly labeled communist.[43] The Conservatives themselves had no doubts as to the nature of Gaitán and his movement. They defined his efforts in the Congress and later in the UNIR as a "social program with a communist flavor" and noted that the movement attracted thousands of Liberals who were tempted by the Communist party but would not join for "sentimental reasons."[44] This position echoed that expressed in the supreme organ of official liberalism, *El Tiempo* of Bogotá. In June it claimed that the "extreme left tendencies" of Gaitán and his followers placed them outside the ideological limits of the party and threatened its unity by driving a wedge between the Liberal leadership and the Liberal proletariat. *El Tiempo* stated flatly that those in the Liberal party who wanted to pursue socialist doctrines were free to do so but that they should stop calling themselves Liberals.[45]

Though a practice that would soon change, the Liberal leadership initially worked to exclude all those of "socialist inclination."[46] These were precisely the people that Gaitán's early movement enticed. Some were members of the Communist party.[47] Others were radical noncommunists, such as Raúl Eduardo Mahecha C., one of the principal leaders of the 1928 banana workers' strike and director of the worker paper *Vanguardia Obrera* in Ciénaga. He claimed that the majority of people desirous of social justice were tired of the traditional parties' deceptions and apprehensive of the Communists for being too wedded to the line from Moscow. They consequently flocked to Gaitán's "socialist camp."[48] Given both such attacks from inside the party and his wide popular acclaim, Gaitán's next move was predictable enough.

Beyond the Bounds of Official Liberalism

Gaitán's exodus from the Liberal family was the direct result of his isolation within the party and his failure to transform it into the popularly oriented entity he and many others believed it naturally should become. Gaitán began to espouse the ultimate heresy that the Liberal and Conservative parties were the same in their disdain for real popular mobilization, and that neither had a greater goal than simply holding office. As early as April 1933 he and other prominent left Liberals met to discuss the creation of a national, leftist political association outside the traditional parties and the Communist party.[49] Its primary concern would be establishing the "base for a campaign of social agitation that would develop in Colombians a class consciousness."[50] Though this initial effort collapsed because of other Liberals' reluctance to break with the party, Gaitán officially split from the Liberal fold in October of 1933. With another student of Ferri, Carlos Arango Vélez (who had long respected Lenin), he founded the Unión Nacional Izquierdista Revolucionaria.[51]

Even though UNIR was organized in late 1933, it burst upon the Colombian consciousness in February 1934. On the fourth of that month Gaitán attended an Unirista rally in Fusagasugá, Cundinamarca, in the heart of coffee country where UNIR, the Communist party, and the Liberal party all actively carried on organizing drives. That day, a Sunday, roughly two thousand people from the surrounding countryside came to hear Gaitán's address, even though Sunday political meetings had been prohibited by the governor to quiet tensions over upcoming elections. When Gaitán began to speak, the Liberal-controlled police tried to break up the rally and the Uniristas resisted. At that point a group of Liberals allegedly attacked the crowd and in the clash that followed four Uniristas were killed and many wounded, forcing Gaitán to take refuge in a supporter's house as a gun battle raged outside.[52] The incident, in which Gaitán himself was nearly killed, received notice in the press throughout Colombia and greatly enhanced UNIR's national image.[53]

Other interpretations of UNIR have stressed Gaitán's role, the national organization, and the official ideological line, giving a view from the inside and from the top. They have also tended to emphasize developments in coffee-producing departments. The general institutional picture of UNIR, accordingly, is rather clear. Its founding charter proclaimed the "struggle for socialism, because the country cannot be developed on the basis of individualist criteria." It was not designed to be a political party in the strict sense but rather a "'free organization tending only to the realization of its ends,' which it defined as building cooperation and solidarity in the country" while raising consciousness. And in March 1934, speaking in the assembly of Cundinamarca, Gaitán asserted that "Unirismo is not a political party. Unirismo is an autonomous, independent force of preparation and struggle, guarding the firm principles of the left."[54] Chief among these were land reform, social justice, and democracy.

UNIR did, nevertheless, seem like a party to many of its adherents and critics. Gaitán deemphasized his successful law practice and devoted most of his time and much of his own money to its service. He stressed discipline, mass mobilization, and a hierarchical organizational structure of local "teams," "legions," a "Central Committee," and the "Directing Commission" made up of Gaitán and his intimates. This organizational structure has prompted many observers to draw parallels with fascist mobilization. It is just as likely, however, that Gaitán took his "legions" from the same place Mussolini did: ancient Rome. Gaitán, after all, was an enthusiastic student of history. Yet while Il Duce looked to Caesar, Gaitán looked to the Tribunes. UNIR also had organizations for internal control, defense of members against employers and political violence, organizing strikes, public relations, and education.[55] Gaitán "encouraged the use of hymns, uniforms, insignias, and decorations." UNIR came to be known as the "Revolution of Soap" because of his stress on hygiene.[56]

The strategy of "state intervention" in the nation's economic and social

organization occupied center stage in Gaitán's cast of programs and policies, presented in the "Manifesto of Unirismo" and the "Platform of Action for UNIR," documents that amplified concepts he earlier presented in
Las ideas socialistas.[57] Gaitán was conspicuously influenced by Marx in
his materialist stress on the economic bases of politics and social relations,
and by Uribe Uribe in his advocacy of "socialism of the state." After a
rigorous constitutional reform, the state would furnish the general economic orientation through control of prices, rent, and credit while implementing a progressive tax structure, land ownership limitations, and re-
straints on private capital. It would implement a broad agrarian reform,
giving control of the land to those who work it, provide an all-encompass-
ing social security network, and give workers a voice in the control of their
firms and industries while regulating disputes. Command of the state apparatus, therefore, was essential to his plan. But instead of being simply
the customary prize of traditional Liberal and Conservative struggles of
old, Gaitán envisioned the centralized state as the focal point of planning
and policy execution. Through supervision of education and its reorienta-
tion toward technical and practical training, Gaitán hoped to raise the
general level of merit and ability. He also advocated recognition of the
rights of illegitimate children, the establishment of civil divorce, and full
political franchise for women.

This program, so noticeably supervised from the top, is one of the obvious grounds for characterizing UNIR's mobilization as a controlled, paternalistic affair. Most scholars have noted Gaitán's "heavy hand" in the
control of his organization, though Sharpless tellingly observed that "democracy within the movement appeared to function primarily at the local
level."[58] Given Gaitán's own misgivings about the supposedly low level
of mass preparedness for political participation and the "authoritarian
spirit" admitted by even his most energetic apologists, the standard interpretation is not off the mark.[59] It should not, however, be overstated.
Gaitán did not earn his position on the Liberal left by underestimating the
pueblo's capacity for popular mobilization. Nor should the topdown view
of the movement be mistaken for the whole picture.

The general impact of the official ideological line among Uniristas is
uncertain. The movement's newspaper *Unirismo,* for instance, was more
prone to cover the doings of Uniristas than to probe deeply into ideological issues.[60] But the most obvious wrinkle is the simple fact that his supporters had their own ideas. Their preoccupations, expressed perhaps in
simpler terms, were no less identifiable. Viewed from the bottom, therefore, the idea that Gaitán effectively forced his will upon the UNIR and its

members stands in need of considerable qualification. Such a perspective will also illuminate the class nature of its social base, the tensions between its official and popular ideologies, and the importance of its urban and national manifestations.

One thing Gaitán and UNIR certainly did was keep pressure on the Liberal establishment. Throughout 1934 the *Diario Nacional* presented generous amounts of favorable coverage of Gaitán and UNIR. Its editors approvingly presented Gaitán as a stinging gadfly whose goal was to push liberalism left. Explaining why he founded "a new party," they pointed out that in revolutions, "economic democratization" must be carried out before "political democratization" can really work. He was also calling liberalism back to its roots. When liberalism arrived in power in 1930 it had had the potential to present a valid leftist program; "until recently" the Liberal party had been the party of the masses, "of the *plebe*."[61]

UNIR was a moral force on the left, which, as opposed to the old parties, was "uniting the *pueblo* to save it morally and economically."[62] A "fervent soldier of UNIR" in ardently Unirista Pereira understood that the primary goal had to be the ideological struggle, "if we do not want to continue with the fossilized practices of the old parties." If intellectuals wanted to be called "revolutionary," how could they be afraid to situate themselves "on the red carpet of Revolution, in the spirit of the left?" He insisted that "to be of the left and flourish in the shade of the right is to sin against the most elementary principles of political morality."[63] In Armenia an Unirista insisted that they pursue "moral defense" from a "leftist tendency."[64] Another in Bogotá compared their struggle to that of "the young warrior David." They were men who had "suffered the rigors of economic slavery." UNIR promoted "universal economic development" that would bring "the complete triumph of the workers." Even though UNIR did not use the "violent language" of the Communists, its struggle was, nevertheless, "class struggle" and therefore "political struggle."[65]

The movement was particularly strong among Colombia's "popular" classes. Gaitán himself argued that "class struggle per se does not exist at this point in our country," and instead affirmed "the struggle of interests."[66] And in another often quoted phrase, he asserted that "we are not enemies of riches but rather of poverty."[67] These positions do not, however, negate an identifiable "class" nature to UNIR's mobilization. Aside from the problems involved in trying to distinguish a well-defined structural separation between the popular characteristics of "working class" and "middle class" in this context, the fact remains that Gaitán discovered his bedrock support among both these categories. In the cities and towns he attracted professionals, small to middling merchants, large numbers of artisans, and workers dependent upon the wage, from both the organized minority and the unorganized majority. In the countryside he attracted small holders, squatters, and landless rural workers, though most notably in regions where land ownership tended to be the prerogative of a small number of individuals or families.

Though they covered the social spectrum, these groups constituted the "popular classes" Gaitán found eager and waiting. A lawyer in Barranquilla assured Gaitán that the paper *Unirismo* was a great success among intellectuals in that city.[68] Another lawyer in radical Pereira spoke of the great support from obreros and campesinos for UNIR.[69] Other activists supported his "revolutionary socialist" politics and clamored for UNIR to provide representation for workers and leftists.[70] Workers themselves recognized that he was their "most outstanding champion and defender," and turned to him for economic justice.[71] This status Gaitán maintained with care, as he demonstrated in a routine acknowledgment to inquiries about UNIR, claiming "to labor constantly in defense of the working class."[72] With such a complex social base, strains were of course inevitable, as an examination of Unirista popular ideology makes clear. Not only were there tensions within Gaitán's thought, as evidenced by his views on property, but also between some of his ideas and those of his followers. These conflicts in turn underscore the degree to which many Uniristas sought to remain autonomous of their caudillo.

While Gaitán's followers were hardly a monolithic whole ideologically, they consistently displayed a steadfast concern for social change through collective means. To many his name represented the ultimate symbol of this objective, even if the form envisioned for this change to take and the rhetoric used to describe it were often quite different. One Unirista contrasted "scientific socialist revolution" and its aim of tearing down the old society to build a new one with "evolutionary Liberalism," which uses the existing system to seek a new path for "collective aspirations."[73] Another claimed that one day "not far off," the Colombian people would "smash the barriers that block their way, throw to the ground the old party structure, and once and for all put an end to the *oligarquía*." Gaitán and his "social revolution" had opened the breach by making Colombians aware of their social rights.[74] And another held up the name of the tribune as the guide to "socialization of land" and "justice for the poor" through a "fraternal social union whose base is an ordered distribution of the fruits of human labor."[75] The theme of significant change by collective action, thus, remained a constant, even if no consensus existed for the means to bring it about.

And there is direct evidence confirming radical strains of "independent," "collectivist" UNIR, as demonstrated by the case of Cartagena. In a speech, intended as merely the first in a series of conferences on "inherent questions for our movement of social vindication," one proto-Gaitanista elaborated on Gaitán's ideas. The speaker focused his "interpretation" of UNIR on a discussion of contrasts it displayed with liberalism, which, he claimed, sought to exhibit false similarities with UNIR to maintain its influence. First he characterized liberalism's historic development after the French Revolution as the defense of individual liberties. With its focus on the individual rather than the collective, "continuing the anarchic use of productive energies," it ignored "the benefits of unity." Under the twin banners of "natural rights" and "individual rights" occurred the accumulation of capital leading to the "slavery" of the contemporary worker. This, he argued, was what was meant by "economic liberty," the "right" to sell one's labor to the "powerful." "Individual liberty" with such "artificial limits" as prescribed by the laws of the existing system, excluding "economic liberty," is nothing more than "deception."

UNIR, on the other hand, was the "enemy" of the current regime. "The society UNIR envisions cannot exist within this Liberal state: a society of national consciousness, knowledgeable of the needs of the Colombian people, seeking new directions through the cooperation of the productive classes, always vigilant of their own defense and that of the ideal of justice." UNIR's struggle, the speaker claimed, was to bring about the recognition of the "value of the producer." Recalling (and slightly altering) Gaitán's dictum, he stated that "UNIR is the enemy of poverty and friend of riches," but only within the context of "justice for the producer in relation to what he produces." As the "manifestation of collective socialism" UNIR was not against "small individual property" but instead sought the "socialization of the large firms . . . and big capital" in order to create a "directed, social economy." Ending his portrayal of the "revolutionary" content of UNIR, he quoted Gaitán in the Cámara: "If we want to make the revolution, we must have the courage to face the problem with wisdom and throw to the ground our decrepit laws that inhibit just transformations."[76]

Popular participation remained the ideal, but disputes arose over the degree to which it could be implemented. The "UNIR of Cartagena" called openly for intensified popular involvement as they declared solidarity with a railroad workers' strike in Medellín. They resolved to make "*obreros, campesinos,* and *empleados*" aware of the proceedings of the burguesía, which sought to ignore worker rights under the law, and thereby bring them into the UNIR.[77] While Alejandro Amador y Cortés could observe that, "The *pueblo,* with that instinct that seldom misleads them, have finally realized that they now have a leader . . . capable of working profound transformations," he could also despair of success and fret that without "education for the masses" they would continue to fall prey to the "insincere promises of their eternal exploiters."[78] Other educated political activists showed concern over the "intellectual preparation" of workers elected to city councils.[79]

Questions of Land and Property

Most studies have underscored UNIR's struggles over land tenure in rural areas, especially Cundinamarca and Tolima, coffee-producing regions where land ownership tended to be concentrated in a few hands. In these areas UNIR had great success in organizing strikes, land invasions, and rural worker unions while pushing for tenant farmers' rights to plant their own coffee and titles for squatters on unused private land.[80] Because of this mobilizing activity, UNIR is rightly remembered as a radical movement especially attentive to questions of property.

Concerns with land tenure and property began with Gaitán himself. Throughout the early 1930s he had sought far-reaching reforms on property questions as a member of the Liberal leadership. Such activity did not go unnoticed. In May 1932 the "owners of improvements" on land in Cundinamarca saluted Gaitán, "worthy exponent of the left and excellent defender of the interests of the laboring and working masses." They also invited him to come for a tour of their hacienda to get an idea of their situation.[81] In July a coffee grower named Gutiérrez agreed that everything Gaitán had said in a recent speech about "the situation of the coffee workers" was truthful. In the coffee estates of Cundinamarca, Gutiérrez had witnessed with a heavy and sad spirit "the supreme injustice that in the name of liberty and rights they commit against their workers, especially the [women] coffee pickers." There "the most elemental notions of human charity are unknown, cruelty blots out any sense of justice." If he had not been absolutely sure he was in Colombia, he would have thought that he was in "Rome, living in its abominable era."[82]

In 1934 Gaitán continued to push for reform from the outside. In a famous speech in the Congress concerning the events at the hacienda "El

Tolima" (where campesinos organized by UNIR attempted to occupy the vast sixty thousand-acre—and largely empty—holding, and police harassed their encroachment, ultimately killing seventeen and wounding many others), he stressed the need for new laws that addressed the structural problems of property ownership.[83]

He argued that "the conflict [at El Tolima] was a direct and natural consequence of the economically feudal state" in which Colombians lived. He was therefore indignant that in the press the cause was attributed to "communism" and "pure demagoguery," when the Uniristas were in fact "enemies of communism." El Tolima, close to Ibagué, was acquired by one Martín Restrepo in 1892, and it was administered by the co-owner, Hernando Jaramillo. Of the latter it was said that he was cultured and generous; not surprisingly, he married the daughter of Restrepo. Gaitán posed a question. What was the situation, under this regime, of the campesinos, "so-called renters, but really more owners than either Restrepo or Jaramillo," many of whom had been on the land for ten to forty years? (Like any good lawyer, he already knew the answer since many of the campesinos had been in his office). When Jaramillo arrived, he started imposing conditions. Thus began, said Gaitán, "the struggle between capital and labor, between latifundistas and workers, between the master and the servant!" Jaramillo proceeded to throw out the people he did not like, with the help of the police, scandalously under-paying them for their improvements to the land.

At this point Gaitán proposed, in his words, "an audacious assertion." He began by asking if there was "a justification under law for throwing these *campesinos* off the land, *campesinos* who had opened virgin land over which these pretenders had no original title?" He answered, "Absolutely." He admitted that Jaramillo was acting in accordance with the law and that the authorities were obliged to help him. Then he pointed out that "laws are transitory, and they have causes: economic phenomena," and can therefore be changed. (Thus speaks a lawyer-radical, not legal-fetishist.) Returning to his narrative he asked, why would campesinos not resist such a state of affairs? This was not the work of agitators—agitators cannot bring movements out of a vacuum. Strikes in Medellín, Cundinamarca, Fusagasugá, Bogotá, Ibagué, etc. did not erupt "thanks to the desires of demagogues" but rather from "grave economic problems."

Gaitán finished by speaking of Heriberto Amador, the police officer in charge of the conflict who, it was said, would be named director of the national police. This seemed natural to Gaitán since there was a precedent: after the *matanza* of the bananeros, Cortés Vargas was named to the same job. Brilliantly, Gaitán got in his stab and reminded everyone of his role in the 1928 affair.[84] The *Diario Nacional,* a citadel of left liberalism in its own right, was glad to see Gaitán keeping the pressure on, but even they seemed uncomfortable with his militancy. In speaking of the bloody struggles over the hacienda El Tolima (as well as those at El Chocho) they recognized Gaitán as the "very intelligent captain" of UNIR. They agreed there was a tragedy but denied that the government was sending assassins to deny colonos "distributive justice."[85] Left Liberals in Cali were less timid. In 1933 they rejoiced that Gaitán had initiated a frontal attack on the "individualist system of property ownership" and insisted that "it is absolutely necessary to change the constitution" to save and protect the rights of the colonos, victims of "the most abominable exploitation."[86]

UNIR's successful rural mobilizations in Tolima and Cundinamarca notwithstanding, Unirista currents also existed in Huila, Caldas, Valle, Antioquia, the Santanderes, and the Atlantic coast, including many urban areas.

Urban UNIR

In urban centers the admittedly short-lived UNIR enjoyed significant support. Bogotá, Barranquilla, Medellín, Pereira, and Cartagena all boasted "Casas Uniristas," which directed the movement's local activities and provided educational and legal services to members and their families.[87] The pages of *Unirismo* give a glimpse of its successes in Barranquilla, Cartagena, and Santa Marta.[88] It is true that the national organization directed most of its resources toward rural mobilization and little to the cities, and thereby caused considerable irritation. But this very lack of attention from Gaitán and the national organization, given the extent of UNIR's influence in many provincial cities, is a strong indication of the independent nature of the movement beyond Bogotá, especially among workers and their advocates.

In Medellín, Pablo Balcázar, the publisher of a magazine called *TODAMERICA,* followed Gaitán's "defense of workers' interests" and was very interested in UNIR. His *revista* waged a campaign in favor of empleados and obreros to obtain new social laws, "in this new era of social transformations," and supported UNIR. He called Gaitán "the Colombian Clarence Darrow . . . and as a socialist leader . . . the most virtuous paladin of our democracy in formation."[89] In Santander, supporters read the paper and were happily surprised "that the Colombian proletariat" now had "an authentic and genuine spokesman for its interests." They spoke of "the oppression of the worker by the *hacendado* and/or the capitalist."[90] Left Liberals in Cali, noting that "the enemies of the worker have been the *gamonal,* the *latifundista,* and the traitor *politiquero,*" called the "Manifiesto del Unirismo" a "transcendent document" and gave UNIR extensive coverage regarding working-class issues throughout its short life.[91] But independent workers' groups were also active in Bogotá. A construction worker and municipal employee, who was a communist militant from a very left-Liberal family background (his father idolized Uribe Uribe and Herrera), later referred to groups in Bogotá affiliated with UNIR. These groups, which he identified as "liberalism of the left," carried on "arduous struggles" with communists "in their fight over the masses of the *municipio.*"[92]

Moving outside the Liberal party to create the UNIR, Gaitán pursued the left-Liberal agenda of reform through state intervention. Gaitán was surely the central figure, but his role did not negate genuine popular mobilization among the Uniristas. Its multiclass composition demonstrated markedly radical strains. And while UNIR was particularly strong in the coffee regions of Tolima and Cundinamarca, the movement also had a significant following in cities throughout Colombia, which would blossom in the 1940s.

Return to the Fold: Looking to Gaitanismo

Gaitán's return to the Liberal party in mid-1935 caused one of his chief lieutenants to accuse him of treacherously deserting the popular movement to further his own political career. Fermín López Giraldo, leftist activist from Tolima and inspector general of UNIR, quit the movement when Gaitán ran on the Liberal list in the Cundinamarca congressional election of May 1935. A year later he published his memoir, detailing the short history of the movement and lambasting Gaitán for hypocritical opportunism.[93] His was the first of several accusations that UNIR was abandoned by its leaders. Evidence exists, however, that suggests other supporters held more tolerant views of Gaitán's decision to bow before political realities.

Gaitán's move outside the Liberal party demonstrated the problematic interconnections on the Liberal left. Ultimately UNIR's proximity to the more radical elements of the Liberal party was both its greatest weakness as well as its cardinal strength. In 1933 a university student—who identified himself as an "almost blind follower of these ideas of renovation and egalitarian justice" that Gaitán advocated "for the good of the humble class"—illustrated the problem. He believed that "while there exist tattered and hungry multitudes, thirsting for equality and justice," the "intellectual should always be on the side of those who suffer and hope," on the side of the "collective needs." Men like Gaitán created the "moral context." He spoke of "a definitive program, that is liberalism, that is leftism, that is Unirismo." He, like many Liberals, was a faithful follower of Gaitán's ideas, but still did not call himself an "Unirista." He was not sure what the new party stood for and did not understand the need to divide the Liberal party, and indeed, did not believe that doing so was Gaitán's goal. He called on UNIR to march with the Liberals against "injustice" in the "cause of proletarian *reivindicación.*" He asked if Gaitán did not agree that the Liberal program was turning to address a "new economic content that recognizes collective needs."[94]

Liberals delivered their most devastating blow to UNIR as an organization by usurping much of its program and, consequently, stealing its momentum. (One can also argue, and this was the paradoxical situation in which Gaitán and the Uniristas found themselves, that bringing about such a usurpation was their stated goal.) From the moment of its conception, one of UNIR's greatest problems was its difficulty in making appeals beyond "certain groups of the population" and overcoming strong attachment to the old parties.[95] And by 1934 many loyal members of the mainstream Liberal party came to express the same basic concerns manifested by more militant currents on the Colombian left, helping bring about a fundamental change in the party's direction. Liberals in Santa Marta argued that the "'social revolution'—in both its most belligerent and constructive forms—is today at the center of the republic's political agenda and has taken on the character of a categorical imperative." "New generations" clamor for a "transformation in the repertoire of political ideas." "All these disparate voices" called for a "transformation of social relations."[96]

The rhetoric and program of official liberalism, therefore, had been pushed to the left. Those who had shown sympathy for UNIR but never abandoned the Liberal party heralded the change with enthusiasm, as Liberal editorialists made evident. Speaking of the "land problem," one argued that economic "discrepancies" not only existed between squatters and land owners but also among squatters themselves, a situation that necessitated "distributive, social justice."[97] Noted left Liberal Armando Solano, who as noted earlier had learned his own lessons about jumping the Liberal ship, condemned Liberal disunity for opening "the road to reactionaries of all stripes." He echoed Uribe Uribe stressing that "Liberalism must march resolutely to the Left . . . and abandon the politics of indifference . . . always agitating for intervention for popular interests and economic democracy."[98] Among many Uniristas the fact that the Liberal party had taken its agenda was hardly a cause for melancholy. For them Gaitán's return to the Liberal party was a source of pride, the return of a conqueror.[99] The fervently Unirista newspaper from Pereira, *Pluma Libre*, demonstrated this as they took the name "UNIR" from their masthead. Gaitán, they argued, had fulfilled his mission of social agitation and consciousness raising. The Liberals now knew they were accountable.[100] They also took López Giraldo to task for his book, *El Apóstol Desnudo*, for being politically naive.[101]

UNIR also endured serious violent repression throughout its short life. In Fusagasugá itself many Liberals believed that violence against UNIR was justified.[102] In Barranquilla police persecuted Unirista workers, and the "bourgeois, capitalist press" (*La Prensa* and *El Heraldo*) ignored repeated attacks on the person of the that city's UNIR secretary.[103] In Caldas an Unirista complained of the Junta Liberal de Pereira, which manifested the "reactionary character of official Liberalism." He lamented the "repression of workers" that was carried out by the mayors of Palestina, Chinchiná, Santa Rosa de Caldas, and Pereira. These officials "believed that they could extirpate the causes of social disequilibrium through dastardly terror."[104] And of course, one of the most infamous incidents was that which occurred at El Tolima in August 1934.

As he made the transition back into liberalism, Gaitán found many Liberals accommodating. In Santa Marta the "chief of that powerful leftist political collective" was welcomed to join in common electoral cause with the Liberal party.[105] In the city council elections of Bogotá, UNIR considered an alliance with Liberals, socialists, and perhaps communists in a united front against the Conservatives.[106] Many Liberals continued to view Gaitán as a symbol of the left. He occupied "a preferential place" in their "intellectual world . . . for his work advocating socialist ideas." His name was still the rallying call for the "revolutionary ideal . . . of a true Liberal" and since 1929 "the standard bearer of a just and noble cause."[107] A telling Liberal criticism of UNIR, though perhaps unjustified, also helps explain Gaitán's decision to end the movement. With the exception of its founder, owner of a well-cultivated mind, Liberals claimed to have not seen another outstanding figure in the movement, for the most part made up of "the illiterate inhabitants of the great estates of the interior."[108]

In a letter that could easily have been written twelve years later, Efraín Rojas Trujillo informed Gaitán that in Neiva they had created a "Centro

JEG," with four "popularly elected" board members of which he was president. The "worker element and the majority of liberalism" in Neiva and the nearby towns were supportive of the "leftist politics" that Gaitán and President López headed. They worked unwaveringly for his ideas, "justice and the redemption of the working classes, and the progress of the nation's institutions." He called Colombia "this land martyred by the *gamonales* [political bosses] and saboteurs of suffrage."[109] He prophetically expressed the social composition, ideology, and political concerns of mature Gaitanismo. And in 1936 Juan Julian Donneys demonstrated the continuing spirit of UNIR. He characterized strikes in Cali as "a clear proof that the Colombian *pueblo* was acquiring class consciousness." UNIR "had not died," he assured Gaitán, and asked him to "receive the salute of a worker."[110]

The Unirista experiment ended abruptly in 1935, but its influence would be felt a decade later when Gaitán consolidated his following within the Liberal party. By that time his rhetoric had changed but much of the movement's radicalism was conserved in the concerns of the Gaitanistas, who still represented the same social groups, indeed, were often the same people as the Uniristas. By emphasizing UNIR's social base and popular ideology, it becomes apparent that the movement was not simply Gaitán's creation. Rather, UNIR represented a widespread mobilization rooted in the left-Liberal tradition. And the extent of popular participation within UNIR belied Gaitán's own low opinion of consciousness among the masses. As evidenced by the conflicts between his ideology and the views and actions of his followers, the movement was not as controlled from above as many now seem to believe. In 1935 the Liberal party had taken on the Unirista agenda but had killed neither left liberalism nor the currents of popular mobilization it represented. Ironically, one of the slogans of UNIR, "muerte al pasado, revolución hacia el porvenir" (death to the past, revolution toward the future) demonstrated that the young Gaitán believed he could circumvent Colombia's problematic past of partisan struggle. But he came to realize that his movement took its power from the left-Liberal tradition.

4

The Lopista Interlude

Revolución en Marcha, Pause, and Crisis, 1934–1946

Though requiring some effort, Lopista Liberals reminded themselves in 1946 that their nation "was not born . . . on the seventh of August, 1930." They believed, however, that Colombia embarked that day on "the path toward the future." The post-1930 Liberal Republic, they claimed, had been constructed solidly upon the foundation of "the rights of the worker"; that "in effect, with the Liberal ascent to power" they realized "a new conception of the state." No longer was it solely the guardian of equality before the law, a mere "spectator in the economic struggle," but rather a source of "special protection" and "justice" for "the worker."[1] They based their case on the accomplishments of President Alfonso López Pumarejo's first administration of 1934–1938. While the Liberals' presidential victory in 1930 was undeniably a watershed in Colombian political history, it proved only the opening act of a dramatic performance that would climax with López's "Revolución en Marcha" (Revolution on the March). His program is still remembered fondly by many Liberals as the first significant attempt to engineer social change in Colombia through reform. Others characterize it, however, as a tragic cooptation and subversion of the cresting 1930s wave of popular mobilization. Critics argue that its social reforms were nothing more than a deceptive illusion that effectively derailed both the Communist party and UNIR. But whatever interpretation one accepts of the López years, their importance to an adequate understanding of Gaitanismo cannot be denied.

The most notable studies of Alfonso López Pumarejo have concentrated on the events of 1935–1937, while the major studies of Gaitán have emphasized the post-1944 struggles. Few attempts have been made to relate these two men and their movements, and as yet only limited analysis has been offered of the relationship between Lopistas and Gaitanistas.[2] These groups, however, were intimately related.

In the mid-1930s, the traditional Liberal-Conservative dichotomy faded in importance relative to the struggles between right and left Liberals. As noted in the previous chapters, liberalism did not comprise a homogenous mass but, rather, represented a battleground between the elite Liberal establishment and the champions of a more popular party. Given the centrality of this conflict, Herbert Braun's assertion that Gaitán occupied "the middle ground" is misleading because Gaitán and those mobilizing under his banner often found themselves beyond the frontier of sanctioned political and social policies.[3] Alfonso López was certainly the early leader of the post-1930 generation of radical Liberals and immensely popular (among left Liberals and Communists), though as the bulwark of social peace and controlled mobilization, he was the real "man in the middle." His orchestrated "revolution" set the stage for more radical movements later by creating unfulfilled expectations. Indeed, the roller coaster of emotions and aspirations produced by Liberal reform played a crucial role in the spectacular flowering of Gaitanismo. This chapter, therefore, will demonstrate that the eclipse of López Pumarejo and the hopes he represented, combined with a growing mood of disillusion and discontent with (and perhaps contempt for) the traditional political parties, permitted Gaitán and his mobilization to step forward as Lopismo's logical alternative and successor.

Enter López

In 1929 López was one of the first Liberal notables to foresee the end of the Conservative Hegemony.[4] He was also instrumental in engineering the selection of Olaya Herrera as the coalition candidate, a palatable and less offensive offering to the perpetually fractured Liberals and to skittish Conservatives in Congress and elsewhere in government. López knew, however, that his day was at hand. A member of a prosperous banking family, López had no university education but gained experience working in finance, the coffee trade, and especially politics. Starting in his youth, later apologists would stress, he traveled throughout the country "by mule, train, and plane" studying the needs of its people.[5] He made a name for himself in the late 1920s attacking the Conservative government's economic practices, and under Olaya Herrera he was the official leader of the party after the president himself. By 1934 the emergent Liberal majority was strong enough to allow for his own markedly partisan candidacy. Through his advocacy of state intervention and reform, he subsequently became the unlikely focal point for popular aspirations, but as jefe supremo of liberalism, he enjoyed support of a more traditional nature.

Though the relevant struggles at this time were more and more between Liberals, not all currents in liberalism contributing to the jubilant feelings of promise were new ones. Many Liberals instinctively saw Conservatives as their primary enemies, as they had for nearly one hundred years. They characterized fifty years of Conservative government as "living under the terrible Conservative yoke" and saw the Liberal administrations as "true emancipation from *godismo*" ("godo" being the derogatory nickname for Conservatives) and its "feudal legislation."[6] Many reproached the government, therefore, for allowing Conservatives to hold important offices under Liberal administrations. Members of "the class that counts within liberalism, those who mobilize the people, organize the elections, and hobknob with the popular masses" (that is, the political professionals), were tired of the policy of "ideals for the Liberals and jobs for the Conservatives."[7] The "old enemies" were not worthy of such considerations."[8]

But the spirit of a redirected liberalism in the early 1930s, as revealed by left-Liberal support for Gaitán and UNIR, also manifested itself within the party, and especially among the supporters of the heir apparent. Alejandro López, one of the party's important economists, envisioned a "real and sincere democracy" in which the "democratization of the land" would be made a reality through state intervention.[9] José Antonio Osorio Lizarazo spoke of a dynamic "Liberal spirit" of "action, energy, and realization." In his view, liberalism could not "be timid in the application of the new principles of social justice and public administration. . . . Journalists and orators, candidates and apostles all have proclaimed the new age."[10] And intellectual Juan Lanao Loaiza complained that aside from a few "deficient" laws on accidents in the work place, unions and collective security, and the eight-hour day, "the country has not taken steps in favor of the great majority of Colombians who work."[11] He hoped that now things would be different. As in the case of support for UNIR, however, this new sense of hope and anticipation was not limited to well-known intellectuals.

On the traditionally Liberal Atlantic coast, expectations of the new liberalism surfaced everywhere. In Barranquilla even centrist Liberals had a more militant concept of popular "revolution." As opposed to the barracks coups and armed rebellions of the nineteenth century, the "masses" were now "mobilized" with the "moral force of progress" toward more "constructive" ends.[12] In Sincelejo it was understood that the "Liberal

Republic" would "remedy social injustices" and "establish a new order," that it would "guarantee a more equitable distribution of the public and private wealth . . . liberating the peasant and worker from exploitation and deceit through the implantation of just legislation, respondent to proletarian aspirations, democratizing the land and the factory."[13] In Cartagena many believed that liberalism in power had a "moral obligation to proceed as a revolutionary party." They contrasted the nineteenth-century Latin American use of the word for civil war and armed movements with modern usage, stressing that "in the present century 'revolution' stands for modification of the social structure." Liberals in office were not obliged to give all Liberals public jobs but rather to pass and enforce laws to ensure "social justice" and "raise the standard of living of the popular classes."[14] The "masses," they affirmed, "even if sometimes late, always recognize those men who serve their interests," and the "Liberal program" was obviously "the only one for the working class."[15] In Aracataca, the Liberal party, "as the mass party," was expected to "show its democratic fundamentals and social preoccupations and give form to the new political era," assuring the material progress of "collective life."[16] And in Santa Marta others defined Liberal democracy as government of, for, and by the people that strove for "social justice."[17] The general sense of what liberalism was about, though hardly seamless, underscored that "without economic equality, society can never nourish democratic virtues," that, indeed, democracy itself "is a myth."[18]

All such expectations focused in large part on Alfonso López and his "program," which supposedly encompassed these ideals to constitute the clearest expression of liberalism. He wanted, it was said, "the betterment of the working classes and the elevation of their standard of living."[19] His presidency seemed to signify the implementation of a truly "authentic democracy" and a "transformation of the spheres of government."[20] Many Liberals took him at his word, when as president elect he called for reports on the state of the nation from the Liberal assembly of Tolima, and they wrote to him concerning their regions' "collective needs."[21] Liberals were tired of political representatives who spent their time taking care of friends and families and hoped that his "Liberal Revolution" would be more than the same old "ridiculous political scuffles" and would lead to new practices.[22]

López's administration, for its part, seemed attentive to the new mood, as it immediately demonstrated with new governmental policies. In December 1934 there was another major strike in the *zona bananera* of

Magdalena, where little appeared to have changed since the first strike. The workers' demands were largely the same as in 1928, and United Fruit once again refused to negotiate, though this time the banana workers' union had the support of organized labor in both Santa Marta and Barranquilla, something it lacked before. The real difference, however, was the government's reaction; this time it sided with the work force against the multinational corporation. By capitalizing on the weakness of an industry in decline, López ran little risk of antagonizing the United States while simultaneously gaining working-class support and demonstrating his nationalistic backbone. Governor of the department, Manuel Davila Pumarejo, met in November with the workers' representatives and found their demands for pay in the national currency, medical care, fair weights and measures, and safe drinking water to be "just." He went on to remind the government "of the significance of the word 'strike' in the *zona bananera* since 1928."[23]

López himself exhibited this new attitude repeatedly to his subordinates. In September 1934 the governor of Tolima wrote affirming that in most of the department's municipalities the situation was "analogous" to that of the "Hacienda del Tolima" (the one made infamous by Gaitán). He argued that the government must find "some solution other than having the *guardias* fire on the *campesinos*." On the "feudal" hacienda El Tolima things had only gotten worse after a bloody incident in which the owner tried to evict a tenant. The renters, "despite the deaths, insist on defending what they consider to be their own, that is, the value of the improvements they have made to the property." Since the owners wanted coercion used to enforce "unjust laws," the governor asked, "What shall we do?"[24] López answered by saying, "It seems to me that you understand very well the spirit of this government's policy concerning social questions and labor conflicts between agricultural property owners and renters." By not intervening violently, the governor had "saved the government from being compromised" in a matter where the laws would have to be changed.[25] (Gaitán's looming presence was quite tangible in this exchange.) And in November López chastised the governor of Caldas for his back-room handling of a "point of order" in Armenia between two Liberal groups. Liberals, he argued, found their best defense in being impartial and demonstrating superiority over their predecessors, and by appealing "directly to the Liberal masses . . . through the public forum" while avoiding specially orchestrated arrangements.[26] The stage was therefore set for intercession from the top.

The Revolución en Marcha and Its Consequences

López promoted an agenda that focused upon state intervention and constitutional reform. Through state welfare, implementation of universal male suffrage, benevolent dealings with urban workers and organized labor, and education and agrarian reform, López effectively won the support of large portions of the "popular classes." The reformed constitution of 1936 authorized the state to intervene on behalf of workers, while law 200 of 1936 attempted to adjust landholding patterns and incorporated Gaitán's ideas on the social responsibilities of land ownership. López's program was obviously related to other reform plans, namely the New Deal, that arose from the economic constrictions of the Great Depression. But Colombia, like other developing nations, was not affected by the world economic crisis in the same way as the core industrial countries. As imports fell, domestic industry in the late 1930s experienced spectacular growth, allowing López to bankroll his expanded central state through progressive tax reforms without overly antagonizing the owners of capital.

Interpretations of the Revolución en Marcha vary in their assessment of its central social dynamic of overtly attempting to curtail class conflicts through controlled mobilization. The most detailed study of López's first administration underscores how it increased popular participation in the political process. Alvaro Tirado Mejía portrayed López and his movement as a true watershed in Colombian political history: the entrance of the masses and the end of oligarchical democracy (López, as well as Gaitán, spoke of the oligarquía). His "Liberal Revolution" used legal, constitutional means to establish a new political order through, among other things, the extension of the vote, unrestricted by the property and literacy qualifications of the 1886 constitution, to all adult men. Yet clearly evident in this study is the acceptance that López was the dynamic partner directing the mobilization from on high to prevent disorder.[27]

More critical students have emphasized this point, though arguing that instead of disorder, the Revolución en Marcha prevented real popular mobilization. Since the late 1950s at least, the Colombian left has argued that liberalism in power contained the general agitation for genuine popular democracy but paid the price of splitting the party in the 1940s.[28] More recently scholars have echoed the position that independent mobilization was stymied, while providing abundant evidence that the actual concrete results of reform under López were little more than illusion.[29] But to say that the Revolución en Marcha was only an overt and consciously planned maneuver to subvert "real" change is simultaneously to ignore an undeniably progressive current in liberalism and to give the oligarquía too much credit for manipulative prowess. One of the reasons the movement fell short, after all, was the tenacious resistance by the privileged to any notion of reform. Moderately inclined Liberals saw López's reforms as "precise, practical, and realistic," but the right of both parties called them "revolutionary" and "of the extreme left."[30] In his work on López and Liberal radicalism, Richard Stoller astutely argued that Lopismo had some truly radical elements (as opposed to those who see it as mere cooptation), that López's Revolución was not seen in a favorable light by the Liberal right, and stressed the "new language" of the López government.[31] And studies of the Liberal implementation of interventionist policies have stressed macro-economic motivations, largely ignoring the strength of popular demands—though Liberal leaders were also pushed from below.

With the benefit of hindsight, one can demonstrate that the reforms López brought about were actually quite modest, and never really probed the limits of state intervention. The truly important consequence of the Revolución en Marcha, however, was its key role in heightening the widespread atmosphere of expectation for social change. To many progressive Liberals, middle-class intellectuals, the Communist party, and large parts of the working class, the reforms of 1936 represented a significant breakthrough. Even decades later López was remembered as the "progressive . . . defender of the working class who assisted in union organization." Indeed, many union members affectionately considered him the real president of their organizations.[32] Banana workers were full of hope about his "progressive revolution."[33] The Federación Sindical del Magdalena, created for "the unification and moral, intellectual, and economic betterment of the working class," offered its services to the new "democratic government." They did so in recognition of the social nature of López's efforts and their "benefits for the entire working class of the nation."[34] When the Church attacked his reforms in the press, he purportedly received "unconditional support" in Barrancabermeja.[35] From Toro, Valle, two hundred Liberals sent a manifesto of support for his constitutional reform, which they believed would make Colombia "a truly democratic state, complete with guarantees for all its citizens, where rights and justice are forces of cohesion that unite all social activities."[36] In a particularly concise example of what made López's activities attractive to both the middle class and working class, supporters in Cartagena praised electoral reform, protection of national industries, religious toleration, and especially his "concern for the well-being of the workers and the destitute classes, while avoiding the violation of private property."[37]

While general working-class attitudes toward López, the Revolución en Marcha, and the politics of reconciliation were undeniably ones of approval, workers' support was neither unconditional nor blind. In Santa Marta Liberal unions continued to stress the centrality of class struggle. They lamented that the working class of Colombia was still divided between the Liberal and Conservative labels for "superficial" reasons.[38] While they railed at the legislature for labeling the Third National Congress of Workers held in Cali as a "reunion of international communism," they could also attack it for condemning the idea of class struggle, the spirit of which "inspired the congress in Cali." Addressing "reactionaries of all breeds" they argued that the representatives' condemnation was inane because "as long as there is one class that exploits and another that is exploited, as long as workers encounter the privilege and inequality of the owners of capital obstructing the path to their just aspirations, the struggle is inevitable."[39] Making a case for politically oriented unions, they condemned law 83 of 1931, which prohibited them, while suggesting that the legislators had not lost sight of the fact that the workers would remain divided between the traditional parties. "Our politics," they stressed, "must be the search for better collectives."[40]

Critics have shown that the impact of Liberal reform was never very great in the lives of most Colombians. The Revolución en Marcha did, nevertheless, establish a legal basis for a more activist and socially interventionist state while nurturing popular expectations for social justice. And though the "revolution" of the Liberal republic was controlled, it did not negate all independent mobilization, which would later be channeled through Gaitán.

López and the Communists

López's government was both a curse and a blessing to the newly formed Communist party. On the one hand, the Communists (along with UNIR) represented competing currents of popular mobilization that were displaced by the official Liberal party. Indeed, it is widely accepted that Liberals delivered their most devastating blow to such popular movements by usurping much of their program.[41] On the other hand, the Liberal government under López made the Communists' organizational successes possible.

The alliance was hardly an easy one. The Communists did not immediately embrace López or the Liberals. In fact, their natural inclination was to spurn and attack them. But, because of its internationalist orientation, especially adherence to the "Popular Front" strategies advocated by the Comintern, the Communist party followed an erratic and, what seemed to many, contradictory course. In July 1935, while calling for solidarity against international reaction, Communists condemned a possible military action against Venezuela, arguing instead "for the transformation to a civil war against national and international exploiters."[42] In November, however, the leadership in Bogotá called for a "change of tactic" to cultivate "a uniform alliance of the forces of the Left," and therefore suspended their attacks on López's government.[43]

But, ultimately, there was nothing surprising about the relationship between Communists and the popular wing of the Liberal party in the 1930s. U.S. State Department analysts at the time recognized that the "development of the Communist party" coincided with "the period of Liberal government," and that some Colombian Communists' grasp of socialist ideology was less than orthodox.[44] And from the beginning it was clear that the areas of Communist strength in the Magdalena region, in Cali, and Bogotá were also left-Liberal areas. One U.S. State Department official went so far as to claim that some of Colombia's "alleged Communism is in reality nothing more than a pronounced liberalism which, as elsewhere in Latin America, is denounced by the Conservative element."[45]

Left Liberals could approvingly note the work of Communists. In 1934 the editors of *La Tribuna* in Barranquilla (later Gaitanistas) plugged the work of a young Communist city councilman, Augusto Durán, for having been the standard bearer of the "exploited working classes" and representing them to their satisfaction.[46] And Communists could sound like Liberals. At the second Communist convention of Magdalena in 1944, the participants offered their "respectful greetings" to López for his part in the nation's journey toward progress, and saluted Roosevelt, Churchill, and Stalin.[47] Liberals in Magdalena acknowledged that while the Colombian Communists' attachment to the Third International was unfortunate, it nevertheless had "aspired to harmonize . . . the tendencies of the left," and had acted as a "sincere and loyal friend of liberalism."[48]

López accepted the Communists' support but never actively sought it out, nor did he go out of his way to make the Liberal party a comfortable place for them. Marco Palacios has argued that Lopismo was given a "revolutionary image" by its Communist "fellow travelers," but that López kept them at arm's length and in general weakened their movement.[49] And López was not alone in this attitude. Even in Barranquilla, the Colombian city most known for its radical sympathies, evidence existed of firm anticommunist feelings. In November 1936, the Liberal-dominated city council asked the national government to prohibit the entry into Colombia of individuals "who profess communist ideas," because communism threatened "the democratic postulates of nation, property, home, and order of western civilization."[50]

Yet, undoubtedly, López made possible the Communists' most impressive conquests during the 1930s in the field of union federation leadership. Summing up the range of Colombian Communist activity from the perspective of 1943, U.S. State Department officials noted that the years of the Liberal Republic witnessed a "tremendous expansion of labor unions, under the sympathetic eye of a government" that had "leaned heavily for its votes upon the lower income brackets." "The most striking aspect of labor organization . . . from the point of view of political and social change" was not the individual unions but the general organizations, especially the Confederación de Trabajadores Colombianos (the Confederation of Colombian Workers, CTC). "Toward the penetration of the central union authority, and similar general labor meetings," the Communists "bent every effort."[51] Though the CTC was composed of Liberal, Catholic, and Communist unions, the Communists were perhaps the most powerful block within the federation.

And after the CTC, the most important federation to the Communists was FEDENAL (the National Federation of Maritime, River, and Port Transportation Workers). The river workers enjoy a legendary status among Colombian workers due to their powerful mobilizations during the 1930s and 1940s.[52] Their successes arose from the strategic position the river occupied in the Colombian economy, and the resultant leverage river workers wielded to their own advantage. The Magdalena connected the coastal regions to the highland interior and served as the means by which coffee, Colombia's major export and lifeblood after 1910, found its way to the world market. Any work stoppages along it, consequently, became immediate national crises. The Magdalena's shipwrights, sailors, pilots, mechanics, and stevedores are central to Colombian labor history because they were the only Colombian workers ever able to impose a closed shop on their employers. Their achievement forced the owners of the river's ships, shipyards, and docks to hire only laborers affiliated with unions of FEDENAL.

The reality of a river workers' federation took shape under the benevolent gaze of the López administration. His government urged companies to the negotiating table after a four-day strike paralyzed the river in June 1937. In July, government arbitrators oversaw the signing of a pact between the companies and the federation's forty-two unions, making a closed shop a reality on the Magdalena.[53] Less than a year after its foundation, FEDENAL had, with government assistance, established a firm grip on the river's labor market. Anyone wanting a job first had to join an affiliated union. Despite cracks in its solidarity, FEDENAL's strength was shown in the survival of its closed shop during the years of reaction against the Revolución en Marcha after 1938, when FEDENAL's unions cautiously used the strike as an effective defensive mechanism against the companies' intransigent refusals to honor the pact of July 1937.[54]

During its relatively short period of dominance, FEDENAL was the model other Colombian labor organizations aspired to emulate, and the pride of the Communists. Augusto Durán, city councilman in Barranquilla, senator from Atlántico, and secretary general of the Communist party (renamed the Partido Socialista Democrático, PSD, in the 1940s), served as the secretary general of FEDENAL. The federation was not, however, completely autonomous. FEDENAL possessed no significant strike funds and was constantly threatened by disunity.[55] It could not, therefore, easily prosper without the aid of the Liberal government, as the slogan "with López and with our own efforts" made clear.[56]

The Communists in Colombia made a Faustian bargain with López. After they threw in their lot with the Revolución en Marcha, they had trouble distancing themselves from the political establishment. Ironically, despite the Communists' generally pro-López posture, the Liberal party never extended to them more than token acceptance. And though the arrangement did serve their purposes, ultimately Colombian Communists found that they stood too close to liberalism for their own good when they later had to confront a powerful competitor on the Liberal left.

A Mayor of the People and the Drivers' Strike of 1937

The Communists were not alone in their problematic collaboration with López. Gaitán also demonstrated the tensions between the Liberal establishment and those on the left, in particular through his experience as mayor of Bogotá. Though Gaitán returned to the Liberal party in 1935, the position he and other left Liberals occupied there remained a problematic one. Despite the atmosphere of expectations created by the rise of López, the more radical elements of liberalism were never entirely welcomed home by its leadership. In Barranquilla, for example, "Liberals of the extreme left," characterized by the American consulate as "in reality communists," were barred from holding meetings in the Casa Liberal in September 1936.[57] Gaitán had been an elected member of the Bogotá city council since 1930 and was therefore well acquainted with local problems in 1936.[58] And López, in spite of his own vast popularity, could not comfortably ignore the other most well-known and popular Liberal politician. At that moment Gaitán was successfully defending the administration's policies against attacks by the right wing of the Liberal party and the Conservatives. López therefore appointed Gaitán *alcalde* of Bogotá, though not without some opposition within the Liberal party. The governor of Cundinamarca would not accept the new mayor and was forced to resign.[59]

Colombians anticipated Gaitán's appointment with intense excitement.[60] The *Diario Nacional* of Bogotá editorialized that the presence of Gaitán, "a man of great energy, capability, and prestige," in the *alcaldía* would be the solution to a "crisis of considerable maturity." They argued that Gaitán had been "the standard-bearer of proletarian rejuvenation" and lauded his record on the city council, among other places. Though "oligarchic groups" would attempt to deny Gaitán the alcaldía, for many Gaitán was already the real mayor, "the pupil, the brain, and the arm of the capital."[61]

On May 22 supporters held a huge rally in Bogotá to celebrate his appointment. Darío Samper spoke of Gaitán's appointment as "the taking of the capital by the Colombia left" and noted that "the banking oligarchy had opposed it to the last." Geraldo Molina, representing organized labor, spoke of the triumph of the "popular front" that had agitated for Gaitán. The old governor of Cundinamarca represented the interests of big landholders, who did not want to see the alcaldía in other hands. He pointed to needs Gaitán should address: problems of the "barrios altos" that sprang up on the mountainsides over Bogotá, municipal control of telephones and electricity, better sewers and more schools and clinics in worker neighborhoods, extension of bus lines out to worker neighborhoods. Gaitán answered that while he was in charge of the municipal executive, "the word 'impossible' would be erased from the municipal dictionary and replaced with 'stimulate.'" Under his administration the "incompetent" would be shown the door and the "indelicados" who availed themselves of public funds would go to jail.[62]

The position, which Gaitán occupied only from June of 1936 through February of 1937, was widely believed to have been awarded him as an opportunity to fail. On the Atlantic coast, for example, "local comment" held that Gaitán's appointment "was made with a view to ruining him politically."[63] Though Gaitán himself was aware of the risks, he took the job as an opportunity to demonstrate his administrative abilities.[64] But he refused to accept the assignment humbly from the hand of the new governor of Cundinamarca. On June 8, seven years (to the day) after demonstrations he led against the Conservative government, he marched through Bogotá to city hall at the head of a throng of supporters and, in the words of the *Diario Nacional,* "took possession" of it in the name of the pueblo.[65] Speaking of the prospects for change, one commentator noted that it was "not possible to stop the torrent of enthusiasm."[66] This statement applied to many places throughout the nation.[67]

During his short tenure as mayor, Gaitán concentrated his efforts on improving the city's infrastructure, paying special attention to the needs and problems of the pueblo. Bogotá's "popular" and working-class neighborhoods were under heavy strain from population growth and migration from the countryside, and their residents made their needs known to the new mayor.[68] Gaitán moved to improve sewers and transportation to and within the neighborhoods, provided electricity, and extended streets and pavement; he initiated public housing projects in two new areas; he also attempted to improve public health facilities and education.[69] Gaitán quickly strove to improve efficiency in the mayor's office, instituting centralized communication and time clocks for municipal employees. Also in the name of efficiency, he attempted to remove partisan influences from the municipal administration by offering bureaucratic jobs to Conservatives of ability.[70]

Popular support for Mayor Gaitán extended far beyond Bogotá, while his prestige and influence among large sectors of the party's base continued to grow. In Medellín, Colombia's second city, the municipal workers' union commended his work, while in Barranquilla, Colombia's third city and principal port, he was heralded as "teacher and chief of the left." With his efforts to transform Bogotá, Gaitán was a modern "Nehemiah," who rebuilt the walls and "defended the people of Jerusalem." Speaking of a rally there on December 23, 1936, this supporter called it "a spontaneous mass expression of loving approval" for the first citizen of Bogotá, demonstrating that people were "conscious of his actions."[71]

As will be shown, such support throughout Colombia, before and after the Bogotá bus and taxi drivers' strike of 1937 (the incident that cost Gaitán his job), belies the conventional wisdom, which holds that Gaitán lost the support of the working class—and therefore his appointed position as the mayor of Bogotá—due to his insistence that the drivers wear uniforms. Yet unswerving workers' support throughout Colombia for "the mayor of the people" before, during, and after the strike belies such a conclusion. Seeing the episode in this new light has long-range implications for the interpretation of Gaitanismo in the 1940s, since commentators have repeatedly pointed to the strike and its outcome as evidence that Gaitán's movement was not truly a working-class movement. In fact, the strike and its aftermath demonstrated the fundamental connections between Gaitán and the Colombian working classes.

After acknowledging his frantic activity as mayor, commentary has most often turned to Gaitán's "authoritarian" nature. Gaitán undoubtedly wanted firm control of the city's administration and its workforce. As in UNIR's "revolution of soap," he insisted on the use of "soap and razor," even though many city workers had no easy access to washing facilities. He also detested and discouraged the use of the traditional ruana, or wool poncho, considering it a symbol of backwardness, even though overcoats cost five times as much.[72] This tension within Gaitán's personality—between the leftist advocate of popular democracy and the righteous, uncompromising reformer—came to a head in his decree requiring the use of uniforms by the city's bus and taxi drivers.

Gaitán issued decree 425 of 1936 mandating that taxi and bus drivers wear officially sanctioned shoes, hats, shirts, and overalls. Claiming to represent one thousand drivers, the Asociación Nacional de Choferes condemned Gaitán's decree as a violation of their rights.[73] Gaitán responded by showing a decidedly stubborn streak. Major newspapers printed the didactic commentaries in which he answered the drivers' contention that uniforms violated their "individual liberty" by arguing that "established habits are not acquired rights." He personally did not understand liberty or democracy in the "anarchic sense" and argued that if people were not materially and morally prepared for certain liberties, "they should be rejected as contrary to the public good."[74] When the Asociación went on strike over the order, Gaitán called in the police to enforce it. After a few tense days, the whole episode came to a sudden close. President López acted with little warning and had the governor of Cundinamarca fire Gaitán on February 14, 1937.

Other students of the strike have largely accepted the supposition that Gaitán lost the support of the city's drivers and, seemingly, the working class.[75] The sheer amount of approval and support pledged to Gaitán during the crisis, however, illustrated the power of his name among popular elements of the Liberal party and the organized working class in particular. While many workers were sympathetic to the drivers' concerns (though not all were), the issue of uniforms was not generally considered sufficient cause to attack Gaitán. Even before the actual strike itself erupted, workers reacted to rumors that Gaitán could possibly resign with demonstrations in his support.[76] On February 11 the crowd that met in Bogotá to support the mayor was estimated at twenty thousand. After his dismissal, "enormous" crowds called for Gaitán's reinstatement and the governor's resignation.[77]

Ample evidence also suggests that Gaitán commanded a more significant portion of workers' sympathy than did the striking drivers. The radical socialist (and left-Liberal) working-class paper *Pluma Libre* of Pereira, for example, proclaimed him the defender of "the proletarian classes" and stood by him throughout the ordeal.[78] Juan Lozano y Lozano, a Liberal intellectual with close ties to the party establishment and never one of Gaitán's cheerleaders, noted that the mayor had with him "a conspicuous portion of the labor organizations."[79] And of considerable significance, Gaitán received the backing of the other major drivers' union in Colombia, the Sindicato Central Nacional de Choferes, which called on drivers to "abandon those leaders who would use the issue of uniforms to disguise their reactionary politics . . . which destabilize the administration of the mayor, preparing for the blackest reaction." They labeled drivers concerned with the issue as "aristocratic elements aggrieved at being workers" who considered uniforms "degrading."[80]

In fact, there was nothing remotely like a solid working-class block of opposition to Gaitán.[81] Railroad workers declined to join the drivers in a sympathy strike, and drivers in Cali also would make no show of solidarity, citing the Bogotá drivers' indifference to the fate of the union outside the capital.[82] In heavily unionized Girardot, the majority of the local unions were at Gaitán's service, ready to sacrifice for democratic institutions.[83] While representatives of the large Bavaria Brewery union visited with the mayor, many buses and cabs cruised the streets, indicating that the strike lacked overwhelming support.[84] In a message from "the workers of Bogotá to the workers of Barranquilla," in which the costeños were warned "not to be deceived," union leaders characterized the strike as the creation of "right-wing reactionaries antagonistic to democratic government." In response they had organized a large demonstration in support of Gaitán's "labor in defense of the working class" that had "provoked the reaction of fascist forces."[85] The letter was also sent to the workers of Cali.[86]

Gaitán even received the backing of his old rivals on the left, the Communist party.[87] (Some Conservatives went so far as to argue that Gaitán received his principal support from the Communists.)[88] In a flyer from the central committee, they affirmed their defense of working-class interests but condemned the "adventurous and subversive" strike.[89] Striking drivers, many yelling "death to Communism and Russia, long live Colombia *libre*," clashed with Communists who were organizing a pro-Gaitán rally in the central Plaza de Bolívar outside the mayoral building. Afterward both groups taunted each other with "vivas" and "mueras."[90]

The workers who supported Gaitán justified their position by maintaining that the drivers' action was not a good strike because it advanced no significant economic ends. In fact, it was a bad strike because it served the ends of the enemies of the working class. According to the Confederación Sindical de Colombia, the strike had furthered no real working-class interests such as "raising salaries, eight-hour working days, or forcing bus and taxi companies to comply with social legislation."[91] The Communists agreed, and argued that the strike did not have a "revolutionary character in the interests of the working class."[92] Railroad workers in Medellín called Gaitán "one of the most robust figures" of Colombian democracy and asserted that his labors as the mayor of Bogotá had impressed the entire country. They interpreted uniforms for drivers as a "social improvement" and evidence of good administration by Gaitán. They would continue to support him in his work and pointed out that "the enemies of the workers" were most pleased by the strike and its outcome.[93]

Left Liberals not only supported Gaitán but also had strong ideas about the strike itself. The most conspicuous theme among their interpretations concerned right-wing manipulation.[94] In fact, conspiracy theories began to circulate even before the strike had actually come to a close. Supporters wrote from all over Colombia to pledge their "unrestricted support" to the mayor of the people in the face of "the dark machinations of the enemies of democracy."[95] Workers blamed right-wing intrigue for sustaining the strike (though the conscious working masses, it was argued, knew better).[96] Workers who were not "reactionary" nor "fascist," and applauded his "democratic" efforts, supported Gaitán's government.[97] Most left-Liberal and union papers pointed to right-wing influence.[98] Conservative papers overwhelmingly followed the anti-Gaitán line laid down by *El Siglo* of Bogotá, owned by the leader of the most reactionary sect of the Conservative party, Laureano Gómez. Some went so far as to chastise Gaitán for arrogance, bloodshed, and intransigence.[99] Finally, right-wing manipulation and reactionary motivations were directly related to the political questions raised by the strike. The traditional Liberal/Conservative antagonism was unquestionably at work, though not a few Colombians recognized that so too were elements of the inter-Liberal struggle between the Liberal establishment and the dissident left Liberals.

Many Liberals were not prepared to admit in public that a significant portion of the Liberal leadership was glad to see Gaitán pushed out. It was less troublesome to place all the blame on the "dark machinations" of right-wing forces largely beyond the Liberal party. Such was the case with the socialist left Liberals at *Pluma Libre,* who remained respectful of President López. They demonstrated the tendency in many working-class organs defending Gaitán to see in the drivers' strike a Conservative plot to create problems for democratic government, to which López unwittingly succumbed.[100] While the Confederación Sindical de Colombia admitted that such political analysis was "outside the orbit" of their normal union concerns, they felt the need to unmask the plot behind the defeat of "a mayor of the people" and, tellingly, defend López and democratic government against fascist manipulation.[101] Liberals in Manizales believed that the government merely committed a huge error in firing the mayor of Bogotá in an attempt to avoid violent clashes.[102]

Side-stepping the direct question of López's responsibility, *El Espectador*'s editors nevertheless commented on how suddenly (and strangely) Gaitán had been kicked out of the mayor's office. They believed that firing him so fast was not the answer; "not only was it a very grave error, it was an inexcusable injustice."[103] *El Tiempo*'s influential columnist, Calibán (pen name of Enrique Santos—brother of Eduardo Santos, owner of the paper, and leader of the right wing of the Liberal party) expressed pseudo-astonishment over the affair. While calling the strike "unjustified," he dismissed as "absurd" the contention that the drivers were fascists and or pawns of the Conservatives. He argued simply that the drivers had made a bad mistake, while Gaitán had overreacted.[104]

Yet one of the Liberal establishment's own mouthpieces, Juan Lozano y Lozano, openly admitted that Gaitán had been "sacrificed by the regime." The Liberals in power could get away with Gaitán's dismissal, who everyone recognized as "the best mayor" Bogotá had had "in a hundred years," because the "forces of the left" were divided.[105] *El Empleado,* a union paper in Girardot, was sure that the strike "was a political game" that left little doubt as to the "enormity of the malevolence it caused." They hinted "that if in the beginning there was no hidden agenda," things had been allowed to run to unnecessary extremes.[106] And *Relator* keenly observed that Gaitán's dismissal would mean a "drastic interruption" in his "gigantic work of material progress and social transformation." The government had "surely sacrificed the great portion of prestige the mayor gave them" to "reestablish order."[107]

Gaitán, at any rate, believed that the Liberal establishment had set him up for a fall. In a speech before the Congress in which he defended himself, Gaitán pounded away at two themes: that he was not a fascist; and that he had been misused.[108] He began by asking: "What is fascism? The negation of violence? No! Fascism is the theory of force. . . . Who is fascist? He who argues that the law must be observed or he who lets violence overtake it?" He asked if his supporters at the respected *El Espectador* in Bogotá and *El Relator* in Cali were fascists. After reading from letters by drivers complying with the uniform order, he said that in their words, "the strike was nothing more than a reactionary plot," and his speech met "fervent applause." Gaitán left open the question of who had been involved in the plot.[109]

The strike had a lot to do with the traditional divisions (and connections) of Colombian politics. Conservatives undeniably seized upon the drivers' action as a wonderful opportunity to attack one of their worst enemies in the Liberal party, and in the process rob the Liberal government of legitimacy. Yet the episode was more than an old-fashioned face-off between Conservatives and Liberals. It also exposed the widening divisions between the Liberal establishment and the increasingly discontented left wing of the party. It proved to be another of those fairly common instances in Colombian history where the elite of both parties could agree on policy, in this case that alcalde Gaitán had to go. The "forces of reaction" had a very clear hand, but so too did the Liberal establishment, as Calibán (perhaps inadvertently) recognized. The drivers may ultimately have been pawns of the "fascist" wing of the Conservative party, but their strike also served López in (temporarily) eliminating Gaitán. In the context of the uneasy reintegration of left Liberals and the Liberal leadership during the post-UNIR years, the drivers' strike foreshadowed the rupture of the 1940s.

Almost before it was over, commentators recognized that Gaitán's time in the alcaldía had been a watershed. After calling Gaitán "absolutist, arrogant, imperious, ambitious, and brusque," one characterized his term of office as "a grand essay in government" that inevitably would have some errors. Yet Gaitán's passion and hard work were beyond reproach. In a few short months he had accomplished such important work in worker neighborhoods that for that reason alone he should be praised. But also fundamentally, he introduced "morality" into municipal government.[110] Gaitán's supporters were slow to let go. An estimated ten thousand pro-Gaitán supporters showed up to the rally on February 17 while leftists in Congress protested his dismissal.[111] Even Calibán noted that Gaitán had emerged with his public career intact and could look to the future.[112]

The strike represented a glaring inconsistency. Gaitán seemingly, and *Relator* of Cali explicitly, condemned the drivers' "resistencia" against authority, even though before and after Gaitán was the champion of such resistance. This is perhaps the best example of Gaitán's dual personality regarding authority: Gaitán the order-loving lawyer and Gaitán the subversive revolutionary. Gaitán's hubris as the stern father caused him and many of his supporters to ignore the legitimate concerns voiced by the striking drivers. Workers, however, were politically sophisticated enough to see beyond the strike. True, there had been a core of drivers decidedly against the decree and probably many others who were not pleased by it, such as the worker who complained that "a good *ruana* costs six pesos but a bad overcoat costs thirty."[113] Yet *El Empleado* of Girardot pondered, with some insight, that "tomorrow these same strikers, the great majority of whom have in the past been such fervent partisans of Doctor Gaitán" might "feel uncomfortable without their *caudillo* in the municipal executive and want him back."[114]

Pause and Crisis

In December 1936, at the industrial exposition of Barranquilla, Alfonso López decreed a "pause" in his revolution. By that time the constitutional reform, centerpiece of his program, had been approved. He declared that thanks to state intervention, "peace and calm" reigned in the countryside and workers enjoyed better salaries, while their legally appropriated indemnities were not a strain on businesses. The institutional changes his government had made provided Colombia with the ability to confront the problems of the twentieth century.[115] López's "pause" turned into full-scale retreat under the administration of president Eduardo Santos.

Among Lopista Liberals, the successor of preference to Alfonso López was Darío Echandía, the minister of government. Because of his contentious career and the extreme emotions he evoked, Gaitán was still not considered presidential material. The more conservative faction of the party, in contrast, backed Eduardo Santos. The choice between Santos and Echandía, many believed, was nothing less than that between turning back to the old elite-dominated liberalism of the past or continuing on toward a more democratic future.[116] Santos's brand of elite liberalism found expression in the words of his supporters. Speaking on local radio in Armenia, Santista senator Carlos V. Rey "denigrated the working class," which Liberal icon Benjamín Herrera called "the flesh and blood of Liberalism," by referring to it as an "ignorant and irresponsible rabble." Echandía partisans saw this as evidence that Santismo disdained the "illiterate multitudes" while their would-be candidate "esteemed, respected, [and] found shelter in the great mass of humanity."[117] Echandía represented a progressive continuation of the Lopista program but nevertheless avoided radical positions that might have been considered alarming. His liberalism did not "cower before the advanced doctrines of social justice, which as philosophical postulates are in constant evolution," but as "defender of the collective" he stood for "a moderate state intervention that would regulate the relations" of capital and labor and establish a "just equilibrium."[118] Gaitán, however, was not forgotten; left-Liberals were reminded that he "fought at Echandía's side."[119]

Yet few knowledgeable observers doubted that Eduardo Santos held the Liberal establishment trump card. Candidate of choice among many powerful leaders of liberalism distressed by the party's popular direction, he effortlessly grabbed liberalism's ultimate prize. Even the Conservative party was content enough with Santos to forego a candidate of its own. Santos and the Liberal currents he represented brought a deathly chill to the type of mobilization associated with the early 1930s. He manifested his characteristic antagonism to the left from the outset of his rise to power. In 1936, for example, he attacked the union congress held in Medellín for looking beyond workers' reasonable interests and instead attempting to create "a political machine that may augur dark days in the future." The congress went even further than "that terrible Popular Front" when it proposed the nationalization of the banks.[120] Santos represented the moneyed elements of both parties and the continuation of their interests through maintenance of the status quo (or as he put it, "the coexistence of different forces and parties"), and therefore welcomed Conservatives into his government.[121] Even the rhetoric of democracy, social justice, and state intervention fell aside as the economic and political elites reasserted their supremacy. Many members of the capital-owning and politically influential class felt that they had allowed enough compromise and reform.

When Alfonso López officially announced his desire to seek the presidency again for the 1942–46 term, he confronted a modest swell of opposition within the party, of which Gaitán was a part. Yet throughout Colombia, popular Liberal and working-class agitation for his return to power to complete the "revolution" had already begun as early as 1938. On the Atlantic coast, optimistic Liberals noted that while "the situation of the working masses" upon his return to office in 1942 was "desperate," the people of Colombia were favored by "a government that cared for their interests."[122] A general Liberal social policy for López's second term, it was hoped, would include reforms to extend protections already established by Colombian law, "to suppress the arbitrary barriers between the middle class and the proletarian class," and to protect their rights, whether they wore an overcoat or a ruana.[123] These expectations, however, were shattered with astonishing suddenness. The López that progressive and radical Liberals encountered after 1942 bore little resemblance to the leader of the Revolución en Marcha idealized in the popular imagination. His concerns had been chiseled down to the uninspiring foundation of Liberal union, party organization, and the political stability of the nation.[124]

The ripening atmosphere of disillusion was apparent even in early 1943. Not referring to López directly, left Liberals in Barranquilla called for "Liberals of action and not just words" to bring order to "the chaos which false apostles have bequeathed us."[125] A little later, summing up López's first year back in office, they pointed out that his government was not producing the fruits the Colombian people had hoped because he returned with Liberal advisers lacking real popular followings in the party and among the pueblo.[126] The U.S. consul there noted that while a pro-López rally in front of the Barranquilla town hall on September 27 was affected by the late hour and ugly weather, "it is believed that, on the whole, the recent demonstration in support of President López did not result in demonstrating an impressive degree of solidarity or political weight." His strength among the "Liberal element" of the coast remained "unproven."[127] Others were less guarded in their assessment of his situation. One Gaitanista claimed that in Barranquilla there existed a profound discontent with López's government[128] and that he had been "justifiably abandoned by Colombia's workers."[129] In spite of a bow to the power of his *mística* among Liberals, observers commenting on a quick visit he made to Santa Marta noted a "profound dismay" at the lost opportunity to effect change.[130] In Cartagena he was no longer known as the "agitator of ideas but rather the creator of chaos."[131] Years later, the twilight of the López period would be remembered by many disenchanted left Liberals as "an atmosphere of artificial peace constructed upon deception."[132] Racked by scandal and opposition (which had even generated an abortive coup attempt), López absented himself from power in 1944 and withdrew permanently from the presidency in 1945 in favor of first designate, Alberto Lleras Camargo.

López's short return to office and withdrawal were symptomatic of the change of fortune FEDENAL, the most celebrated of Colombia's labor organizations, would experience in the postwar period. By the mid 1940s, the importance of the river as a means of transportation had come under mortal pressure from more reliable methods of transport, especially improved roads and rail. The northern railroad eventually linked Barranquilla to the center of the country and to the growing network of national roads.[133] River workers also faced new threats from changing technologies, such as cranes, to load and unload steamships. By 1945, therefore, the river workers' organizational vitality was declining, despite the fact that FEDENAL remained the most powerful federation within the CTC and the very symbol of organized labor.[134] Given this descent and the unstable political climate, it was an inopportune moment for the federation to flex its muscles. The Communists in charge of FEDENAL, however, felt their patience and cooperation during the war years deserved reward. The federation once again demanded that companies observe the pact of July 1937 and that they raise salaries, which had not been adjusted since 1942. They also took heart that at that moment the country was experiencing other significant labor actions.[135] The PSD was confident that FEDENAL would prevail yet again.

The strike, which began on December 17, 1945, and ended on January 4, 1946, immediately became a confrontation between the Communists in FEDENAL and the state.[136] Acting president Lleras Camargo refused to negotiate with the strikers. He called the strike an action against the government and eventually declared it illegal. Liberals in the government attacked unionized river workers as a "privileged" sector of the working class that was abusing its "advantages." The PSD, which considered the strike a critical encounter, quickly found itself isolated from its left-Liberal allies. Important Liberal federations of the CTC condemned the strike and offered their support to the government. Even FEDENAL itself fractured, with several of its important unions refusing to participate. The strike collapsed. The Ministry of Labor allowed the strike breakers to retain their jobs and be incorporated into unions, effectively ending the closed shop that FEDENAL had achieved nine years earlier.

The PSD (and much of the Liberal left) had simply bet on the wrong horse after 1942, though at the time this was not immediately clear. Their collaboration with López and support for the Revolucíon en Marcha, it must be remembered, had paid off. Through their alliance with the establishment Liberals in the 1930s, the vote had been dramatically expanded, workers made significant gains, and the PSD had created their stronghold within the nation's labor organizations, especially within the CTC and FEDENAL. But the Communists in particular paid a heavy price. Antonio García argued that the Communists remained the creatures of López, even during the "black period" of his second administration when Gaitán was the "true" leader of the people. They fell prey to their own "terrible myth" concerning the accomplishments of the Revolución en Marcha.[137] In July 1945 the PSD was still plugging Darío Echandía in *Diario Popular* as the only hope of Liberal salvation because he would continue the work of López. They seemed to be in a state of denial concerning López's abandonment of the left. By 1945 it was clear that reform under Lopista liberalism was at an end. Left Liberals now looked to new champions.

Liberal Struggles, Gaitán, and the Popular Memory

Liberal radicalism did not end with the Revolución en Marcha.[138] The currents of left-Liberal conflict and agitation with official liberalism that Gaitán represented did not evaporate with the demise of UNIR. Workers in Santa Marta never ceased to believe that the "paternal classes . . . would not miss the slightest opportunity" to control the working class.[139] Left Liberals in Barranquilla continued to speak of awakening the consciousness of "revolutionary and impassioned Liberal youth" to rejuvenate the party's militancy. They wanted to establish a Liberal nucleus within the party in Atlántico, whose goal was the creation of "a new orientation for liberalism."[140] Left Liberals pointed to the "transcendent" example of Lázaro Cárdenas in Mexico and his expropriation of the U.S. and British oil companies, a course that "showed the way to other American nations."[141] Such Liberals, whether middle-class intellectuals or working class, were ready to go beyond the "sterile and pointless" controversies of the López reelection campaign. They wanted "authentic democracy" that sought, not only the power of public office, but also to carry out the "ideals" of liberalism, which emphasized "the elevation of the intellectual, economic, and moral level of *el pueblo*."[142] And while many Liberals disagreed about the means, popular Liberal aspirations continued to focus on the pursuit of "social justice."

Gaitán remained the focal point of left-Liberal struggles within the official party. He absorbed the blow of his humiliating dismissal as mayor of Bogotá and continued on with a resiliency that bespoke the magnitude of his popular following. In September 1937 Gaitán was reelected to the city council by working-class neighborhoods in spite of the opposition of *El Tiempo*.[143] His popularity was clear in neighborhoods all over Bogotá. The residents of the workers' neighborhood La Providencia named a school after Gaitán in August 1937. Northern workers' neighborhoods, considering his "civic struggles" in the interests of the "working classes," thanked him for his work in the *concejo*. They protested against the continued "attacks by reactionary elements" against him. Another called him the "authentic defender of the working and undervalued classes." Those "high" on the mountainsides praised his "love of the oppressed classes and defense of their interests"; in the neighborhood named after him Gaitán was called the "unwavering combatant for the working classes." This spirit remained strong years later when a neighborhood remembered his "brilliant labor" as alcalde.[144]

Organized labor organizations in Bogotá also remembered Gaitán. Municipal workers thanked him for his advocacy, as did transport workers, "in benefit of all the working classes." Mail and telegraph workers commended his "disinterested service in the name of the *reivindicaciones* of the undervalued classes of society." Electrical workers, knowing that Gaitán had accepted the call to defend their organization, gave him their complete confidence in his ability to defend the "working classes." Bogotá's shoe shiners thanked *concejal* Gaitán for his support of their petition.[145] And in an extreme act of unself-conscious irony, the Asociación Nacional de Choferes asked in 1938 for his opinions for their new paper, *El Conductor,* on (among other things) whether they should have to pull a twenty-four hour shift every third day, and whether they should have to deposit twenty pesos with the company.[146]

Though Gaitán held several positions of authority under the López and Santos administrations, he was one of the few prominent public figures of the Liberal party who escaped "the stain" of official corruption and scandal, especially that of the second López presidency.[147] As minister of education, Gaitán was remembered as full of energy and ideas, advocating a "campaign of cultural extension" through the "nationalization of primary education."[148]

On the eve of his appointment as minister of labor in 1943, workers in Barranquilla thanked and praised him for his "noble campaign" in the Senate against a law by the then minister of labor that "would not only restrict and regulate the exercise of the right to strike but would also strangle its use in practice, with grave consequences for working-class interests."[149] Answering a letter from Humberto López Gaviria of the publication *Liberación,* organ of the Federación Nacional de Comunicaciones, Gaitán made his position on the importance of struggle through organization quite clear. In an article published in *Liberación,* he understood López Gaviria to hold that unions are "dangerous forms of class struggle because they can lead to revolution" and that workers should employ more "humble" forms of "collective demands." Gaitán answered that he, on the contrary, did "not see unionism nor other organizations of struggle" as "abominable" but rather as "basic rights . . . that working men have acquired through consciousness of their position." Organization, in his opinion, was the "most precious element of struggle they have."[150] As minister of labor, Gaitán the activist believed in identifying social problems and proposing plausible solutions. This he demonstrated when he spoke of the "the biological reality" of Colombia's popular classes before the Congress. He believed that struggle over working conditions and wages were not sufficient when infant mortality was 160 per 1,000, when Colombia had 3,500,000 cases of malaria, and intestinal parasites racked 95 percent of the population that lived at lower altitudes. He then upbraided many representatives for showing less interest in such social problems than in the "hatreds of yesterday."[151]

Throughout the Lopista interlude, therefore, Gaitán endured in the popular memory as a symbol of struggle, despite alternating periods of attack and deliberate disregard by the traditional political culture. Gaitán's devotees closely followed his career over the years. A union activist writing from Barranquilla, who had been a founding member of both the telephone workers' and "Germania" workers' organizations, commented on his support for the then minister of labor in his different public positions. When Gaitán was mayor, he claimed to have been the instigator of "two demonstrations in his homage" and also one of the last to quit the "Plaza de Bolívar, theater of events." He also approved of Gaitán's efforts as minister of education.[152] Writing from Santa Marta soon after Gaitán was dismissed as mayor of Bogotá, one admirer assured him that notwithstanding the obvious attempts "to negate . . . and obscure his admirable labors benefiting Bogotá and the working class," his enemies would "never be able to erase the memory of his work from the peoples' consciousness."[153] To some in the party, Gaitán represented the ultimate expression of true, anti-Conservative liberalism.[154] The former Unirista socialists of *Pluma Libre* reaffirmed their admiration for the caudillo four years after UNIR's dissolution.[155] Left Liberals in Cartagena wanted "the prestige" of his name at the head of their independent electoral list.[156] And among the working class in particular, his appeal showed no sign of waning. In 1938 workers deflected Liberal "arrows . . . launched against the prestige of a man . . . that with his voice and pen accused the assassins of the bananeras while others maintained a silence of complicity"; he was the "symbol of reform" and defender of the new liberalism.[157] Indeed, memory of his denunciation of the killings in Ciénaga received constant mention.[158]

After 1944 liberalism stood in disarray and Jorge Eliécer Gaitán inherited the legacy of popular aspirations associated with the spirit of left-Liberal reform. By then "the opinion of the working masses" was no longer "seduced" by the discredited politics of the Revolución en Marcha. "Genuine Liberals" who thought with their "own heads" believed instead in the "sincerity" of Gaitán's "revolutionary ideas."[159] López had opened the door to change but then refused to pass through the portal. Reforms on paper gave legitimacy to the struggle that began to take a new form between 1944 and 1946. Lopistas were becoming Gaitanistas, and controlled mobilization could no longer maintain the social peace. In the words of Gonzalo Sánchez, the Gaitanistas "picked up the banners which Lopismo had left in the middle of the road."[160] Gaitán and his movement were ready to change Colombia.

5

The *Pueblo*

Gender, Race, and Class in the Liberal Republic, 1930–1946

Gaitanismo cannot be understood apart from the social makeup and class nature of the Colombian pueblo that swelled the ranks in Gaitán's campaign for president between 1944 and 1946. Populist, multiclass political phenomena such as Gaitanismo often receive unfavorable comparisons to more homogeneous (i.e., working-class) movements. Yet the Gaitanistas' accomplishments in terms of political mobilization were quite impressive. In particular, they mobilized women, racial and ethnic groups, and classes traditionally on the fringe of political life. These different groups were tied together by Gaitanismo's message advocating amplified Lopista social and economic programs combined with a more popularly oriented political system. It resonated with popular demands for *justicia social, democracia,* and the completion of the Revolución en Marcha.

A theoretical model that automatically privileges the confrontation between capital and the working class obscures the power of Gaitanismo. This necessary bow to the movement's complex social composition should not, however, lead to the unwarranted extreme of denying its essentially "popular" class character. And though the movement was made up of different social strata, the urban working classes played a central role in Gaitanista mobilization, as did many landless rural workers. That Gaitanismo displayed serious overtones of class struggle was clear both to Gaitanistas who challenged Colombia's oligarchic democracy, and to the oligarquía itself.[1] Indeed, the existence of middle-class or "petty-bourgeois" elements within the multiclass mix of Gaitán's following did not negate its more radical qualities. It is certain that the different classes occasionally played divergent roles within the movement and exhibited tensions over direction and emphasis. Strains also arose from the conflict between Gaitán's ideas of social equilibrium and the class demands of many of his followers. Yet, in Colombia's rural society of the 1930s and

1940s, urban working-class and middle-class interests were more similar than dissimilar. The distinctions between these groups proved rather vague in practice and the barriers between them porous. Gaitanistas habitually spoke of the middle and working classes as similar or even the same. And groups without firm political rights, be they members of the "middle sectors" or women, have often been known to make alliances with workers as in populist movements.[2] Finally, these mutual connections, as well as their shared separation from the elite, were enhanced by the question of race since most Colombians, whether indio, mestizo, or negro, understood the connection between their skin color and their membership in the pueblo.

This chapter will show that Gaitán's dichotomous vision of struggle between the país político and the país nacional, between the oligarquía and the pueblo, reflected the class reality of Gaitanismo. Such a statement does not deny that his conceptualization belied the complicated inter-class alliances Gaitanismo involved. While the pueblo was made up principally of the "popular classes," generally identifiable as "subaltern," its composition was not exclusively determined by a shared relationship to the means of production. But Gaitanismo nevertheless found its inner drive in something approaching class, race, and gender conflict. For most Gaitanistas, the struggle between the pueblo and the oligarquía was that between the largely dark-skinned "productive masses" of common men and women in conflict with the "owners" of political and economic power. Though obvious cultural divisions existed within the pueblo, they did not impede political alliance. Rather, the pueblo was an ideological construct in which the working classes and middling classes, men and women, black, brown, and even white, saw themselves united by Colombia's political traditions and ideas of popular nationalism and popular mobilization.

Women and the Liberal Left

Though traditionally on the social and political margins, women in Colombia came to exercise an important role on the Liberal left in the 1940s.[3] While women still lacked the vote, the Gaitanistas actively sought their support as political participants. Yet in doing so, the Gaitanista leadership found that women were hardly passive agents waiting to be given political consideration. Many women demonstrated themselves to be militant, radical, and sophisticated activists who used Gaitanismo for their own purposes, especially as a vehicle to carry on their struggle for women's suffrage.[4] No less significantly, however, women who were far from being radical feminists would mobilize in support of Gaitanismo. Even more than Gaitanistas in general, women within the movement were a multiclass and heterogeneous lot. But while their economic and political interests were in no way monolithic, they united in the struggle for their most basic rights as citizens. This struggle found echoes in the broader Gaitanista mobilization in both the Gaitanista preoccupation with democracia and in terms of the social tensions present within the movement.

Magdala Velásquez Toro has argued that in Colombia, "oppression and discrimination against women" have historically transcended social class. This was still largely the case in the 1930s and 1940s, when women found their place in society not much changed from that of the nineteenth century. In 1930 a woman lost all economic rights upon marriage and could only practice a profession with the permission of her husband. The Catholic Church in Colombia continued to take an active interest in managing women's lives, to the point of dictating propriety in fashion. Education was severely limited for women, and of course, they still had no political rights.[5] But perhaps the most dramatic examples of the considerable disadvantages women suffered relative to men could be found in the workplace. Thirty-three percent of industrialized workers were women, yet they tended to be found in the more "traditional" roles in food preparation and in textile manufacture.[6] Significantly, the most common jobs for women workers in the coffee business were looked upon as extensions of feminine domestic roles. Women were more likely to fall into the less well paid category of *obrera* than that of *empleada*. This was true even in industries like tobacco and textiles where the huge majority of the workforce was composed of women. And no less significantly, those women who happened to share the "the same occupational category" with men could expect a notably inferior rate of pay.[7]

Despite the absence of economic, social, and political equality for women in Colombia, however, some observers argued in the 1930s that concern for "*el problema femenino*" appeared less intense than in other parts of Latin America. On the eve of his first presidency, Alfonso López Pumarejo attributed the lack of a perceptible awakening among Colombian women to "archaic vestiges of colonial culture." Women activists in Colombia echoed this belief while blaming Colombia's relative backwardness, compared to "the rest of the world," on Colombian women themselves. Women were supposedly "unconcerned with their own problems" and "unenthusiastic" about receiving the vote.[8] Later, Gaitanistas who wanted to bring women into the movement felt frustration at what they considered to be the traditional backwardness of women. One organizer in Cartagena lamented that the women's organization there had progressed little because "unfortunately, women in Cartagena feel little inclination toward political questions."[9]

There were, not surprisingly, men in both the Liberal and Conservative parties opposed to political rights for women. But even among women themselves there were doubters. One upper-class young woman writing her law thesis at the Catholic Javeriana University cautioned against immediate suffrage for women. While claiming that it was not her "aristocratic ideas" that led her to this position, it was her "sad conviction" that Colombia's "bajo pueblo" lacked the sufficient degree of "civilization and culture" to merit voting rights.[10] And not all breeds of left liberalism were in the forefront of struggle for women's rights either. In Santa Marta, generally progressive Liberals counseled that it would be more advantageous if "women were to remain in the sacred position" they already occupied, in "the sanctuary of the home, far from the dirty realm of politics."[11]

Such resistance to and disregard of "el problema femenino" notwithstanding, militant currents of feminism and advocates of women's rights existed in Colombia. In the 1920s, "although not calling themselves feminists," Betsabé Espinosa and María Cano "broke with the established roles for women, especially in the realm of organizing workers."[12] Lola Luna has argued that between 1930 and 1957 women leaders in Colombia were quite active in the press, before Congress, and in their struggle for the vote.[13] And during the 1940s, in the vanguard of feminist activism marched a group of women based in Tunja, Boyacá, led by Liberal intellectual Ofelia Uribe de Acosta. Between October 1944 and October 1946 they published *Agitación Femenina,* an "ideological and combative review." Prominent female and male intellectuals aired their views in its pages while working-class and middle-class women from every part of Colombia sent letters.[14] Their journal was different from others of its kind since they had no interest in "embroidery, fashion, cooking, or cinema." They were women "long on ideas and short of hair."[15] Their objectives were political and the chief among these was women's suffrage, though Uribe de Acosta did not consider hers a "war of the sexes."[16] Not surprisingly, they associated themselves with leftists, left Liberals, and Gaitanismo. In an exchange of letters in mid-1946, Ofelia Uribe and Gaitán made their mutual goodwill evident.[17]

The pages of *Agitación Femenina* railed against the complacency of elite liberalism. While nominally Liberal, the editorial tone was generally one of irony concerning the official Liberal establishment. They admired López's accomplishments but believed that liberalism should be more openly "a force of the left."[18] Their archrivals were the old boys at *El Tiempo, Sábado,* and *La Razón* in Bogotá. When Calibán, columnist at *El Tiempo,* called women's suffrage nothing less than the return of "barbarism," *Agitación Femenina* asked if it had been a misprint.[19] Such misogynist attitudes even found official expression. A minister of López's government called the vote for women a sign of "social rupture and the disorganization of the family." Women, he said, were neither Liberal nor Conservative, they understood no political creed, but were simply women.[20]

The vote was an issue that united disparate classes of women, yet *Agitación Femenina* placed itself on the radical left. As will be seen, such ambiguous relationships and cross-class alliances reflected the general situation of Gaitanista support. In its program of action published in *Agitación Femenina,* the Feminist Union of Colombia claimed to represent secretaries and clerks, women writers and journalists, women teachers, professors, professionals, nurses, and, of course, workers. They advocated equal work for equal pay, protection of children, and the incorporation of women into the life of the nation.[21] A selection of *Agitación Femenina*'s adherents, however, displayed a radical bent when voicing views on the vote. One argued that women did not aspire to "men's rights" but rather to "people's rights." Another asked how an illiterate man could really exercise superior judgment to a woman of the same condition. And another maintained that women outside their campaign were "poor of spirit" and let men do their thinking for them.[22]

Many left Liberals were eager to embrace women as political participants and chief among them was Gaitán, who had advocated women's suffrage as early as his UNIR days. A campaign film from 1945, itself an innovation in Colombian politics, made clear Gaitanismo's overtures to women as political actors. While the camera panned a crowd of thousands in which women were noticeable, the voiceover stressed that women were not simply on the margins of the movement.[23] One of Gaitán's chief lieutenants, José María Córdoba, claimed that the presence of women in the Gaitanista struggle displayed its spirit of justice and gave a more complete idea of national consciousness.[24] The pages of *Jornada,* the movement's newspaper, declared that women Gaitanistas were an eloquent and healthy demonstration of the awakening collective consciousness. "Women in Liberalism," reprinted in *El Estado,* argued that Colombian women had "a clear conception" of their "political mission and social responsibilities." The Colombian woman, with the "intuition innate to that sex," understood that the republic needed her cooperation. Women's participation in politics was seen not only as "convenient" but also necessary. Gaitanismo aspired to the "moral force of women" in its struggles for democracy.[25] It should be recognized that Gaitán and the Gaitanistas' interest in women was atypical even among radical populists in the period. Alan Knight noted that while populisms proclaimed the value of the common man, they rarely championed "the common woman."[26]

Women on the Atlantic coast in particular demonstrated their political sophistication and left-Liberal mística. In general the northern coast enjoyed greater contact with the wider world, which produced an atmosphere where progressive ideas were more available.[27] A woman in Barranquilla, for example, sent a telling letter to Agitación Femenina, saying she saw no basis for belief in the so-called "fragility of the weaker sex." The goal of women ought to be "the abolition of woman's slavery to laws created by the delirium of 'masculine supremacy.'"[28] That Gaitanismo was popular among costeñas, therefore, is not surprising. With pictures of Gaitán and one of his local captains on her "humble" wall, a self-described negra in Barranquilla, descended from Liberals who had spilled their blood for the Liberal cause, assured Gaitán that the oligarquía knew Gaitanismo would prevail.[29] Fifty-nine Liberal women in Montería affirmed that women had to be involved in the realization of the common ideals of liberalism.[30] Liberal working-class women of Barranquilla added their voices to those of the "suffering classes" to applaud Gaitán for his support of justice and morals and "the defense of human values."[31] A woman who represented the women of the banana zone encouraged women to join Gaitán, because without the inclusion of both men and women, democracy would be in danger. The time had arrived for women to enter the fray and conquer their rights long denied them by ignorance and the bad faith of politicians. Fortunately, she concluded, the Liberal pueblo, with its "knowing instinct," would respond.[32] "Feminist Civic Committees" were organized in Barranquilla, Cartagena, and Santa Marta, as well as cities and towns throughout Colombia, to work for the right of women "to elect and be elected."[33] "Gaitanista Feminist Committees" were organized all over the coast.[34]

Women participated in Gaitanismo in numbers unprecedented in Colombian political history. On the eve of the presidential election of 1946, an estimated crowd of forty thousand people turned out in Bogotá in support of Gaitanismo and women's issues, in which female factory workers, women professionals, and society women participated together.[35]

Women militants took an active role in organizing their own participation within the movement. In most Gaitanista municipalities, José María Córdoba argued, the faithful "spontaneously began to install Gaitanista committees of both sexes," with the women being just as active as the men.[36] Women of different races and classes embraced Gaitán's movement, as many had Lopismo and the Communist party, because it spoke to their political concerns.[37]

Questions of Race and National Identity

Though students of human physiology can now demonstrate the "nonexistence" of race as a genuine distinction between different varieties of Homo sapiens, ideas of race in Colombia remain (as Alan Knight has argued for the case of Mexico) "embedded deep in social relations."[38] Belief in the primacy of biological determination in human society continues to thrive throughout Latin America, in both negative and positive forms. The question of race and the process of *mestizaje* are concepts around which Colombian ideas of national identity have persistently revolved. There long have been, however, important differences in the ways that members of the elite and the pueblo, respectively, have dealt with race and identity. And even among the pueblo questions of race have evoked uneven responses. The predominantly white Bogotano elite of the 1940s continued to exclude people of color from consideration in discussions of nationhood, while members of the "popular classes" regarded "Indian blood" as an essential part of being Colombian. But the question was not the relatively straightforward one of whites on the one hand and mestizos and Indians on the other. Colombia also has a sizable population of Afro-Colombians, which greatly complicates the issues of race, national identity, and Colombia's unifying myth of the "mestizo society." Gaitán understood this ambiguity and exploited it.[39]

Mestizaje in Colombia, as in other parts of Latin America, refers especially to the mixing of European and Indian lineages. And in this regard Colombia has witnessed a high degree of race mixture. Jaime Jaramillo Uribe characterized mestizaje as the dynamic social factor "por excelencia" of the seventeenth and eighteenth centuries.[40] Because of northern South America's smaller population, depopulation from the conquest, mining, and disease was even more complete than in Mexico and Peru.[41] Mestizaje, however, originally held negative connotations that have survived well into the twentieth century. One Colombian social scientist declared in the 1950s that mestizos were a "race" of "contradictions," of "impulses," and of "doubts." It was a race that did not know its place and had not found its "destiny." "Mestizos" formed an unstable and "incomplete" people who found themselves in conflict with "superior cultures." The "mestizo race" was still in its "biological adolescence."[42] Various conceptualizations of mestizaje have been drawn along similar lines, with all the attendant racism.[43] Such ideas had deep historical roots in Colombia.

Negative judgments about race and race mixture, however, were slowly muted in the late eighteenth century as "Spanish separationist policy began to give way to a new integrationist current."[44] The process accelerated after independence as many Latin American nations refined their national identities. Perhaps the best example is Mexico of the 1920s, in which the revolutionary state adopted "indigenismo" as the official ideology. Yet indigenismo was wedded to mestizaje from the beginning since the goal of the *indigenistas* was to "mestizo-ize" the Indians.[45] Under the auspices of the revolutionary state, the mestizo was exalted as a member of José Vasconcelos's "raza cósmica."[46]

In contrast to the Mexican case, however, Colombian elites never openly embraced the idea of a mestizo nation as official ideology and did not attempt any co-optation of the idea of race as the post-revolutionary Mexican state did. To be sure, nineteenth-century elites in Colombia wanted to create a consolidated nation by incorporating its Indian populations into the greater body politic. Yet they had a very specific process in mind. By the 1850s and 1860s, Frank Safford has noted, elite Colombian writers and commentators were keen to integrate the "dominated, non-European peoples into a dominant European-modeled culture, economy, and polity," but largely for reasons of economic development. Elite concerns for the political integration of Colombia's Indian and Afro-Colombian pueblo "had receded to the background" since the 1820s. (This was, of course, in stark contrast to the political agenda of the left Liberals.) By midcentury, Colombian elites displayed "a pronounced tendency to treat Amerindians as stupid and to see lack of economic drive as a proof of that stupidity." Elite authors who dealt with race "invariably . . . depicted the Indian population as less intelligent than Europeans or mestizos." They also continued to believe, "as had some of their late colonial forebears, that racial amalgamation between Amerindians and whites would result in an improvement on the Amerindian original."[47] For Colombian elites in the nineteenth century, therefore, mestizaje meant "whitening" the Indian (and, eventually, the Afro-Colombian) population. They wanted race mixture, but with the goal of eliminating dark skin, its "ugliness," and the backward cultures and economic behaviors associated with it. This delusionary racist fantasy clearly survived into the twentieth century. In a travel pamphlet published in 1945, Colombia was depicted as of generally "European ancestry, chiefly Spanish" with only a "small number" of blacks, living mostly in the coastal lowlands.[48]

Elite misgivings about race aside, many Colombians too have sung the praises of their nation as a crossbred mestizo society, a "raza cósmica."[49] Jaramillo Uribe has even argued that miscegenation, which he says happened in Colombia in a "particularly rapid and complete" fashion, is that which gives Colombian society its cohesion.[50] As he demonstrated, modern writers have emphasized the high degree of race mixture in large part because of Colombian desires to portray the nation as a unified whole. (This exercise in turn is based on the questionable assumption that a racially mixed society is automatically a more harmonious society.) In the 1940s Luís López de Mesa credited miscegenation with saving the nation from "grave complications."[51] And a popular general history text from the 1980s argued that Colombia is a racial and cultural "hybrid" and stressed the themes of integration, coherence, and "acculturation."[52]

Yet Colombia's status as a "racially mixed nation" is rather problematic, given the spatial segregation of different racial groups. Each "regional type" is generally recognized to have different dominant racial elements. For example, the *antioqueño* is "tri-ethnic" or black and mulatto, mestizo, and white. The *caucano* is mulatto; the *tolimese* is mestizo; and the *costeño* is black and mulatto.[53] In a more recent work, Orlando Fals Borda has demonstrated that the racial composition of the coast is also really "tri-ethnic."[54] In Gaitán's day, Colombian racial distribution still reflected its historical development, in which "the Andean highlands held the majority of whites and indians, the Amazon plains and jungles were dominated by indians, and the coasts had a strong black element with not inconsiderable numbers of indians."[55] In fact, the population of Colombia has not historically moved toward anything like complete racial integration. In Antioquia James Parsons demonstrated continuing racial segregation in the mid-twentieth century in his work on Antioqueño colonization. Lynn T. Smith painted a similar picture for Colombia as a whole in 1950.[56]

But especially problematic for champions of the "mestizo nation" thesis is the question of where Afro-Colombians fit in. Areas in Colombia strongly identified with their African influences began to emerge in the eighteenth century when slavery made a weighty demographic contribution to Nueva Granada. Thus were formed certain "core" regions of black and mulatto population. As Jaramillo Uribe argued, "Popayán, Cali, el

Chocó, the North of Antioquia, and the Atlantic coast became the social centers of slavery in Colombia where *negro* elements left a deep impression on the society and the character and conduct of its inhabitants." As the colony revitalized mining in Cauca and Antioquia and started producing in earnest such commodities as honey and sugar, Cartagena became a major slave trading port. By the middle of the eighteenth century in some places, specifically Cali and Cartagena, "the slave and free black populations equalled or surpassed the numbers of other groups."[57] Despite their weighty numbers, however, people with African ancestry would not be readily accepted as "Colombian." Blacks have been seen as "people of the jungle" who exhibit a pronounced "sensual vigor." Their intellectual powers have not been seen as great in some circles, nor are they credited with creating any culture of significance.[58]

It follows that the idea of "Colombianidad" is tied to race in arbitrary, confusing, and deceptive ways. While Colombians have long seen their population as racially integrated, it is still the case that "skin color darkens, education decreases, sweat increases" as one passes from the elite down to the lower levels of Colombian society.[59] Poetic accolades for mestizaje notwithstanding, "darkness" continues to be a relative handicap within Colombian society for both blacks and mestizos, despite the persisting fiction of Colombians' general blindness to race. Peter Wade argued that the "idea of a 'racial democracy' in Colombia is still pervasive, and despite refutations of this myth from academic and popular circles alike, some people of all colors and classes can still be heard to avow the insignificance of race as an issue, especially as far as blacks are concerned."[60] Indeed, this tendency to deny the existence of racism and racial inequality has been encouraged by the fact that "raza" refers to both race and culture. As is the case in many parts of Latin America, people can change their racial status to a point. One student noted that for "the Indian the change means going from being non-Colombian to being Colombian; for the Negro it means going from the twilight zone of barely Colombian to complete Colombian."[61]

There is no question that Gaitanismo was a "dark" movement. The terms "pueblo," "plebeyo," "chusma" (rabble), and even "país nacional" all had strong race as well as class connotations. The caudillo himself was referred to maliciously as "el negro Gaitán" in elite circles. His dark complexion and facial features marked him unmistakably as a mestizo, and he could never forget that his heritage set him apart from the rest of the social, economic, and political gentry. Alone among Colombia's prominent political movers, Gaitán was denied membership in the patrician "Jockey Club," in no small part due to his appearance.

Yet what was a liability among "gente decente" was an asset among the Gaitanistas. Gaitanismo was, in essence, a movement of outsiders, and no one in Colombian society was more on the periphery than its darker-skinned citizens. In addition to the appeal of Gaitán's left-Liberal ideas, therefore, his experience as a racial outsider resonated with the pueblo. As early as 1932 an admirer told him that he was "a son of the pueblo" who would never turn his back on his "origins." Gaitán had been "born in the thriving heart of the *raza*."[62] As a consequence Gaitán subtly turned his "darkness" to his own political advantage. Herbert Braun has shown that during his presidential campaign, most of Gaitán's pictures "show a dark-complected Gaitán, his eyes half closed in the culturally recognized sign of suspicion and distrust held to be characteristic of *malicia indígena*. . . . After having been vilified for so many years as *el negro* Gaitán . . . [he] was now forcing his image on every Bogotano."[63]

And there was no real doubt about the connections between dark skin and the Liberal party. Ideological currents in liberal thought antagonistic to slavery assured that it was no accident that the heavily Afro-Colombian areas in the northern regions of the country and Valle de Cauca where slaveholding was predominant during the nineteenth century would later be left-Liberal strongholds. Indeed, "the mere fact that final emancipation had come under Liberal auspices helped the Liberal Party to capture and maintain the overwhelming allegiance of the nation's blacks."[64] In "mining regions, partisan loyalties coincided with race and class," and the same can be said of other regions with large populations of freed slaves. "The identification of Liberals with the poorer and darker people of Cauca and in the nearby city of Cali was proverbial in the 1840s and 1850s." Quoting Alfonso Romero Aguirre, Gary Long argued that in Cartagena "to be Liberal was almost the same as 'being black and plebeian.'" The same could be said of Diego Luis Córdoba's left-Liberal movement in Chocó on the Pacific coast, which was composed in great part of Afro-Colombians (and politically allied with the Gaitanistas).[65]

Nonetheless, Gaitanista mobilization never mustered overtly along color lines. Race was an omnipresent but largely silent issue. Gaitán observed the Colombian convention of disregarding race when he spoke of the pueblo, while Colombians of all races accepted the dogma of a "mixed nation." One Gaitanista believed that America did not have to worry about "the problem of the races that confronted Europe in the case of the

Nazis in Germany and the Fascists in Italy." Yes, it was true that in the past "los negros" had been treated like beasts by "mother Spain." But this predicament no longer existed in Colombia, he argued, "given the racial promiscuity" that "produced the mestizo."[66] And as Gaitán had significant followings among both highland "cachacos" and lowland "costeños," the geography of Colombian race distribution did not come into play in a forceful way. Finally, given Gaitanismo's emphasis on democracia, the question of race in connection to being Colombian was treated as "irrelevant" within Gaitanista discourse.

There was, however, one telling exception to the tacit agreement among Colombians to ignore racial questions, and it demonstrated the intimate relationship between the emotional ideas of race and nationhood. Gaitanistas clearly demonstrated a xenophobic and even racist nationalism directed against Gabriel Turbay, the official Liberal candidate in the 1946 presidential election. Turbay's family came from Lebanon and, as in other parts of Latin America, were called "turcos" because they carried passports of the Ottoman Turkish empire. This tendency was one of the principal reasons that some of Gaitán's opponents characterized him as a "fascist." Gonzalo Buenahora, a medical doctor and Liberal politician in Barrancabermeja, has argued that while Turbay was in many ways part of the radical, left-Liberal tradition, he was still at a disadvantage because of his "foreign blood" in the eyes of the Colombian pueblo, unaccustomed as they were to seeing "*turcos . . .* taking the reins of power."[67] Gabriel Turbay Avinader, many pointed out, was "really" Gabriel Caram Elmeraguar. He was one of those "foreigners" who "for reasons never well explained, changed their names when they arrived in the country."[68] But instead of demonstrating a "fascist" strain, the Gaitanistas' use of race allowed them to turn a liability into a nationalistic weapon against the official Liberals.

Given the relationship between the civil wars and political mobilizations of the nineteenth century and the rise of left liberalism, to be unable to establish a connection to these was, for many Liberals, unforgivable. That, as much as race, established Turbay's "non-Colombianess." In Cartagena a group of Gaitanistas lambasted the oligarquía for attempting to elect as president "a nationalized immigrant" who had "no roots in our country and whose ancestral blood was never spilled on our soil" in the civil wars of the nineteenth century.[69] *El Estado* of Santa Marta noted that popular sentiment rejected Turbay because, while he was Colombian by constitutional virtue, he was not by "heart," "blood," or "race."[70] A druggist in Bolívar claimed that Colombians would never be able to forgive the

Liberal leadership for offering to a "turco" what "by right belongs to a son of the womb of Colombia."[71] Some saw a "turco/oligarquía" conspiracy against the pueblo. One thousand "pure Colombians" in Cartagena condemned the "oligarquía" and the "turcos" for robbing the "poor working pueblo."[72] (In an interesting twist, Gary Long hinted that "turco" was as much a "class" as a "race" epitaph, associated in the popular mind with immigrant businessmen who began to violate the moral economy of work shared by Colombian artisans in the 1930s.)[73] In Magdalena Gaitanistas were warned that "dirty *turcos*" wanted to steal votes from Gaitán and sow discord among their ranks.[74] Gaitán and the leading Gaitanistas did little to discourage such feelings.

Gaitán, on the other hand, was called a "patriota," a "pure Colombian."[75] He pertained to "the Colombian *raza*," to which he belonged "without a hint of mixture."[76] One lifelong Liberal who could trace his activism back to Herrera pointed out that "the only thing the plutocracy can say about Gaitán is that he is 'indio'; this is true, and he does not deny it, as others deny their true nationality."[77] While speaking of the "treachery" of Gabriel Turbay, a Liberal and Gaitanista in Atlántico fumed that even the Conservatives had never allowed a "foreigner" to be president, "even if he had been born in Colombia."[78] Members of the middle class in Atlántico would rather abstain than "vote for a candidate not completely Colombian."[79]

The questions of race and nationalism, therefore, cut in many different ways, depending on whether one viewed them from the point of view of the elite or of the pueblo. Gaitán was denigrated as "*el negro* Gaitán," and had always been on the outside of Colombia's elite political inner circle because of it. Yet his followers stressed that his was the "blood" of Colombia, and his ancestors had "spilled" their blood for the patria. Gaitán was, consequently, a "pure" product of the Colombian "race." The idea of race was an ill-defined but nonetheless very powerful notion in the minds of the Gaitanistas. For them there was a "Colombian race," the differences between mestizos and blacks notwithstanding. Even though Afro-Colombians did not necessarily possess "Indian blood," they were still accepted as a part of the pueblo by virtue of their dark skin, their obvious non-elite status, and their undeniable contributions to the mobilizations on the Liberal left. These were the underlying components differentiating between elite and popular conceptualizations of what it was to be Colombian.

Gaitanismo was certainly a mass movement, perhaps the first of its kind in Colombia, ushering many new components into the political milieu. As a national movement, it was one of the first movements to transcend the traditional parties and the focus on Bogotá. Gaitanismo heeded the voice of the "popular classes," the masses, on an unprecedented scale. "Everyone" in Duitama was Gaitanista; Liberals and "many Conservatives were Gaitanista."[80] And the movement welcomed women, mestizos, blacks, and mulattos, until then largely ignored by the political establishment. But not only was Gaitanismo a mass movement; it was also a class movement.

A Multiclass Movement of Popular Character

Not unlike other Colombian political movements, Gaitanismo was a complex phenomenon that could count adherents among the professional politicians, the small-scale commercial class, intellectuals and the traditional professions, private and governmental white-collar employees (empleados), and even rural small holders and landless agrarian workers. It found some of its most significant and numerous support, however, among the organized and unorganized urban and industrial workers and artisans. This is not surprising, given the beginning of Gaitán's political career as the hero of the bananeras debate and his long history of judicial activism on the part of workers. Students have long recognized the multifarious nature of Gaitán's "populist" movement. A sympathetic observer in the 1950s identified its social composition as "the workers of the cities, the most radical sectors of the rural population, and the most progressive part of the petty bourgeoisie."[81] Yet while the diverse elements that composed the movement are generally recognized, characterizations of its class nature have ranged from radical leftist mobilization to fascist demobilization. These judgments have hinged upon the degree of participation attributed to the working class, and the nature of the middle class's contribution.

Herbert Braun made some general statements about the social composition of Gaitanista mobilization. He understood it as a "class movement," but one of a very restricted nature. He characterized Gaitán as "a petit bourgeois whose thinking was shaped by his own place in society." Gaitán spoke to "a small and insecure class of professionals, small property- and shopowners, and private and public employees."[82] In the light of the mass nature of Gaitanismo, however, Braun's narrow definition of the pueblo seems restrictive in the extreme. And there are, in addition, problems with the notion of "petit bourgeois." As Alan Knight has pointed out, the promiscuous usage of the 'petty bourgeois' category is fraught with analytical dangers and confusions. For, even if the class (sic?) can be identified in terms either of its relationship to the means of production or of its espousal of a distinctive liberal or 'Jacobin' ideology, the fact remains that it was grotesquely fractured along social, cultural and geographical lines.

Knight argued that the *ranchero,* a rural "petty bourgeois," was a "Jekyll and Hyde character" regarding his political behavior, and the same can be said of the more urban varieties.[83]

A central issue in this conundrum, therefore, involves the character and behavior of the "middle class" within Gaitán's pueblo. This question of the nature of the middle sectors is generally a thorny one for historians who study such movements, since many openly yearn for the comforting dualism of the struggle between the proletariat and the bourgeoisie. It is difficult, however, to reconcile such dualism with the Colombian experience of the mid-twentieth century, given the tenacious survival instincts of the "secondary classes."[84] Any model requiring a "pure" working-class movement is almost impossible to apply to actual historical situations, yet some historians of Gaitanismo disqualify it as a "working-class" movement because it encompassed other class elements. There has also been a tendency to interpret middle-class participation as particularly unwholesome. Daniel Pécaut argued that the movement was not a workers' movement because it was as much of the small businessmen and artisans, of Liberal public employees, and intellectual elements of liberalism as it was of the lower pueblo. Indeed, one of Pécaut's principle themes was that multiclass Gaitanismo suffered from a grievous lack of "class synthesis," which restricted Gaitanismo's more radical tendencies. In a similar vein, Mauricio Archila recognized Gaitanismo's multiclass influence among workers but went on to argue that the movement acted as a "debilitating" influence on working-class organization because it weakened its "class identity." And finally, Charles Bergquist has argued that Gaitán "embodied in his program and in his person, in his demagogic political style, and in his passionate and often violent oratory the social and ideological schizophrenia of the middle class." Bergquist acknowledged that, unfortunately, within "the great undifferentiated mass of people in the *país nacional*" Gaitán's "message also appealed to a largely unorganized working class deprived of an autonomous vision of its place in society."[85]

The pedigree of this interpretation is not difficult to trace. Looking to Marx and to Lenin, social theorists have often viewed the working class as less corrupt and innately more radical than social strata of a middling nature.[86] In fact, the working class and the middle class are generally viewed as opposed to one another. There are, of course, good historical grounds for stressing the cultural and political divisions (at certain times and in certain places) between the working and middle classes, stretching from the counter-revolutions of France, Germany, and Austria in 1848, to Pinochet's coup in Chile in 1973, and to Thatcherite skilled workers in Britain and Reagan Democrats in the United States during the 1980s.[87]

The difficulty arises when this frequent manifestation of class struggle is elevated to the level of historical "law." Thus Lenin characterized "labor aristocrats," among whose ranks were many artisans, in terms of "opportunism." They used their position as a "middle stratum" to benefit at the expense of other workers. Labor aristocrats, the most skilled and highest-paid workers, enjoyed higher rates of savings and some degree of "respectability." They also had social and cultural pretensions relative to other laborers.[88] From their favorable location, Lenin argued, these "petty-bourgeois" artisans infected the proletariat proper with their corrupting tendencies.[89] And Marco Palacios argued that in the case of Colombia, artisans occupied a space "between the pueblo and the 'gente bien.'" He admitted that the categories *artesano, comerciante,* or *agricultor* were "ambiguous," though he stressed that from these groups emerged the small industrial and commercial sectors. He identified a strong split (in both social and political terms) between workers in the "proletariat," on the one hand, and "artisans," whom he lumped in with the "small merchants."[90] Yet as Eric Hobsbawm contended, no class or segment of a class is automatically more radical than another. Artisans, for example, "could be politically or socially radicalized when their position was threatened or undermined."[91] Labor elites are often the "nursery of the left," and "labour activists" often come "disproportionately" from the ranks of the labor aristocrats.[92] Such radicalism was also apparent in other groups in the Colombian middle sectors in the 1940s.

The traditional Marxian economic definition of class, so comforting to historians, must therefore be tempered by considerable allowances for the complexity of Colombian social, cultural, and racial reality. The pueblo proved extremely interconnected in practice. Gaitán recognized this reality and employed the rather more elastic and inclusive dualism of país político and the país nacional, contrasting the oligarquía with the pueblo. Both of his related dichotomies placed the primordial divide between "the popular sectors" and "the elite," and not within the pueblo itself, and there were good (very historically grounded) political, social, and racial reasons for doing so. This division would be paralleled by E. P. Thompson with his "field of force" idea. Thompson described a magnetized plate on which iron filings grouped themselves at one pole of attraction or the other, with other filings in between that seem to point one way or the other. This was how he understood eighteenth-century society, "with, for many purposes, the crowd at one pole, the aristocracy and gentry at the other, and . . . the professional and merchant groups bound by lines of magnetic dependency to the rulers, or on occasion hiding their faces in common action with the crowd."[93]

The fact that Gaitanismo attracted both property owners and those dependent upon the wage is one of the reasons that interpretations of it have varied so much. This has long been a central problem in the interpretation of populism. Yet the convergence of these groups' interests has not gone unnoticed. Ernesto Laclau linked the pueblo to "a specific contradiction"—the people/power bloc confrontation, "whose intelligibility depends not on the relations of production but on the complex of political and ideological relations of domination." Laclau emphasized "the relative continuity of popular traditions" and identified many examples of struggle of the people against oppression. From this tradition "class struggle" takes its spirit.[94] And Daniel James noted that the "formal rhetoric of Peronism was not one which saw society in primarily class terms. . . . The critical division in society [was] between 'the people' and 'the oligarchy.'" This situation, critics have argued, represented "a non-class potential appropriate to a movement led by dissident elite sectors which functioned primarily as a channel for integrating the emerging urban masses within an expanded polity without fundamentally altering the class relations of such a society." Yet James pointed out that "such notions coexisted and were interrelated with elements which made the consolidation of capitalist ideological hegemony extremely problematic."[95]

This dualism goes to the heart of populism and gives force to the notion that strict Marxist interpretations place the break in the wrong place. Alan Knight recognized that as a concept, populism refuses to disappear, and suggested that populism be defined as a political "style" that embodies a close connection to "the people" and employs a "them versus us" understanding of politics. He stressed the all-important dichotomy populism invariably involves: the people versus an other, usually an elite (social, political, economic), though it can be foreigners, traitors, and so on. By recognizing this duality always found in populism, Knight also argued that the fact that populist movements were multiclass (as have been most successful parties in most places) did not negate their ability to create political polarization with strong class implications.[96] In U.S. history as well, the political dynamic has often been that between the "powerful" and the "powerless," between the small farmer, the working man, and the "middle-class taxpayer," on the one hand, and the "bureaucrats," the "fat cats," and the "Big Men" on the other. Michael Kazin stressed the language of populism as its most basic defining element, "a language whose speakers conceive of ordinary people as a noble assemblage not bounded narrowly by class, view their elite opponents as self-serving and undemocratic, and seek to mobilize the former against the latter." The idealism (and even radicalism?) inherent in this language of populism quite naturally produced "battles between us and them" over "the meaning of Americanism itself." Populists "voiced a profound outrage with elites who ignored, corrupted, and/or betrayed the core ideal of American democracy: rule by the common people." This "stark dualism" in the U.S. political tradition was of considerable age, as outlined by late-nineteenth-century populists who drew the distinction between Hamiltonians who advocated centralized government for the moneyed interests, and the Jeffersonians who opposed them in the name of the people.[97]

Shop owners, urban artisans, and rural small holders in Colombia obviously had some access to the means of production. But these members of the "middle class," and/or their immediate family, may also have had one foot in the world of wage labor. The middle sectors, including white-collar empleados, certainly were "closer" to their working-class neighbors than they were to verifiable members of the economic or political elite in real economic terms. The experience of Gaitán's own father is a case in point. Richard Sharpless argued that he "was that most anxious of men, the petit bourgeois who above all wants to appear prosperous and respectable, but who only succeeds in staying a few pesos away from actual poverty." Herbert Braun noted that neither parent "produced goods that others needed and that might give them a niche in society. . . . Closer to falling into the proletariat than rising into the bourgeoisie, they strove desperately to keep up the outward appearance of respectability."[98]

And there was nothing new about this situation. David Bushnell demonstrated that foreign visitors in nineteenth-century Colombia observed "that the middle sectors (clerks, small tradesmen, and independent artisans) and the well-to-do did not really live much better than members of the working class."[99] Francisco Gutiérrez Sanín was even more explicit in his discussion of the "movimiento plebeyo" in the early 1850s. He recognized the muddled nature of the social classes involved in the pueblo and opted for a more inclusive and "flexible" approach. "Social struggle" was not carried out around clearly defined class interests, yet he located the crucial social divide between "los de abajo" and "los de arriba." He noted that "conventional categories" of social analysis are, in practice, "incredibly varied and complex" and, by implication, perhaps artificial. Gutiérrez Sanín rejected the "temptation" to lump artisans "into a middle class, in the middle of the road" between elite and pueblo. Artisans lived "immersed" in the plebian culture with all its duality.[100] The same can be said of other middling groups in the 1940s.

Finally, as Herbert Braun acknowledged, Gaitán himself blurred the distinction between working class and middle class: "His contemporaries were uncertain whether he had a middle-class or a working-class background. But there was little question in their minds that he was a man of the pueblo."[101] Indeed, a supporter in Pasto pointed out the obvious: Gaitán "came from the pueblo, and for that reason the pueblo acclaimed him."[102] The key point is that these middle sectors in Colombia shared many attitudes and behaviors with workers, and this translated into political alliance.

Gaitán, therefore, did not invent his inclusive idea of the pueblo out of thin air, nor did he arbitrarily stress the dualistic confrontation with the oligarquía (to disorient workers and anger Marxist historians); rather, he was expressing a widely recognized historical social reality. In 1931 a "democratic Junta" in Buenaventura called him a "radical socialist" and "exponent of the most authentic democracy" whose ideas and activism sustained the "middle, *obrera,* and *campesina* classes." That same month a middle-class wage earner in Cundinamarca thanked Gaitán for his defense of the "rights of the pueblo" and "the interests of the middle class, the most undervalued and forgotten class by the legislators." And in 1936 the editors of the *Diario Nacional,* that bastion of left liberalism, weighed in with a thoughtful editorial on the structural similarities of and need for strategic unification between the middle class and working class. They were reacting to a piece in *El Tiempo* by Calibán, who argued that "the middle class has its own distinct interests from those of the capitalists and the proletarians, and on occasion, they are opposite to those of the other classes." This statement, they insisted, placed the empleados and the obreros in open conflict and created an antagonism that "does not exist and cannot exist except in the superficial vision" of those who did not see, or refused to recognize, their similar essences. They quoted Engels, noting that if they had distinct social conditions and experiences, "they suffer the same exploitation and are twin victims of a system that denies them guarantees and support." The common game of the industrialists of raising prices when they raise wages worsens the condition of the middle class and should not be a source of antagonism between empleados and obreros. If the middle class opposes pay raises for workers, it is only advancing the interests of the capitalist class at its own expense. Tension between the middle and working classes is produced by the interests of capitalists. "*Empleados* and *obreros* should form a single force, a common front against the common enemy, capitalism. The *obrero* and the *empleado* are instruments of capital, each one in their place: the first as a producer; the second as an intermediary in the process of exchange and consumption." Their answer was "scientific unionism," which would organize the "exploited classes."[103]

In fact, Gaitán's supporters had the recurring habit of speaking of the working class and middle class in the same breath, as two peas in the same social and political pod. (And as discussed in the previous section, race was very much a factor.) During the 1930s, the editors of a workers' paper in Barrancabermeja, later a Gaitanista stronghold, called daily for enforcement of social laws for obreros and empleados.[104] One of the leaders of the ill-fated banana workers' strike of 1928 called Gaitán the man that "the middle class and workers in general" unquestionably needed.[105] Another supporter in Magdalena insisted that Gaitán soon visit the banana zone to confer with the "*obreros* and *empleados.*"[106] The owner-operator of a radio station in Barranquilla assured Gaitán that his campaign had "deep support" among the great mass of "workers and free employees."[107] A labor organization in Cartagena recommended that the "working masses" give Gaitán their support to further the interests of "*empleados,* the middle class in general, and that great mass of the population . . . workers and peasants."[108] A committee representing "retired *empleados* and *obreros*" in Tolima assured Gaitán that both groups were "friends" of the political ideals he represented, and called him the "spokesman of the *clases trabajadoras.*"[109] And union leader Juan Manuel Valdelamar was convinced in 1944 that "the masses, both unionized and unorganized, plus large portions of the middle class" would support Gaitán's run for the presidency.[110]

The Gaitanistas were thus well aware of the social amalgam their movement represented. Asdrubal Amarís, an important Gaitanista from Santa Marta, identified two groups: the small number of individuals and groups privileged with public power (the oligarquía) and the exploited majority without political rights (that is, the pueblo). Among the latter group Amarís spoke of *campesinos,* abandoned to their own meager resources; obreros, deceived and subjected to all manner of humiliations;

empleados, hounded by the deprivation of their situations and unable to act as free men; *pequeños comerciantes,* or small business owners, strangled by influential speculators; intellectuals and professionals, persecuted by the powerful if they failed to cooperate. They were all part of the pueblo, enduring "an anguished moment of their history."[111] According to one group of supporters, the triumph of Gaitanismo would be the triumph of the engineer, the small farmer, the doctor, the small businessman, the mechanic, the teacher, and of the worker over the *politiquero* (a pejorative term for political insider) and the oligarquía.[112] Too, Gaitán understood the diverse makeup of his following, as was reflected in how he tailored his style of speech according to his audience. In his visits to Cartagena and Barranquilla he would alternately harangue and gesticulate in the "popular neighborhoods" and give "scientific conferences" at the universities.[113]

As in other places at other times, the identity of the "middle class" in Colombia was anything but cut and dried. Professionals, especially, have always been a wildcard in the capital/worker dynamic. Many Gaitanistas most certainly recognized the social divide between the middle and working classes. Gaitán himself proudly pointed out that the "ruling classes" of Bogotá were obliged to recognize that Gaitanismo was not composed simply of "people 'without class,'" or "rabble." They saw with their own eyes that the movement also encompassed people of intelligence in commerce, manufacturing, and universities.[114] And as was apparent in the press, the self-consciously middle class often felt a paternal impatience with their "popular" comrades. This tension frequently manifested itself within the movement. The middle-class editors of the left-Liberal *La Tribuna,* for example, believed that Gaitán, then minister of labor, would address working-class issues and "put a stop to the problems" certain union leaders constantly created for the government. Minister Gaitán, then touring the coast, would attempt to establish "the relationship of harmony that should exist between worker and employer."[115]

Yet it is clear that in the case of Gaitanismo, a not insignificant portion of the middle class threw in its lot with the popular mobilization and the working class because it lived on the social and economic edge. A supporter in Barranquilla who had worked for a "respectable *casa de comercio*" for many years claimed membership in "the middle class . . . that is, the most anguished class" and asserted that all the "empleados" were Gaitanistas.[116] In fact, members of the working and middle classes often shared similar insecurities. A multiclass group in Cali wrote to Alfonso López, Gabriel Turbay, Darío Echandía, Gaitán, and even Enrique Santos (Calibán) arguing for renters' rights against property owners and calling for economic morality. Lack of rent controls gravely affected the interests of "public and private *empleados, proletarios, pequeños industriales comerciantes*," who were all "defenseless victims of property owners." They were all for prices controlled by supply and demand, free trade, and competition, yet in rents there was "no competition," especially in cities where there were not enough places to live. They demanded rent control.[117]

So despite unmistakable yearnings for social advancement and cultural feelings of superiority, in the 1940s "middle-class" involvement within Gaitanismo, shoulder to shoulder with workers dependent upon the wage, is strong evidence that many in the middle understood their kinship as part of the pueblo. Indeed, the case of white-collar workers (empleados) was instructive. They often had access to education and other cultural benefits their blue-collar colleagues (obreros) lacked, and management never ceased trying to take advantage of these differences (as the *Diario Nacional* noted).[118] Yet empleados were very likely to see their interests as aligning with those of the obreros. What must be stressed is that in the minds of many Gaitanistas, the identities of "middle class" and "working class" were not clearly differentiated. Gonzalo Sánchez has also recognized this phenomenon and lumped these groups together. He argued that Gaitán directed his efforts to "the middle sectors—to shopkeepers, artisans, and industrial and service workers—to that whole stratum that the Bogotá aristocracy called 'the lower depths of society.'" Sánchez stressed the cohesiveness of the "popular classes" as a "new historical force."[119]

It should also be recognized that, in Colombia, members of the "middle class" commonly acted like "workers." Middle-class radical activism and political mobilization were not new on the Colombian political landscape, nor was middle-class appropriation of collectivist strategies. In 1936 the "Committee of Middle-Class Action" of Bogotá published its platform in the Cartagena workers' paper, *El Sindicalista*. The committee's intent was to form an organization of empleados, small business and shop owners, and rural small holders to "fight for the economic, social, and intellectual interests of that class." They believed it "indispensable" to the success of their campaign for the middle class to organize unions and federations, which in turn would act with "cordial sympathy" toward all worker and peasant organizations.[120] Significantly, Eric Hobsbawm noted that while labor elites in England did aspire to upward social mobility and ascribe to the idea of self-help, they always did so in the context of organization. While individuals in the middle class "improved" themselves one by one as it were, the labor aristocrats had no choice but to do so in a group.[121] In

Colombia, this was true of many members of the middle sectors as well. In Cali in 1934, the "Federation of *Empleados* of Valle" thanked Gaitán and other congressional representatives for defending the "middle class" and spoke of the thousands who were "humbled by their precarious condition" and lacked adequate legal protection.[122] In 1935 organized municipal empleados in Bogotá were worried about "the future necessities intrinsic to their class," yet sounded like workers in calling on city councilman Gaitán to see to the building of schools and homes.[123] (Empleados also followed labor legislation with keen interest.)[124] In March 1944 the National Federation of Empleados in Bogotá wanted Gaitán, the just-resigned minister of labor, as president "because the *empleados* consider him the defender of their interests."[125] And in Manizales the next month, a tenants' society of small businesses and artisans saluted him and wished him well in his "grand social campaign."[126]

Given societal concerns for "social harmony" and "social equilibrium," Gaitanismo did address the worries of Braun's "petit bourgeoisie." Yet the movement embodied different agendas and more radical tendencies, including a role for class conflict. Social accommodation and compromise coexisted with social confrontation. And there were radical strains of Braun's "small and insecure class." One veteran of the War of a Thousand Days and owner of a small neighborhood grocery, "La Democracia," claimed to have accompanied Uribe Uribe on all his campaigns, and saw in Gaitanismo the salvation of the fatherland.[127] Where the movement was weak, Gaitán could count on socially middle-class individuals to spread the faith, as did a captain and pilot on the Magdalena river.[128] The "middle class" in Atlántico considered their "only possible salvation in rallying to the candidate of the majority."[129] And of particular interest was a lawyer, a historically minded, left-Liberal, and self-proclaimed "proletarian of the pen" from Medellín who was dedicated to battling for working-class interests. He was one of the organizers of Unirismo in Antioquia, following Gaitán's "trajectory from the *zona bananera* to the *alcaldía* of Bogotá to the Ministry of Education." "Politics," he argued, "is the art of bringing together and as Gen. Uribe Uribe wrote, it is the process of attracting and not repelling." Yet he was concerned that "this grand movement" would be "bastardized from the moment of its genesis, especially since there exist the two diametrically opposed currents, the *país político* and the *país nacional*."[130]

Finally, the class nature of Gaitanismo also reflected the common understanding that the pueblo represented the "poor" and "humble." Mauricio Archila showed that from at least the late nineteenth century, "obrero" was associated with "pobre," in both the material and spiritual senses (though the latter was more of an elite image). The elite enjoyed a marked social distance from the working classes, but this varied from region to region (Medellín less, and Barranquilla very little, compared to Cartagena or Bogotá). Archila argued that among artisans and other workers, "pobre" was more a part of the image of the pueblo, and pueblo meant working class.[131] And the pueblo "loved" Gaitán, according to one follower, because the light of his torch would "help and comfort the destitute and the weak . . . the workers and the poor and humiliated [*humillada*] class."[132] Among the Gaitanistas however, not only the working class but also "middle-class" members of the pueblo referred to themselves as pobre. Another letter writer agreed with Gaitán's ideas because they were informed by the Liberal mística, the only doctrine on the side of the "humble classes." He, a "humble telegraph operator," had the impression that the Colombian pueblo, or "middle class," saw in Gaitán its only salvation.[133] Liberals in Anapoima, Cundinamarca, proclaimed for Gaitán's candidacy because he had been a "great organizer and leader of the pueblo" and a "defender of the *clases desvalidas*" who understood their "social problems."[134] In Villa de Leiva, Boyacá, a supporter called the pueblo "the unfortunate ones"; "we are *los de abajo*," he claimed, "and those of the *clase media*."[135] In Ipiales, Nariño, another adherent remembered that Gaitán, a leader of democracy since his youth, continued to work in "defense of the abandoned masses of Colombia."[136]

Gaitanismo, therefore, was a "popular" class movement that defied a crisp social characterization. Gaitanistas disregarded the peace of mind of future students of the movement by using terms like obrero, empleado, "workers" (trabajadores), "working class" (clase trabajadora), "middle class," "poor," and pueblo as easily interchangeable synonyms. But this situation arose in part from the important role played by workers within Gaitanismo.

Gaitanismo and the Working Class

The Colombian working class proper has traditionally been described as "weak." The leading proponent of the "weakness" thesis is Daniel Pécaut, who has provided some of the most insightful work on Colombian workers with his *Política y sindicalismo en Colombia* and *Orden y violencia*. Charles Bergquist furthered the idea of the relative weakness of organized labor in Colombia in *Labor in Latin America*. Mauricio Archila questioned the general contention somewhat in his *Cultura e identidad obrera*, but fell back on it in explaining working-class attachment to López and Gaitán. Contrasted to their more robust cousins in Argentina, Brazil, and Mexico, not to mention the industrialized nations of the north, Colombian workers of the 1940s played a comparatively modest role in their society. The economy was still largely agrarian and tied to coffee. The working class, defined as the mass of urban and industrial workers, some dependent upon a wage and some artisan, still comprised a small portion of the overall population, and organized labor a very much smaller part. Yet the working class's central role in the Gaitanista mobilization assured it a significant degree of active influence.

Some students largely deny the connections between Gaitanismo and the working class. Herbert Braun argued that the working class was "not at the forefront of Gaitán's struggle." He conjectured that perhaps it was "too closely tied to López's reforms of ten years before."[137] But as was argued in the previous chapter, Gaitán had inherited the López mística as champion of the working class. Most of Braun's conclusions on the social base and class nature of Gaitanismo rested on his interviews with inner-circle Gaitanistas, from which the rank and file are conspicuously absent.[138] If he had consulted sources that were closer to the popular base of the movement, he might have drawn different conclusions.[139] Be that as it may, for many hardcore militants, the essence of Gaitanista liberalism was to be understood as "the working people" (the pueblo trabajador).[140] The "*vértebra dorsal* of the economic system of the fatherland" was the "*trabajador,* the proletarian in the shop and the forge, the rustic *jornalero,* the *campesino* . . . the exploited *colono.*"[141] Observers of this persuasion equated the pueblo with workers.[142] For many, the oligarquía or país político of Gaitán's dichotomy represented all the corrupt, privileged castes and the pueblo or país nacional represented the "honorable workers."[143]

And there are also problems with the worker "weakness" thesis's implication that Colombian workers were not a significant source of pressure on the status quo. Charles Bergquist was on solid ground in stressing the crucial importance of individualistic small holders to Colombian history. However, his lumping of these "coffee workers" as a less than radical part of the working class, without drawing the distinction between independent small holders and rural proletarians, is somewhat problematic. Coffee workers on the large estates of western Cundinamarca and eastern Tolima without access to their own land, and landless workers in the departments of the Atlantic coastal region and the Valle de Cauca, did not follow Bergquist's pattern of Hobbesian individualism. As touched on

earlier, these areas were Gaitanista, left-Liberal, and Communist strongholds. Rural workers, who not uncommonly thought of themselves as
"proletarians," habitually wrote to give support to Gaitán.[144] In fact, this
interpretive trend is shifting. In a study based on extensive archival work,
Gary Long focused on radical artisans (whom he showed were also solidly
Gaitanista) and directly attacked the weakness thesis by stressing their
central importance to Colombian history in the 1940s. Though artisans
were slowly being pushed out of existence, their radical traditions of mobilization had carried over from the nineteenth and early twentieth centuries to great effect and were, if anything, heightened as their situation
became more precarious.[145]

Gaitán understood the working classes' importance and was noticeably
attentive to working-class issues. He was, after all (as pointed out before),
the most celebrated labor lawyer of his age. It was not uncommon for him
to be "unanimously" named a union's legal representative in conflicts
with their employers.[146] Letters from unions thanking Gaitán for his services are ubiquitous in the Gaitanista correspondence.[147] In 1944, on the
eve of his campaign, a union (after thanking him for his labors on their
behalf) declared that "once more" he had "demonstrated the sincerity"
that guided him "in the defense of the *clases desvalidas*." This "gesture of
social sensibility" placed him "at the forefront of the political leaders of
Colombia."[148] Left Liberals in Tumaco proclaimed for his candidacy precisely because he worked for the benefit of workers and to establish "moral
administration" and a "democratic government that is faithful to the
popular will."[149] In Tolima the pro-Gaitán regional Liberal establishment
proclaimed Gaitán their candidate because his "intelligence" had always
been "at the service of the *clases trabajadoras*" and of democracy.[150] There
his "humble compatriots" supported him as the "paladin of the rights of
the *pueblo humilde* and *trabajador*."[151] Even the Communist dominated
CTC occasionally recognized Gaitán's credentials and asked him to defend
one of their own.[152]

In fact, the politician, the candidate for office, and the labor lawyer had
long been one. In 1939 a labor organization in Bogotá that toiled "in
defense of the *trabajadores*" urged its adherents to vote for Gaitán as
concejal in Bogotá because his list "embodied the aspirations of the *pueblo
trabajador,* as always."[153] And in 1944 a union in Girardot gave him their
support for his electoral campaign since he was the "maximum captain of
Colombian democracy whose government would be a guarantee for the
working classes." (And since he was going to be in town, they wanted his
help with "exaggerated" municipal taxes.) They called on him since he

had "always been the foremost spokesman of the *clases trabajadoras* and *desvalidas* . . . and could undoubtedly understand the injustice" of which they had been victims.[154] Finally, it was no surprise that the *Federación de Choferes* saluted Gaitán for his labors for workers in general and for defending them in particular, while transport workers in Bogotá called Gaitán a "true fighter for democracy" and supported the "Moral Restoration."[155]

All this working-class support, therefore, was not the product of chance. Gaitán devoted a large part of his time to working-class issues. He purposely held his *viernes culturales* or Friday radio chats at an hour when workers could listen. And at the beginning of January 1944, as the newly appointed minister of labor, Gaitán made his "famous tour" up and down the banks of the Magdalena that took a month to complete. His purpose was to gain firsthand information on the "conditions of life and work of Colombian workers and to discuss a general labor code with union leaders." This tour put him in contact with river workers, railroad workers, tobacco workers, and oil workers, among others.[156] Yet even before his appointment to the Labor Ministry, Gaitán's high-profile activity concerning working-class issues was not lost on the pueblo.

There is absolutely no doubting the great appreciation a good part of the organized working class showed for Gaitán's defense of their interests, nor its long duration. In the "radical" 1930s Gaitán's activity was already enshrining his name in the hearts of workers. An imaginative dialogue with Gaitán in 1933 called workers the "stones . . . which support the full crushing weight of the social edifice" in Gaitán's view of the world. "For Gaitán the kneeling *jornalero*" rose higher "than a *hacendado* standing on his feet."[157] An organization of left-Liberal workers in Cali, not uncommonly, named itself after him in 1932.[158] "Various wives of workers" in Bogotá sent a commission of "niñas" to present him with flowers for being "one of the principal *voceros* of the *clases trabajadoras*."[159] Railroad workers in Cali expressed their support for his actions as well as his ideas. Worker neighborhoods in Bogotá gave him their "más efusivo saludo" because he was the "constant defender of the *masas trabajadoras*." Tram workers in Medellín thanked him for "disinterested work that he had "day and night" lent to their cause. Postal workers in Medellín, Cali, and Popayán respectively named him honorary union president, hoped for the "triumph of his ideals," and thanked him for his "valiant labor." And a labor federation in Nariño representing drivers, carpenters, construction workers, shoe makers and shoe repairmen, and textile workers called him the "maximum paladin of Colombian democracy" because of his labor as their representative in the Senate for proletarian interests, and made him an "honored guest."[160]

Worker gratitude and enthusiasm for Gaitán's political activity on the local level—as well as his legal representation of workers—increased, if anything, during the supposedly co-opted 1940s. Gaitán had been, workers were well aware, a Bogotá city councilman almost continuously since the 1930s, and simultaneously headed electoral lists from many different parts of the city. "Worker neighborhoods," such as the Guavio sector, sent their *saludo* to Gaitán and thanked him for heading their list for concejo. His "great efforts for the progress of the city, and especially the workers' neighborhoods," they assured him, did not go unnoticed by the pueblo of Bogotá. The worker neighborhood "La Providencia" proclaimed him their candidate for the concejo because of his "great sacrifices . . . for the benefit of the workers' neighborhoods of the capital." "Popular" neighborhoods in the south recognized his "dynamism" in bringing about "substantive reforms and fundamental public works." And the neighborhood "Lourdes" recognized that as a member of the concejo Gaitán had demonstrated himself to be "the defender of the workers' neighborhoods" and that, when he was mayor, he worked "untiringly for the benefit of the *clases trabajadoras.*" The workers' neighborhoods, therefore, owed Gaitán their support.[161]

On the national level, workers followed his different appointments in the cabinet with great interest.[162] And as an elected representative, his campaign in the Senate against the Labor Ministry's attempts to restrict the right to strike in 1943 was particularly well received. Workers in Manizales commended his "brilliant" defense of the workers' most basic right against the bad faith of the "genuine representative of the reactionary classes . . . Londoño Palacio," the then minister of labor. His defense of the right to strike was echoed by domestic workers in Pereira and newspaper hawkers in Barranquilla.[163] In fact, workers throughout Colombia took note. Workers in Bogotá commended his work in the Senate "in defense of the interests of Colombian workers." In Palmira, he was also saluted for his "brilliant" defense of workers. In Cartago workers offered thanks for his steadfast resistance against the "monstrous project" to "do away with the right to strike . . . the only weapon of defense" possessed by workers.[164]

And as a political movement, Gaitanismo overtly targeted workers in its organizational drives. Samuel Guerrero, an empleado, labor leader, and Gaitanista, habitually distributed campaign literature among Cartagena's unions and put up fliers in "strategic spots throughout the city, where workers pass."[165] Adriano Rangel, a left-Liberal politician and Gaitanista, routinely visited workers' neighborhoods and union halls in Barranquilla distributing *Jornada,* the movement's paper, and left petitions in barbershops for the customers to sign, since people congregated there throughout the day and night to talk politics.[166] The official organization cultivated working-class interest and involvement in the movement, and encouraged the view of Gaitán as the "only evident hope of the working class."[167] José María Córdoba claimed that the country had "greatly suffered due to the idea that government must be composed solely of 'intellectuals.'" Gaitanismo included "honorable working people" and not just the intellectual oligarquía.[168]

Perhaps the best evidence of Gaitanismo's character as a working-class movement was its strength in areas traditionally associated with workers. In fact, urban Gaitanista zones tended to be areas of working-class concentration. Such was the case with Barranquilla, which one worker called "the workers' city" while claiming that "the city was totally Gaitanista."[169] The same might be said of Bogotá or Cali, Ibagué, Pereira, or the decidedly proletarianized oil city, Barrancabermeja. Barranca began to move decisively into the Gaitanista camp after the broken oil workers' strike of 1938.[170] Their support would be dramatically affirmed in Barranca's tenacious Gaitanista uprising after Gaitán's assassination on April 9, 1948.[171] It is true that not all working-class areas were so powerfully Gaitanista. While Gaitán had significant support in Medellín, the industrial workers there were not so solidly in his camp. A Liberal dentist observed that a significant "nucleus of workers" supported him but that in Medellín the Conservative candidate had strong support among "the industrial and coffee sectors, commerce and banking, and the high and low clergy."[172] There are several reasons for this. First, anti-Gaitán union leaders in Antioquia had considerable control. Also of critical importance, Medellín was a traditional and extremely Catholic city, as well as a Conservative party stronghold, which undercut the left-Liberal influence there. Finally, many factory workers in Medellín, in particular the key sector represented by female textile workers, were decidedly enmeshed with paternalistic employers.[173] Yet even Medellín displayed mass support for Gaitán, much of which had to be from the working class.[174] Ultimately, regardless of the problematic case of Medellín, the fact remains that Gaitanismo was well represented in working-class areas, and not a few areas of rural wage labor.[175]

Medellín notwithstanding, another crucial indicator of Gaitanismo's working-class appeal was its ability to attract workers traditionally of

Conservative party affiliation. A worker in construction and hotels remembered that Gaitán's tours of conservative Boyacá in 1946 made a profound impact, recognized even by the Conservatives, and proclaimed that "the current was tremendous." Though Boyacá was (and is) largely "godo," there were significant Gaitanista frontiers in Tasca, Paz del Río, Tasco, and Socotá. Also in Boyacá, tailors and barbers from Duitama, "without regard to political colors," gave their votes to the "moral and democratic restoration" (as Gaitán's campaign was known).[176] In Ciénaga, a large part of the Conservative "masses" supported Gaitán's effort.[177] In Barrancabermeja, the Conservatives were solidly Gaitanista.[178] Writing from Barranquilla, an electrician admitted to Gaitán that he had not ceased to be a Conservative. Gaitán had been, nonetheless, a great influence on his political spirit, and in his opinion should be president for a thousand reasons.[179] José María Blanco Núñez, the Liberal Gaitanista named governor of Atlántico after the election of 1946, found great support for Gaitán among the "popular elements of Barranquilla's Conservatives" (a code word for Conservative workers?) who came to his office "frequently and spontaneously" to proclaim in favor of Gaitán. Many claimed this was only a Conservative tactic to split the Liberals, but he thought this unlikely.[180]

On the eve of Gaitán's campaign, workers and their sympathizers felt pride for the organizational gains they had made since the 1930s, building unions that would defend their economic and political interests while securing better working conditions. In the early 1940s organized workers pointed to the dramatic increase in the number of unions and the size of their collective membership.[181] Yet there was also a strong element of working-class anger at traditional Liberals. Resolution number 26 of the Federation of Workers of Magdalena condemned El Tiempo, and other bulwarks of the Liberal establishment, for denouncing wage increases demanded by the CTC, the Confederation of Colombian Workers, and for backing the organization of Catholic unions that would split the working class.[182] Their platform, therefore, called for expanded organization to counter employers' efforts to break unions, "real" distribution of land to colonos through the enforcement of existing ordinances, higher wages, enforcement of the legal eight-hour day, and a moratorium on colono debt.[183]

Gaitán's reemergence onto the national political scene as a presidential candidate was met by many workers with enthusiasm. The Union of Pilots and Navigators of Barranquilla supported his attempt to initiate a "democratic system" at what they characterized as "such a critical moment for the working class."[184] In 1945 the events of December 6, 1928, in Ciénaga retained their significance for "the proletariat of Colombia." The "bloody bodies of workers machine-gunned" ignited the "first cry of protest demanding justice and attention to social problems."[185] In the banana zone, the workers never forgot that it was Gaitán who raised his voice to denounce the massacre.[186] But workers in other parts of Colombia also remembered the "hero of the banana zone" as the "defender of the proletarian class."[187] In the months preceding election day, a profusion of organized and unorganized workers wrote to Gaitán to pledge their votes and support, often in opposition to their union and political leaders. These included bus and cab drivers, founders, bakers, tailors, barbers, electricians, textile and other factory workers, brewery workers, petroleum workers, rural wage workers, mixed workers' unions, railroad workers, and river workers.[188] Most spoke of him as the "authentic representative," "defender," or "savior" of the working class.

One of the best illustrations of the working-class presence in Gaitanista mobilization and its autonomous nature was provided by a key group of workers, those of the Magdalena River. Their eventual decline in numbers and strength did not preclude highly effective patterns of struggle. Throughout the 1930s and 1940s, the river workers proved themselves adept at political, as well as shop-floor, maneuvers. Indeed, while in a forceful position to exert pressure on their employers, the river workers sought governmental intercession to sustain successful shop-floor struggle. The river workers both helped bring about and benefited from the Liberal Party's labor policies of the 1930s, which ultimately led to FEDENAL's closed shop. So when their power to control the river's labor market was smashed in the strike of 1945, the workers of the Magdalena showed, yet again, their understanding of the connections between union organization and mobilization in national politics. With defeat on one front, the river workers opened another by swelling the ranks of Gaitán's radical populist movement. One broken strike, albeit an important one, did not spell the end of their leverage. The river workers' struggles from 1930 to 1945 had shown them the connections between shop-floor and political action. These lessons made their participation in Gaitanismo second nature.

For years, Gaitán had been busily building support for his movement with special attention to the cities and towns of the Atlantic coast and up the Magdalena. And for years he had been involved in the affairs of the river workers. In 1935, for example, unskilled port workers in Gamarra, Cundinamarca, wrote to Gaitán for his legal expertise and expressed a wide range of worker interests, including concerns over work rules and workers' rights, the dignity of artisans, the need for legal representation, and their understanding of the need to organize. They addressed him in his capacity as the "indisputable *jefe* of *obrerismo* and creator of the grand socialist party called UNIR." They owed much to Gaitán because of his "audacious reforms."[189]

Gaitán's status among the workers of the Magdalena, therefore, was not fortuitous. Skilled and unskilled river workers gave Gaitán ample support for his independent campaign. In 1944 "three unions in the industry of river navigation" reminded him of the consideration he had shown them while he was minister of education, help they would not forget.[190] Scores of unions pledged their members to go "to the attack" (*¡a la carga!*) with Gaitán, a slogan that became his rallying call.[191] In Puerto Berrío, the stevedores were totally devoted to the Gaitanista cause.[192] In fact, river workers were simply following the general trend within the movement of autonomous mobilization. Throughout Colombia, supporters formed "Gaitanista Committees" to sustain the campaign. Many of these entities were made up of professionals and educated workers. Yet others were like the one in Honda, where the committee was composed of "poor workers," only one of whom could read.[193] Many of these workers belonged to unions that lacked legal recognition and therefore had no official affiliation with federations like FEDENAL.

The case of the river workers begs some questions: What was the nature of the working class's weakness? Was the working class really an "orphan," as Archila claims, in the post-López period? The working class alone was weak, yes, but Gaitanismo helped it transcend that weakness. In joining multiclass Gaitanismo, workers enjoyed and added to the movement's political strength, which found its power in its inclusiveness. Given their relatively small numbers in Colombian society, organized workers had little choice but to pursue their interests through political alliance with the urban middle classes. This was not, perhaps, ideal, but it was also not the product of manipulation or faulty class consciousness. To condemn working-class participation within Gaitanismo seems preposterous since between 1945 and 1948 it offered the best hope to date of actually obtaining the promises of the Revolución en Marcha.

After 1944 Gaitanismo would unite diverse regions and mobilize groups traditionally ignored by the political establishment. Though they lacked the vote, women played a significant role in the movement. Colombia's black, mulatto, and mestizo population naturally gravitated toward "el negro Gaitán." And Gaitanismo represented the "popular classes" in accordance with Colombian social realities. Gaitán's pueblo, though multiclass, found its class character strongly influenced by the urban working classes and rural proletarians, while members of the middle sectors were also capable of disquieting demands. That Gaitanismo was a "class movement" was never doubted by the Gaitanistas. "Middle-class" interests did not prove antithetical to "working-class" interests, as demonstrated by their mutually advantageous alliance within the pueblo against the oligarquía. The middle class and working class did not share a clear relationship to the means of production, but Gaitanismo nevertheless found its inner drive in class conflict—that of the darker-skinned pueblo against the political and economic oligarquía.

1. Rafael Uribe Uribe. (Author's collection.)

2. "To the reconquest! Before with the rifle, today with the cédula" (meaning the vote). Left-Liberal popular mobilization, armed and electoral, in the nineteenth and twentieth centuries, as seen from late 1946. (Author's collection.)

3. Emblem of UNIR.
(Author's collection.)

4. Alfonso López Pumarejo, leaving for the United States after stepping down as president midway through his second term in office. (Photo by Sady González, courtesy of revista *Número*.)

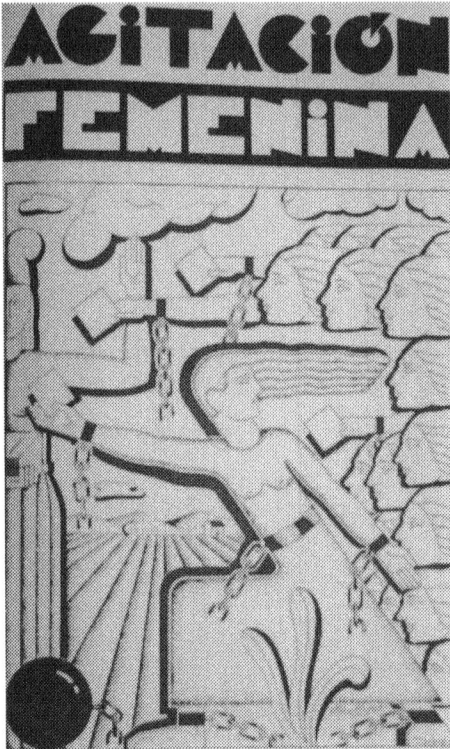

5. Women breaking their chains and voting. Cover illustration of *Agitación femenina*. (Author's collection.)

6. Demonstrating the obvious race and class overtones of the old Liberal/Conservative divide in 1947, the parties face off as boxers. Liberalism is portrayed as a large Afro-Colombian, Conservatism as an old white (presumably elite) man, clutching a rosary. (*Jornada.*)

7. Decked out in oligarchic finery, Carlos Lozano y Lozano, Alfonso López Pumarejo, and Gabriel Turbay. (Biblioteca Nacional.)

8. Gaitanista rally in the Plaza de Bolívar, Bogotá, at the height of Gaitán's campaign, April 13, 1946. (Photo by Sady González, courtesy of revista *Número*.)

9. Gaitán broadcasting one of his "Viernes Culturales" from the Teatro Municipal of Bogotá. (Photo by Sady González, courtesy of revista *Número*.)

10. The famous image of a defiant Gaitán on a campaign poster. (Author's collection.)

11. Calle 12, Bogotá, November 12, 1945, with a campaign poster in the lower right-hand corner. (Photo by Sady González, courtesy of revista *Número*.)

12. Gaitán pictured with Rafael Uribe Uribe and Benjamín Herrera, revered apostles of the left-Liberal tradition, and veterans of the War of a Thousand Days. (Courtesy of Pascual Del Vecchio R.)

13. Gaitán arriving in Barranquilla and carried in on the shoulders of his supporters. (Courtesy of Pascual Del Vecchio R., who is wearing the white fedora.)

14. Gaitanista support in Barranquilla. *(Jornada.)*

15. Procession of Mariano Ospina Pérez, August 7, 1946. (Photo by Sady González, courtesy of revista *Número.*)

16. Cocktail party for Gaitán at El Embajador, May 7, 1947. (Photo by Sady González, courtesy of revista *Número*.)

17. Alberto Lleras Camargo in the Senate, leading the last-ditch effort by the Liberal elite against a surging Gaitanista tide within the Liberal party, October 22, 1946. (Photo by Sady González, courtesy of revista *Número*.)

18. Political cartoon depicting the oligarchic nature of elections as seen by the Liberal pueblo. (*Jornada*, Feb. 4, 1947.)

19. Representing the extremes of Colombian politics, Gaitán faces Laureano Gómez. Roberto Urdaneta, Ministro de Gobierno, is smoking. (Photo by Sady González, courtesy of revista *Número*.)

20. The Manifestación del Silencio in the Plaza de Bolívar, Bogotá, February 7, 1948. Note the banners from different cities and regions. (Photo by Sady González, courtesy of revista *Número*.)

21. Plinio Mendoza Neira, Roberto Gacia Peña, and Gaitán in his library, April 8, 1948. It is perhaps the last photo of Gaitán alive. (Photo by Sady González, courtesy of revista *Número*.)

22. Gaitanistas in the Carrera Séptima, Bogotá, anxiously await news of Gaitán's condition after he was shot. (Photo by Sady González, courtesy of revista *Número*.)

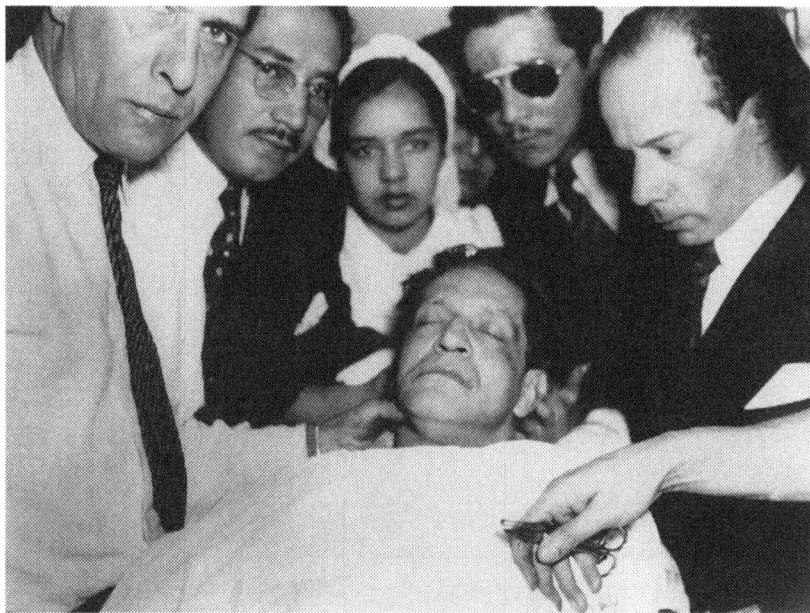

23. Pedro Eliseo Cruz holds the head of Gaitán after his death in the Clínica Central. (Photo by Sady González, courtesy of revista *Número*.)

24. Gaitanistas armed with machetes, knifes, clubs, hammers, and whatever was at hand on April 9, 1948. After looting stores, they were also drinking heavily. (Photo by Sady González, courtesy of revista *Número*.)

25. Marching toward the presidential palace among armed Gaitanistas are, among others, Darío Echandía, Carlos Lleras Restrepo, Víctor J. Merchán, Alfonso Araújo, and Jaime Posada. (Photo by Sady González, courtesy of revista *Número*.)

26. Memorial service for Jorge Eliécer Gaitán in the Parque Nacional, April 20, 1948. (Photo by Sady González, courtesy of revista *Número*.)

6

The Moral and Democratic Challenge

Oligarchic Political Practice and Gaitanismo, 1944–1946

By 1944, Colombian liberalism was a house divided. It came as no surprise, therefore, that Gaitán's campaign for president between March 1944 and May 1946 ignited the long-smoldering feud between the Bogotá-dominated party establishment and left Liberals who now spoke openly of Gaitanismo. Though some historians still dismiss popular challenges to the power of the oligarquía in the 1940s, many of Gaitán's contemporaries recognized his undertaking as truly without precedent.[1] His was the first independent, mass-based, popularly oriented mobilization of its magnitude in Colombian history. In the context of the Liberal Republic's crisis of leadership and direction, Gaitán and his supporters saw the perfect opportunity to go on the offensive and grab the Liberal nomination for president. If the Liberal party acted on the Gaitanista demand for a popular convention to pick its candidate, Gaitán's supporters reasoned, he could not lose. When the party leadership predictably decided to follow tradition and impose its own candidate, Gaitán had little choice, or inclination, but to continue on as an independent Liberal candidate through his campaign for the "Moral and Democratic Restoration of the Republic." His left-Liberal movement had a life-force of its own. To prove his position among the Colombian masses once and for all, Gaitán had to split the Liberal party.[2]

Undeniably, Colombia's political system in Gaitán's day exhibited a long-established practice of civilian rule, spirited electoral politics, the rule of law, separation of powers, and orderly transitions of power between competing parties. It had a distinct heritage of popular participation that was given a powerful boost in the constitutional reform of 1936. It was a political system, in fact, that enjoyed a great deal of legitimacy, and in the 1930s and 1940s, Colombia could rightly claim to be one of the most democratic countries in the world. Yet, it was also clearly an "oligarchic" system that sustained a forcefully hegemonic political elite. For all its popular vigor, the system was prone to domination by powerful groups and individuals. Though never a monolithic bloc, the jefes naturales of the Liberal party establishment were given to arbitrary decisions and less-than-democratic procedures. And at the system's heart on the local level was a proficient mechanism of political control, namely the techniques of electoral manipulation employed by the *gamonal* (the boss). While gamonales of both parties were always aware of their own personal interests and ready to play local, departmental, and national interests off one another, they did deliver the votes to the national parties.

As noted earlier, political hegemony can be seen as a shared framework for negotiation and struggle over questions of power, but a framework that also tends to influence, or even control, the process. Focusing on the presidential campaign and election of 1946, therefore, this chapter probes the mechanics of oligarchic political practice within this framework (often fragmented in itself), while highlighting the accomplishments (and failures) of the Gaitanista enterprise in challenging the system, especially in urban settings. Gaitanismo in the 1940s, as opposed to Unirismo in the 1930s, was a more urban mobilization. This was not due to any waning of interest in land problems on Gaitán's part, but rather because more political space and opportunity for electoral success existed in towns and cities. While the Gaitanistas did not completely overcome their need for a caudillo to unify their movement, nor solve the problem of violence in Colombian politics, they explored new relationships for leaders and followers. Gaitanismo united diverse cities and regions of Colombia, no mean feat in an especially fragmented nation. As already demonstrated, it mobilized classes, ethnic and racial groups, and women traditionally on the fringe of political life. And the Gaitanistas employed mobilization techniques never before used in Colombia. The Gaitanista grassroots political organizations that fixated on the purity of the franchise opened up Colombia's political system to more democracy by challenging the elite political hegemony of boss politics (rural and urban, on the local and national levels) employed by the traditional parties. To be sure, Gaitán and some of his followers in the political profession were not above using gamonal tactics for their own ends, but in general, Gaitanistas were intent on ridding the system of gamonal influence. Belying the usually pessimistic characterizations of Colombia's oligarchic democracy, the Gaitanistas demonstrated the sophistication and radicalism inherent in Colombia's popular political culture.

Mature Gaitanismo, representing the party's left-Liberal tradition of rebellion for democratic rights and social justice, emerged in 1944 during a tense period of discord, popular frustration, and class conflict. The hostility of the oligarquía to any amplification, or even continuation, of reform assured that Gaitanismo would generate a furious social confrontation, both within the Liberal party and throughout the larger society. Gaitán's independent run for the presidency exposed many cracks in Colombia's political structure and social fabric, and demonstrated how radical movements of change could arise from within the elite-dominated political parties. Though he lost the election and split the Liberal vote, giving the Conservatives the presidency for the first time in sixteen years, he demonstrated the depth of his movement. Gaitán proved himself the popularly anointed leader of the Colombian left and, soon thereafter, of the Liberal party itself.

Popular Acclaim and Elite Repugnance

Gaitán's presidential bid provoked reactions that tended to rather telling extremes. The Liberal pueblo (and a significant portion of the Conservative pueblo) displayed widespread enthusiasm. The Liberal political elite, in contrast, exhibited a near universal mixture of fear, anger, and loathing. (The Conservative elite's reaction was more nuanced. They feared him, praised him for denouncing the Liberal establishment, used him, and most assuredly hated him.)

Gaitán had been receiving popular encouragement to seek the presidency for some years. In 1939 a "humble *campesino*" declared himself behind Gaitán all the way to the president's chair.[3] Later in the same year a proto-Gaitanista with the national postal workers' union noted that while the Liberal leadership would not "recognize the true leaders of democracy," Gaitán had long been the "axis of Liberal politics," and he awaited Gaitán's political resurrection on the national scene.[4] In 1941 Milton Puentes, who would later write Gaitán's campaign biography, compared him to Colombia's political (though mostly Liberal) pantheon: he was like Bolívar in the "indomitable" way he pursued his goals; like Vicente Azuero in the "intensity of his thought"; like José María Obando for "the love" he was "given by the masses"; and like Uribe Uribe in the "majestic elegance of his words." He argued that the moment was ripe for Gaitán to take the presidency.[5] And in 1942 two policemen (most of whom where Liberal, whereas the Conservatives dominated the army) encouraged Gaitán to run, noting that his "political current" was "extensive" and supported by the "working masses." They did not doubt his ultimate victory, given his capacity "to organize our nation." He would wrench power from the hands of the "privileged castes" of the *oligarquía*.[6]

In 1943 workers from Bucaramanga who wanted Gaitán in the presidential palace summed up his biography and in the process demonstrated their frustration with Liberal reform. Even in his early years, they noted, he had struggled for Colombian workers while in his head "aristocratic ideas never found shelter." Gaitán as a youth was always concerned with "the problems . . . of the sons of the *pueblo*"; as an adult his "democratic thought" produced many "fantastic ideas, always focused on the revindication of the oppressed classes." They remembered UNIR, devoted to the progress and support of the "abandoned and forgotten classes," and also his time as mayor of Bogotá, during which he "introduced reforms" for the benefit of "the urban workers." In the Cámara and the Senate he challenged the leaders of both parties, "crossed swords with adversaries of influence and renown," and was also the "premier penal jurist of the country." Through it all, Gaitán had been "one of the principal champions of the working classes." In a thinly veiled reference to López, they spoke darkly of "others" who had hidden under the cape of "fraternity and equality" but were really only demagogues who availed themselves of the people's ignorance to fool and exploit them. "Now" was "the hour of social revindication," they argued. The people were "tired of empty promises"; they suffered from "hunger and thirst for justice"; the moment had arrived "for moral and material liberation." Following Gaitán as *jefe único* would mean "abandoning the paths of error" to redirect the nation's course "down the great way of progress, to fight for the just cause of worker salvation." They supported Gaitán for president because he had always "raised his voice in protest" in favor of the working class, the class for which he was "apostle . . . and defender," the class "exploited not only by Colombian magnates but foreign capitalists as well."[7]

In a similar vein in 1944, a Liberal radio newsman in Caldas lamented that López had "defrauded the hopes" of Colombians. He claimed to have been pro-Gaitán since UNIR and now called for Gaitán's candidacy. Gaitán would "continue to struggle against the *camarillas*" that controlled the party. His voice would be raised against the "candidates of the impertinent and dominant *oligarquía*."[8] And during that same week an editorial writer in Ibagué expressed the spirit of the moment, exposing what Gaitán was tapping into, while making connections to the glorious (radical) Liberal past, with its traditions of resistance and moral indignation. He looked back with pride and honor to the "romantic Liberal generation now almost extinct," whom he called "visionary apostles, defenders of the moral integrity of the party." They fought with "protest on their lips and a rifle to their chests." He could still hear "echoes of the bells" ringing the triumphs of "revolutionary arms." Their "*mística* Liberal" was grounded in their "fervor for Liberal teachings" and "deep respect for its doctrinal traditions of the collective." He noted that the final battle had yet to be fought but that the moment was at hand. It was imperative for Liberals to "return their eyes to the ever-open book of history" that revealed the "thesis of the political revolution of Liberalism." The party's philosophical base (read: left liberalism) had been infiltrated by an ideological "Trojan horse." "A la carga!" as "someone" had said, "A la carga, yes" (that someone having been Gaitán, who, as pointed out earlier, used the phrase as his rallying call). The party had to remain "loyal to democratic postulates and to the will of the *pueblo*." The supposed leaders of the party "there on Olympus" were "kindlers of disasters" who pretended to be "guides." Yet they caused "moral calamities."[9] And a month later, for a tenants' association in Bogotá, Gaitán's candidacy represented democracy, awakening class consciousness, working-class interests, and class struggle. They were with him in his fight.[10]

A supporter in Ibagué informed Gaitán that the local Liberal establishment was solidly Gaitanista. The majority of the congressional deputies from Tolima were Gaitanista, as well as the representatives in the departmental Assembly, and all the members of the departmental Liberal Directorate. In Ibagué there was no support, he claimed, for Carlos Lleras and only a "ridiculous minority" for Gabriel Turbay, comprised of oligarchic elements. The pueblo was Gaitanista, "from the *pequeño comerciante* and the *empleado* to the humble *obrero*." All this support notwithstanding, they were worried that the National Directorate would instruct them to move against Gaitán. Incidentally he noted that the local Communists continued "being more papist than the Pope" regarding their support of the old Lopista Liberal establishment, calling Gaitán a "dangerous leader."[11] In Caldas another supporter assured Gaitán that "despite the difficulties, in this and neighboring *municipios*" the force of a Gaitán candidacy would carry it to victory.[12] In Cúcuta, regardless of the wishes of the local Liberal leaders, workers were already organizing for Gaitán in a popular assembly of "united workers' unions."[13]

All of this popular activity and enthusiasm for Gaitán stood in stark contrast to the reaction of the Liberal leadership and their retainers. In a moment of honesty Juan Lozano y Lozano, a journalist, public intellectual, and Liberal insider, demonstrated how the Liberal establishment saw Gaitán. "If Carlos Lleras would be the best governor," he argued, "Gaitán would be the most legitimate president, in that he would be the most popular." "Popular" he clarified of course, among the pueblo. The "ruling classes, comprising a small minority," felt for Gaitán "an invincible repugnance." The pueblo, who had watched Gaitán at their defense for twenty years and more, knew that he was the "most tenacious and ardent defender of their interests" and that he had "the most profound feelings and comprehension of their problems." It was evident that Gaitán was the only candidate who "implicitly" carried "in his life and in his ideas" the potential for "radical change in Colombian life." The revolution of López "would be sugar water in comparison to the revolution Gaitán would carry out." And this was the point of the whole piece: Gaitán, the radical populist, would be a dangerous leftist leader. A Gaitán government would be a frightening "leap into the abyss." Lozano y Lozano strikingly demonstrated both elite fears and the depth and class nature of Gaitán's support.[14] In Ipiales a supporter astutely noted that it was "natural" for "the professional politicians" to be against Gaitán.[15]

Such fears were echoed in the Lopista press in both the capital and in the provinces. In Manizales in March 1944, for example, a Liberal paper with working-class sympathies that had been a cheerleader for the Revolución en Marcha argued that Gaitán was too far left. Commenting on the different Liberal candidates, they asserted that Gaitán moved "on the left margin, intoning the hymn of authentic democracy" yet unable, they argued, "to attract workers and campesinos from outside the Liberal party." He presented himself "as the prototype of the true revolutionary who would abandon the old routines . . . and lead the national administration down new paths." This was "much to say and pretend to do" they believed. They advised that his way would be "prejudicial" for the country. He would bring about "a revolution" in the nation's economic and political systems, and no one could be sure if such a direction would be wise. On May 6 they declared Liberal Manizales Turbayista and called Gaitán a demagogue.[16]

Campaign and Election in a System under Stress

Gaitán opened his campaign with a speech at the Municipal Theater in Bogotá in which he differentiated the país nacional from the país político and explained his definition of the oligarquía. The "country of nationhood" encompassed the people "who worked, who labored in the interests of their families, who sought the education of their children, who were concerned with real, daily problems of living, whose lives were involved in a constant struggle."[17] The "political nation," the oligarquía, was a minority concerned with votes, contracts, or cushy appointments. The oligarquía was composed of those men who made the important decisions and their flunkies who "penetrated into the neighborhoods, the towns, the assemblies," the "local bosses who arranged elections for the benefit of the political country in exchange for profits."[18] From the very beginning, therefore, Gaitanismo took aim at a political system far removed from the concerns and will of the majority of Colombians. Gaitán ended his speech with the clarion call of his movement, "Pueblo . . . a la carga!"

Early posturing among the would-be candidates in the Atlantic coastal department of Magdalena demonstrated the general flux endemic to the Liberal party in the mid-1940s. In March 1944 *El Estado* of Santa Marta gave parallel coverage to both Gabriel Turbay and Gaitán, with preference to the former, but noted that Gaitán continued "his constant political activity" and received "*adhesiones* from all the departments."[19] They considered Turbay, the early favorite, the best hope for Liberal union.[20] In early 1945 *Vanguardia* of Santa Marta still hedged its bets by saying positive things about both Turbay and Echandía, but admitted that Gaitán and his "attractive program" could not be overlooked.[21] Dionisio Rincones Ponce observed that Turbay had some support in Magdalena's government and business circles while Gaitán commanded the loyalty of "the great mass of workers and peasants, 'los descamisados' in general." Many people in Turbay's camp recognized Gaitán's great popular appeal but were afraid to declare publicly for him because of their subservient position in relation to the oligarquía.[22] In late 1945 another Gaitanista claimed that the Echandía forces were disoriented and that Turbay's candidacy had been discredited in the eyes of the "*pueblo,* the masses," because it awakened "no patriotic emotions."[23] In December 1945 Rincones Ponce claimed that Turbayismo in Magdalena was largely "without troops."[24]

In the early phase of the campaign both Carlos Lleras Restrepo and Darío Echandía threw their hats into the ring, but quickly withdrew them because of intense pressure from the Gaitanista masses.[25] As Gabriel Turbay remained the only other Liberal of stature besides Gaitán in the race in late July of 1945, the Liberal party leadership met privately and then declared Turbay their candidate at the elite Teatro Colón. This action represented the fruition of the Gaitanistas' worst fears. As early as May 1944, the president of the Comité Gaitanista of Atlántico complained to Eduardo Santos in an open letter about the "irregular manner" in which the Liberal leadership was preparing for the upcoming national convention. As a representative of the Gaitanistas of Atlántico he also claimed, with considerable justification, to represent the majority of the department's Liberals. He accused the National Directorate of attempting to subvert the "expression of the popular will" by orchestrating the undemocratic selection of the Liberal presidential candidate.[26]

Gabriel Turbay, born in Bucaramanga, was an intellectual and in early adulthood came much closer to being a doctrinaire Marxist than Gaitán ever was.[27] But despite his radical sympathies, he worked his way up through the ranks of the Liberal party in the traditional fashion. Turbay was therefore more reliant on the old Liberal political networks and had little popular following of his own, which did not seem to bother him. As Juan Lozano y Lozano quipped, Turbay was only disposed to take the Liberal nomination if it were offered with the proper pomp and circumstance.[28]

Establishment Liberals expressed their opposition to Gaitán's campaign with anger when they realized that he meant to challenge their decision. Many important members of the party's hierarchy continued to believe that Gaitán's drive was an attempt to position himself for a prominent appointment in the next administration and that he would eventually bow to the official candidate. This apparently was Turbay's belief until the very days before the election. But the editors of Eduardo Santos's *El Tiempo* and Juan Lozano y Lozano's *La Razón* immediately initiated counteroffensives. They called Gaitán a traitor to the party, and even a crypto-socialist who masqueraded as a Liberal.[29] *El Tiempo* largely ignored Gaitán's campaign and only covered it during negotiations with Turbay in April 1946. Most often they only spoke of him to attack him. Less than a month before the election they called Gaitán's candidacy "the fruit of personal agitation" and not really Liberal. Turbay, the official candidate, was the real representative of liberalism, they insisted. In column after column, *El Tiempo*'s Calibán attacked Gaitán as a demagogue or worse.[30] *La Razón,* another bulwark of the Liberal establishment, was by January 1946 100 percent pro-Turbay, preaching the dangers of Liberal division.[31]

Other major Liberal papers followed the establishment line to varying degrees. *El Diario* and *El Correo,* both Liberal dailies in Medellín, were both Turbayista in 1946, yet they refrained from attacking Gaitán. *Vanguardia Liberal* of Bucaramanga, on the other hand, was very Turbayista in 1946 and disdainful of Gaitán. *La Nacional* in Barranquilla went even further in claiming that Gaitán's appeal was "personal" and that with his skills as orator he mobilized "passions, and not ideas."[32] They agreed with Calibán that Gaitán was not only a danger to liberalism but also to democracy.[33] The editors of *El Liberal* in Bogotá understood full well the dangers of Liberal division. Staking out a lonely neutral position in favor of a Liberal "frente nacional," they rejected both Gaitán and Turbay. "Neither" could unite liberalism, they argued; both had their "group of supporters, but no more than a group." They proposed acting president Lleras Camargo.[34] One important exception to the anti-Gaitán current among the big Liberal daily papers was Bogotá's independently minded *El Espectador,* which continued to give Gaitán largely impartial coverage as they had done since the late 1920s. On April 9, 1946, they noted that for Gaitán his candidacy was not an electoral battle but rather "a revolutionary assault by the Liberal and Conservative masses on the historical parties, on big industry, on the bourgeoisie."[35] The crux of the matter for elite Liberals was what they considered to be Gaitán's emotional appeal to the *chusma,* the rabble. Gaitán stirred up and manipulated the masses to such an extent, they argued, that "respectable" citizens were struck with fear at the sight of Gaitanista demonstrations.[36]

In spite of the rough handling they received during the FEDENAL strike of 1945, the Communist leadership continued to support the official Liberal candidate. In perfect step with the Liberal establishment, the PSD attacked Gaitán and his movement as a Colombian variety of fascism. This dynamic, as pointed out earlier, was a common one between populists and communists in Latin America as both groups struggled for popular support. And as in other places, this political confrontation was driven along by the question of nationalism. Juan Manuel Valdelamar, one of the Gaitanistas' most astute leaders on the coast (though he was also a Communist leader), argued that Gaitanismo's "national character" was one of the principal reasons that both the PSD and the oligarquía feared it.[37] Nationalism and patriotism were important in all populist movements, but in the case of Colombia, isolated and given to entrenched party loyalty, it was especially pronounced.[38] Most Colombians identified more with Liberal and Conservative struggles than with Communist and Fascist ones.[39] In the 1930s the Communists' assertion that the idea of *patria* was only a bourgeois construct, making them "citizens of the world" and brothers to all workers, offended the national pride of many otherwise sympathetic Colombians.[40] The idea that "the worker has no fatherland" seemed absurd to many on the Colombian left.[41] And at the time, Liberals consistently characterized their Communist rivals as too close to the Soviets and as essentially "foreign," claiming that Communist activity, perpetrated by "agents of Moscow," was "outside the law."[42] And Gaitán himself was hardly above inciting fear against Communist activity as dangerous intervention into the life of the patria by a "foreign organization."[43]

In the end, the Gaitanistas' successful appeals to national identity only kindled the PSD's natural inclination to call them fascists.[44] The Communists could point, after all, to the seeming alliance between Gaitán and the rabid leader of the most reactionary sect of the Conservative party, Laureano Gómez, who gave Gaitán coverage in his paper *El Siglo* in a successful attempt to split the Liberal party. Throughout late 1945 and into 1946, accordingly, the Communists pounded away at Gaitán in speeches, memoranda, and their party paper, *Diario Popular*, as a demagogue and a threat to the Colombian working class. Augusto Durán, then secretary general of the PSD, declared that those masses who did follow Gaitán did so because he had "a powerful throat."[45] The Communists argued that since he had been a mayor and ministers of labor and education under Liberal governments, he was himself a part of the oligarquía and a "proto-fascist." Those who followed him were merely Liberals who had been pushed away from the governmental pork barrel or people who had been deceived.[46] Resurrecting the title of Fermín López Giraldo's 1936 polemic, they called him the "naked apostle," a representative of the most reactionary forces of Colombia. Gaitán, they argued, disoriented the working class by camouflaging his hatred of the people in phrases appealing to the interests of the people.[47] He was "the screen" behind which hid antidemocratic reaction.[48] Gaitanismo was nothing more than "demagoguery and lies."[49] As Durán said in a speech in Barranquilla in September 1945, "Hitler and Mussolini also deceived the people with the demagoguery of moral restoration." Gaitán was simply Gómez's frontman.[50]

Spurned by liberalism's leaders and their Communist allies (the former calling him "socialist" and the latter "fascist"), Gaitán concentrated his efforts on mobilizing the disparate groups and social strata attracted to Gaitanismo into a viable political movement. Most importantly, Gaitán and his followers had to build an electoral network (especially in towns and cities) that could rival the long-established Liberal and Conservative political machines. The most spectacular illustration of this effort during the campaign came with the "Popular Convention" in Bogotá on Sunday, September 23, 1945.

The convention represented Gaitanismo's ultimate expression of legitimacy and popular muscle. The fruition of a year and a half of campaigning, it was the best example of Gaitanista utilization of mobilization techniques. In overt contrast to the controlled, elitist, and secretive way in which the official Liberal party leadership chose its candidate, Gaitán's popular convention was a dramatic spectacle. Thousands of Colombians from all over the country took part in what was the first instance of direct mass participation in the selection of a presidential candidate.

The event was meticulously planned. The central organizational committee demanded that urban and rural workers, shopowners, and peasants outnumber políticos in the delegations to the convention, and they organized transportation to the event. In the days before, Gaitanistas held parades and processions in the city center and in working-class neighborhoods. On the 23rd, fireworks and marching bands ushered in the convention. Beginning at the tombs of Rafael Uribe Uribe and Benjamín Herrera, revered prophets of left liberalism, Gaitanista leaders gave patriotic speeches and the multitude of supporters marched to the city's bullfight ring, the Circo de Santamaría. When Gaitán arrived in the late afternoon, the capacity crowd of twenty-five thousand delegates (surrounded by thousands of spectators outside the arena) cheered as flowers and paper flew, doves were released, and bands played the national anthem.[51]

The speech Gaitán delivered was one of the most important of his career.[52] He launched his address by noting that "unheard clamors for justice" were "silently, methodically but inexorably forming new concepts of social equilibrium . . . and more just systems of living." He then made distinctions between popular Gaitanismo and establishment liberalism. The former, he claimed, represented the will of the people, while the latter consisted of machine politics that sabotaged the moral and democratic legitimacy of the Liberal party and of Colombian society. The party bosses, representing the oligarquía, undermined the moral and social contracts of the Colombian social organism. While technological advances made a higher standard of living possible for all of humanity, the oligarquía had undermined such promises by commandeering the economic base of society for their own selfish ends. But as fascism in Europe had just been defeated, so would the forces of corruption, political manipulation, and immorality that had taken root in Colombia's institutions. Gaitanismo aimed to restore the democratic and moral legitimacy of the Liberal party. After the speech, Gaitán led a procession of roughly forty thousand supporters though central Bogotá.

One of the principal battlegrounds of Gaitán's mobilization and campaign was within the organized labor movement.[53] The Gaitanista leadership naturally saw one of their most important objectives as challenging the PSD's dominance of the CTC. Though they had encouraging signs of possible success, the Gaitanistas faced serious Communist opposition. On the eve of the disastrous FEDENAL strike in 1945, the Gaitanistas attempted to take control of the CTC at its seventh national congress. In this objective, the Gaitanistas failed. The Communist leadership of the CTC persuaded Liberal labor leaders to hold the line against "fascist" manipulation.[54]

Yet Communist leaders in both the PSD and the CTC never came to grips with the Gaitanista sympathies of many unions.[55] In Barranquilla and in the surrounding countryside, workers and peasants followed Gaitán, often as not, in opposition to their leaders.[56] As José María Córdoba later argued, the "poorly led" CTC never caught on that the proletariat, for the most part still unorganized, saw Gaitán as their "only salvation."[57] On his tour of the river ports in March 1944, the astute Juan Manuel Valdelamar "felt the pulse of the unionized workers and drew the following conclusions." In general, the unions affiliated with FEDENAL and the CTC continued to follow the line set down at the congress of Bucaramanga the year before, agitating for the return of López to power. Yet Valdelamar maintained that under the surface, most of the workers all the way down the river to Barranquilla and Cartagena spoke in favor of Gaitán's candidacy. The anti-Gaitán line pushed by the Communist leadership in its memoranda and the *Diario Popular* had proven to be a failure, even among the mass of the party faithful.[58] Similar splits between union leaders and the Gaitanista ranks emerged throughout Colombia. In Ibagué, the president and secretary of the "Casa del Pueblo," which claimed to speak for the city's unions, asserted that workers there were not with Gaitán. Yet the important tailors' union of that city argued that "thousands" of workers in the department of Tolima were standing up to "worker *caciquismo*" and these "pseudo-leaders of the workers" and supported Gaitán's campaign.[59] In the department of Nariño the local railroad union created a *Comité Pro-Candidatura* Gaitán, even though their organization could not officially endorse him because the national organization had not done so.[60] In the municipality of Santa Marta, Dionisio Rincones Ponce believed, perhaps optimistically, that at least 70 percent of the workers were Gaitanistas, and almost all of them were unionized. "The influence of the *caciques* notwithstanding, the great majority of the workers and peasants" of Magdalena were Gaitanistas.[61] In Sevilla, for example, a group of more than one hundred pro-Gaitán workers and peasants even went about forming their own organization, the Union of Various Professions. They organized to represent the interests of workers and peasants to date unorganized or poorly served by the CTC.[62]

Watching the growing fragmentation within the Liberal party and its popular base, Conservative party leaders skillfully waited for the proper moment to act. In the early phases they cultivated Liberal division and capitalized on Gaitanismo to attack the government. A Conservative and Catholic labor leader later remembered that since they wanted change in 1946, they naturally took advantage of the Gaitanista phenomenon.[63] *El Deber,* a Conservative paper in Bucaramanga, appropriated Gaitán's critique from his radio address of March 14, 1944. With his "voice of protest and punishment" he spoke "like a prophet" of the defects of the current Liberal regime. This was not a "traditionalist leader" nor a "Conservative orator," it was "nothing less than the *caudillo* of the Colombian left, the Tribune of Liberalism." He was just repeating, so they argued, what Conservatives had been saying for years, pointing to the economic, social, and moral crisis.[64] In their March 30 editorial they provided a typical case of Conservatives speaking of Gaitán and the problem of the oligarquías, meaning the Liberal government. The *Diario del Pacífico,* a Conservative paper in Cali, also adroitly played the "split Liberalism" game. They asserted that Gaitán was supported by a rough coalition of "extreme right" Conservatives and "a group of Liberals on the left," and argued that it was "useless" to deny the force of his candidacy. They thought that it was unlikely that he would pull out, when he was "convinced" that he was "the most popular of the candidates."[65] Throughout February of 1946 they seemed to support Gaitán. On March 9 they warmly welcomed him to Cali, and, ironically, on March 11 they gave the best coverage of the massive Gaitanista support in Cali.

Isolated, ignored, and attacked in the official Liberal press, Gaitán had happily accepted the coverage given his movement in Laureano Gómez's *El Siglo.* Gaitán and Gómez overlooked the extreme differences between their respective worldviews and formed a short-lived marriage of political convenience for the purpose of attacking the official Liberals. But the differences were, nonetheless, enormous. Christopher Abel pointed out that both Gaitán and Gómez railed against corruption and spoke of a "reconquest" and both stressed their moral authority. Yet in contrasting their different concepts of "morality," Daniel Pécaut argued that Gaitanista morality was "of the tradition of the inexorable march of 'universal forces,'" while Laureanista morality had nothing to do with "historical laws" but rather saw the world in terms of a struggle between the forces of good and evil. Gaitanismo "perceived the possibility of unchaining the collective forces" of society. Laureanismo inhabited a "mythical universe" that was the battleground for a "fight to the death between irreconcilable forces." And James Henderson noted that Gómez emphasized "the organic and hierarchical characteristics of society," and traced the origins of Colombia's crisis back to the Enlightenment, and even more, to the demise of the monolithic Christian world in the sixteenth century. Since for Gómez the only route to salvation was through the Roman Catholic church, he was antagonistic to all breeds of liberalism, and insisted that those who disagreed were not only wrong, but evil.[66]

When in late March of 1946 the Conservatives launched Mariano Ospina Pérez as their first presidential candidate since 1930, they found the Liberals utterly divided. Ospina Pérez, the son of a powerful and wealthy family in Antioquia that had produced two Colombian presidents, ran as a candidate of reconciliation. Though the Conservative move was a surprise, it was not without precedent. Most instances in Colombian history in which one party took power from the other resulted from a divided ruling party; the parallel with the Liberal rise to power in 1930 became uncomfortably apparent to Liberals.

As election day drew close, Liberals frantically tried to mend the gap between official liberalism and Gaitanista left liberalism. Without reconciliation, the Conservatives would be assured of the plurality of votes necessary to win the election. Most distressing was the common knowledge that behind Ospina loomed the despised influence of Gómez, leader of the most militant wing of the Conservative party, who many Liberals believed sympathized with Italian Fascism and German National Socialism.[67] At the beginning of April 1946, Gaitán met with Turbay, López, and Santos to consider a possible solution. At a series of private meetings between Gaitán and Turbay, they discussed concrete economic and political reforms designed to increase popular participation in Colombia's institutions that had to be accepted before Gaitán would withdraw from the race.[68] They discussed forming a Liberal "anti-oligarchy pact" in which Turbay would stand for president in 1946 and Gaitán in 1950.[69] Such wording quickly alienated the party's leaders and both López and Santos turned against a merger. And, more importantly, Gaitán's followers definitively rejected such a compromise. At one of his periodic radio addresses at the Municipal Theater immediately following his meetings with Turbay, Gaitán faced an ugly crowd that would hardly allow him to speak. He quickly realized that there was no turning back.[70]

Liberal opinion makers responded differently to Gaitán's decision to stay in the race, reflecting Gaitanismo's varying strength in different regions. A common reaction in places where Gaitán did not command a decisive majority of Liberals was demonstrated by *El Demócrata* of Bucaramanga (Turbay's hometown). On April 12, 1946, its editors were pro-Turbay, yet respectful of Gaitán, approvingly calling him a "lively . . . and eloquent" critic of past Liberal governments and of the oligarquía. They asserted that Turbay and Gaitán could join forces for the good of Colombian democracy.[71] Yet on April 21, they emotionally lashed out when it was apparent that Gaitán would not step aside. They turned nasty and attacked anyone who would vote for Gaitán, denying his campaign the status of Liberal or popular, asserting that he could never deliver on what he offered the "humble classes," and labeling him a demagogue and traitor to Liberal ideals.[72]

Relator of Cali (an extremely left-Liberal town) followed a different trajectory between January and May of 1946. While *Relator* was the main local Turbayista paper, trying desperately to build support for the official candidate and save the election for the Liberals, it tellingly remained "pro-Gaitán." As in Barranquilla and Ibagué, many of the local Liberal leaders in Cali recognized the depth of Gaitán's support. They refused to follow the example of the Liberal leadership in Bogotá (and of the PSD) in attacking Gaitán. In January they published abundant attacks on the Conservatives but no word on Gaitán, seemingly in denial. They quoted liberalism's intellectuals who were proclaiming Turbay the next president, and as late as the beginning of March *Relator* was still largely ignoring Gaitán, though it was clear that he was a specter haunting the whole process. On March 9, 1946, over a large picture of Gaitán, they gave him a warm welcome on page one. While still very pro-Turbay, they recognized his campaign and its base in a "combat-hardened sector of the *pueblo*." They called him "a son of democracy" and praised his legal and political expertise, his intelligence, and his knowledge of the Colombian pueblo. *Relator* was honored by its cordial, firm, and long friendship with Gaitán.[73] They were very attentive to the talks between Turbay and Gaitán in early April, but by mid-April, their tone was frantic. On April 29 they continued to predict a victory for Turbay but refrained from attacking Gaitán.

The outcome of the May 5th election shocked the Liberal notables and their allies within the PSD leadership. Ospina Pérez won the election with 565,260 votes, while Turbay came in second with 440,591. Gaitán trailed relatively close behind with 358,957 votes.[74] Most significantly, however, Gaitán overwhelmingly carried the urban masses (at the expense of the official Liberals and politically bankrupt Communists). He won most major urban centers and departmental capitals, including Bogotá, Barranquilla, Cartagena, Santa Marta, Cali, Neiva, Ibagué, Quibdó, and

Cúcuta, and even narrowly missed carrying Popayán, a traditionally Conservative city. The only significant urban area that Gaitán did poorly in was Ospina Pérez's home town, Medellín. But while it also was a Conservative party stronghold, and while Gaitanismo in Antioquia suffered from incessant bickering among its leaders, the movement had a massive following even there that election returns, due to massive fraud, did not reflect.[75] Gaitán enjoyed outright majorities in the departments of Atlántico and Bolívar on the northern coast, and won majorities of the Liberal vote in Magdalena, Cundinamarca, Huila, Cauca, Valle, and the intendancy of Meta.[76] Many of Gaitán's enemies realized that even with the Liberal party's entire political machine turned against him, they could not crush Gaitanismo. They had to embrace it or doom the party to division and impotence for the foreseeable future. And the Gaitanistas themselves sadly realized that while Ospina and the Conservatives had been expected to out-poll them, there were also "silent anti-Gaitanista forces" within the party that voted against Gaitán.[77] The old Liberal divisions were alive and well.

The election showed that while Gaitán owned the cities, the Liberal machine still controlled the countryside and many of the small towns, where the majority of Colombians continued to live in 1946. It was, nevertheless, a watershed in Colombian history, the most serious electoral (and social) threat to the hegemony of the Colombian political elite in living memory. Gaitán's independent candidacy and its aftermath would finally force the Liberal leadership to recognize his political strength.

Contested Mechanisms of Oligarchic Rule: The *Gamonal* System and Its Discontents

While the national government's ability to project its power remained decidedly frail in the 1940s, the oligarchic mechanisms of political control in Colombia were quite potent. They allowed for continued elite domination of the traditional parties and the state. These mechanisms, however, had long been challenged and their power mitigated by the high degree of popular participation in Colombia's political system.

After the constitutional reform of 1936, all male Colombians could vote for president and members of Congress on the national level, and for Assembly deputies on the departmental level. Yet the legal structure of authority in Colombian politics remained hierarchically arranged. From the top, the appointment power of the executive was vast. The president appointed both cabinet ministers and governors of the departments. His appointed governors, in addition to controlling the armed forces in their regions, appointed lieutenant governors, *secretarios* (who served as departmental level cabinets), and municipal mayors. The lieutenant governor then appointed the police commander of the region, who controlled the departmental police force. Local leaders, however, had considerable say in who would be mayor, and of crucial importance to local politics, members of the town council (concejo) were elected. To run for office, one had to have his name inserted on a party list (usually headed by a well-known local or national leader).[78]

As these legal structures demonstrated, Colombia's political system still reflected its early *caudillista* development on the national level. Fals Borda defined caudillismo in Latin America as a "particular type of authoritarianism" that "filled the political void" left by the demise of the colonial state. Those who employed it believed that the situation required a strong hand because the majority of Latin America's inhabitants were not prepared for out-and-out democracy. The "real *caudillo*" was not content with local power and sought national influence, though he was seldom able to pass power on to his chosen successor. Since the classic image of the caudillo was that of a charismatic military leader on horseback, Colombian leaders of the twentieth century were not caudillos in the traditional sense, but strong elements of caudillismo remained in Colombia's political structure in Gaitán's day. Caudillos, and their twentieth-century descendants, executed the important function of integrating national and regional politics, and "transcending" local economic and political interests.[79]

Yet the truly enduring element of Colombian politics was gamonal (also called cacique, jefe político, and, on occasion, caudillo) control on the local level.[80] It was in this way that political life was "dominated by an oligarchy" that tightly controlled "the principal means of political influence and the avenues of social mobility."[81] Hegemony seldom entails a solid oligarchic corps in lockstep at the head of dominated subaltern masses, but almost always represents a contested political process of domination and struggle. In Colombia the hegemonic political system clearly incorporated popular elements and participation that ensured its legitimacy, so it therefore also had to have concrete political arrangements to maintain control. Gamonalismo was the mechanism at the heart of the hegemonic system. (And when the gamonal's political control failed, he would often resort to violent repression.)

Individual gamonales sought control of the local coffers, such as they were, because the system provided limited but sufficient spoils to warrant their attention. They also had considerable influence over the local judiciary, which could be turned against their rivals.[82] Charles Bergquist noted that at the level of the municipio "local strongmen, Liberal or Conservative, manipulated economic power and ties to the national party to distribute favors and the benefits of control over police and the courts."[83] Gamonales, therefore, served as the conduits for the distribution of resources from levels of government beyond the municipio. Carlos Miguel Ortiz Sarmiento characterized gamonal power as a function of this role as the one to meet the needs of neighborhoods and families, and as the link between communities and the departmental and national legislatures, in particular for "extraordinary" spending on things like roads and bridges or the construction of hospitals. Often the amount a locality received depended upon the political ability and personal connections of the gamonal and/or on his membership in the legislative bodies.[84]

The social foundation upon which local gamonal control rested in the nineteenth and early twentieth centuries, therefore, was the patron-client relationship, an interaction between "actors of unequal power and status" who form stable, reciprocal relationships.[85] The gamonal was usually not one of the largest landholders. Most of these lived in Bogotá or the provincial capitals and commercial centers and were not directly involved in politics on the municipal level. As a rule, local politics and its coarse nature were considered beneath the dignity of Colombia's decent folk.[86] And extensive land holdings by themselves did not guarantee political power. Rather, networks were built on knowledge of local needs. Whether a government official, a majordomo, a merchant, or a landowner (and as Mary Roldán has pointed out, gamonales could also come from the ranks of bar owners, civil engineers, and in Antioquia especially, parish priests),[87] the gamonal enlisted his followers to fight or to vote on the side of his party. The gamonal wielded power through his local influence, with *chicha* (corn beer), and with his revolver.[88]

The gamonal also generally controlled access to public employment through the city council. He could name both "positions of prestige," such as secretaries, administrators, and directors of departments, and "subsistence employment," such as drivers, nightwatchmen, trash collectors, and labor for public works projects. At the same time, friendship with the gamonal could make the difference between jail time or walking free.[89] None of these elements are exclusively Colombian. As Christie observed, what set Colombia apart was the prevalent role of violence and religious pressure.[90]

The reciprocal nature of the patron-client relationship in the rural setting thus helps explain the manner in which the lower classes were traditionally incorporated into the national political process. Their mobilization in support of the two dominant parties grew from the mutual benefits
accrued by the parties involved. Popular approval was purchased with
alcohol, roasted meat, bread, access to land, and occasionally, public employment. Peasant participation in politics, as in most machine systems,
was not without its logic.[91] Such practices did, nevertheless, result in significant leverage for the local elite, the more politically inclined landowners, and for gamonales. Following common practice, the owner of the
finca "Gomezlandia" wrote to Gaitán in 1945 concerning the votes of his
clientes. Though he claimed that past experience had taught him that
meddling in elections was largely unfruitful, he offered Gaitán 350 votes
if the caudillo would help him legally obtain two four-ton trucks.[92] As this
example shows, rural *patrones* often owned, in a literal sense, the votes of
their dependent employees. Ortiz Sarmiento told of landowners and
gamonales who kept the *cédulas* (roughly equivalent to voter registration)
of "their people" locked in their offices, and who escorted them to the
polls. In many towns as well, voters felt obliged to follow the lead of their
gamonal to maintain their employment, or to obtain it.[93]

Yet economic and political elite control was anything but absolute. The
national elite was not "cohesive and united" and was incapable of always
"prevailing against demands from the sub-elites."[94] Indeed, the oligarquía
was divided not only on the national level, but exhibited a "dual power
structure" of elites split between the national and local levels.[95] Eduardo
Posada-Carbó has pointed out that during the Conservative Hegemony,
even with the support of the army, police, and Church, the government's
ability to control the political process was limited. This was clear regarding the "so-called electoral machinery . . . controlled from the center."
Presidents and their appointed governors "were far from omnipotent."
Thus the oligarquía was not monolithic and could not always prevail
against the popular classes. Nor, for that matter, against the gamonales,
who were not exactly synonymous with the oligarquía. Conservative and
Liberal elites feared that earlier experiments with universal suffrage in
Colombia only favored the power of gamonales or the Church.[96]

The structure of Colombian politics, therefore, allowed significant political space for autonomous participation and influence by the pueblo. As
discussed earlier, popular military mobilization could at times be very
threatening to the elite. And perhaps even more important was Colom-

bia's long tradition of institutional democracy, which created a popular political culture that emphasized democratic values. Malcolm Deas stressed that despite "restricted suffrage" and "insignificant urbanization," politics were "ardently" practiced on a wide scale from the early days of the Republic.[97] And as Posada-Carbó has shown, "elections in what are considered 'pre-modern,' 'pre-democratic' societies have not received much scholarly attention." He argued that "they tend to be identified exclusively with the practices of patronage and clientelism, or merely with fraud and coercion. At a more sophisticated level, elections in these societies are perceived as mechanisms of social control or as conferring legitimacy to the oligarchies and the political systems."[98] Yet Colombian politics did not prove to be an unfailing force of elite control, nor was real political mobilization the exclusive domain of the relatively small, fully vested voting sector of the population.

Though most male Colombians could not vote directly for president or Congress before 1936, they were in the habit of voting. Even though universal male suffrage, granted in the Constitution of 1853, was quickly restricted for national elections by property and literacy requirements (at first piecemeal and then across the board in 1886) and remained so until the López reforms of the 1930s, there was always an "active political atmosphere."[99] Indeed, elections and popular participation were about more than voting (or voters); they were social events. But most important of all, popular electoral participation for offices on the local and departmental levels remained a significant constant in the Colombian experience. And in practice, restrictions on voting in national elections were disregarded or dropped over time (especially as income requirements became engulfed by inflation).[100] Finally, the oligarquía itself opened the door during the Conservative Hegemony to more popular participation by giving the vote to the Conservative pueblo. In many cases "persons who had neither the property or the literacy qualifications required by law were permitted and encouraged to vote," that is, if they happened to be members of the Conservative party. These were "interesting instances of de facto widening of the suffrage by the Conservatives who in 1886 had restricted it."[101] One should also keep in mind that the same process was undoubtedly in play in areas under Liberal control.

And while participation within patron-client networks predominated among the scattered residents of rural Colombia, the system did not translate smoothly to the urban setting, where currents of left liberalism in the 1930s and 1940s offered dramatic popular challenges to the mechanisms of gamonalismo. Even in nineteenth-century Brazil, a system known for its elite control and patronage networks, voters in the cities were hard to control.[102] What is more, cities in Colombia had always been vital to Liberal politics. Even in very Catholic and Conservative places, such as Chiquinquirá, Liberals in 1922 could count on significant support since liberalism tended to be strong in urban areas ranging from small industrial towns to cities.[103] This trend can be dated to at least the artisan's sociedades democráticas in the 1840s and 1850s, which in good part explain the phenomenon. Artisans, left liberalism, and towns often went together.

In cities, people who had relatively more freedom looked upon the buying and selling of votes as undemocratic. In 1945 a commentator in Sincelejo called boss control of local politics the "gangrene of the *patria*." Though he noted that an "old patriot of the generation now passing" might have believed caciquismo or gamonalismo to work "in the name of peace, social tranquility, and the benefit of all," the writer maintained that caciques more often sacrificed "peace, progress, and dignity . . . for personal profit." There was not, he argued, a town in the entire country where a gamonal did not "impose his own caprices in the interests of himself, his family, or his intimate friends." The cacique "rules in his town or *municipio*" through intrigue and opportunistic games, playing governors, ministers, and even presidents one against the other. The national administration could aspire with "all the best intentions" to create a government "of all and for all through equality and justice, founded on reason." But the caciques who moved "in the shadows" of government thought "in a different way." They controlled the mechanisms of local government and oversaw the flow of public money. The municipal treasury, the property of the "industrious citizenry," became a captive to his personal "whim" as he defrauded the "popular masses." Colombia had always rejected dictators yet lived "under the despotic heel of nepotistic *caciquismo*." Their "electoral code," an "honor to democracy," remained a useless scrap of paper. The problem was not with the constitution but with their hearts. He called for the true rule of law, insisting that Colombians must smite "the serpent of *caciquismo*."[104]

As the observer in Sincelejo pointed out, along with the patron-client relationship (the social and economic foundation of the system), control of the electoral mechanisms was the political cornerstone of gamonal power. Colombians used the word "machine" to refer specifically to gamonal manipulation of the electoral system. It was not a political machine in the same sense as that of Boss Tweed and the Sachems of Tammany Hall. They too were skillful at electoral manipulation, but their "machine" rested more on amounts of city patronage and largess that simply were not available to any *patrón* (rural or urban) in Colombia in the 1930s and 1940s. (Contracts for paving streets could not be given away if most streets were unpaved.) Gamonal control of elections was a problem well known to left Liberals. In 1932 a "leftist" in Neiva made the distinction between legitimate "política" and "la politiquería" (political intrigue) of the oligarchic machines.[105] The same year a member of the "leftist youth" of Magdalena argued that all political action was "useless" without positions on the departmental electoral boards, given the time-honored "corrupt practice of 'he who counts the votes elects,'" which was the basic weapon in the hands of the old Liberal political bosses. Though it was undeniable that at the moment left Liberals "had the support of the masses," this in itself was of little value "without ways to defend electoral rights from the corruption" of those who still directed Liberal politics there "with the collaboration of prestigious elements in Bogotá." Addressing Gaitán frankly, he argued that "if you seriously want the left to take official roles and assume true legal capacities within the country's political realm," it would be necessary to appoint "one of our own" to the electoral board of Magdalena.[106]

There is no doubt that "control of electoral boards was inextricably linked to the question of fraud." Sometimes "outright fraud" was employed, such as the "crude adulteration of the ballot," and other times "more subtle" methods served better, "for example, controlling access to the franchise by drawing up a new registrar before each election."[107] Ortiz Sarmiento identified "five principal forms of fraud" that were frequently employed during the first half of the twentieth century. These included false and multiple cédulas (the principal charge leveled by Conservatives against the Liberal Republic), confiscation of cédulas, obstruction by one party or the other of election verification, theft of ballot boxes, and alteration of election results.[108]

It should be noted, as Eduardo Posada-Carbó has rightly argued, that the assumption that the "party in power ... always carries the election" is "misleading," given the electoral successes of dissident movements (both inside and out of the ruling party). From the point of view of election results, "the traditional bipartisan dichotomy needs to give way to a more complex picture." He argued for "a more competitive scenario in Colombian electoral politics" during the Conservative Hegemony, and points to Liberal successes in the 1920s. The same was certainly true later. Posada-Carbó also noted conflicts between governors and electoral boards. And there was play in the system. "Not all elections were fraudulent, and the degree of electoral corruption varied from constituency to constituency."[109] Fraud was most often employed "in the form of inflated numbers" of votes "in what were considered the 'governmental' departments, those in which government influence was easiest to exercise."[110]

In the 1940s, however, the power of the gamonal and the political machine was still a force to reckon with, as the case of Antioquia would demonstrate. (By the official tally, Gaitán received an unbelievably low 5 percent for the department as a whole on May 5, 1946.)[111] In early 1946 Froilán Montoya Mazo, a político in Medellín, wrote a remarkable series of letters to Gaitán detailing the "dark machinations" of the system and telling of the obstacles "that the oligarchs" were placing in the path of his candidacy. For over a year he had been a member of the local election board in Medellín, but as soon as he started to support the principles that Gaitán represented "and went to the street to fight for them," the board began a campaign against him "the likes of which had not been seen since the days of the inquisition." And despite "clear" rules pertaining to the tenure of election officials, they had succeeded in removing him from the body.[112] He wrote of methods of fraud that he had often witnessed (and very possibly participated in). He argued that it was "the case that a high percentage of the population" supported Gaitán and his "battle for democracy," but it was also the case that the oligarquías, upon realizing that they could not "counteract this avalanche of people, . . . set their hand to manipulating the electoral machinery as their only hope of victory." He noted the truth of the aphorism (as had the leftist youth in 1932), "He who counts elects." Most "electoral organisms" were skilled "at the art of bamboozling" the electorate, and he was intent on demonstrating "how this heavy machine crushes all good intentions and spontaneity out of the will of the citizenry."

Montoya Mazo began with the "cacique político," a category he defined as "he who rules." Generally in small towns this "fatidic personage" sat on the local electoral board, almost always its president, but without fail a principal member." He reminded Gaitán that in such towns it was "easy to know the political persuasion of a citizen" and therefore not difficult to manipulate the makeup of the board or the rolls themselves. This was the key at the local level, and he presented a hypothetical example:

> Say I am a citizen of a *municipio* and known for my adherence to cause B, which goes against the dominant local political interests. Since the local board is comprised in its majority of current A . . . they register me in the electoral roll with my last names inverted:

> Froilán Mazo Montoya. . . . So when I go to vote with my correct registration as Froilán Montoya Mazo, the official in charge of course rejects me since there is an obvious problem. When I demand recourse, he sends me to an election official, who tells me to wait for the president of the board who is the only one who can change it. . . . Thus (de Herodes a Pilatos), the poor *campesino* abandons his attempt to vote.

Then he turned to issuance of new cédulas, which merited special attention because every year a considerable number of individuals reached the legal voting age. He continued to speak to the case of the small town, since "in cities the obstacles are relatively easier to overcome," and presented another example:

> I am a citizen of municipio A and I have just reached my twenty-first birthday. Taking the necessary photos I go in search of my document of citizenship *(cédula)*. The mayor, whose job it is to provide me with this essential document, charges me one peso. As a consequence, if I have the money, I receive my cédula, if not I can not exercise my rights as a citizen. Yet, if I am a friend of the mayor or in his party, I get the document with no further ado.

Speaking of local municipal election boards, Montoya Mazo dispensed with the hypothetical examples and turned to "concrete cases." In Antioquia "the electoral machinery" exhibited the most technically impressive forms of fraud. The Concejo Electoral was made up for the most part of Turbayistas who therefore had great influence over the naming of local boards. Consequently, in the cases of Andes, Venecia, Maceo, Tiriribí, and Medellín itself, the Gaitanistas had very significant public support but no access to the ballot box. Montoya Mazo also told of a conversation he had had with a "jefe manzanillo" ("manzanillo," as noted earlier, is slang for corruption and corrupt politicians) about the current political predicament, during which he mentioned the additional popular support that Gaitán picked up each day and "the fervor and reverence that the pueblo showed for his name." The cacique answered with a flippant and cynical attitude. "I like Gaitán and his politics," he claimed, "and what you say is clearly the reality of the situation. However, I am not a Gaitanista because in truth he may carry public opinion but he does not have the electoral machine on his side, and as you know, that counts for much." And finally Montoya Mazo mentioned other, more aggressive, dirty political tricks such as robbing the ballot boxes, as recently had occurred in Antioquia, where he claimed that government officials had spirited them away to be unlocked with master keys or pried open.[113]

In a typical example of moral indignation at gamonal practice, a costeño politician complained to Gaitán in 1937 about "scandalous" election fraud in Atlántico. The boss, who he claimed was the "absolute owner of electoral power" in his district, disregarded alternative Liberal voices there. In spite of their vigilance, many votes failed to materialize and several ballot boxes were never even opened. Normally, the results were known on the same election Sunday, but in this case, days later, the outcome was still a mystery because the gamonal could not make up his mind about what result he wanted.[114] In San Bernardo, Tolima, seven years later a Gaitanista complained that the pueblo was "enslaved" and "subdued by false promises" by the cacique, who led them "blindly" to the voting box. The local cacique, Antonio Vargas, attempted to hold the campesinos there in "feudal domination." His weapons were "the bribe, the threat, the insult, slander, and lies."[115]

The effects of fraud and gamonal manipulation were clear. The pueblo was, in the eyes of left Liberals, simply misled, or pushed into abstention. A lawyer from Popayán in 1931 complained that demands for real democracy could be thwarted by the old Liberal networks. He lamented that in Popayán "it is a *pueblo* sick with *caudillismo*" (the terms *caudillo* and *gamonal* were sometimes interchanged), which continued to follow "the *caudillo* that exploits them" and was fed by promises that would never be fulfilled. A recent election resulted in "the triumph of the *caudillo* and defeat of the leftist youth and the conscious workers."[116] In 1944 the spirit of liberalism in Tumaco was "discouraged." Zest for the fight was "almost extinguished." There "great and negligible" observers alike were convinced that elections were not determined by "flesh and blood voters but rather the powerful electoral machine" whose "political mechanisms" Gaitán had analyzed and denounced. The people in the political establishment were all resigned that the candidate eventually backed by *El Tiempo* would be the official Liberal candidate, regardless of their lack of enthusiasm. True, the "gentes sencillas" who had been profoundly devoted to López were now "unanimously" convinced that the "man of the hour" was Gaitán. Few observers doubted that he would be supported by the "Liberal masses of Tumaco and even by the Conservatives." The "humble people" of Tumaco would give their votes to Gaitán, though it seemed probable that "the owners of the electoral machine would change them."[117] In 1947 Samuel Guerrero claimed that in the cities of Bolívar, the old boy network of manipulation of "collective sentiments" had brought on the abstention of nearly twenty thousand Liberals. "No one," he asserted, "can keep the *pueblo* from expressing its discontent" in this manner. Abstention in Bolívar was not, in his opinion, the simple result of Conservative persecution.[118]

And when their will was defied, gamonales used the institutional and economic powers at their disposal to coerce compliance. Also, in good Colombian political tradition, they employed violence. In Corozal, Bolívar, for example, two Gaitanista telegraph operators spoke of the local Liberal bosses' threats to punish their "insolence" in questioning the leadership's claim to sole representation of Liberal interests. The Liberal leaders waged a campaign of persecution against the fifteen Gaitanistas in their twenty-one-employee office. As government employees they felt especially vulnerable to such dangers, including "the specter of hunger" stalking their homes, but they intended to support Gaitán nonetheless.[119] In Ciénaga, election authorities withheld the cédulas of various Gaitanistas as the presidential election approached.[120] This tactic was employed especially against the more "humble citizens."[121] Samuel Guerrero experienced both the carrot and the stick from Turbayistas in Atlántico and Bolívar. First his employer raised his salary, trying to get him to break with Gaitanismo, saying "decent people" were Turbayistas. His employers made it clear that they did not want a "Gaitanista manager." Later they wanted him to sign a contract renouncing political activity.[122] And in Coromoro, Santander, Gaitanistas were threatened with "rocks, bullets, and the garrote."[123]

Colombia's system of oligarchic political control had evolved during the partisan conflicts of the nineteenth century, and it retained considerable force in the 1940s. Yet it had never been all powerful. At its side strains of popular political mobilization had developed that always resisted elite hegemony, often with considerable success. In the urban settings of 1946, the Gaitanistas would build on these traditions of popular struggle and defy the gamonales.

Problems and Practices of Mobilization

Despite the insidious power of Colombia's oligarchic political structure, and despite serious internal weaknesses inherent to the popular movement that would become all too apparent, the Gaitanistas utilized the long-standing democratic elements of Colombian politics, exploited gaps in the system, and directly challenged the political elites' hold on power. The scale of Gaitanista mobilization was new in Colombian history and brought many new elements into play. As a national movement, it was the first to move significantly beyond the Liberal and Conservative organizations. Gaitanismo flourished in all of Colombia's major cities and shifted the political focus away from the capital city. Bogotá and its immediate hinterland have received the lion's share of attention from historians concerned with Gaitanismo. Given Gaitán's influence there, such a focus is understandable. Yet his movement exerted profound influence on and found considerable support in other regions. Inhabitants of the Atlantic coast, as well as people in other parts of "the provinces," were abundantly aware of typical Bogotano attitudes concerning their "forgotten regions."[124] Such regions, however, had not been forgotten by Gaitán. Their political value in terms of the votes their growing urban areas could provide made them worthy of his continuous attention. Gaitán received constant reminders that in these cities (and a not insignificant number of smaller towns) he was the man the multitudes acclaimed as the future president of the nation.[125]

Populist movements have often been portrayed as controlled mobilizations. Stirred by charismatic caudillos and directed by coercive políticos, historians have repeatedly argued, such movements were exercises in manipulation and co-optation of the working classes. Not unlike Lopismo in the 1930s, mobilization under Gaitanismo undeniably embodied such top-down and manipulative features. And even when they were personally true to Gaitanismo's more radical currents, some Gaitanista leaders lacked faith in the degree of popular commitment and expressed skepticism over the true strength of the popular movement.[126]

Yet Gaitanismo provided ample evidence of autonomous popular mobilization. Members of the Gaitanista Workers' Front in Atlántico counted 1,200 members and claimed to be growing every day. They traveled throughout the entire department and organized Gaitanista committees in every municipio.[127] An adherent in Barranquilla declared that "the working masses" had awakened from the "lethargy" that the governing elite had so long promoted.[128] Many workers were anything but acquiescent. In Barranquilla, one group of left Liberals affirmed that united with Gaitán, "neither the false apostles of democracy . . . nor their promises designed to maintain the status quo" could "tear the banner of liberalism" from their hands.[129] In Bucaramanga Gaitán was called "the candidate of popular deep-rootedness."[130] In fact, many Gaitanistas believed, as a local organizer in Cartagena insisted, that the moral restoration had to "begin at the bottom and go to the top."[131] One youth league, "typical of the organizations" supporting Gaitán's candidacy, stressed the importance of remaining somewhat apart from other groups in the movement to demonstrate their ability to sustain themselves.[132] And another supporter reminded the caudillo that the people of his poor neighborhood had supported Gaitanismo with little help from the Casa Liberal Gaitanista in Barranquilla.[133]

This was not a controlled mobilization. Gaitán's campaign embodied the left-Liberal mutiny against the Liberal status quo, and represented an inversion of the old political order, "imposing," as one Gaitanista put it in 1945, "the país nacional over the país político."[134] A Gaitanista labor leader noted disrespect for the official Liberal candidate in Antioquia, where workers called Turbayismo "Turmayismo" in their "rude language" (the word *turma* in Spanish refers to the testicle of a man or an animal).[135] Speaking of the "Popular Convention" of September 1945, students in Cartagena predicted that it would be "the best demonstration to the *oligarquía*" that the pueblo would "soon commence its rule."[136] Gaitanistas played up the "panic" felt by the official Liberal leadership. Gaitán's paper, *Jornada,* for instance, emphasized the power of the pueblo "to intervene for its own sake, without asking anyone's permission." The people were hungry and sick, victims of speculation, and exploited by the politicians, but in the streets, things were changing and Gaitán was the symbol of this "revolution."[137] Gaitanismo, while ignored or attacked in the elite Liberal press, loomed as a continuous preoccupation for the Liberal leaders. It offered new direction and leadership to the disoriented Liberal masses.[138] In March of 1946 a delegation from the Liberal Directorate arrived in Usiacurí, a small town in Atlántico, and encountered the majority of its inhabitants in the central plaza. The throng would not let them speak, shouting "we already know what you came to tell us, we know it by heart. . . . We are with Gaitán, *a la carga.*"[139] And in El Carmen, Norte de Santander, Gaitanistas enjoyed an "absolute majority" while the Turbayistas only received a third of their votes. This was despite an all-out offensive by the entire membership of the *Jurado Electoral* and the public-sector employees they controlled.[140]

Left Liberals understood the relative strengths and weaknesses of the Gaitanista pueblo and political establishment. In Ibagué a Gaitanista believed he could say "without exaggeration" that Turbayismo in Tolima had "a directory of four oligarchs, but no sector of the population supported it." In contrast, Gaitanismo had broad support. This was the "political reality of the city and the department."[141] In Medellín Bernardo Angel asserted that Turbayismo in Antioquia would have "to depend completely on fraud to win." It did not have the support of the masses, he claimed, "and everyone" knew it.[142] López and the Liberal leaders repeated the same old tired platitudes while ignoring the crisis of liberalism. His "light" represented nothing more than "the pathetic will-o'-the-wisp, generally indicative of the subterranean presence of decomposing corpses." Gaitán, in contrast, was ready for battle; with nerve and vitality he stood at the forefront of the struggle for Colombia's future. He believed that politics should be for the people.[143] Gaitán, who commanded the Liberal multitudes, would revive optimism with his return to the electoral battle.[144] Gaitán's qualities and accomplishments aside, the "secret of his triumph" would reside in his making "good use of the moment."[145]

The problems Gaitanismo faced had not so much to do with how to draw popular support as what to do with it. Even with little or no financial foundation, Gaitanistas were very often the dominant political entity in a neighborhood, municipio, or region. Richard Sharpless noted that some provincial Gaitanistas "even suggested that official liberalism was so badly discredited and there was so much grassroots support for Gaitán that a local organization was really not necessary."[146] Yet any mobilization, no matter how popular in nature, must have leadership and direction. Analyzing Gaitanismo, "an example of participant democracy," from a tactical perspective, later apologists for the movement focused on Gaitán's mechanisms of central administration. They characterized Gaitán's tactical expertise as an aptitude for turning the Liberal-Conservative establishment's own structures toward more revolutionary paths, the ability to seize the initiative, and the practice of anchoring his organization's politics firmly in the popular base.[147] The problem for the Gaitanista leadership, therefore, was directing the political struggle while retaining the movement's "popular" personality.

As Orlando Fals Borda noted, the caudillo acted as a unifying agent in national politics, and that was certainly Gaitán's function on the Liberal left.[148] For the purposes of day-to-day political organization, Gaitán's role remained an unresolved problem. Gaitán's presence seemed to be an all too vital ingredient. A Gaitanista in Barranquilla lamented that he had been completely deceived regarding the capacity for rebellion among the fickle pueblo. They "needed the continual spur from [Gaitán's] voice to overcome their social inertia," he claimed.[149] And in Bolívar, Gaitán's appearance was needed to awaken the Liberal mística.[150] Juan Manuel Valdelamar reported that "the Gaitanista masses frequently asked" if Gaitán would head the list of representatives for Bolívar.[151] Throughout Magdalena various municipalities clamored for a visit from the candidate.[152] Bucaramanga supporters admitted that the movement there was unorganized. They saw support but warned that the campaign would founder if Gaitán did not show up there.[153] Liberals in Líbano urged Gaitán to visit.[154]

Such reliance on Gaitán emboldened Liberals identified with the Liberal establishment of the López years to deny Gaitanismo's mass support (in solidly Gaitanista Atlántico of all places). Editors of *El Nacional* in Barranquilla claimed in June 1945 that it had "neither masses nor chieftains."[155] This opinion seemed to be supported by the elections for the municipal concejo in October of that year. The U.S. consul in Barranquilla, Leonard Dawson, noted that the Gaitanistas "made a very much smaller showing than was expected," taking only three seats to the official Liberals' nine, and scarcely outdoing the Conservatives with two seats and the Communists' one.[156] Such problems often surfaced when Gaitán himself was not directly involved. Dawson also pointed out that when Gaitán appeared in person to give a speech, the crowds "far outnumbered those of any other presidential candidate, when they held similar meetings."[157] As was apparent after Gaitán's assassination, Gaitanismo never had the chance to outgrow its dependence on him as a focal point for the practice of political struggle.

Gaitán himself expressed the general need for leadership and his idea of its role within the movement. Ever the activist, he stressed the need to create the conditions for a successful mobilization. It was not conceivable, he argued, that "the masses would flock to our movement" if the leadership did not "create the proper climate through diffusion of our ideas and objectives."[158] Herbert Braun demonstrated how Gaitán accused Liberal leaders of not understanding the psychological needs of the pueblo, and the "irrational" motives "behind crowd behavior that he as a positivist did understand. The multitude, he informed them, had to be directed, implying that only someone like himself who was close to the *pueblo* could do so."[159] From Gaitán's personal perspective, seemingly, his leadership was the essential element.

Yet the Gaitanista leadership had to walk a fine line between the need to direct a unified political struggle from Bogotá and the importance of respecting the movement's popular personality as an autonomous political mobilization. The day-to-day management of the campaign fell to José María Córdoba, who diligently sent out instructions on how the faithful should go about mobilizing. Since many Gaitanista leaders were new to politics, little could be left to chance. Córdoba pointed out, for example, that it was "important to prepare the Gaitanista masses and to place determined and enthusiastic supporters throughout the crowd" at demonstrations. He stressed that Gaitanistas "should not let an opportunity pass to shout 'viva' for the candidate of the *pueblo*."[160] Gaitanistas were instructed to put up portraits of Gaitán and signs saying such things as "¡Viva Gaitán! Candidate of the *pueblo*"; "Battle has been engaged! The speculating plutocracy are united with the unscrupulous professional politicians against the *pueblo* and their leader Gaitán"; and "The *oligarquías* want to shut Gaitán out for being a son of the *pueblo*."[161]

This kind of close political management was crucial because many of the movement's activists often had more enthusiasm than practical experience in the nuts and bolts of political mobilization. In Tolima political novices flocked to the movement, where twelve members of the "socially humble class," who were new to the game of mobilization, put together a Gaitanista committee. They had never before directly participated in politics and were not sure of themselves since they did not claim to have the "intellectual preparation that would authorize [them] to make a political campaign." But motivated as they were by the "understanding of what Gaitán's candidacy truly represented for the *pueblo*," they attempted to carry out their humble labor on his behalf. They were poor, and had little time, but still were intent on urban and rural organizational work.[162] And a businessman with dealings in Barranquilla, Cartagena, and Santa Marta "frankly" admitted that he did not command any votes, never having dabbled in politics. But he sincerely believed that Gaitán was the only hope for the economic middle class.[163] Another man in Bolívar, "little versed in politics," had followed Gaitán's "socio-political trajectory" since the time of the bananeras. Though his support of López and Santos had somewhat concealed his sympathy for "revolutionary leftism," he now wholeheartedly supported the "savior of the working masses." He complained of the continuing old boy networking and undemocratic attempts to control the Liberal party by the establishment.[164]

Predictably, such inexperience in political matters led to a good bit of confusion. In Barranquilla a supporter told of "disorder and undiscipline" among the Gaitanista masses because educated voters avoided the polls and the more popular citizens sold their votes for alcohol.[165] While noting the general enthusiasm in Cartagena for the Gaitanista cause, Juan Manuel Valdelamar deplored the poor organization of committees in the "popular neighborhoods."[166] Indeed, far from being dominated from Bogotá, Gaitanistas often expressed frustration at the absence of leadership. One in Tolima was angry at the national organization and at *Jornada* for the "indifference" they had shown to the departmental directorates. They were the ones "fighting earnestly against the official machine, against the *señores oligarcas.*" The majority of their affiliates were "*campesinos* and *obreros*" and did not have the financial resources that the Turbayistas enjoyed.[167]

Gaitanista leaders, however, recognized the urgency of encouraging autonomous political action. Gaitán himself advocated popular activism. In the same letter in which he stressed the need for leadership, he also expressed a vision of autonomous popular mobilization: "We cannot be passengers in a tedious line waiting patiently in the hope that the train will arrive. We must rather be the engineers who confidently guide the train to its destination." The struggle was not simply a political campaign but rather something more profound, an attempt "to create within the *pueblo* a spirit aflame with its own nationality and capacity for progress, with its own works and culture . . . to create within the bosom of the masses the ambition to attempt great conquests and achieve transformations for the common good . . . to awaken a burning passion for ideas." The movement represented "not just one election but a drive to create a spirit of permanent battle."[168] José María Córdoba stressed the struggle at the grassroots level and argued that it was "not absolutely necessary that a committee be composed of distinguished figures." It could be made-up of "simple but enthusiastic workers. . . . We stress efficiency and activity in the struggle over social class."[169]

While the Gaitanistas received guidance, their local committees were of necessity the organizational foundation of the campaign. Gonzalo Sánchez has noted Gaitán's "predilection for 'movement' over 'party,'" manifested in his "preference for popular committees" over "an organizational scheme of directorates and cells." This attitude obviously reflected Gaitán's view of himself as the "sole interlocutor between the masses and the oligarchy, to be played in the setting of his choice, the public plaza."[170]

Yet this structure was as much a function of necessity as choice. In practice Gaitanista leaders in Bogotá had to rely on largely independent mobilization of the faithful throughout Colombia, with all of its shortcomings, because the leadership could offer little more than encouragement and advice. The success or failure of the Gaitanista movement on the local level depended on the efforts of the rank and file. Córdoba constantly reminded Gaitanistas that Gaitán was "a man of action and few [?] but sonorous words. We who follow can only but imitate him with work, work, work."[171] And such committees are, by their nature, more democratic and dynamic than centrally administered directorates, even if less cohesive and disciplined.[172] Throughout 1945 Córdoba reminded activists that it was "important to continue stimulating public opinion and organizing Gaitanista committees in neighborhoods, unions, cities, and departments."[173] Typically he would recommend that they "form a committee" to then pass on adhesiones from their city to be published in *Jornada*.[174] In creating these committees he counseled that all of its members should get together with as many of the Gaitanistas in the area as was possible, so its foundation would be a popular one. "The *oligarquía* designates the composition of its directing bodies from the capital, but we do it differently. We rely on popular plebiscites."[175]

Finally, political inexperience on the part of many Gaitanistas should not be overblown since the tradition of popular electoral mobilization played a central role. Under the Conservative Hegemony it was widely recognized that the key to success was "a good electoral organization." Speaking of the Liberal presidential victory in 1930, Eduardo Posada-Carbó maintained that far "from being a miracle, the mass mobilization . . . at the polls was rooted in a long-established electoral tradition, kept alive in spite of civil conflicts, official malpractice, party divisions, and calls for either insurrection or abstention."[176] This was something the Gaitanistas would prove.

Gaitanista mobilization was spread by dedicated and diligent work. In Pasto the Gaitanistas had installed their "Casa Gaitanista" in an "excellent and strategic place" on the main plaza. They met there, holding conferences and spreading the word, "in gratitude to the ex-Senator for Nariño."[177] In a short period in Ibagué left Liberals had witnessed Gaitanismo spread like an "outbreak of measles." They had gone from a lack of optimism to the assurance of local electoral victory, all based on the "unflagging" organizational work of neighborhood committees, which distributed flyers and proved the power of word-of-mouth promotion.[178] Eduardo Tribiño Sáenz was president of the Gaitanista Committee of San José and worked as an itinerant organizer in Caldas. In each town he "agitated, stimulated, organized committees, and reviewed the capable Liberal personnel there and sent their names to the National Directorate." He also spoke at rallies in the various town plazas. He was very much akin to a traveling evangelist, preaching at revivals and saving souls.[179]

All of this political activity was grounded in the Gaitanistas' recognition that the vote was the most important weapon against gamonalismo. Since the days of UNIR, Gaitán had been the focal point of calls for democratic reform. From his "place on the Liberal left," an adherent in 1934 sent Gaitán an endorsement for his campaign to "radically transform the politics and public administration of the country, which are so morally corrupted by ancestral defects." "Public opinion" would thank him for "bringing morality to our democratic customs" and for leading the fight to reorganize "anachronistic" municipal government throughout the nation.[180] Gaitanistas consequently displayed intense preoccupation with the cédula. In the 1930s, left Liberals at El Mitín often repeated filler such as, "The social work initiated by Liberalism in power can continue its triumphal march if all Liberals procure their cédula electoral."[181] By 1946, however, many in the countryside still lacked this all-important certificate. In the upper Sinú River valley of Bolívar, the huge majority of six thousand Liberals in five districts could not secure their cédulas, despite a sitting Liberal government. Therefore only six hundred voted in the May 1946 presidential election.[182] Speaking of "cedulación," Gaitanistas in Neiva complained of government foot-dragging. They asked the Liberal authorities to send the "foto-ceduladores" to all the places that had requested them (and even asked that they send them to places that had not yet made the request). But the government deferred the process indefinitely (Huila being a very Gaitanista place), claiming that there were insufficient materials.[183] Party leaders in 1947 stressed the need for a party census in each municipio, the need for assistance on the local level to provide the necessary pictures, and argued that the party should pay 80 percent of the costs in 1948.[184] Others stressed the vital importance to the movement of revising the electoral rolls. They had to "wipe from the lists minors and castigate people who had cédulas but had not specified their date and place of birth."[185] After the Conservative ascension to power, the problem became even more acute.[186]

Gaitanistas did not lack evidence that, in large parts of Colombia, the machine was what mattered. On the day after the election, Liberals in the municipio of Chinchiná claimed that they had had support for Gaitán throughout Caldas, but that Turbayista leaders (among whom were the governor and various mayors) labeled Gaitán a Conservative, and fought to the end. In their municipio a member of the election board, a Turbayista named Arturo Salazar Campuzano, reenacted "the miracle of the bread and wine" on election day.[187] He turned 500 votes into over 1,000, using the cédulas of 300 deceased citizens, with many of them returning from the dead to vote two and three times. (Partisan loyalty runs very deep in Colombia.) Also, many hydroelectric workers were intimidated for supporting Gaitán, and some were even fired. In the town of Palestina, the mayor declared Gaitanismo illegal, and threatened to jail anyone who continued to distribute Gaitanista literature.[188] In Huila, Gaitanistas making campaign swings by train were in "a little war of nerves" with the local Turbayistas that included even "false telegrams and derailments." Though they had "all the masses," the caciques, one of whom was the manager of the railroad, had all the money and leverage.[189] Taking on the Liberal establishment was a formidable task because the "forces of the *oligarquía,* rigidly disciplined and obedient," were ready to rally around "one of the clan" to assure the continuance of their power. Through the might of their capital and their monopoly of the elite press, they remained strong.[190]

It was clear, nevertheless, that popular support for Gaitán had created huge rifts in the old system, and these were often most apparent in city councils. In Sincelejo, the movement had the old political establishment "against the wall." The five *manzanillos* that comprised the majority of the concejo, for example, wanted to impose appointees "that the *pueblo* detested," but after a "demonstration that lasted a week" they were withdrawn.[191] For sure, gamonal control of concejos could be very difficult to shake. In Pasto Augusto Esparza G. claimed that the popular will toward Gaitán was generally favorable, though he confessed that mobilization was very weak. He, the mayor, had rebelled against the local jefe político and supported Gaitán. The rest of the political establishment (and especially the city council) was openly hostile. The big problem there was getting the word out. He was not able to publish in the local press and could not get financing for his own Gaitanista paper. And the local radio station supported Turbay.[192] Given gamonal control of the political machine, assessment of Gaitanista support using the vote in local elections can only be done with care (as the case of Barranquilla, mentioned above, made clear). Julio Ortega Amarís in Santa Marta, who believed that Gaitanista leaders should try to get the faithful to vote Gaitanista in concejo elections, made a telling observation when he recognized that the results should not be construed as an actual reflection of Gaitanista strength. More than in presidential elections, the contest betrayed the power of local influence, or "the interests of persons or families."[193] But in the end, the democratic nature of city councils made them more sensitive to popular pressure.

In Barranquilla, Cartagena, and Santa Marta, in Cali, and in Ibagué, the broad support Gaitán enjoyed caused a large portion of the official Liberal establishment to endorse his campaign. This shift in the Liberal party's orientation was obviously not the simple result of a leadership decision. By the mid 1940s, important Lopista Liberals on the coast (as in other Gaitanista regions) recognized that as a result of the Revolución en Marcha, the pueblo had come to expect an increasingly central role in Colombia's political life, and Gaitán represented this aspiration. By March 1946 Samuel Guerrero argued that, among Liberals, only the caciques were concerned with "Liberal union" while the pueblo just thought of Gaitán. He believed even many Conservative workers and peasants on the coast were disposed to vote for Gaitán in defiance of their leaders. Other Liberal leaders too had observed and interpreted the writing on the wall. Francisco de Paula Vargas prophesied to Guerrero that if liberalism did not get behind Gaitán in the election, it would fall.[194]

Francisco de Paula Vargas, generally known as Pacho Vargas, had been a popular Liberal leader in Bolívar since the early 1930s. A mulatto of left-Liberal affinity, *El Fígaro* derisively called him "the dark-skinned *caudillo* of the streets."[195] Early observers argued that he represented a progressive political tendency whose goal was modern democracy and the social good of the citizenry.[196] Appointed mayor of Cartagena in 1935, he declined the position to take his seat as one of Bolívar's senators. In 1935 his name resonated with many Liberals' desire for "true democracy."[197] When he took his seat again in 1937, supporters hailed him as "chief of the leftist current in Bolívar."[198] While some historians have implied that his support for Gaitán was mere opportunism, Vargas joined the Gaitanistas early in the campaign.[199] In Atlántico, José María Blanco Núñez followed the same pattern of backing Gaitán while other Liberal leaders condemned his campaign. Blanco Núñez was hardly a stranger to the Liberal establishment, having served as governor of Atlántico under López in 1935 and 1936, congressional representative, and supreme court justice. Seemingly the consummate insider, he nevertheless joined Gaitán's rebellion at the outset. Also aware of the writing on the wall, Blanco Núñez claimed (somewhat implausibly) that it was simply the case "that neither Gaitán nor I are part of the *oligarquía*."[200]

This success, however, led to a real danger: the encroachment of the país político on the popular movement. Though far from being a controlled mobilization, Gaitanismo did have to contend with manzanillo infiltration. Since they could not beat the movement back, portions of the political establishment attempted to neutralize it from within. This was, according to one Gaitanista, clearly the case in the struggle over the composition of election commissions in Huila. There the "formidable impetus of the movement" had been "chilled and stunned" by the naming of a slate that in its majority consisted of manzanillos. This was "a classic automatic sabotage" of popular democracy. They subverted the movement through the use of "continual delays, or as is rustically said here, 'jugando a la paritaria.'" The políticos believed that agreements between the establishment and the Gaitanistas would sap force from the movement and insure the "thunderous reappearance and complete predominance of the *país político.*" While Huila was "integrally Gaitanista" and "fundamentally partisan to and identified with Gaitán's cause," the delegation from Neiva to the national Gaitanista Directorate "in no way" represented the popular movement, nor for that matter did those from the rest of the department. He called for a new departmental directorate made up of real Gaitanistas.[201] Such splits within Gaitanismo would only increase after May 1946 as the movement had to face the problem of the "false Gaitanistas."

The Colombian political system was indeed dominated by a political oligarchy that skillfully employed the mechanism of gamonalismo to ensure its continued hegemony. Colombia also had, however, a long tradition of widespread popular participation in politics that the Gaitanistas expanded. Despite the unresolved questions regarding leadership, the problems generated by political inexperience, and the weaknesses of political organization, rank-and-file Gaitanistas mobilized the left-Liberal vote and created ruptures in the elite-dominated political system. The movement's more glaring weaknesses were to be found nearer the top.

The Case of Barranquilla

Gaitanista struggles on the Atlantic coast, especially in the city of Barranquilla, demonstrated the complexity of local politics as they alternately meshed with, and scraped against, national politics. In Barranquilla, epicenter of the river industry, Gaitán took a whopping 71.1 percent of the vote on May 5, 1946, his largest majority anywhere, including Bogotá.[202] Yet there, where the movement most clearly defeated the old Liberal establishment, Gaitanismo exhibited instructive dilemmas regarding leadership and the role that political professionals would play. The experience of Barranquilla, in fact, recapitulated the intra-Liberal political dynamic throughout Colombia. It demonstrated that beyond Gaitanismo's broad appeal lay the longer-term problems of Liberal reintegration, political infighting and opportunism, and the ambiguous role played by Gaitán.

The leaders of the Liberal machine could see the approaching storm of Gaitanismo, and many (rather vainly) attempted to defy it. One such leader in Atlántico provided an example of gamonal power and the massive resistance it encountered from Gaitanistas. Rafael Blanco de la Rosa, two-time governor of the department, headed governments that were, in the words of one Gaitanista, "of and for the plutocracy, examples of pure manipulation and deception of the *pueblo*." His administrations, the Gaitanistas argued, insured that representatives to the national Congress would be none other than his cronies and hacks.[203] A peculiar episode on the eve of the 1946 election illustrated the inner workings of this gamonal's network as it came into contact with more popular political currents. On April 23 Tomás Villanueva Ortega, a Barranquilla taxi driver and Gaitanista, picked up Roberto Manotas and another man named Herrera, both there from neighboring Usiacurí. They were in Barranquilla, Villanueva discovered, to attend a political meeting with Señor Rafael Blanco de la Rosa in his factory on 43rd Street. As they arrived, Villanueva recognized various delegations from the different municipalities of the department.[204] When Villanueva heard that they were discussing the presidential candidates, he got out of his cab and loitered between the gate and the door of the building where he could hear what was said.

When he got into position, Sr. Blanco de la Rosa had begun to speak. The gamonal urged the Liberal politicians, Villanueva later related to Gaitanista leaders, to withhold their support from Gaitán because he was an "irresponsible candidate" who only knew how "to insult men of politics in public." Blanco de la Rosa recommended that they "bring all the pressure" they could to bear "to insure the victory of the only legitimate candidate of the Liberal party, Dr. Turbay." Gaitán was unacceptable because he was "a candidate taken from the streets. It would be preferable to elect an onion before supporting Gaitán." This was at 10:25 A.M., as Villanueva knew "with precision," because he looked at his watch as Governor Alberto Pumarejo of Atlántico and Mayor Raúl Fuenmayor Arrazela of Barranquilla emerged from the door. Villanueva made this report to the Gaitanistas of Atlántico because of his concern for the "purity of the franchise."[205]

This episode was significant for several reasons. First, it illustrated the depth of an important gamonal network. Though no longer in an official position, Blanco de la Rosa had officials from all over the department, including the governor and the mayor of Barranquilla, at his beck and call. In 1946, it must be remembered, these were not elected offices but rather executive branch appointments. Many of these men had no popular followings of their own and depended upon such individuals as Blanco de la Rosa for their political careers. Second, while gamonales were accustomed to firm political control of their regions, they now encountered overt resistance "from the streets" in the form of popular support for Gaitanismo. Finally, it illuminated the high degree of political knowledge and sophistication Gaitán's pueblo possessed, and their understanding of the dangers to democracy presented by vote fraud (and other forms of manipulation).

Gaitanismo in Barranquilla made clear the disconnection between the mass support available on the Liberal left and the traditional practices of

Liberal politics. José María Blanco Núñez astutely identified the strengths and weaknesses of the movement and the presidential campaign there. On the one hand, Gaitán's movement "commanded the immense majority of Liberalism in the city, something like 80 percent, all fervently partisan" (his estimate may have been closer than the election demonstrated). On the other hand, the great majority of this support came from "popular elements, almost all of whom had very scant resources to draw upon, including those who made up the directorate" and were therefore at a considerable disadvantage.[206]

The case of Barranquilla also demonstrated the resilience of Colombia's political class and its ability to adapt to the popular threat. This was abundantly clear on the city council. Of course, some politicians were genuinely enthusiastic supporters of Gaitán. Saúl Charris de la Hoz was a Liberal who operated in the "dissident" Liberal tradition.[207] Charris was from a family with local political influence (and considerable land holdings) in Atlántico. He was elected to the concejo of Santo Tomás in 1937, based on family connections, and as such was part of the political oligarquía. But he maintained connections to the anti-López faction on the coast that saw itself as the anti-oligarchy faction because of its opposition to the "aristocratic" López appointee to the office of governor, Alberto Pumarejo. Charris soon withdrew and went to law school in Bogotá. After another stint on the Santo Tomás concejo in 1943 and an encouraging (if unsuccessful) run for the departmental assembly, Charris ran for the Barranquilla concejo as a Gaitanista in October of 1945, and won.[208] Charris de la Hoz, an advocate of "uncontaminated" or "true" liberalism, felt an ideological and "moral" affinity with Gaitán's campaign. He was drawn to its anti-oligarchic orientation, its exaltation of the popular, and its moderate tone of nationalism. Charris was also concerned about the flaws in the electoral system—the "central column of Democracy"—such as predetermined lists, the profusion of white rum, and the purchase of votes.[209]

As noted earlier, in October 1945 only three Gaitanistas were elected to the concejo (Miguel García Caratt, Elías Moisés, and Saúl Charris de la Hoz), and this was in large part due to the unwieldy number of Liberal lists, nineteen in all, as opposed to two Conservative lists and one Communist.[210] In November of 1945, the Gaitanista members of the concejo (pushed by Charris) twice unsuccessfully attempted to get the body to endorse Gaitán's campaign.[211] But by late March 1946 the hurricane of Gaitanismo was clearly bearing down on the city. On March 27 the more elite-dominated departmental assembly of Atlántico endorsed the official candidacy of Turbay. Days later, all twelve Liberal councilmen on the fifteen-member city council of Barranquilla declared in favor of Gaitán's candidacy as the "only one for the Liberal party." They were especially concerned about the dangers of dividing liberalism.[212] Now the other nine Liberal concejales—Néstor Carlos Consuegra, Agustín del Valle, Alfonso Hernández Barreto, Rafael U. Molinares, Honorio Alarcón, José A. Donado, Emilio Lébolo de la Espriella, Ernesto Salcedo, and Carlos Cervantes Núñez—had all discovered the virtues of Gaitanismo in Barranquilla.[213]

Yet such success also presented serious problems. Struggles on the local level for political mastery of Gaitanismo led to fierce infighting among regional politicians. In Neiva, for example, the task of organizing and carrying out "genuine and disinterested labor on behalf of the popular Liberal movement" was proving very difficult, "given mutual distrust and personal rivalries."[214] The Popular Gaitanista Assembly of Girardot called on the Liberal leadership at the local and national levels to put aside their "personal ambitions" and rally behind the "genuinely popular candidate."[215] These and other cases illustrated the problems involved in translating Gaitán's following into a useful political asset and deciding who would control his mística on the local level. There was also the vexing problem of determining what Gaitán's role should be. Some Gaitanistas wanted his direct intervention while others wanted him to stay clear. The practice of Gaitanista mobilization, therefore, proved messy and sometimes ugly as many Gaitanista leaders clamored for Gaitán's support or defied his authority to direct them.[216]

Far larger than most other towns, Barranquilla suffered numerous divisions among the various politicians and political bosses there, a growing number of whom wanted control of or access to the most powerful movement in the region. Throughout 1945, therefore, the quest for solidarity became an ever more elusive undertaking. One activist in Barranquilla spoke of the refusal of Señores González U. and Adriano Rangel "to come to an understanding." The same could be said of Señores Santander Leon y B. and Gerardo Certain. In Barranquilla they had "established a tower of Babel," and it was not possible to continue in such a state. The good of the movement, he argued, demanded harmony and the putting aside of personal animosities.[217] In response to such problems, Gaitán's lieutenants in Bogotá frantically tried to keep the peace. Referring to struggles involving Adriano Rangel, Gerardo Certain, and Elías Moisés, José María Córdoba cautioned in early 1945 that "it would be prudent to rally the forces and not disperse the adherents collaborating with our campaign."[218] Such wise counsel fell on increasingly deaf ears as Gaitanista políticos jockeyed for position within the movement.

Organizational efforts from the capital, consequently, solved little. Answering a letter from Gaitán to himself and Santander León y B., Gerardo Certain reported that commissions Gaitán had named in Barranquilla had not produced the desired results. They had not arrived at a definite plan of action, "given the diversity of opinions among the members."[219] Answering the same letter, Santander León y B. too complained that the commissions had "created a tower of Babel," that only Gaitán could put to rights, being "the father of the situation." Many people had worked and sacrificed for the movement but had been overlooked by Bogotá, "like tired and spent beasts of burden."[220] These letters demonstrated the tension between those Gaitanistas who believed Gaitán's personal intervention was needed and those who wanted him to keep his distance. The latter group came to be known in Barranquilla as the Gaitanista "dissidents." On January 23, 1946, Nestor Carlos Consuegra spoke on local radio arguing against Gaitán's participation in the creation of Gaitanista candidate lists, advocating instead a freer hand on the coast. He pushed a list headed at that time by Alonso Hernández Barreto while accusing Elías Moisés of treachery to the movement. The concerned follower who reported Consuegra's activities called on Gaitán to come to the coast and tell the pueblo who was in charge and show that Consuegra's group were not "dissidents" but rather "traitors."[221]

After the election, rivalry among Gaitanistas in Barranquilla heated up even more, and it became increasingly apparent that Gaitán was just one of several important players. A representative of Atlántico spoke of the rivalry between Nestor Consuegra and Elías Moisés and their respective minions. Their disagreements, which revolved in great part around the degree to which Gaitán should be involved on the local level, caused substantial discontent within the movement. He warned that the pueblo might react by abstaining from the polls, and that the oligarquía was ever ready to capitalize on the resultant anarchy within the ranks and "fish in the torrent for votes and lesser *caciques*."[222] A worker wrote to Gaitán to lament the "political chaos" among the leaders of Gaitanismo in Atlántico. Workers, the "genuine Gaitanistas," wanted nothing more than union at Gaitán's side. As their spokesman he pleaded with Gaitán to put the situation straight so their infighting would cause no more "decay in the mystical fervor the masses felt for Gaitanismo."[223] Elías Moisés complained to Gaitán that in Atlántico there were entirely too many people who wanted the senator and representative spots, while "nearly everyone" wanted to head a list. After discussing the rival lists of would-be senators and representatives, he pointed out that without unity, the Gaitanista cause would lose votes. Moisés asked Gaitán to personally intervene to weed out weak Gaitanista candidates, namely the Consuegra ticket.[224] Gaitán answered with his increasingly common response to such pleas, saying that "with respect to elections to representative bodies, it is the place of the *pueblo* to indicate the persons who it deems fit . . . to represent it."[225]

This rivalry illustrated the diversity and independence of Gaitanismo, and the profusion of problems Gaitán would not and could not personally smooth over. By February 1947 the American consulate in Barranquilla identified a three-way power struggle for control of the Liberal party in Atlántico. The old-line Liberals were headed by Edgardo Manotas Wilches, with backing from the former governor Alberto Pumarejo, then a senator. The Gaitanistas were led by Nestor Carlos Consuegra, who as a city councilman "presented plans for the city of Barranquilla to take over the Empresas Públicas Municipales, as well as the American-owned electric light and telephone companies." A third group was a largely Gaitanista loose-cannon faction headed by Claudio Martín Blanco, the brother-in-law of the Gaitanista governor of Atlántico, Blanco Núñez.[226] After Gaitán visited Barranquilla that month to announce his desire to run as a congressional deputy for Atlántico, a clear breach ensued between Nestor Carlos Consuegra and Elías Moisés, though "the actual difference of opinion between these two men" was not known to the consulate.[227] By March the contest for voters in the upcoming elections had boiled down to an encounter between three coherent factions. Alberto Pumarejo ran for senator and had the support of Barranquilla's main paper, *El Heraldo*, with the support of roughly thirteen thousand voters. The "official Gaitanistas," led by Claudio Martín Blanco for senator, Elías Moisés for representative, and Gaitán himself for deputy, reportedly counted on ten thousand votes. The "dissident Gaitanistas" around Nestor Carlos Consuegra commanded seven thousand votes.[228]

The case of Barranquilla revealed the untidiness of democracy. Most Gaitanistas on the coast, however, probably would have argued that such confusion was a necessary evil. An observer in Barranquilla noted that "undoubtedly the clash of personalities and personal agendas" manifested itself in Barranquilla "in crude and intolerable ways." But on second thought, he recognized that at the moment the remedy perhaps would have been "worse than the affliction." He went on to speak of Liberal infighting and the resultant thirty Liberal electoral lists for the city council elections.[229] Many Gaitanistas continued to believe that despite the confusion within the movement, the best insurance against the evils of the oligarquía was getting the entire pueblo involved in the selection process. Anything else would allow the continued betrayal of their interests.[230] As Gaitanismo opened up the political system, Gaitán became just one of many different actors.

In June 1946 "a Liberal youth interested in the union of the party" offered his ideas on the meaning of liberalism and caudillismo. "Liberalism, by temperament and in its essence" was a party of "rebellion." "A single *caudillo* can win laurels" but his departure can be "disastrous." Throughout Colombian history "many different political collectives in our country have had *caudillos*," and this has been the fundamental factor in Colombia's "historical political development." This has meant "great triumphs but no less stupendous failures, a consequence of the logic of the fall of a great leader." This can lead to anarchy. No less dangerous is the tendency for a caudillo's "unlimited aspirations" to corrupt a party.[231] As he indicated, Gaitanistas were aware of the political pitfalls of reliance on Gaitán, but they were not sure what to do about it. Despite this central weakness, however, in the 1940s the Gaitanistas built on the left-Liberal tradition of popular political mobilization and dramatically challenged the oligarquía's system of boss political control, especially in cities and larger towns. With the constitutional reforms of the 1930s, especially the broadening of the franchise, popular elements came to the fore. In Gaitán's time there had been no complete break with the past. Machine politics had never been practiced in terms of issues and continued to function throughout Colombia, as it always had, with its primary goal focused on winning elections (by whatever means) and dividing the spoils. Left Liberals did not end gamonalismo, nor did they completely avoid employing patron-client relations themselves. But whereas machines only inadvertently acted as agents of social welfare, providing no vision of a new society, the Gaitanistas had very definite ideas. Given the prevalence of regionalism in Colombia, Gaitán's presence as the personalistic "caudillo" was still necessary to transcend the hold of local politics and unite the Liberal left. Yet the Gaitanistas were learning to turn the old system to their own ends. Their resistance to gamonalismo's basic practice in Colombia's cities caused political leaders to use their power in more self-conscious ways, while generally weakening the entire system of machine politics. The final tally in the 1946 election was undoubtedly low due to various forms of elite manipulation and fraud. Yet even with the game rigged against them, the vitality of the Gaitanistas' popular mobilization shone through.

7

Collective Vibrations

The Ideologies of Gaitanismo

The allure of Gaitanismo sometimes seemed otherworldly. Juan Manuel Valdelamar remarked that in Bolívar, "All the *campesinos* have a portrait of Gaitán in their homes, and daily they tend it with a *mística* that approaches adoration."[1] Nonetheless, the quasi-religious and mystical reverence Gaitanistas professed for their caudillo found its origins in the gritty substance of Colombian social reality. New social conditions within Colombia during the 1930s and 1940s created ideological niches for the germination of alternative ideas (some having been planted long before) about the economic and political relations of Colombian society. Gaitanista ideology, therefore, sprang from the Gaitanistas' collective understanding of the world and from their shared notions of how it ought to be. It constituted a system of belief and community of discourse that oriented Gaitanista social and political action. These ideas reflected popular understanding as well as ideological connections to more well-heeled intellectual traditions. And in the context of the disillusion, frustration, and political chaos of the mid-1940s, the Gaitanistas understood the radical nature of their popular mobilization.[2]

Much like the nature of its social composition, however, Gaitanismo's ideological character is still a matter of dispute. Gaitán's detractors on the left have long claimed that the movement he came to lead merely channeled discontent through the existing political establishment, blunting its impact. Students of Colombia rightly emphasize the persistent influence of the Liberal and Conservative parties as one of its most unique characteristics. Marx characterized such influence as the tyranny of the "prejudices" or "fixed ideas" of the past. In Colombia continued popular attachment to and hegemonic submersion within the traditional parties, so the argument goes, has prevented the oppressed of society from recognizing their collective and mutual interests and, consequently, from creating more appropriate political arrangements. As with all populist movements, Gaitanismo exhibited elements of both continued elite dominance and of popular resistance.

Studies grounded in this assumption, however, often over-accentuate the enduring sway of the Liberal and Conservative parties, while at the same time slighting their more progressive and radical elements. Helio-doro Cogua Pulido, a lifelong Gaitanista, claimed that with Gaitán's appearance, many people began to emerge from their "feudal slumber."[3] Allegiance to the ancestral parties abated perceptibly in many instances as Gaitanismo slipped from the recognized track of Colombian history. Of course the shift was not complete, demonstrating that Gaitanista intimacy with liberalism could be a source of weakness as well as strength. For many Gaitanistas, "godo," the derogatory nickname Liberals gave to Conservatives, equaled "oligarch."[4] Gaitanismo encompassed a bewilder-ingly complex and, perhaps, contradictory mixture of ideas, suggestions, and demands. Such ambivalence manifested itself in the confusion many intellectuals felt over the true ideological nature of the movement. Yet left-Liberal Gaitanismo effectively retooled the nature of the Liberal/Conservative dichotomy for many Colombians. The contest was becoming one between the pueblo and the oligarquía, as argued earlier, with serious overtones of class struggle. The Gaitanistas' dichotomy demonstrated the possibility of an alternative political system based on class interests rather than political labels.

Gaitán's influence has long been attributed to charisma, and his ability to stir emotions with fiery oratory. Even today it is difficult to listen to recordings of his speeches and not feel his magnetism.[5] Students of Gaitan-ista ideology have also overwhelmingly looked to Gaitán as the source of his movement's ideas. Yet the significance of "the moral and democratic restoration" rested upon more than Gaitán's personal outlook or his art-fully delivered and emotionally charged words. Ultimately, Gaitanismo's ideological outlook rested on a long-established intellectual tradition and matured in an interactive process between leader and masses, which played itself out in Colombia's mass media and in the movement's corre-spondence.[6]

This chapter will show that Gaitanismo, rooted in the left-Liberal tra-dition and cultivated in the heated milieu of social confrontation during the 1920s and 1930s, blossomed into an ongoing and broad-based ideo-logical crusade against the hegemonic structures of power within Colom-bian society, before and after the election of 1946. Far from being a collec-tion of ideas handed down by the intellectual strata of the movement,

Gaitanista ideology reflected popularly held notions that Gaitán identified, articulated, and eventually came to symbolize. Gaitanismo demonstrated the relationship between people in the streets advocating simple yet forceful ideas, who opened space for the intellectuals and insiders who wrote their manifestos. Colombians in the 1940s exhibited conspicuous popular agitation for increased democratic rights and more popularly controlled institutions. This process, in turn, was closely connected to widespread demands for social and economic justice. The ideas of democracy and social justice were intimately related in the minds of the rank-and-file Gaitanistas. Gaitanista morality, consequently, derived its power from the social and economic content of Gaitanista ideology.

This chapter also attempts to resurrect the meanings of "democracy" and "justice," "socialism" and "morality," pueblo and oligarquía, and in the process show how they were understood and used by the Gaitanistas in focusing their movement. Now these words seem to have lost much of their original power since repetition and disillusion have taken their toll. These terms, nevertheless, had radical meaning for Gaitán's followers. The desire to fight, as it was commonly put, for "the well-being of the less favored classes of society" seemed more tangible to the Gaitanistas than vague references to class struggle and revolution.[7] Understood in this light, the popular ideology of Gaitanismo helps restore the movement's original status as a radical popular mobilization.

Echoes of Left Liberalism

By 1944 it was clear that Gaitanismo represented a pronounced intellectual tradition in Colombia that may be referred to as a homegrown left. This tradition largely explained the enduring strength of the official Liberal party, as well as Gaitán's challenge to it. Colombia was obviously not isolated from the currents of mobilization manifest in Latin America in the 1930s and 1940s, but the peculiarities of its history assured that the form Gaitanista mobilization took would be idiosyncratically Colombian.

The enduring influence of the Liberal party was indeed strong. It was not uncommon for a Gaitanista to have been a left Liberal from birth. Heliodoro Cogua Pulido's father was a "radical Liberal" and fought in the Liberal guerrilla army led by Generals Rafael Uribe Uribe and Benjamín Herrera for Liberal "principles and ideas." Ofelia Uribe de Acosta's parents "were Liberals" while she herself was "a leftist radical Liberal." One Gaitanista in Magdalena "had struggled since childhood at the side of his father" for Liberal ideals. And another in Barranquilla received her Liberal ideas "in the cradle," since her entire family was, not surprisingly, Liberal.[8]

And as discussed at the beginning of this study, Gaitán and the Liberal left traced their lineage through the writings of Rafael Uribe Uribe, who was the prism through which nineteenth-century liberalism refracted into Gaitanismo. "Uribe's ideals," as the ideological bases of liberalism were often called, proved to be an ambiguous heritage, but more radical than some students have admitted. As in the 1920s and 1930s, many who called Gaitán the leader of the Colombian left saw him as a reviver of the glorious days of Uribe Uribe and Herrera.[9] Uribe, and perhaps to a lesser extent Herrera, were not only remembered as great Liberals but also as defenders of the working class. In 1947 the Liberal National Directorate honored Uribe Uribe as "the precursor of the new currents of economic democracy within Liberalism."[10]

Uribe Uribe and Herrera were continually remembered in the left-Liberal press. Throughout August 1939, for example, the formerly Unirista and decidedly socialist weekly *Pluma Libre* marked the twenty-fifth anniversary of Uribe Uribe's assassination. During the last years of his life he "resuscitated the social politics" of traditional liberalism, and with his "social ideals" had been the "life-giver of democracy." The "democratic spirit which characterized his struggles" was the same that now inspired "the Liberal masses in the battle for the collective well-being." And in *Pluma Libre*'s pages the Confederation of Colombian Workers paid homage to Uribe's memory because of his concern for "the productive classes" and for his "social and political conquests" in their interests.[11] In February 1944 *El Estado* honored Benjamín Herrera, one of the "giants" of liberalism, because he stood for the "ideal of democracy and justice." And in October 1945 they noted the anniversary of Uribe's death, whose figure became more important with every passing year.[12]

Many prominent left Liberals and Gaitanistas made repeated references to Uribe Uribe's statement about the necessity of liberalism becoming "socialism" to avoid eclipse. In 1935, for example, as José Antonio Osorio Lizarazo noted what he called the dynamic nature of the Liberal party, he reminded Liberals of Uribe's dictum. And José María Córdoba believed that Gaitanismo found its historical pedigree in Uribe's turn-of-the-century observation, which he paraphrased thus: "If liberalism does not want to disappear in the near future, it must enrich itself in the fountainhead of socialism." Left-Liberal activist and intellectual Gonzalo Buenahora characterized the liberalism of Uribe's day as a "revolutionary party," and saw Gaitán as the one called to rejuvenate it and remind Liberals of Uribe's ideals. Especially, as Uribe said, "if liberalism does not drink from the spring of socialism, it will disappear."[13]

Among the Gaitanistas, Gaitán was seen as the intellectual and moral descendent of Uribe Uribe. He was the "heir of the great men" of the left-Liberal tradition. The "spirits" of Herrera and Uribe Uribe accompanied him. An old Liberal warrior, who placed Uribe Uribe and Herrera at the top of the list of Liberal "heroes," looked to Gaitán to reorder the "undisciplined" current regime, which had been converted into "roscas [corrupt oligarchic networks, or cliques] mansanillas [sic] oligárquicas."[14] Indeed, Gaitán's name was often included among these Liberal heroes as an equal. On their letterhead the Liberal Gaitanista Command of Mompós included the phrase, "Gaitán hoists the banner of Uribe Uribe and Herrera." In Magdalena they called him "friend and defender of the proletarian classes," the most outstanding advocate of "social transformation" since Uribe Uribe himself. Thousands in Bolívar would follow Gaitán "to the grave," in the name of General Rafael Uribe Uribe and the other caudillos of the last war. After the election of 1946, prominent Gaitanistas in Cartagena were ready to follow Gaitán in the "reconquest" of the presidency to "realize in its totality" the Liberal ideals of Uribe and Herrera. The Liberal Committee of La Jagua de Ibirico in Magdalena praised Gaitán for "defending the same principles of Simón Bolívar, Santander, Uribe Uribe, Benjamín Herrera and Olaya Herrera." Gaitán was seen, as an important supporter in Cartagena assured him, as the champion of "the tradition of justice . . . which liberalism represents."[15] Gaitán, for his part, actively sought the mantle of Uribe Uribe and the left-Liberal tradition.

A Radical and Popular Mobilization

Some students of Colombian history have emphasized the divide between the "radical" 1930s and the "populist" 1940s. Charles Bergquist held that the collective mentality of the early 1930s succumbed to a Hobbesian, small-holder individualism in the years that followed. He argued that the Colombian labor movement lost "its explosive and ephemeral strength in the late 1920s and early 1930s" to suffer "institutionalization and de-radicalization" at the hands of the Liberal governments between 1930 and 1946. Bergquist noted that "many coffee workers and small producers" were successful in their struggles to "win control of the means of coffee production," and he contended that collective labor struggles were largely abandoned as a result.[16] Marco Palacios echoed this interpretation, calling Gaitán a "vender of illusions" in the 1940s.[17]

The collective spirit of change Gaitanismo represented after 1944, however, was a natural outgrowth of the struggles of the 1930s and of the left-Liberal tradition. Given wide access to land, the means of production in Colombia's coffee-based economy, and the small size of the organized proletariat, working-class alliance with multiclass political movements was not surprising. As pointed out earlier, it was a mobilization within the context of structural class weakness, but a popular mobilization nonetheless. The critique Gaitanistas offered of Colombian society clearly did not bode well for the existing social relations of production, and many among the oligarquía saw its dangerous implications and potential. The Gaitanistas demonstrated that radical movements could arise within the traditional party system.

One of the general themes of Bergquist's *Labor in Latin America* was that radicalism in Latin America is most likely to flourish where the means of production is owned by foreign capital.[18] The areas generally accepted as radical in Colombia, specifically the zona bananera of Magdalena, the oil production center of Barrancabermeja on the Magdalena river, and the coffee regions of western Cundinamarca and eastern Tolima along with the sugar plantations in Valle (all dominated by large landholdings), are often referred to as anomalies within a nonradical Colombian whole. Barrancabermeja and the banana zone, especially, are classic examples of the foreign penetration Bergquist pointed to in support of his thesis. Along the same lines, Mauricio Archila identified a "radical popular culture," specifically in Viotá, Caquetá, the zona bananera, and Barrancabermeja, though he too argued that it "did not spread" to other regions.[19] And Marco Palacios, who called Gaitán's "appropriation" of the bananeras a "classic case" of "co-optation of discontent by Liberal populism," asserted that after 1930, only "a few enclaves of radical subculture remained." Within this group he included organized labor on the Magdalena, the "indigenous south" of Tolima, Barrancabermeja, and the coffee haciendas near Viotá, Cundinamarca.[20] Yet Gaitanista mobilizations throughout Colombia are evidence of a more generalized "radical culture." Interestingly enough, all of these "radical" areas were Gaitanista strongholds; ironically, though, Gaitán's influence in other regions of Colombia is often referred to as proof of their inhabitants' less-than-radical tendencies.[21]

Gaitán always claimed to be a socialist, though, for political reasons, more overtly in the 1930s than in the 1940s. Gaitán had learned of the continuing dangers of straying too far from the Liberal label, while he wanted to distance himself from his Communist rivals in the PSD. And as demonstrated in earlier chapters, the overlaps between left Liberal and socialist allowed Gaitán to blur the distinction.[22] Whether or not historians allow him and his followers this status, however, is perhaps less important than the fact that rank-and-file Gaitanistas considered themselves to be leftist, radical, and even revolutionary. The editors of *El Estado* in Santa Marta maintained that Gaitanismo's insurrection against the old parties had "all the characteristics of a true revolution." Gaitán led the "cry of rebellion" against the political culture that "undermined the meaning of democracy."[23] And there is no doubt that Gaitán's followers (and enemies) regarded him as a radical, a portrayal that followed him throughout the 1930s and 1940s. Gonzalo Buenahora noted that while Gaitán "was never a Marxist," he nevertheless "founded a revolutionary party . . . UNIR." José María Córdoba argued that Gaitán's "battle to revolutionize Colombian political customs should be understood . . . as a radical transformation." Osorio Lisaraso insisted that Gaitán's goal of fundamental national transformation was what "inspired liberalism of all ages." By 1947, thanks in large part to Gaitanismo, Conservatives believed that liberalism was "converting" into Communism.[24]

Nor is it only in retrospect that the (non-Communist) radicalism inherent in Gaitanismo was apparent. In the weeks before the presidential election, a group of leftist intellectuals in Santander produced a manifesto that laid out their reasons for supporting Gaitán. They lamented that contrary to their wishes, there was no viable, independent party of the left, yet they advocated political action in an imperfect world. As "Colombian socialists" they noted that the "electoral *cacicazgos*" had attempted to "strangle the spirit of the traditional parties and their Communist (or *socialista-democrático*) apprentice," subverting their "ideology, organizations, programs, and morality." So they saw two alternatives: to either go "where the *pueblo trabajador* of the different parties congregated" or to "remain neutral," though such so-called neutrality would reward "Conservative reaction." Ospina Pérez represented those who wanted an "economy free and uncontrolled" that conformed to "oligarchic economic ideals," which worked to "enslave" the "small-holder *campesino, the obrero* of the workshop or factory, and the *artesano* or *pequeño industrial*." The "minority movement" of Turbay was comprised of "the *manzanillesco* apparatus of Liberalism" and the jefes who had no ideas of their own. He was the candidate of the "Liberal *oligarquías*" who were defending "a system of privilege" and an "electoral order" that could only survive through the manipulation of the "mechanisms of government." The caciques would not permit a truly democratic system and preferred, "over the interests of the party and the good of the system," their own personal interests. Such leaders were intent on "maintaining the vices of liberalism with the tools of politics," but were ultimately building "on a base of sand." They predicted a "negative insurgency expressed as voter abstention." The *manzanillaje* of the Liberals and Communists defended a "monstrous deformation of the nation's political life," namely, the "concentration of power in the hands of the *oligarquía*" at the expense of the "pueblo trabajador." The "powerful popular movement" that followed Gaitán saw in him not merely the leader of an electoral campaign but also "the leader of a conquest of power . . . for the restoration of democracy and the social liberation of the *clases trabajadoras*." This would be "social democracy without *caciques* or *oligarquías*." The state would be the "servant of the *pueblo*"; it would "enslave the economy so that man can be free." They believed that "one of the great postulates of modern democracy is that man should not be at the service of the economy but rather the economy at the service of man." They saw no better objective than "the active struggle against the economic and political *oligarquías*" for the "liberation of man from need." They therefore supported Gaitán for president.[25]

As the intellectuals from Santander recognized, the Gaitanista collective self-image as a radical mobilization found its origins in the aspirations of its popular base. (And as will be demonstrated below, these ideological trends, in turn, found their way into the Gaitanista program.) Insightfully, one Gaitanista insider argued that Gaitán's candidacy originated "deep within the popular consciousness." "From the core of the Colombian collective soul," echoed Gaitanistas in Santa Marta, emanated "a powerful longing for transformation and social betterment and change, which Gaitán recognizes and interprets." Seventy-two Liberals in Honda, who marched "decidedly toward the left," declared their continued support for Gaitán in October 1946. Gaitanismo represented "a movement of the revolutionary left" on the path toward transforming Colombia's institutions, "through legal and constitutional means," into "an effective democracy." It would be a state in which existed not only the right to work but also the right to find permanent work equitably compensated. Gaitanismo correctly interpreted the "popular desires" and "symbolized the anguish and rebellion of the dispossessed classes."[26] In Santa Marta Gaitanismo was a movement that aspired "to fundamental change of the nation's systems of rule," based as they were in "deception." It was not a movement oriented toward simple, immediate, electoral goals as the oligarquía believed, but a push for "authentic democracy."[27] In Barranquilla a fervent Gaitanista called Gaitán "the candidate of Liberal leftism." In the united march of the campesina and working class, the words "solidarity" and "fraternity" ceased to be empty of meaning.[28] Some of Gaitán's leftist allies in Cartagena, the Partido Liberal Izquierdista, proclaimed their basic ideological stance and support for Gaitanismo on their stationery. Printed at the top in red ink was the slogan, "Liberals and democrats of Colombia unite!" Along the sides, also printed in red ink, it read: "Gaitán has the support not only of the majority of the Liberal party but also the majority of *el pueblo colombiano*." To refuse Gaitán support was to encourage the "anti-popular offensive" and "reaction."[29]

One of the best pieces of evidence for the popular spirit of the movement was Gaitán's declaration, "El pueblo es superior a sus dirigentes" ("The *pueblo* is superior to its leaders"). Herbert Braun admitted that it "was the most far-reaching of all his slogans, for it pointed to an overturning of the social order," though he then argued that this statement was not really a representative remark and soon forgotten.[30] The phrase, however, went to the heart of Gaitanismo, as a few examples demonstrate. In early 1944 Gaitán's followers on the coast seized upon this phrase as a characterization of their movement. In a piece entitled "Liberalism Is Democracy," the editors of *El Estado* used Gaitán's speech on March 14 to comment on the chaotic political situation and the possible remedies. Gaitán, they argued, cut directly to the problem. He claimed that Colombians were offered a false dichotomy, in which the Liberal establishment claimed that only a change of government was needed, and outsiders claimed that no real solution could be found within the morally and intellectually bankrupt political system. The first was "duplicity," which ignored the deep and organized currents of dissatisfaction. The second was a "cruel" underestimation of the pueblo's capacity for mobilization. Neither of these positions acknowledged what Gaitán and *El Estado* of Santa Marta considered to be the truth of Colombia, that "el pueblo es superior a sus dirigentes." In the same month, at the other end of the country, a local político in Nariño agreed that "it is indisputable that our . . . *pueblo* is superior to 'los blancos,'" as the holders of political, social, and economic power were called in local slang.[31]

In the coming years, Gaitanistas would often remind the caudillo of this statement. While assessing the movement's strengths and weaknesses in Cartagena, Julio Vélez Micola of the departmental Liberal Directorate, noted that enthusiasm for Gaitán was widespread, given his realization that "el pueblo es superior a sus dirigentes." Writing from Barranquilla, Samuel Guerrero spoke of "this great *pueblo*, that is very 'superior a sus dirigentes.'" In 1947 organizers in Cartagena echoed Gaitán: "As he has said, and repeated continuously, that phrase engraved upon the popular soul: 'el pueblo es superior a sus dirigentes.'"[32] Even decades later, Gaitanistas would repeat the maxim with reverence.[33] The fact that it became something of a mantra signifies its deeper meaning to the rank and file of the movement.

The movement never completely reconciled the tension between those followers who advocated struggle and those who sought "equilibrium." Gaitán, in his guise as the conciliator, wrote a long letter to banana workers in Magdalena, the main theme of which was the search for the mutual interests of the workers and the company, while quickly finding a solution.[34] Some followers chose Gaitán because of their fear of social upheaval. The Comité Liberal de la Clase Media del Atlántico embraced Gaitán as their presidential candidate because Liberal leadership and policies had failed, creating "anarchy" and "chaos." The general state of degeneration had carried the nation into social conflict and exposed it to the dangers of both "communism" and "the *oligarquía.*"[35] *El Estado,* for example, was somewhat contradictory in the policies its editors advocated. At times it sounded rather militant; at others, as when commenting on the manifesto of the Liberal Gaitanista Directorate, *El Estado* agreed with the need to avoid "deep disequilibrium." The moral restoration would be hard to defend if carried out by way of violent suppression of innocent people and disrespect for the constitution and law.[36]

Yet, as discussed earlier, foremost among Gaitanismo's dominant social elements were urban workers and artisans. Changing and uncertain economic conditions in Colombian cities in the 1930s and 1940s pushed these groups toward radical political movements, be they Liberal, Conservative, Communist, or Gaitanista. In Barranquilla, famous for its working-class and leftist character, Gaitanismo found some of its most ideologically focused and militant adherents. In the Rebolo neighborhood of the city, "as in other neighborhoods," resided a "great number" of ideologically "conscious workers" who supported Gaitán.[37] In Cartagena also, Gaitanistas running for office had "the confidence of the workers" because they advocated the "revolution of ideas" headed by Gaitán.[38]

So while the Gaitanista mentality accommodated both conflictive and conciliatory messages, the more powerful ideological current among the mass of supporters was that of struggle against the status quo. Supporters in Antioquia told Gaitán that "day by day enthusiasm for his campaign" was increasing among "the belligerent men of the Liberal party" who dreamed of a free nation. They railed at the "political parties" that spoke of "democracy" but offered "dictatorship," contrary to the interests of the "oppressed" and "working" masses.[39] Some adherents even went so far as to characterize theirs as a violent struggle. In Cartagena, a "soldier of Colombian liberty" pledged his last drop of blood to rid the country of the oligarquía, ending with "*a la carga,* death to the exploiters of the *pueblo.*"[40] In Barranquilla another "soldier" and member of "the rebellious youth" was ready to fight in whatever form necessary and to spill his blood for the fatherland and the cause.[41] While a radical supporter in Ipiales believed that the moment was not ripe for overt "social revolution" (that it would be a long struggle), he still recognized that "it is more beautiful when the fight is from below [*desde abajo*] rather than from above [*desde arriba*]." They had to continue no matter what with the struggle; "and if there is blood, so much the better. Blood creates *mística.*" Blood, which is emotion, was stronger in Colombia than reason.[42] The rank and file of his movement, after all, associated him with Uribe Uribe, who tried to take the government by force during the War of a Thousand Days. Gaitán generally called for nonviolent political action, but his rhetoric often projected stark images of conflict and struggle, while his rallying call, "a la carga," was the military command for the charge. Under pressure from Conservative attacks in 1946–48 such images became more overt. In the Colombian political context at the beginning of la violencia, no political mobilization could really be devoid of tendencies to armed action.

The view of Colombia history in the 1940s as nonradical, as articulated by Charles Bergquist (and others), is in need of revision. Gaitanismo represented a strong critique of and dangerous challenge to the economic and political status quo. The movement drew upon widespread radical feeling, which was not bottled up in isolated enclaves. While Gaitanista ideology accommodated both conflictive and conciliatory messages, the more powerful was that in defiance of Colombia's structures of power, which reflected the process of its formation.

Interactive Ideology

Gaitanista ideology was not a homogenized commodity handed down by the intellectual strata of the movement, nor was the ideological relationship between official and popular Gaitanismo the one-way flow students of populist movements sometimes describe. Gaitanista ideology reflected popularly held notions that Gaitán identified and articulated. Gaitanismo's ideological perspective derived from an interactive process between leader and masses, which played itself out in Colombia's mass media and in the movement's correspondence.[43]

It is true that Gaitán and his lieutenants carefully attended to the job of consciousness raising by mobilizing the mass media. One of the more innovative methods the Gaitanistas employed was that of radio, which proved highly effective in spreading the Gaitanista message and also gave leaders in Bogotá considerable control over its content. Gaitán paid close attention to the process of Gaitanista ideological formation through the airwaves, and his Friday radio talks, or viernes culturales, were heard throughout Colombia. As Gonzalo Buenahora remembered, workers "would return from work, bathe, and listen to Gaitán on the radio." In this way phrases like "down with the Liberal and Conservative oligarquías" worked their way into common usage.[44]

The U.S. consul in Barranquilla pointed out that Gaitanista-organized events on the coast sometimes drew small crowds because many people stayed home and listened to the radio broadcast of Gaitán's coinciding rallies in the capital. Concerning a rally he himself had attended, he observed that "there were many others who listened to him over their home radios. I was downtown that evening, and all along the street, I could hear the blare of the radios in private residences, bars, cafes, etc."[45] Another witness noted that Gaitán could count on substantial audiences for recordings of his speeches rebroadcast on the "Voice of Barranquilla." During one he drove through the city's "popular neighborhoods" and realized that most radios were tuned in to Gaitán's talk.[46] Organizers of Radio Barranquilla's program "Jornada Gaitanista" claimed to influence 50 percent of the public opinion on the coast, and especially in Atlántico.[47] This process was aided by newspapers sympathetic to the movement, which often reported on Gaitán's radio addresses and summarized their content.

The use of radio, nevertheless, faced both political obstacles and logistical hurtles. In Barranquilla, Gaitanistas spoke of the oligarquía's attempts to "sabotage" Gaitán's programs.[48] And in Cartagena the movement's Sunday broadcasts were often missed because most of the towns in the department had no electrical service during the day.[49] The Gaitanistas therefore had also to rely on more traditional means to spread their message. The other most common form of mass communication in Colombia during the 1940s was naturally the press. Newspapers proved significant not only because they efficiently spread and reflected Gaitanista ideas but also because of their relatively autonomous nature. Gaitanistas publishing papers, or writing in them, generated their own ideas.

As noted earlier, most of Colombia's big Liberal dailies were either cool to Gaitán's 1944–46 campaign (some outright ignored it) or were openly hostile, following the lead of *El Tiempo* in calling him a "fascist" (though at other times they called him a "socialist," which was considered, perhaps, worse). Newspapers in Colombia during this period were intensely political, but this did not impede their talent for switching allegiances quickly when expedient. *El Liberal* of Bogotá, for example, curtailed its sympathy for Gaitán when he decided to run against the official Liberal candidate. Provincial Gaitanista supporters consistently maintained that the elite newspapers of the capital and elsewhere were anti-Gaitán and controlled by the oligarquía. But as one important Gaitanista in Cartagena said, despite the "conspiratorial silence" about Gaitán's successes in the Liberal press of the capital, the pueblo was with him.[50] Speaking of the "campaigns of the enemy press" against Gaitanismo in Honda and the department of Tolima, one steadfast activist believed they would come to naught. "People conscious of our movement are alerted against such hoaxes."[51] And another in Santa Marta maintained in July 1947 that *El Tiempo* and *El Liberal* of Bogotá continued their "suicidal labors." When Gaitán was elected president of the Senate, he received only "diatribes" from the elite press. Yet while "the organs of the *oligarquía*" still cultivated their political deceptions, the Liberal masses had turned their backs on such campaigns.[52]

Gaitán understood the virulence of the elite Liberal press's opposition to his campaign, so he founded his own nationally distributed left-Liberal newspaper, *Jornada*. It was no coincidence—indeed it was powerfully symbolic—that *Jornada* was produced on the old printing press that had turned out *Diario Nacional* in the 1930s. From March 1944 until early 1947 it appeared as a weekly, after which time it converted to a daily format. In February 1944 Gaitán described his alternative news source, saying that it would "call things by their names and attempt to break up the systems of disinformation which hold the national consciousness in oblivion." Its primary concerns were to be corruption (el manzanillaje), dirty business deals, dirty political systems, bribery, and, of course, Gaitán's campaign.[53] *Jornada* effectively served as Gaitán's mouthpiece. José María Córdoba characterized the paper as "the organ of the movement," the medium through which Gaitanistas stayed abreast of the course of the moral restoration. A self-styled "soldier of Colombian liberty" admired *Jornada* as the only "free" paper in Colombia, which contained many cruel and bitter truths in its pages. Lopista democracy, he claimed as an example, was deaf to the real cries of distress, and its social laws had proven ineffective.[54] While this was largely true in Bogotá, where

Jornada was the main Gaitanista paper, its role in the rest of Colombia should not be exaggerated. Even though *Jornada*'s influence also spread through reprints in other Gaitanista papers, the production and distribution of *Jornada* proved difficult and sporadic in practice. It often lacked funds to purchase paper, and many towns and neighborhoods complained that it seldom reached them. In Pasto, Augusto Esparza quipped that its distribution was so irregular there that it had the character of "a clandestine publication."[55]

Given such impediments to *Jornada*'s circulation, the importance of the local and independent Gaitanista press never diminished. Such papers played a vital role in the Gaitanista mobilization, and they were never as easy for the leadership in Bogotá to control. In Barranquilla, the American consul informed his superiors that neither of the city's leading dailies were supporting Gaitán, though two weeklies, "both scandal sheets," gave him support and seemed "to be increasing their circulation" on this basis.[56] While he did not specify the names of the papers, he probably had *La Tribuna* and *Protesta Liberal* in mind, two intensely left-Liberal papers. *La Tribuna* under Rodolfo Ponce had been active on the Liberal left since the early 1930s. *Protesta Liberal* was new to the scene but claimed influence in the worker neighborhood of Rebolo or "Zona Negra."[57] They promoted Gaitán's campaign in their pages and even plastered his messages on billboards, walls, and in theaters.[58]

Some papers showed a good deal of initial hesitance in supporting the independent candidacy, but they quickly acknowledged the writing on the wall. In Santa Marta the brothers Julio and Asdrubal Amarís, who had often supported Gaitán in the 1930s, published *Vanguardia*. Though rather paternalistic in tone, it was a hardcore Liberal paper of leftist orientation. It carried substantial amounts of working-class news, often published messages from unions to the government, and even covered the activities of the local communists, reported by PSD member José G. Russo. During the first half of 1945 *Vanguardia* hedged its bets by reporting on both Turbay and Gaitán. By October, however, it stood solidly behind Gaitán, recommending a Gaitanista "convention of the people" on the Atlantic coast, in which the caudillo could reaffirm his program.[59] In giving such support, they got in front of but did not create the movement. The fact that more and more Liberals came over to Gaitán before the presidential election is good evidence that the real dynamic of the movement came from its social base.

A large number of small papers rallied to Gaitán or sprang up to support his campaign. Many more were founded after the election of 1946. A study of Barranquilla's press during the mid-1940s characterized the fortunes of such papers and the conclusions reached can be applied to other regions of Colombia. "These different publications had ephemeral lives because most found their origins and goals in short-term electoral politics." They therefore had limited financial backing, which permitted few editions or numbers, often spread over long, irregular intervals. This situation was especially illustrative of the many weeklies that sprang up and, as often as not, did not find their way into any archive.[60] Most Gaitanista publications were of this breed and had limited circulation, short runs, and are next to impossible to find today. Their significance lies in demonstrating the kind of grassroots support Gaitán could expect.[61]

Gaitanista ideology, therefore, was not produced in a social vacuum. It reflected popularly grounded ideas that had their roots in the left-Liberal tradition and first found partial political expression in López's Revolución en Marcha. Gaitanista themes were further matured in an interactive process between Gaitán and his followers. The mechanisms of such a process are never clear-cut or easy to reconstruct, but the case of Gaitanismo provides an extensive paper trail. In addition to the vibrant Gaitanista press, the correspondence between Gaitán and the members of his movement readily exposed Gaitanista concerns and how they influenced the caudillo. Many different layers of Colombian society generated ideas; Gaitán received sophisticated political discussions not only from politicians and lawyers but also from medical doctors, engineers, teachers, union leaders and activists, workers, artisans, shopkeepers, and peasant small-holders. In 1938 slightly more than one out of two Colombians was literate, that is, 56 percent of the population, though the rate of literacy was much higher in cities and particularly high, 70 percent, in Atlántico and Barranquilla.[62] But the movement unquestionably represented more than just the literate; a large percentage of letters were from organizations claiming wider influence (such as labor unions and local political committees) or actually had multiple signatories, sometimes in the hundreds. Even allowing that as with any political movement "activists" who might write a letter are a minority, it is clear that the Gaitanistas' correspondence represented broad ideological currents.

It is also important to note that the production of Gaitanista ideology was not a simple case of leadership aspirations for social "equilibrium" diluting rank-and-file tendencies toward "radicalism."[63] "Radical" elements of the "official line" were also in evidence. José Maria Córdoba, perhaps the most militant member of Gaitán's inner circle, often sounded a militant tone while answering the continually increasing correspondence.[64] Writing as Gaitán's campaign surged into high gear, Córdoba told one correspondent that the country had entered a new age, in which the pueblo would, "through reason or force," bring to power the men capable of redefining Colombian politics.[65] And stressing more Gaitán's role as a proponent of class struggle than of social conciliation, Córdoba later wrote that "Gaitán became an omen of foreboding for the upper classes. His 'the rich should be less rich so that the poor can be less poor,' constituted an expression as powerful to them as the biblical proverb, 'it is easier for a camel to pass through the eye of the needle than for a rich man to find salvation.' Gaitán referred concretely to the struggle between the people who work . . . the *país nacional* . . . and the speculators and salon stuffed-shirts . . . the *país político*."[66]

The Gaitanista worldview was the product of interactions on the ideological level between Gaitanista leaders and the rank and file. As this process unfolded in Colombia's growing mass media, Gaitán lost ultimate control of the movement's ideology. His became simply one of many important voices on the Liberal left.

Charisma and Program

Many students of the movement have emphasized the importance of "emotion" and "charisma." It is necessary, therefore, to sort out the attraction of Gaitanista policies and actions from Gaitán's emotional appeal. This is essential to a basic understanding of his *mística*. Those who would use emotion and charisma alone to explain Gaitán, the "demagogue," and his mobilizations of the 1930s and 1940s should be disturbed by the motivated and enthusiastic mass following of the comparatively uncharismatic Alfonso López. To call them both charismatic is to stretch the term to meaninglessness.

Richard Sharpless, who stressed the popular and radical nature of Gaitanismo, still fell back on the conventional divide between leader and masses common in the study of populism, and argued that the "primary ingredient was Gaitán":

> In this respect Gaitanismo was part of the caudillo tradition characteristic of Latin American politics. The tradition had its roots in the seignorial relationships of the hacienda culture. In its modern manifestation as Gaitanismo the patron-client relationship continued in the dependence of the Gaitanista masses upon the leader for both direction and inspiration.[67]

For Sharpless and many other students, "personalism" was the glue that held the newly urbanized Gaitanista masses together. Medófilo Medina also located Gaitanismo's "cohesive element" in Gaitán's "charismatic leadership." The movement's chances for lasting influence, therefore, were considerably dampened with his death.[68] Later in his analysis, Sharpless mused about the degree to which Gaitán contributed to social and political tensions in his run for the presidency and afterward.[69] The active assumption here is that charismatic orators whip up action with emotion and that people have to be incited to defend their interests.

Such assumptions were common currency in Gaitán's time. According to Antolín Díaz, an early apologist, Gaitán's opponents unjustly characterized his "clamor for justice" as demagoguery.[70] Upper-class and educated attitudes toward the "popular classes" were indicative of a general antipopular mentality. While making no direct mention of Gaitán, *El Fígaro* of Cartagena voiced fear of the popular classes and their newfound leaders. The growing concerns over social problems had called forth a new class of demagogues, they warned, called "sons of the *pueblo*" or "representatives of the working classes." These men exploited "the most base of passions." The son of the pueblo was simply "an ignorant and audacious fellow without a conscience." He dedicated his time preparing "spiritual toxins" to "inflame the primary instincts of men." As the "great majority of the public at large, the masses" were "children, easily charmed with the most inoffensive baubles," the son of the pueblo had no trouble inciting their "animal instincts." He knew how to convince them that they were "exploited." Though in January 1946 *El Fígaro* argued that Gaitán was no demagogue, by April they claimed that he appealed to the most "detestable passions" of the pueblo.[71]

But notwithstanding the views of the "better sorts," Gaitanismo and its popularly influenced program represented something rather more profound. According to a Communist tailor who worked in Barranquilla, Gaitán's words touched the intimate misery and pain that were realities of life for the Colombian people, while a Gaitanista in Cartagena spoke of the deep pull of democracy and the "rational ideals and program of scientific Liberalism."[72] In Boyacá an adherent argued that the influence of Gaitán's "effervescent words" and the mística that it produced were not produced "by his voice but rather his philosophy," which was creating "a new orientation for the Liberal party." The "humble campesino," with all his "hopes for advancement," saw in Gaitán "the legitimate defender of his interests."[73]

The appeal of the Gaitanista program, therefore, was virtually self-evident,[74] and Antolín Díaz spelled out the reasons for the mass appeal of the caudillo's initiatives. Gaitán "passionately used his legal skills for social justice, for the well-being of workers and employees, and to readjust the country's economy," taking from the profits of the great industrial enterprises to raise salaries and wages. He worked on the part of the consumer, the worker, and the small property owner, bringing pressure on the government to take action against the high cost of living.[75] Speaking of the movement's program, Gaitanista insider Francisco Chaux argued that Gaitán had "socially practical programs" aimed at the pueblo's actual problems. Gaitán understood the Liberal party as a political instrument that he intended to utilize in "raising the economic level of the *pueblo*." Gaitán intended to "realize social equality based on study, competence, and work"; to make women the equals of men before the state; to create a social, family wage based on an index of the cost of living; and to implant a system of obligatory social security.[76]

Though Gaitán's agenda has been characterized as "a vague program of reform," his followers saw potential for real change.[77] A lawyer in Cartagena in 1943 remembered his student days of a decade earlier and his sympathetic feelings toward Gaitán's early movement. Having recently encountered an outline of Gaitán's political program, he believed that "popular faith" in Gaitán's mística would be reborn and that a presidential term would be the logical outcome.[78] At a campaign rally on April 29, 1946, Liberal activist José Mar claimed that the political caciques had not realized the extent of the social phenomenon of mobilization fermenting amongst the Liberal masses. The people would no longer follow leaders who had grown accustomed to ignoring the popular will; therefore, they were against everything that smacked of "deception and exploitation." The moral and democratic restoration of the Republic had made inroads into the popular consciousness because "working men of all categories . . . want to freely and responsibly choose their leaders." Gaitán's mística was the result of a "patient and constant process" that would ultimately end in a rebellion against the país político.[79] And a group in Barranquilla echoed these beliefs, arguing that unlike "genuine liberalism," which Gaitanismo represented, politics as usual "sucks away all capacity for idealism," the real basis of politics.[80] To his credit, Sharpless noted that at the base of Gaitán's personalism was his ability to "demonstrate genuine concern" for the "common people." "He had proved this objectively by the many initiatives he had made on their behalf during his public career" and instilled in his followers the "spirit of his concern."[81]

Populist programs were always grab bags. They included a wide variety of economic and political reforms that attempted to effect change in systems where social and economic structures of the past remained intact. Populists were compelled by popular aspirations for change and impeded by elites who sought to forestall it. Earlier studies have argued that populist movements effectively derailed authentic efforts to transform Latin American societies. Such was the case with Alfonso López's Revolucíon en Marcha (Laclau's "populism of the dominant classes"?). In the minds of many Colombians, its promise had yet to be fulfilled; a good number even believed it had been betrayed. Their interest in Gaitanismo, therefore, was not coincidental. While the specifics of Gaitán's proposals fell short of overturning the social relations of production in Colombian society, its general thrust was in the direction of social and economic justice through increased political power for the majority.

Concrete expression of Gaitanista concerns found articulation in the Plataforma del Colón, a policy statement sanctioned by the popular convention of January 1947, and the Plan Gaitán, a legislative package submitted by Gaitanistas to the national congress in 1947.[82] While the overall Gaitanista agenda was reformist in appearance, it introduced concepts that proved radical in the Colombian context. Its implications clearly threatened the privileged role of the elite in politics and the economy. The Gaitanista initiatives went far toward empowering the majority of Colombians traditionally on the sidelines of power and influence.

The plataforma, a general blueprint for Gaitán's vision of the Liberal party as a democratic and interventionist party of the masses, carried the subtitle, "Political democracy cannot exist without economic democracy" (p. 329). Liberalism, to be a party of the pueblo sustained by democratic civil rights for all, would voice the concerns of the nation's majority. But political rights alone would be no guarantee. As long as the oligarquía held their monopoly control over the nation's wealth, they could exert undue influence within Colombia's political and financial institutions and protect their collective interests. For the Gaitanistas, therefore, the necessary precondition for the creation of "political" democracy was the existence of "economic" democracy. In practice, the establishment of "economic" democracy would mean much wider distribution of societal resources through state oversight and broader ownership of Colombia's productive forces. Production, the plataforma declared, should be for man and not man for production (p. 341). The plataforma represented a general statement of how Gaitanismo would realize this image of Colombian society.

As did the Revolución en Marcha, the plataforma echoed Uribe Uribe by delegating the central role to the state. The state would intervene to ensure balanced and socially responsible economic development and to protect the interests and well-being of those members of society who were economically disadvantaged. The overall goal was to create what the Gaitanistas called "egalitarian social harmony" by bringing the nation's different economic interests into a workable equilibrium (p. 338). The Gaitanistas argued that the existing administrative mechanisms of the state were not up to the task and outlined new ones. The plataforma called for a general economic planning agency and proposed institutes to direct development on the regional and municipal levels. These bodies would be staffed by a technically trained corps of career civil servants.

The key to the Gaitanista vision rested on increasing Colombia's productivity in a socially conscious manner. Selective progressive taxes, it was hoped, would stimulate investment meant to increase employment and economic growth, while nonproductive wealth would be heavily taxed. Colombian-owned industry would be protected, though "excess" profits would be confiscated by the state. The state would demand representation on the directing boards of private companies and reserve the right to intervene in their operation. The state would closely control the nation's financial markets to ensure productive use of capital. It would also greatly expand its role in credit distribution to bolster the more feeble spheres of the economy, especially targeting agrarian small holders and small business cooperatives. Public services, including electricity, water, telephones, and public transportation would be nationalized and price controls would be installed on food and rent.

The plataforma also addressed issues of immediate relevance to Gaitán's working-class and middle-class supporters. The Gaitanistas called for a minimum wage linked to the cost of living at a socially defined level for the support of a family, with supplemental income given for each child; profit sharing with employees; equal pay for women; state management of the labor market; state protection of an independent labor movement; a labor code that guaranteed the right to strike, collective bargaining, and state-supported legal aid to workers; the extension of social security to all workers and campesinos; and a national public health system (pp. 342–46). And not to be forgotten, the Gaitanistas meant to distribute land to those who actually made it produce, productive squatters or colonos (pp. 334, 339–41). The rural aspects of Gaitanismo have yet to be plumbed, but election returns notwithstanding, Gaitanismo had significant rural support, which was logical given the fact that UNIR was largely an agrarian movement. While the urban setting proved more conducive to Gaitanista mobilization, Colombians consistently addressed land problems in their letters to Gaitán throughout the years.[83]

It is no mystery where the basic substance of the plataforma came from. Liberals of Gaitanista leaning had interconnected political, economic, and social agendas. They wanted clean politics, equality of political opportunity, and some even called for an end to the "hereditary hatreds." They wanted the nation's natural resources used for collective interests, an equal distribution of the nation's riches, and limits on inheritance. They demanded the intervention of the state for economic rationalization and importation policies aimed at satisfying domestic needs and defending the consumer. They wanted housing, education, and hygiene for campesinos, unions for workers, and a system of state intervention for reciprocal rights and obligations between labor and capital.[84] One Gaitanista, in his "capacity as a worker," had had the opportunity to personally experience the social problems that confronted the working class and had witnessed the advantages and disadvantages of the government's social legislation. He was convinced that the state should continue to intervene.[85]

There was no dearth of popular contributions. In Atlántico there were calls for the "definitive implementation of the minimum wage" (especially for women, who they claimed suffered most), construction of hospitals, and investment in agricultural infrastructure.[86] In Barranquilla a concerned Gaitanista wrote that "it is a secret to no one that the Liberal masses, and especially the workers, are discontented." He stressed the need for new ideas. "Only a blind man or a fool" could continue to believe that the classic liberalism of the past century had the staying power to be the basis of action for liberalism of the 1940s. Liberals of "hunger and immediate need" required a strong government of intervention.[87] In Santa Marta Liberals called for a defined social agenda, aimed at raising the "material and cultural levels" of workers and peasants.[88] In Magdalena Gaitanista Liberals called for a more cohesive social policy while commenting on the IV Workers Congress of 1943 held in Bucaramanga. Noting that while emphasis on social policies during the preceding decade of "national evolution and revolution" had come to occupy a preeminent position in national discourse, it was still the case that Colombia lacked a comprehensive system of social legislation.[89] They advocated an amplification of the Liberal program of the 1930s.

After the election, Gaitanistas continued to voice similar concerns. To a portion of "the *pueblo* in Barranquilla," Ospina Pérez's government was the same as those "of the past," offering "promises and more promises." Worried about the cost of living and tired of "false promises," they demanded that Gaitán push his programs for "the class which works."[90] The organized Gaitanistas of Cartagena wanted "a program of action . . . and effective practice" to resuscitate the Liberal faith, and would no longer stand for obstructionist politics.[91] Among the fifty-two points of the new ideological platform of liberalism under Gaitán's leadership, the Gaitanistas in Santa Marta stressed: liberalism is the party of the pueblo; liberalism fights for the political rights of women; liberalism proclaims solidarity with the forces of the left in the common struggle for democracy; liberalism advocates the popular election of mayors and governors.[92] In Barranquilla an anonymous labor activist assumed that in the post-election congressional struggles, Gaitán would command the brigade that would defend "the interests of the fatherland and of the working class." Speaking specifically of Law 95 of 1946, which provided that after twenty years of service, regardless of age, bank employees would receive a pension of two-thirds of their last salary, the writer wanted to know why the rest of the nation's workers were excluded. He advocated extending the law to all workers, but with pensions of 100 percent of the last rate of pay. Though he recognized the existing social laws as a great improvement over the past, the writer was sure that Gaitán's program for the "oppressed classes" would bring advances of a more transcendent nature.[93]

Finally, while Gaitanista demands for social justice might not have seemed as radical as more direct critiques of society, Gaitanista proposals concerning the question of property were as radical as any advanced in Colombia in the 1930s and 1940s. Given a powerful small-holder ethic in Colombia and the centrality of coffee to its economy, even the relatively urban Gaitanista movement of the 1940s could not ignore small farmers. In 1931 a group of costeños in Atlántico wrote describing problems that, they understood, occurred in other parts of the nation. "Capitalists," or those with money and influence, followed the common practice of "acquiring" land and letting campesinos develop it to a certain level. They then pushed off the cultivators and herded cattle over the property, which "before the eyes" of the agonizing farmers would destroy "the fruit of their labor."[94] The question of property, therefore, spans the years and, as shown in chapter 3, never ceased to be a point of ambiguity for Gaitanismo. Yet for Gaitán and his followers, it was not an object immune to redistribution. Even the moderately left Liberals of El Estado who definitely recognized private property also stressed the importance of state intervention for "the just distribution of the fruits produced by the owners and the workers."[95] Eighty Gaitanistas from Tumba Toro in the municipality of Morroa, Bolívar, declared their allegiance to Gaitán and awaited his triumph in the struggle "to change Colombian life." They endured a "semi-slavery" in their region in which the "rich owners of the land refuse to rent it."[96]

On May 1, 1947, *Jornada* spoke of the heroic deeds of the "army of labor" to build the nation and its necessary battle within the organization of society for dignity, rights, and "the bread to survive." Colombian democracy, the editors argued, had to transform itself to be just. Workers still had faith in its principles, but the political process had to go beyond its old concerns to really address their hopes and needs. Fatherland and justicia social were the "words in the mouths of millions."[97] Important as Gaitán and his charismatic presence were to the movement, emotion alone did not motivate the faithful. Gaitanistas were drawn to the movement's program, which they themselves had a hand in creating.

Gaitanista Discourse: Democracia and Justicia Social

Gaitanista concerns and values surfaced in Gaitanista language. Certain terms and images so permeated the letters and other writings of the Gaitanistas as to qualify as obsessions. Democracia and justicia social, if their near universal espousal by Gaitanistas is any indication, were the bedrock concerns of popular Gaitanismo; both of these ideas were intensely charged moral issues for the Gaitanista faithful.[98] Social justice attained through democracy, therefore, represented the key to understanding Gaitanista ideology. From this root other basic terms in the Gaitanista lexicon have clear and logical meaning. No longer are such words and phrases as el pueblo and la oligarquía (and their peculiarly Gaitanista variants, el país nacional and el país político), "socialism," and "morality" to be dismissed as vague or deceptive. These simple but powerful concepts constituted the elements of a concrete political consciousness.

Democracy, many exasperated Gaitanistas argued, did not yet exist in Colombia. The Liberal party was still controlled by the oligarquía, despite the efforts of reform during the 1930s. In the minds of left-Liberal Gaitanistas at *La Tribuna,* the customary practice of professional politics continued to manifest itself as "the art of deceiving and defrauding the masses." Gaitanismo, therefore, demanded "genuine" democracy. The opinion of the people, they claimed, should be regarded as the voice of God. Its editors saw two groupings within liberalism: the old political insiders who would continue the closed, personalistic system, and those "true leaders" of the people whose support rose above "deep roots in the popular consciousness."[99] A woman writing to *Agitación Femenina* pointed out that a government that denies three-fourths of the nation's inhabitants their rights as citizens, especially "voice and vote," could not really be considered "democratic government." Another echoed her, saying that a "true democracy" such as Colombia prided itself on being, cannot exclude participants because of their class or gender, or it ceases to be one.[100] Women in Cartagena, proclaiming their faith in Liberal ideas, nevertheless intended to broaden Colombian democracy. They wanted to realize "total democracy," not the "incomplete democracy" then in existence in which women had no say. That was why they supported Gaitán.[101] Prominent Gaitanistas in Cartagena asked for pause (after the election) to focus on the real objectives in retaking power, emphasizing the rejection of "oligarchical practices."[102] For many Gaitanistas, "pure democracy" and "true Liberalism" were one and the same.[103] "Genuine Liberalism" and therein genuine democracy, others maintained, found its true expression in Gaitán's ideas.[104]

And closely related to agitation for democracy were concerns for social and economic justice. Rafael Azula Barrera, an early commentator, noted Gaitán's "confused," though direct, appeal to popular economic aspirations.[105] And the Gaitanistas themselves provided ample evidence for this observation. As early as 1932 radicals who wanted to move beyond the two traditional parties to a new party based on class expressed their hostility toward "all injustice." In 1939 Liberals in Manizales proclaimed themselves followers of Gaitán's "democratic and just ideology." In 1940 a left Liberal in Tumaco lamented that in Colombia there was "no distributive justice." Gaitán was not "a capitalist" but rather "an intimate friend of social and economic defense."[106] A group of Liberals in Magdalena supported Gaitanismo "as real Liberals who have always been on the side of just causes." From their "naturally leftist and revolutionary position in the nation's press," the directors of *Agitación Femenina* called for a "more just tomorrow." The editorialists of *Vanguardia* advocated the "high ideal of humanity and social justice," which should be supported through state intervention and enforcement of work contracts and labor legislation. They defined "social justice" as the maximum degree possible of well-being for the majority, or inversely, the smallest possible amount of misery.[107] A Colombian international leftist activist who had worked with the "masas trabajadoras" in Nariño maintained that left Liberals had to transform the "primitive emotions of the cry of disobedience" into a concrete "economic" understanding of the "Colombian reality." Liberal city councilmen in Cauca were pro-Gaitán because of his "humanitarian social doctrines." For the inhabitants of Turbo, the "social question" was one of "permanent struggle for justice" and to "raise the standard of living." In Barranquilla Gaitanistas were the "friends of social justice."[108]

Democracy and social justice were closely related in the minds of Gaitanistas at all levels of the movement and, indeed, could not be separated. José María Córdoba argued in his memoir that Gaitán's work represented an attempt to transform Colombia's "political customs" and realize an "economic democracy."[109] Luís David Peña, one of Gaitán's original apologists, held that at the core of Gaitanismo was the belief that Colombian democracy could not be effective unless it "advanced toward economic democracy." He argued that the "essential liberties of speech and thought" could not be exercised within a social structure in which the economically powerful could dominate the weak.[110] Antonio Garcia called Gaitán a "historically necessary man" who rebelled instinctively against the accumulated injustice of centuries. Gaitanismo expressed, in his opinion, the moral outrage of socialism, and its constant objective was economic, political, and social democracy.[111] The editors of *El Estado* held that Gaitanismo was not merely political but was nurtured by "a deep and sincere sentiment of distributive justice." They later stated flatly, echoing the plataforma, that "political democracy is inoperable without economic democracy."[112] In Riohacha, a merchant described his and his community's reaction to one of Gaitán's radio addresses speaking of the struggle between the pueblo and the oligarquía. The people, he claimed, had faith in Gaitán's voice as "the revolutionary force" propelling Colombia toward "economic democracy and social justice."[113] From Barranquilla, a "son of Colombia" called for the "economic and social well-being" of the nation.[114] And one supporter, who gave his address as "the Liberal and Conservative *pueblo* of Colombia," lived in the provinces in an atmosphere of "superstition, misery, and sectarianism." Yet in just such a place, one could most feel the deep pull of democracy and understand the "rational ideals and program of scientific liberalism." He also longed for implementation of the "economic politics" of Gaitán's program, as did others in Cartagena.[115] In Cartagena Gaitanistas believed that "justice and democracy" were "embodied in the popular movement of moral and democratic restoration of the republic."[116] In Girardot at the beginning of his campaign, a supporter hoped for the triumph of Gaitán's "truly democratic ideals" since he represented the spirit of "fraternity and justice."[117] In 1947 Gaitán's "voice of justice" still showed the way down the "paths of democracy."[118] Under Gaitán, a supporter in Tolima asserted, the pueblo could "breathe freely and possess its social and political rights."[119]

Social justice attained through democracy, therefore, represented the ultimate tenet of Gaitanista ideology. Though not calling for the immediate end of the current relations of production, Gaitanista demands represented an intuitive critique of the system.[120] Based on these simple but powerful concepts, Gaitán's *mística* constituted a system of belief that orientated Gaitanista social and political action. Democracy meant an end to elite control of the political institutions of society. Social justice meant an end to economic inequalities, thereby bringing a higher material standard of living for Colombians. Letters from the rank and file repeated variations on these themes. A "working man" declared his support for Gaitán's campaign because it represented "the betterment of our democracy and the well-being of the *pueblo.*"[121] In Cartagena a group of Gaitanistas proclaimed Gaitán the standard bearer "of justice and democracy, embodied in the popular movement of moral and democratic restoration of the republic."[122] In Ciénaga another supporter believed that politics as usual had "disfigured" Colombian democracy by allowing small groups to dominate the process while ignoring fundamental social problems.[123]

One letter brought several of these themes together at once. A medical doctor in Cartagena (and member of the Liberal directorate of Bolívar) wrote to Gaitán and the Liberal leaders of the coastal departments concerning his vision of a just and democratic society. The well-being of the fatherland could only be possible under the stable rule of the party that represented the "great popular majority." The Gran Partido Liberal, through its "essentially democratic nature" and its principles of liberty, equality, justice before the law, and "faith in God," would "bring harmony to the relationships between rulers and ruled, and between workers and employers," applying to all the concept of "distributive justice, the essence of the most pure ideology." The party no longer struggled for bureaucratic power but rather democratic government, "by, of, and for the people." In his view, the party had erred by putting too much power in the hands of a few men and needed more democratic selection of leaders. He finished, predictably, by recalling the words of Uribe Uribe who said that to remain in step with the rhythm of the times and retain its status as the principal representative of the majority, the Liberal party would have to renovate its principles in the fertile soil of socialism.[124]

Gaitán himself became the focus of these concerns. A militantly leftist supporter in Cartagena assured Gaitán that for the Liberal and Conservative pueblo of Colombia, he was "the apostle of social justice."[125] When Gaitán spoke in Santa Marta on December 12, 1945, *El Estado* characterized his movement as revolutionary in content, not merely political, and nurtured by "a deep and sincere sentiment of distributive justice."[126] After the election, in Barranquilla the "friends of social justice . . . men, women, and children, their eyes filled with tears," flooded into the streets to show their support for Gaitán's campaign.[127] A supporter in Honda observed that "though limping, justice will arrive."[128] A politician in Cartagena, calling Gaitán the "expositor of leftist ideology and apostle of justice," supported his "national renovation along the paths of social justice and economic equality."[129]

The connections between democracy and social justice were reflected in the opposition of the pueblo and the oligarquía; this was not an overt vision of class struggle but tended toward it. The pueblo, while used by Gaitán as a multiclass grouping, in practice had a more specific meaning. As noted earlier, for many Gaitanistas the essence of Gaitanista liberalism was to be understood as "the working people." The existence of the oligarquía, on the other hand, negated "real" democracy.

Gaitanistas believed that democracia, properly understood and practiced, could produce justicia social. The existing political system, therefore, was not dismissed as utterly bankrupt. But while politics retained a tenuous degree of legitimacy, the Gaitanistas introduced ideas assuring that political struggle was grounded in popular, even class-based interests. By insisting that democracy and social justice had to go hand in hand or not at all, they offered a thinly veiled, intuitive critique of the existing relations of production. Theirs was not an overt attack on capitalism, but the Gaitanistas conserved their interest in "socialism," which was caught-up with their ideas of democracia and justicia social. Democracy meant an end to elite control of the political institutions of society. Social justice meant an end to economic inequalities, thereby bringing a higher material standard of living for Colombians. They did not have a detailed economic structure in mind, but it was certainly not unfettered capitalism either.

These ideas were intensely charged moral issues for the Gaitanista faithful. Gaitanista morality, however, always had a strong economic flavor. Thus the "moral" in the "moral and democratic restoration" was in perfect harmony with popular Gaitanista concerns. Milton Puentes's biography of Gaitán written during the presidential campaign hinted at the economic underpinnings of Gaitanista morality. Under liberalism's "canopy of humanitarianism" gathered all who sought "the social and economic good of the collective." This explains Gaitán's assertion while speaking in Cartagena that "human history has been the struggle for morality."[130] Gaitanistas in Barranquilla with *La Tribuna* called for "morality" over all else. Municipal councilmen need not be individuals of "robust mentality" as long as they were honest and served the public

good. Another Gaitanista in Barranquilla pledged to aid in Gaitán's ideological struggle to liberate the "working classes and the middle class" who
suffer from "immoral politics." A textile worker and communist militant
in Barranquilla, typical of those who supported Gaitán, voiced the common sense of moral outrage that the movement represented. Though he
claimed to be no intellectual, only a worker who rose to a leadership
position, he felt the exploitation of his class as soon as he began work in
the 1930s.[131] Left Liberals with *La Opinión* in Ibagué in 1944 demonstrated their desire for real political change and a more popular Liberal
party by venting their moral indignation. The camarillas and roscas of the
oligarquía had brought the nation to a crisis, and the party should move to
combat the speculators who were a danger to "morals." (It was not a
coincidence that the same day there was a big headline and photo dealing
with Gaitán's campaign.) They covered his speech in the Teatro Municipal
in Bogotá at the start of the campaign, calling it "the tonic of sincere
truth" about the culpability of the oligarquía in ruining the Liberal party,
and quoted him saying "we are ready to give battle to the system." They
too wanted to "purify Colombia."[132] A Gaitanista in Pasto claimed that
the Colombian pueblo "in its majority" saw that the country's "moral,
political, and economic structure has been shipwrecked in the stormy seas
of personal interests."[133]

Gaitanista discourse represented Gaitanista political consciousness.
Concerns with democracy and social justice expressed by Gaitán's followers found their origins in the thought of Uribe Uribe, and partial reflection
in the Revolución en Marcha. This amalgamation of influences found
their way into the Gaitanista program. The popularity and force of the
"moral and democratic restoration" were good indications of the popular
moral sense of outrage prevalent among the Gaitanistas. Gaitán had come
to symbolize their interests.

Symbolic Gaitanismo

As Gaitán so tellingly affirmed, "No soy un hombre; soy un pueblo" (I am
not a man; I am an entire people.) Gaitán understood that he had become
the symbol of struggle and action, justice, democracy, hope and change,
workers' rights, and the left-Liberal tradition. Admiration for the caudillo
was very often expressed in New Testament messianic terms. Supporters
interchangeably called Gaitán a "new messiah," "the only salvation of the
oppressed classes," "the apostle of social justice," the "savior," and the
"redeemer" of Colombia.[134] One group in Bolívar proclaimed that "as

Jesus came into the world to save us from sin, so came [Gaitán] . . . to defend the working *pueblo* against the mortal sins of the *oligarquías*." Another supporter foretold the "resurrection" of the Liberal party under the redeemer Gaitán, "crucified by President Lleras and sold by that Iscariot, Eduardo Santos," while Gaitán's "visionary" supporters in Mompós held that liberalism could only be saved if the "popular will united around a steadfast leader" who, "with the lash of his tongue," would "drive from the temple of the party the business interests which had plunged it into anarchy and chaos."[135]

In their manifesto to the Liberals of the department, the Gaitanistas of Atlántico explained the "promise" of the movement and why it had the sympathy of the "struggling masses." Gaitán's campaign embodied the "legitimate hope" of the pueblo because it sought to put into practice "the ideals of economic and social redemption" and because he had always preached against injustice.[136] A poem by a self-styled "Gaitanista fanatic" called Gaitán's popular candidacy "the roar of the oppressed *pueblo,*" which struck fear in the hearts of the oligarquía.[137] For the editors of *La Tribuna* in Barranquilla, Gaitán's candidacy had been "deeply etched into the Liberal consciousness" because he "represented the banner of struggle and action."[138] Among the cowboys of Bolívar, Gaitán's name was "pronounced with affection . . . as the symbol" of their "economic redemption."[139] For Liberals in Tolima, his name was a "symbol of the surging movement of the masses" since he sought "the salvation of the republic, reign of order, of justice, and morality."[140] Gaitán had shown the "trabajadores, obreros, and campesinos" of Colombia that he was the true representative of their aspirations and "defender of their social rights." He was the embodiment of the "Liberal and democratic spirit,"[141] the "symbol of justice" in the tradition of Uribe Uribe and Herrera.[142] For Liberals in Tumaco, Nariño, Gaitán was a healer who had begun the process of "purification" of the patria of the "sores left by the *oligarquías*." He would usher in "a new era of justice, progress, and well-being."[143] For hundreds of "Liberal citizens" of the municipio of Fresno in Tolima, Gaitán and his movement represented the "only authentically popular expression."[144] He was characterized as the liberator and defender of the pueblo, of the exploited and subjugated, and especially of Colombia's workers and proletarians.[145]

Longtime Gaitanista judge and politician in Magdalena, Dionisio Rincones Ponce, called Gaitán "a symbol" who represented "the aspirations of a people" while understanding its "anguish, suffering, and needs." Those people who believed the movement would end with Gaitán's electoral defeat on May 5, 1946, deluded themselves, he argued. Gaitán was not the leader of merely an electoral campaign. He was also the leader of a "revolutionary enterprise" whose immediate objective was "the fundamental change" of Colombia's political customs while acknowledging that "man is the fundamental factor of the economy" and had to be spared from his misery.[146] Proclaiming Gaitán a "symbolic figure," Gaitanistas in Popayán knowingly summarized the symbolism of Gaitanista ideology. It was not a case of "infantile personalism." Gaitán's supporters were "adults." The movement's ideology was "its banner and star." It led "the *caudillo* to express the many vibrations of the collective with his voice." Gaitán was not, they affirmed, the demagogue the elite press claimed. Gaitán represented the "promise" and "spirit" of "transformation." The movement's program, contrary to elite criticism, was more complete than any liberal program before it. "Men of the left" now could "fight in defense of something concrete and fundamental." Now the "political fossils" were separated from the Gaitanistas, not only by their hate but also by doctrine. Ideology, they claimed, is "greater than the leader. It can survive him; ideology does not die."[147]

The basic substance of the Gaitanista world view reflected an amalgamation of the left-Liberal tradition, of Gaitán's ideas, and of popular demands. Popular Gaitanista ideology reflected popularly held ideas that new urban social conditions allowed to emerge in a forceful way. The Gaitanistas' shared moral sense of social justice and demands for more popularly based political representation unified their mobilization and drew them to Gaitán, the symbol of their aspirations. Gaitán served as a catalyst for the movement's ideological content, but he did not bring it down from the mountain. It matured through an interactive relationship on the ideological level between Gaitanismo's leadership and its rank and file. Gaitán's influence, commonly attributed to his charisma, resulted from the hope he offered of completing and expanding the promise of the Revolución en Marcha. Though a derivative of the Liberal tradition, Gaitanismo offered a popular, and radical, alternative to the two established parties in the mid-1940s. Gaitanismo was a popular mobilization that effectively challenged the hegemony of the economic and political establishment. In the mouths of the Gaitanistas, "democracy" and "social justice" proved to be powerful stimulants for popular mobilization.

8

The Dilemmas of Liberal Integration in the Twilight of Politics, 1946–1948

Many of his critics believe that as Gaitán pressed closer to power, he allowed the official Liberal party to lethally absorb and neutralize his left-Liberal movement. Following the presidential election of 1946, after all, Gaitán quickly adopted the language of Liberal unity to meet the threat of the minority Conservative party intent on holding power after 1950 through violence and intimidation. And as Gaitán picked up the mantle of liberalism's jefe único, he increasingly evoked the legacy of the "hereditary hatreds" and worked openly with the Liberal oligarquía. Yet this chapter will demonstrate that among the Gaitanistas, the battle to remake Colombian politics along more democratic lines continued.

Between 1944 and 1948, the Gaitanista mobilization divided into two major phases. The first was Gaitán's 1944–46 presidential campaign. The second was the problematic reintegration of liberalism with its left-Liberal wing. The Gaitanista drive to recreate the Liberal party after May 1946 took place within the context of the Liberal *reconquista* of presidential power. As official liberalism and Gaitanismo warily drew closer together, popular forces of change vied with the Liberal establishment for control of the party. This process, the big narrative, presented a backdrop for various subplots in which Gaitanistas struggled over the political organization of their movement. Gaitanismo continued to suffer serious internal battles over leadership, policy, problems of the vote, how to change the mechanics of Colombian democracy, and to what end.

Still intent on recreating the Liberal party as a truly democratic and popular organization, the left-Liberal goal since the time of Uribe Uribe, the Gaitanistas continued to challenge the oligarchic mechanisms of Colombian politics after the 1946 election. The historiography has tended to view the mobilizations and conflicts of the 1930s as radical and those of the 1940s (especially post-1946) as retrograde. Yet the political victories of Gaitanismo throughout 1946 and 1947 demonstrated that the popular rebellion against traditional Liberal political practice had breached the party's defenses. As Gaitanismo merged with liberalism, it must be admitted, the movement absorbed less democratic elements. Opportunistic politicians took up Gaitán and his policies, leading to the common claim that new supporters were really "false Gaitanistas." To evade this charge, the clamor for Gaitán's mark of approval became at times a contradictory din. But left-Liberal Gaitanismo maintained a basic continuity between its "radical" and "populist" phases, even in the 1946–48 period.

Gaitán never openly abandoned his old positions. True, Gaitán had learned the political lessons of UNIR and was now ready to make the compromises that power required. But if he changed his rhetoric, he remained focused on the basic issues dear to left Liberals. And while Gaitán was the leader and best representative of the political forces manifesting themselves during his lifetime, he did not create them and he did not control them. His movement's development and its violent suppression after 1947, therefore, had as much to do with the unresolved struggles of Colombian history as with his opportunism and his death.

Lingering Elite Resistance and Continuing Struggles for Democratic Liberalism

The Liberal establishment did not lose gracefully. The party's top leadership plainly could not endure the indignity of yielding to the popular caudillo and attempted to ignore the implications of Gaitán's dramatic showing in the presidential election. Most refused to bow to his political authority until the Gaitanistas had trounced them in the March 1947 congressional elections. They indulged in such fantasies even while the consummate Liberal oligarch, Calibán, had admitted that Gaitán controlled the allegiance of the urban masses and that the Liberal party could not regain power without him.[1]

Retreating into a dreamlike state of denial, many top Liberals apparently wished Gaitán would simply go away. The absence of a significant discussion of Gaitanismo in the semi-official history of the Liberal Republic published in 1946 is telling.[2] In frustration, one Gaitanista in Boyacá justifiably lamented that Liberals should realize that they had not been defeated by the Conservatives but rather by precisely these "delusions of grandeur" of the "roscas Liberales," who believed that their domination of Colombia was "eternal."[3] Another in Santa Marta pointed out that despite the Gaitanistas' political victories throughout 1946 and 1947, the "organs of the *oligarquía*" persisted in their illusion that the movement was on the wane.[4] In Pasto Liberal union was a bust because the old políticos resisted integration with Gaitanismo and the popular will. They refused to recognize "that Liberal politics in Colombia" were now "directed by new, essentially democratic criteria, different from the old politics of *rosca*," based on the "corrupt offer" of payment for the campesino's vote.[5] And in Cúcuta, a Gaitanista pointed prophetically to the Liberal leadership's scorched-earth policies. There the Liberal organization was "absolutely null," due to its fragmentation. The "Liberal oligarchs" preferred to sow "anarchy" among the Liberal ranks and work against both the interests of the collective and the ideal of social justice rather than join Gaitanismo.[6]

Gaitanistas understood the reasons for continuing resistance on the part of the oligarquía, but they also sensed its political futility. In an open letter, fifty Gaitanistas of the Atlantic coast condemned the editors of *El Tiempo*, *El Liberal*, and *La Razón* of Bogotá for their "systematic" campaign against Dr. Gaitán. The pueblo understood these attacks, they argued, as a common cause the Liberal establishment made with the Conservatives. They hated Gaitán because he had stripped them naked before public opinion. They envied his mística and his movement, "the largest in Colombian history," and felt panic at the thought that the pueblo no longer gave its "natural obedience" and that Gaitán would be president. These attacks, however, would prove sterile and even suicidal, because the old Liberal establishment would be tagged as "open enemies . . . of the oppressed classes." They attacked not only Gaitán but also the pueblo, who were finally "awake."[7] Writing in Bogotá, Hernando Téllez noted that what Liberal union there was resided in the "base of the party, that is to say, in the masses." The elite of the party still would not forgive Gaitán. *El Tiempo* did not "lose any opportunity to demonstrate that it would not pardon Gaitán any failing." *La Razón* held to its "tireless opposition to Gaitán," and even *El Espectador,* he claimed, now showed "universal hostility" to Gaitán.[8] Commenting on the crisis within the party, Gaitanista Liberal leaders in Saboyá argued that given "the diversity of personal interests in play," there had been a "clear and disconcerting dismissal of the public will" by the "antidemocratic and unpopular" national Liberal leadership. The establishment in Bogotá, they believed, was in league with the "provincial *caciques*" and "at the service of the exploiters." They noted that "three hundred and sixty thousand Liberals" voted for Gaitán and that the number under his banner had doubled. They recognized that while "the *caciques* were responsible" for the defeat of liberalism, the "Liberal proletariat, urban and rural," was abandoning its old leaders and following Gaitán. They wanted unity to stay the course, to continue to work for the humble and suffering campesinos, empleados, and obreros; to hold on to power in the Congress and the Judiciary; to fight fraud and violence; to assert individual rights; to let the oligarquía know that the "vigilant *pueblo*" followed Gaitán.[9] In Paz de Río another Gaitanista noted the division among Liberals between the "notables" of the "center" and those who followed Gaitán "in a new direction," the "Liberal *pueblo*" that sought "just causes."[10]

Post-1946 Gaitanismo has for some observers remained an unrecognized mobilization. Daniel Pécaut alleged that after 1946 Gaitán became a Liberal of the establishment and largely betrayed the character of his movement's popular mobilization.[11] Some of Gaitán's contemporaries concurred, continuing to argue (decades later) that Gaitán was simply an old-style caudillo and that his crusade therefore died with him.[12] There have been, however, some dissenting voices. Gonzalo Sánchez argued that while Gaitanismo's reincorporation back into liberalism affected the movement's options for "autonomous development," it is also true that "the Liberal party did not prove immune to Gaitanista penetration. . . . Gaitán introduced class struggle into the workings of the Liberal party."[13] The case can be made, therefore, that while Gaitanista and Liberal leaders fixated on the party's comeback, the Gaitanista masses had something else in mind.

The popular movement remained, at its core, a struggle to recreate the Liberal party as an agent of economic and social justice through democracy, and continued to find its strength in its rank and file. Richard Sharpless, among others, has stressed the centralized nature of Gaitanismo's crusade and Gaitán's role within it. He argued that "despite the popular base of the movement, despite its themes of democracy and mass participation, the movement was essentially personalist; that is, it was a movement in which Gaitán was the center, the matrix, the voice who gave the movement its definition and form. . . . This was both its greatest strength and its greatest weakness."[14] Indeed, in the words of one prominent *barranquillero,* thanks to Gaitán, Gaitanismo exhibited a "messianic" force throughout Colombia, successfully challenging the political establishment and becoming "the defining axis."[15] But while Gaitán was surely the central figure, Gaitanismo was the manifestation of a political current that had taken many forms since the nineteenth century. Left Liberals, Socialists, Communists, and Lopistas (often the same people) all sought more representative democracy, and in 1946 Gaitanismo proved to be its most concrete expression.[16] Liberals on the coast argued that liberalism suffered from "anarchy," "discontent," and "profound apathy" because the leadership had become conservative in power and "defrauded their supreme aspirations."[17] Gaitanismo therefore (as a principal Gaitanista maintained soon after Gaitán's assassination) had wrought a transcendental metamorphosis of Colombian politics by putting the pueblo at the center of the Liberal party's agenda. It made the popular will the basis of its organization while striving for judicial, political, social, and economic democracy.[18]

The new, more popular liberalism emerged slowly, evolving from the pre-election rebellion, through the elections of March 1947, and on into the twilight of politics as Colombia became engulfed by civil war and class struggle. Before May of 1946, the Gaitanista portrayal of their struggle took the form of an easy-to-understand dichotomy: the candidate of the oligarquía challenged by the candidate of the pueblo. Gaitán had, after all, argued that the Liberal convention at the Colón Theater was not legitimate because it did not obey the Liberal party's own statutes and took place behind the backs of the pueblo. Instead of a candidate of the people, liberalism had produced a candidate of the oligarquía.[19] In creating this dichotomy, Gaitán hit upon a powerful, if dangerous, organizational tool. As one Gaitanista in Atlántico echoed Gaitán's own words, "In reality it is a struggle between two groups, representative of two different approaches to government within the same party. . . . These two groups are the supporters of Gaitán and the partisans of the *oligarquía*." The old forms of fooling the people, he argued, would soon be thrown out by the advance of democratic concepts and practice.[20]

After the election of May 1946, the acts of disrespect against the Liberal leadership by the Gaitanista masses increased in number and intensity. Popular pressure was brought to bear on the political establishment with unprecedented force, particularly in regions where the bulk of the electorate went with Gaitán. In the municipality of Suan, Atlántico, for example, where the Gaitanistas got 206 votes, Turbay got 82, and the Conservatives got 57, the pueblo was no longer a victim of the "tyranny and deceit of the *caciques* and the *gamonales*." The pro-Gaitán Liberal leaders there had successfully built a political block that would work in the general interests of the people. They did not consider the loss of the presidency a defeat because it would help "orient Liberalism along better paths."[21] In Magdalena the mutiny against both the national and local leaders proved especially conspicuous. There "the *caciques* suffered massive defeat" at the hands of the relatively inexperienced Gaitanistas, whose courage and persistence proved too much for the "idlers of the *oligarquía*."[22] As Gaitán himself stressed often, the struggle was not only against the Conservatives but also against the Liberal leadership, who in reality were different sides "of one single front."[23] While Eduardo Santos was in Santa Marta in December 1946, one Gaitanista approached him on the street and from two meters away shouted, "Viva Gaitán, abajo Santos," at which point "the oligarch blanched noticeably."[24] Julio Ortega Amarís reported that on this visit to Santa Marta, Santos was "completely rejected by the *pueblo*," having his elite-sponsored rally fall flat.[25] Asdrúbal Amarís believed that the first stage of the battle for national restoration was complete, for while the Liberals had lost the presidency, Gaitán had launched an era of new political practices. "The Liberal worker and peasant masses" watched with anticipation.[26] While Gaitán was in Magdalena in February of 1947, supporters there stressed his role as the truly popular Liberal leader. For "while the great opportunists feast at the banquet of farce, Gaitán walks the country to be in contact with the *pueblo*."[27]

The postpresidential election period witnessed a high degree of militant popular political mobilization, despite the evident obstacles. In Cúcuta, "Liberals of the left, warrior Liberals, socialists all," who represented "the living force of democracy," were ready "to give battle for the reconquest at the head of the popular forces," but they would not "support unpopular candidates." In their region "the rebellion of the *pueblo*" had "a positive character." They identified "a strong current, the most rough and ready among the Liberals, with the backing of the popular forces," that would go to the elections. These "new men, new names," pressed forward, whether or not they were wanted by "the eternal *caciques*." They would support these rebels because it was "preferable to fight in opposition than to accept the way it was before May 5th."[28]

After the election, the Gaitanista base was still solid, and many adherents presented more demanding themes in their letters. Workers in Magdalena wrote to affirm their continuing faith in Gaitán, using familiar language. They hailed him as the "authentic representative" and "defender of the proletarian classes" and peasants.[29] In Barranquilla workers also "continued at the front" of Gaitán's movement.[30] In Chocó they continued to support Gaitán because he worked to "elevate the economic and social level of the *clases laboriosas*." In Valle miners, who were "a good number of suffering and abandoned workers," would continue to give their "fervent votes" to Gaitán because of his "effective and decisive" work for the "Colombian *pueblo laborioso*."[31] On April 21, 1947, Barranquilla witnessed "grave disorder" after some of the city's labor unions organized a rally to protest the cost of living. Shops were sacked and people wounded, and eventually the army deployed troops on the streets "to prevent worse disasters."[32] Workers writing to Gaitán became, perhaps, more insistent in their calls for action. Now that many believed it only a matter of time before Gaitán would be elected president, they focused their attention and energy on more immediate needs. One union in Barranquilla wanted protection for its *personería jurídica* against modification by the new Conservative government. Another wanted his help in obtaining wage increases related to the cost of living and other "just" benefits.[33] Indeed, the economic needs of the working class and the honesty of local elections came to the forefront of demands made by Gaitanistas.[34]

Now Liberal groups were becoming evermore unrelenting in the naming of their own candidates. Organized workers in Bogotá, for example, wanted to name candidates for the concejo who would represent "a radical change" from the men who routinely served on the body and who would help "guarantee a real campaign in defense of worker neighborhoods" in the capital.[35] Rank-and-file Liberals, therefore, unleashed a host of candidate lists on Gaitán and the Liberal leadership.[36] For decades left Liberals had chafed at gamonal domination and now wanted to have a direct role in candidate selection. Their primary response (launching their own lists) unfortunately did not always facilitate effective democratic mobilization. Going from the authoritarian (but orderly) boss system to the open anarchy of multiple competing lists of candidates at times severely handicapped the movement. Gaitanistas also offered advice and rather insistent encouragement. A Gaitanista in Villa de Leiva complained in December 1946 that the pueblo was "in limbo," and that Gaitán had to get on with implementing his program. The pueblo had to be further mobilized, with special attention given to market days.[37] In Ibagué another railed at "Sunday Gaitanistas" who did not help to get out the vote.[38] Indeed, in Cúcuta Gaitanistas spoke of "problems of organization" among the Liberal forces, since many were afraid to declare their allegiance, were racked by doubt, and who only joined when the way seemed safe and the movement enjoyed a national presence among the pueblo.[39]

To solidify the Gaitanista resistance, and perhaps get control of it, Gaitán began to speak of another popular convention as early as the days immediately following the election. The convention would be a beautiful reality, one enthusiast believed, with each municipality directly electing delegates—a manifestation of force and discipline.[40] The popular convention, essentially a clone of the 1945 prototype, finally took place in January of 1947 and once again occurred outside the bounds of official liberalism. The event largely succeeded in its goals of discrediting the Liberal oligarquía, clarifying the Gaitanista program, and preparing the definitive assault on the país político in the March elections. The week it unfolded was dubbed "Week of the *Reconquista* of Power." Once again, bands blared, delegates from every part of Colombia crammed into the Circo de Santamaría, Gaitán gave an emotional and moving speech, and then led a procession of thousands through the streets of Bogotá to the Teatro Colón.[41] There he and the most important delegates worked for three days to produce the central document of official Gaitanista ideology, the Plataforma del Colón.

For the Gaitanistas, the key feature of the convention distinguishing it from a traditional Liberal affair was its democratic nature. They hailed it as "the first national assembly of the Liberal party with authentic elected representatives of the Liberal *pueblo*." Though not all municipalities sent their representatives nor was the voting process without flaw, the oligarquía could not deny, they argued, that the assembly was "an authentic expression of the popular will." Now the Liberal party's representatives reflected its social base, could produce truly democratic statutes, and would fight for "the well-being of the less favored classes of society."[42] The Popular Liberal Convention, united to study the problems of the party and define its future political orientation, saluted the democratic pueblo, the worker and peasant masses, and the revolutionary youth, intending to maintain the spirit of liberty that animated the ideals of Colombian democracy.[43]

Gaitanismo emerged from the convention aware of its own power. It rolled on to savage the Liberal party lists headed by Santos and Lleras Restrepo in the March congressional elections. The Gaitanistas took 448,848 votes to the official Liberals' 352,959 votes.[44] Gaitanistas on the coast pointed out that "if Gaitán is today the chief of the Liberal party, it is because his policies and supporters carried the day on March 16, not because of his pretty face nor because the *oligarquía* gave their consent for it to be so."[45] Gaitanismo had wrenched control of the Liberal party away from its natural leaders.[46] Most of the Liberal notables withdrew from public life, and even left the country. Eduardo Santos went off to Paris in a huff, defying Gaitán to survive without the political bosses. López and Lleras Camargo had posts in New York and Washington and simply did not return. Lleras Restrepo, as Herbert Braun put it, "retired to private life and to a career as delegate to international conferences." Calibán did not abandon the country, but admitted that he would travel abroad more often. Of the principal Liberals, Plinio Mendoza Neira alone could forge a personal relationship with Gaitán, and Darío Echandía joined the Gaitanistas, though without enthusiasm.[47] By June Gaitán was declared jefe único.

Communists as Gaitanistas and the Disintegration of the PSD

Communist leaders were just as unforgiving as the jefes naturales. But as the election of 1946 showed, their refusal to support Gaitán, and their monumentally ill-conceived attempt to label him a "fascist," seemed absurd to the majority of Colombians on the left and even to many of the Communist faithful. As a consequence, Gaitán proved himself the popularly anointed leader of the Colombian left and decisively eclipsed a splintering PSD in 1946–47.[48]

Connections on the left had long been apparent. While Gaitán's followers did not see him as an enemy of private property, religion, or the family, he was nevertheless known as an advocate of "leftist Liberalism" of a "socialist tendency," under which economic relations could be regulated.[49] It is no surprise, therefore, that Gaitán was identified with the left and with Communists.[50] Decades later a mason remembered that Gaitanistas were also called "Communist."[51] This association even rubbed off on some of his decidedly non-Communist supporters.[52]

In fact, for some time, many Communists (leaders as well as the rank and file) were also Gaitanistas. One of the best representatives of such duality was Juan Manuel Valdelamar, who was an important Communist party member and union organizer throughout the 1930s and 1940s. In 1936 the Liberal paper *El Mitín* of Cartagena gave an account of a rally at which he spoke against "Yanqui" imperialism and the bourgeoisie, themes he had expounded upon "for many years."[53] Analysts at the U.S. State Department described him on a list of Colombian Communist party members "and their known activities" in 1947. They characterized Valdelamar as "Indian [in another report they called him "negro"], age about thirty-four, formerly a barber, once accused of theft, an acknowledged leader of the Communist party but expelled in May 1944. Very intelligent and very dangerous."[54] At one time he was president of the Cartagena chapter of the Communist party and a member of the national directing bodies of both the PSD and the CTC, serving as the secretary general of the latter. In 1942 he ran afoul of the CTC leadership while representing the federation to the river workers of the Magdalena. Apparently advocating a more militant line of action than the federation, he "violated his instructions" and committed "union indiscipline," leading to his dismissal. The PSD commended his ouster, stressing that union discipline was necessary to defend worker interests with "Nazi subs off the coast terrorizing our cities," and kicked him off their board and out of the party as well.[55] Even after he was expelled from both the CTC and the PSD, however, he remained an important leader of his union in Bolívar and eventually found his way back into the PSD. By the early 1940s, Valdelamar was carrying on a lively and informative personal correspondence with Gaitán, whom he backed with few reservations. His was not an isolated example.

There was much evidence of Communist rank-and-file sympathy for Gaitán. In Cartagena Samuel Guerrero reported having spoken to various "militant members" of the Communist party there who were "disgusted" by Durán's opposition to Gaitán's candidacy. Prophetically, he held that if Durán and the other leading *compañeros* continued, "contrary to the political principles of genuine Communism," to oppose the "popular candidacy" of Gaitán, they would soon split the party.[56] In Santa Marta Eduardo Octavio C., a Gaitanista telegraph operator with a penchant for writing letters to the editor of major newspapers, lived next door to a Communist union hall. He was a "good friend" of Carlos Arias and José Russo, both prominent members of the departmental and national Communist organizations, and regularly took them copies of *Jornada* to read. One afternoon in early 1945, sitting with Russo outside his house, Octavio asked if the PSD's reluctance to back Gaitán was not a "death blow to their political aspirations." Russo reportedly looked around uncomfortably and declined to answer.[57] A Communist militant and labor organizer active in Barrancabermeja in the 1940s later remembered popular displeasure among party members over PSD support for Turbay because "the mass of the radical oil workers were Gaitanista." Those sympathetic to the Communist party, therefore, took a dim view of the party's decision to favor Turbay, "candidate of the *oligarquía*." From that point onward, the party's influence decreased considerably.[58] In April 1946 representatives of the PSD traveled to Barranquilla to encourage support for Turbay but faced serious opposition from rank-and-file Communists.[59] Barranquilla union leader Ramón de la Hoz, remarking on FEDENAL and the PSD's support of Turbay, expressed a feeling repeated often, that it was a disaster for a party of the left to support the candidate of the oligarquía and appear unrevolutionary.[60] Communist militants active in Barranquilla at the time remembered the support for Turbay as "absurd politics" because "the proletarian masses were with Gaitán."[61]

A telling defection from the Communist party was that of Carlos Giacometto del Real, a prominent Communist leader from Magdalena.

Giacometto exemplified the general overlap common on the Colombia left, having been a Communist, a Lopista, and a Gaitanista almost simultaneously.[62] As he wrote to Gaitán in July of 1947, he left the ruins of communism to enter Gaitanismo, the only movement "capable of confronting reaction."[63] Such defections became increasingly common as the PSD broke into tiny, antagonistic groups.

As Gaitán took control of the Liberal party, the PSD rapidly plunged into extinction as it split into three rival Communist organizations led by Augusto Durán, Gilberto Vieira, and Diego Montaña Cuéllar. This rupture was in large part due to the inability of the old leadership to admit Gaitán's victory in mobilizing a powerful, leftist movement.[64] Despite their all-out campaign, Gaitán's showing in the presidential election of 1946 decisively proved the impotence of the PSD. They were reduced to calling for, in the words of a State Department observer, a "Popular Front" of Communists and Gaitanistas, in a "union of all democratic forces . . . to defeat the Conservatives in the March 16, 1947, elections of Senators, Representatives and Departmental Deputies." While "the Communists sought in vain to win Gaitán's followers," the "bitter hatred felt by top Communist leaders" for Gaitán, especially Durán, had not abated. In private, the PSD continued "to revile him as an irresponsible demagogue."[65] Yet many rank-and-file Communists and rogue leaders believed that Durán was "entirely too aloof from the people" and that he had "forgotten that he was a laborer and a product of the Magdalena river."[66]

The party line immediately after the presidential election, according to the U.S. State Department, was that "the masses which follow Gaitán" were "sincere" and had to be won over. "Gaitán himself, on the other hand, is an out and out demagogue, slightly demented" who suffered from delusions. The Communist leadership finally recognized the Gaitanista masses as "of the same character as the Communist masses" and, it was believed, "could be easily won over once Gaitán has been exposed as an instrument of the Conservatives to keep the Liberals divided." But one confidential source pointed out that "Gaitán's attitude toward the Communist masses is similar to Durán's toward the gaitanistas: Gaitán hates Durán but seeks to win over the Communist masses."[67] Valdelamar smugly noted that just as the Communists originally attacked López as a demagogue but on seeing his mass following abruptly turned to support his "revolution," now they wanted to ally with Gaitán, who months before they denigrated in apocalyptic terms.[68]

And it was lost on no one that the Gaitanistas "had not come to the Communist door, but rather, vice-versa."[69] During the elections of March

1947 "the Communists made almost all the concessions, and the election results proved that Gaitán had stolen many of their votes." This was not surprising since in August 1946 the CTC had imploded, resulting in a stalemate between Communist and Liberal unions in which "two rival committees were established" though "neither side was able to obtain official, legal recognition."[70]

The Gaitanistas gleefully chronicled Diego Montaña Cuéllar's withdrawal from the Communist party in March 1947. Accompanied by "numerous" worker leaders, Montaña Cuéllar made "grave accusations against Durán and Vieira" for their campaigns of personal ambition, which had wrecked the party. In an interview with *Jornada,* he said that the PSD no longer represented the authentic aspirations of the working class.[71]

As he pulled out of the party, Giacometto del Real spelled out the deficiencies of Colombian communism, "for which there are no solutions." Colombian Communist leaders had come to view the party as an institutional base for personal power and influence. Short of a social revolution in the United States, nothing could shake them from their idle life as high-living "functionaries," subsidized by the working class. In his opinion, little of substance could be found separating Durán, Vieira, and Montaña Cuéllar. Their battles were simply power struggles that failed to advance the cause of the Colombian revolution. The three competing Communist parties had sunk into a morass of endless infighting and expulsions, denying them any hope of relevance. When he joined the Communist party in 1937, he had not supposed it to be composed of "a chorus of archangels," but at that time it seemed the most legitimate advocate of justice. This was no longer the case. Giacometto believed that the only viable action for an "honest Communist" was to join the Gaitanistas. Therefore he and "numerous ex-members of the PSD" were organizing the Acción Colombianista to work within liberalism to assist Gaitán in the reconquest of power because, "if we are Marxists, we should also be realists." Gaitán was the undisputed leader of liberalism and of the masses. While they were aware that liberalism encompassed "tremendous forces of reaction," it also contained progressive elements, and represented the most viable catalyst of struggle.[72] Commenting on the "letter" and Giacometto's organization "Acción Colombianista," the editors of *El Estado* noted the rupture of the PSD with an attitude of self-satisfaction.[73] Describing his movement in a letter to their editorial board, Giacometto declared Gaitán the "captain of *el pueblo.*" His group fought for unified liberalism, an autonomous union movement, peasant leagues, and to make Conservative workers aware that their real enemies were not the Gaitanistas but rather the Liberal and Conservative oligarquía.[74]

When the PSD finally admitted the depth of Gaitán's support, it was too late. As they suffered politically for first opposing, then supporting Turbay, they lost credibility for opposing Gaitán and then supporting him. Ironically, as Gaitán moved closer to the Liberal establishment, he gained the Communists' grudging support. The PSD found itself eclipsed and absorbed by a rival, indigenous, leftist movement.

False Gaitanistas

Despite the reactions of the jefes naturales and the Communist leadership, many Liberal políticos decided to jump to Gaitanismo soon after the presidential election. After May 1946, therefore, the question of who could call himself a Gaitanista became a highly contested one. The infiltration of the movement by "false Gaitanistas" increasingly alarmed the faithful. A member of the "studious youth" on the Liberal left in Tunja who, for example, was "ready to give battle for ideas and not for the bureaucratic interests" that divided the party, railed at the "false Gaitanistas" invading the movement.[75] An "old Gaitanista" in Ibagué fumed at "false Gaitanistas," who he claimed were only there for personal advancement.[76] Gaitanistas not uncommonly contrasted "true Liberals" ("Liberales de verdad," i.e., left Liberals) with professional politicians joining the movement.[77] And a group of concerned adherents in Atlántico were not surprised by the conduct of so-called Gaitanistas, whom they believed worked against the "essential spirit of our faith and convictions."[78] To some Gaitanistas, any professional politician was suspect, and perhaps with good reason. Gonzalo Sánchez noted that after failing in their attempt to paint Gaitán as a fascist, establishment Liberals "tried another route, which, in the end, proved more effective." In penetrating the Gaitanista ranks they sought to "neutralize" the movement or at least "to accentuate its internal tensions." It was only at "that price" that "Gaitán became the leader . . . of the Liberal party in 1947."[79] Indeed, one of the principal reasons that Daniel Pécaut argued against the popular nature of Gaitanismo after 1946 was this invasion of Gaitanismo by the país político.[80]

Undoubtedly the problem of opportunism nagged the movement as political professionals flooded in after the election. Some observers even began to muse whether Gaitán himself had become a false Gaitanista. As one Communist rival later maintained, once Gaitán became the jefe único of the Liberal party, he was no longer the man who said, "If I stop, push me; if I retreat, kill me"; his movement rather naturally attracted opportunists.[81] Since neither the Liberal machine nor Gaitán's network could prevail alone, political leaders created strange but expedient arrangements. As the old political system meshed with mass-based, idealistic Gaitanismo, both were altered. A telling indicator of the trauma Gaitanismo underwent was the prevalent atmosphere of intrigue and accusation. Yet even if Gaitán turned away from the popular character of Gaitanismo (and it is not clear that he did), the movement itself retained a good deal of its radical nature.

And it was also the case that bringing the political professionals over was seen by many as quite an achievement, not unlike Gaitán's return to the party in 1935 was seen as the ultimate success of UNIR. Long-time Gaitán disciple Dionisio Rincones Ponce identified two classes of Gaitanista among politicians. The first encompassed those "of the heart, animated by their humanitarian and patriotic feelings," whose "capacity for sacrifice" elevated them above political "vulgarities." The second class contained Gaitanistas "of calculation," there to benefit from Gaitán's popularity. Though unfortunate, the existence of the latter variety demonstrated the victory of the movement.[82] Some Liberal políticos immediately switched to Gaitán, far ahead of the Liberal leadership. One elected official from Medellín claimed to have been the "first anti-Turbayista of Antioquia," but had wanted party unity in his department and voted for the official party slate. Yet on May 8, 1946, he proclaimed his allegiance to Gaitán as jefe único.[83] Even Fermín López Giraldo, who was infamous for condemning Gaitán as the "naked apostle," returned to the Gaitanista camp "like a prodigal son."[84]

There had been problems with infiltrators even before May 1946. Gaitanistas were ever on the lookout for political chameleons who might slip into the movement's ranks and dilute its authenticity as a popular mobilization. As early as 1945, a lawyer in Barranquilla fretted over one such case in which an alleged Gaitanista impostor was spreading falsehoods about the movement's inner workings and trying to "capitalize on sympathies" that were rightfully Gaitán's.[85] Gaitanistas such as Carlos J. Moreno, who could not tolerate any deals with the oligarquía, saw it as their principal duty to support Gaitán and attack the "oligarchical systems of government." He disapproved that Adriano Rangel and Elías Moisés, who called themselves Gaitanistas, had declared support for Martín Leyes, a known Turbayista.[86] He even railed at Blanco Núñez for going to a "banquet of the *oligarquía*" in honor of governor Alberto Pumarejo,

Gaitanismo's "number one enemy" in Atlántico.[87] And for many, welcoming former enemies proved difficult. In Atlántico "chaos and discontent" reigned, according to Santander Leon y B., because many people could not accept an "ex-militant of the Communist party." He accused Adriano Rangel of being a "false friend" of Gaitanismo who entered the movement to further his own selfish interests.[88]

Yet there was no general agreement about who was false. Another group, for example, had no problem with Adriano Rangel who, they said, respected their organization and small paper, *Frente Nacional*. They did, however, have their own list of false Gaitanistas. The presence of one Roberto Jimeno Collante among the ranks of the faithful was "an offense to the Moral Restoration." With him they included Alonso Hernández and Nestor Carlos Consuegra as opportunists without ideas.[89]

After the election of 1946, the enemies of false Gaitanismo voiced recurring concerns. As one of the faithful warned Gaitán in November 1946, he was sure Gaitanismo was "headed for disaster" if Gaitán continued "turning his back on the original soldiers of the movement." It could not be forgotten that they were "the base and pillars of the movement."[90] A "son of Colombia" was greatly dismayed at the "slow but steady fusion of the *nacionales* and the *políticos,*" which was causing many followers of the movement like himself to leave their ballots blank. He believed that "just as the fruit of old trees is, by the laws of nature, degenerate," a regression to the old party politics would yield a putrid harvest.[91] Gaitanistas in Magdalena warned that eleventh-hour infiltrators were swarming the ranks.[92] In Bolívar Carlos Tamara warned that if "genuine Gaitanistas" did not get themselves taken into account, "the *país político* would easily push them to the margin." The movement there was suffering an "avalanche of candidates who had never been, nor ever would be, Gaitanistas."[93] Since 1944 a coherent group of rebels had fought for the moral restoration in Bolívar, according to one longtime supporter. Yet, after the oligarquía had been defeated by Gaitán, many old gamonales and caciques "camouflaged themselves as Gaitanistas, infiltrated the ranks, and took over positions of authority," pushing many of the true leaders aside. This situation was breaking the discipline of the movement.[94] In August 1946 *El Estado* denied "rumors" that the movement was being infiltrated by the país político.[95] But by January 1947 they voiced their concerns about the health of the Liberal union and about attempts of "the enemies of Gaitanismo to sabotage the movement." The oligarquía still hoped to disrupt the democratic reorganization of the party, and "in the middle of the anarchy and confusion . . . continue their old ways." What was happening in Magdalena, they warned, was happening throughout the country.[96]

The necessity of coexistence with the old political culture, therefore, pitted professional politicians (some of whom were "false" and some of whom were not) against many rank-and-file Gaitanistas new to the compromises involved in politics. In a municipio in Tolima, where in the past the Liberal machine had denied Gaitán even a single vote, old Liberals were jumping on board so fast in July 1947 that it had become a hotbed of reconquista.[97] In Ibagué the concejal Germán Torres Barreto wanted to make the council "a political trampoline for his personal ambitions." Some members who were "Gaitanistas of long duration" and who represented "elements of the left" tolerated his maneuvers because they did not want to see the failure of Liberal union. Yet they were growing weary of Torres Barreto, who "on more than one occasion plagiarized the phrase of Louis XIV" by saying, "El Concejo soy yo" (The *concejo* is I).[98] False Gaitanistas in Cúcuta who had never worked in favor of "the popular cause" were really forces of the old guard fighting against the recognition of the popular slate of Gaitanistas for the convention. They brought "anarchy to popular Liberalism" and did not contribute "to the popular victory." As opposed to the "popular forces of the Left," which had always supported Gaitán, the old Liberal políticos of the department wanted to join the movement even though they were "more reactionary than the Conservatives."[99] In Mompós the Gaitanista municipal directorate resisted nominations of old machine politicians to their body made at the last minute by Pacho Vargas. The nomination of these gentlemen caused considerable "resentment and indignation" among the faithful because of their close ties to the city's oligarquía. They, who had been the enemies opposing Gaitán's campaign and had recently been defeated, "smiled disdainfully" at the true Gaitanistas and informed them that their directorate no longer had a reason to exit. Such "indecency and immorality" angered those who could say with pride that they had been with Gaitán from the beginning. Their allegiance had not been given without a price, as one of their number—who lost his job as a postal administrator rather than renounce Gaitán—could testify. They were not "May 5th Gaitanistas."[100]

Such struggles, as noted in chapter 6, produced a turbulent contest for Gaitán's approval. In the municipality of San Bernardo del Viento, Bolívar, departmental assembly deputy Antonio Zapata Olivella claimed to represent the Gaitanistas there against the "feudal politics" of one José Santos Cabrera. Cabrera owned a large portion of the municipality's land, perpetuated the exclusive cultivation of rice to the detriment of many poor colonos, and controlled the city council through fraud. He had jumped on the Gaitanista bandwagon to weaken the forces of the pueblo.[101] A group running for the city council and seeking the Gaitanista mantle, however, claimed that Zapata was one of the people claiming to be Gaitanistas who did not "understand our movement and its patriotic ends." He was only in the movement to "divide the *pueblo* . . . [and] disorient the masses."[102]

The case of gamonal Juan Barrios in Ciénaga demonstrated the byzantine maneuvers often involved. A longtime adherent complained that before May 5th Juan B. Barrios had been a determined anti-Gaitanista, who "publicly denigrated Gaitán's person and the movement in a vulgar fashion." He was "an opportunist of the worst class . . . with leftist pretensions." He dealt falsely with his political contacts and "pertained to the old school of politics," which used the system "to corrupt and round up flunkies."[103] The city's central Gaitanista committee reported that during the presidential campaign, Barrios rudely attacked Gaitán's "illustrious name," and only after Gaitán's success pretended to embrace the banner of moral restoration. He even went so far as to brag that he joined Gaitanismo while really practicing something else, "mocking the authentic electoral will of the masses."[104] And circuit court judge Juan N. Payares, a self-proclaimed friend of Gaitanismo from the beginning, counseled that it would be dangerous to let Barrios head the ticket for senator. They believed in Ciénaga that he was likely to turn on the movement.[105]

Within the bigger picture, Barrios was an example of the Gaitanista political dilemma: to mix or not to mix. As Dionisio Rincones Ponce deciphered the situation for Gaitán in June 1946, the old Liberal machine in Magdalena was split into two camps before the 1946 presidential election. One was commanded by José B. Vives and the other by Pedro Castro Monsalvo. The more unattractive of the two factions was that of Castro, "the perfect *manzanillo,* a true oligarch," who had grown rich from his influence over the departmental government. Vives, though an old-time politician, was an honorable man and not corrupt. In the election they both united in their support of Turbay and by June had "naturally split apart again." Both wanted to be elected senator, but since within the liberalism of Magdalena there existed "a great force . . . which triumphed in the last election, namely Gaitanismo," Vives proposed a deal. In order to "definitively liquidate Castro" he would join his senatorial ticket with the Gaitanista deputy ticket. Juan B. Barrios would also run for senator, and while he was sure to lose, he would "certainly take a large number of votes from Castro." With these musings Rincones Ponce consciously ignored "whether or not the Gaitanistas of the department would accept such a mixture," but he was sure that Castro's machine was "the most hated." He asked Gaitán if they should "accept this combination . . . or go to the March elections without a mixture of any kind." Gaitán sidestepped the issue and simply answered that they should "prepare and organize for the popular convention"; they as yet had not given any thought to the congressional elections.[106]

By late 1947 Gaitán offered a typical answer to angry letters of accusation and complaint about false Gaitanistas. In Montería the president of the Popular Liberal Committee was up in arms about the candidacy of one Antonio Navarro for a local office saying, "The *pueblo* has grown tired of suffering deceptions."[107] Gaitán replied that as he had said many times, the struggle was not simply over local offices and bureaucratic positions, "but rather a complete revolution against the old political and administrative systems." And at that moment he did not advise struggles between Liberals.[108] In other words, Gaitanistas had to keep their eyes on the prize. Only so many deals could be cut, however. Gaitanistas would only go so far in cooperating with their former enemies, and many were not willing to sacrifice the movement's goals simply to retake the presidency for the Liberal party.

Reintegration and *La Reconquista*

After May of 1946, Gaitán's principal concern was Liberal reconquest of the presidency. For this to happen, the Gaitanista Liberal movement had to reunite with the official party. On the night of May 5th, a Conservative asked Gaitán what he would then do, and Gaitán replied "the battle has just begun. Until now, we Liberals have been fighting amongst ourselves."[109] The push for Liberal unity came as early as May 1946 in the official Gaitanista line. José María Córdoba indicated that the Liberal party could not give up its control of the national Congress nor the judiciary, nor could the Conservatives be allowed to continue in the presidency in 1950. "Dr. Gaitán and this directing body are earnestly striving to bring about the union of all the elements of liberalism. We must be prepared for the future battles with the traditional enemy."[110] And given the rising level of political violence throughout Colombia as Conservatives asserted their control, Gaitán's return to the Liberal party was more than just an opportunistic maneuver; it was a matter of survival.

In June 1946 a former concejo secretary for Tunja optimistically saw great potential in rallying the party behind Gaitán as jefe único. From

1930 to the present, he argued, Liberals were all "travelers in the same ship" that had navigated the high seas of government. Yet for some time the ship of state had been "anchored in the still waters of ambition . . . with torn sails, and more than one captain." He also hoped that Gaitán would usher in a period of heightened democracy, calling for the national directorate of the Liberal party to be formed "in a more popular and democratic way, finally opening its deliberations."[111] The boat image was a popular one. In left-Liberal Líbano, Gaitán was "at the helm of the good ship Liberal" guiding it through the rough waters of "envy, ingratitude, and passion" to the safe haven of electoral victory.[112] A better image of liberalism after 1946, however, would have been of two eighteenth-century ships of the line, lashed together to form a giant catamaran, but whose gunners continued to fire into each other.

Many Gaitanistas were decidedly uneasy with the idea of reintegration. The president of the Popular Liberal Committee of San Juan y Chaparro, Guaguarco, Hilarco, and Boca de Hilarco (in the municipio of Coyaima in Tolima), which represented 263 Liberals "in the popular movement" who still worked for the "restoration," was a good example. He assured Gaitán that he was embedded "deeply in the consciousness of the Liberal *pueblo*" because of his "program for the workers." He reminded the caudillo, however, that their main goal remained to change the political system and fight the domination of the caciques. "The Liberal oligarchs, who do not want to be called Conservative" were really the most reactionary in their actions. They quoted the "illustrious doctor" Jorge Uribe Márquez: "In the popular consciousness a storm of quiet anguish was building, that upon explosion will break the national equilibrium."[113]

Daniel Pécaut interpreted this convergence as the end of popular Gaitanista mobilization. He recognized that Gaitanismo represented the death blow to Lopista liberalism and took the banner of social mobilization away from the CTC and the PSD. But he portrayed the movement as a largely destructive phenomenon, "irresistible, yet at the same time, fragile." Gaitanismo laid waste to the old political organizations but, he argued, had little more than Gaitán's voice to hold it together. Pécaut interpreted Gaitanismo's attachment to the Liberal party as a sign of its weakness, that it could not create an independent movement of its own. Gaitán's involvement with the Liberal party doomed the movement to lose its soul in the endless struggles between the traditional parties.[114] Gaitanismo, in other words, no longer had any pretensions to being a popular movement. There are problems with this interpretation, however. It discounts Gaitanista popular ideology, ignores the connections on the Colombian left, and overlooks that Gaitanismo was part of a larger current of popular mobilization.

The uneasy unification of official liberalism and Gaitanismo altered both in dramatic ways but, as already demonstrated, did not spell the end of popular mobilization. There were, moreover, reasons why Gaitanistas had little choice but to rejoin official liberalism. If there had been any doubts about the existence of an oligarquía during the Liberal Republic, after 1946 they evaporated as the Liberal masses encountered a "flesh and blood" oligarquía.[115] Immediately after the election Colombians witnessed a wave of spontaneous strikes and heard calls for Gaitán to assume the presidency. Gaitán, however, insisted that the results be recognized by all.[116] Recognized they were, but social unrest and labor actions increased in number and intensity throughout 1946 and 1947. The most dramatic episode was the general strike of May 13, 1947, which Gaitán himself ambivalently supported. Pécaut pointed to this tricky episode as evidence that Gaitanista populism was incapable of a class "synthesis." He noted that Gaitán first seemed to call for the strike, but with the proviso that it be employed if the Conservatives would not share power. Ultimately Gaitán did not work for the strike; he remained quiet and on the sidelines. Days later he called it "illegal" but also "just." The strike was quickly crushed. The Conservative government detained 1,500 workers on May 13 alone and suspended the CTC's *personería jurídica* for three months. Pécaut identified the strike as the final blow to the organized working class, which, he argued, Gaitán had abandoned.[117] But an alternative interpretation is that Gaitán opted for the political struggle, believing that direct mobilization of the still relatively small working class would be to no avail. And to pursue the political struggle, Gaitanismo had to rejoin the Liberal party.

As a united liberalism turned against the traditional foe, it was not, however, a mere return to partisan struggle. In fact, even in the nineteenth century the hoary Liberal versus Conservative altercation always had popular overtones, and now it had the more overt flavor of the Gaitanista dichotomy between the pueblo and the oligarquía. Under the conditions of the late 1940s, the "hereditary hatreds" had more ambivalent meaning; the old dichotomy was anything but pure. Thus Gaitanistas compared Gaitán and Gómez as they spoke on the same night. The leader of liberalism demonstrated his faith in the great undertaking of making politics more popular, supported as he was by the "democratic majority." Gaitán looked with confidence to the future while Gómez saw only darkness and danger. Gaitán spoke before the pueblo while Gómez spoke alone in his office to a microphone, "directing phantom armies."[118] Unfortunately for Colombia, these armies would soon prove all too real.

But even if political reality necessitated the attempt at reintegration of the different currents of liberalism, many recognized the odds of success as long ones. In Ibagué a Liberal político bowed to the reality of Gaitán's popularity there (even if rather late). He freely admitted that he was not one of Gaitán's followers, had indeed fought him, but faced with the Conservative threat would make an attempt at "this impossible union."[119] And even once Gaitán was recognized as the leader of liberalism, the divisions were still apparent just below the surface. In June of 1947 important Liberals still clearly disagreed about the goals of liberalism.[120]

Finally, whatever understandings Liberals could come to amongst themselves, it was clear that space for productive political activity was becoming quite restricted. Even the principal concern of the Gaitanistas in the still Liberal-controlled Congress of 1947, namely electoral reform, was dead on arrival. Its failure showed that in the atmosphere of increasing partisan tension and real and potential violence, the political system was becoming incapable of finding solutions. With the political stalemate in Congress, Gaitán continued to mend bridges with official liberalism, but his primary goal now was to build support in the streets.[121] Having defeated the jefes naturales and subdued many of the gamonales, the Liberal left found an even more implacable foe.

The Vengeful Return to Political Violence

Gaitanismo retained a good deal of its radical vitality, even under the increasing weight of the false-Gaitanista freeloaders. This reality was borne out by the fact that it was not easy to control and eventually could only be repressed by violence and civil war. Throughout Colombian political history, Eduardo Posada-Carbó argued, as "elections became more competitive, the role of the opposition in conditioning the level of fraud became as critical as that of the government." And it was just one of several factors.[122] This was the key to the political origins of the Violencia. Gaitanismo was simply too big of a movement for unadorned fraud and gamonal manipulation to be carried out decisively. On the local level, therefore, the Liberal oligarquía and their political majordomos resurrected various types of violence and threats of violence. Such pre-election brutality against Gaitanistas was evidence of serious intra-Liberal class struggle. This was not old-time political violence between multiclass parties, but rather factions of the same party that represented different social, political, and economic interests. After May 1946 the Conservatives, with the collusion of important elements within the Liberal party, many Gaitanistas believed, moved toward outright repression.[123]

In Santander left Liberals spoke on the eve of the presidential election of official "outrages, abuse, . . . cruelty, and monstrous cases" that were reminiscent of "the inquisition" or "the dark times before the French revolution." They identified two dozen paid "villains" and "assassins" in the nearby town of San Gil that were making life a terror. One Gaitanista's mouth was broken with a bottle in a most savage fashion; another was in grave condition after being stabbed; and another was strangled with a garrote; many others "were knocked around and left crippled in their beds . . . all under official sanction." These "unheard of abuses" were committed against "poor workers . . . Liberals" that carried (his emphasis) "THE DESIGNATION GAITANISTA!" This was the sole reason these victims were persecuted "with such caveman savagery." These were "acts that would not even be performed in a cave of gorillas" and that would require one "to be a medical doctor not to vomit." They asked, "Must Liberals be killed for the victory of the Liberal party?" They ended by pointing out that even the police, not just thugs, were carrying out raids against Gaitanistas, "giving Colombian democracy the most black, dismal, heinous, and fetid tunic of dishonor."[124]

Repression against Gaitanistas in Caldas was carried out by a very powerful cacique. Samuel Jaramillo was director of the municipal Liberal directorate, president of the concejo, president of the *jurado electoral* and of the Casa Liberal, secretary of the Sindicato Obrero, and prominent representative of the public employees. In addition, all the members of the Liberal Directorate and the concejo were Turbayistas. It was no surprise, therefore, that the vote in Quimbaya was not what it could have been because of the repression by "agents of the government . . . in the service of the illegitimate candidate." The "persecution against the Gaitanista element" there was "without precedent." By order of Bernardo Carrasquilla, the mayor, and Efraín Parra S., a local police sergeant, Gaitanista literature was banned during the last week of the campaign and many prominent Gaitanistas were carted off to jail. All Gaitanista notices were torn down. Turbay was declared the only legitimate candidate, and out of fear, many campesinos would not vote for Gaitán.[125] This case was hardly unique.[126]

Sometimes persecution by caciques was meant to settle personal scores. Carmen de Vidal and her family suffered for years the "odious and torturous power of the *caciques*," the story of which was a long history of "perverse interpretation" of the politics of López. She, her husband, and their children lived in peace along the Ferrocarril de Nariño until one Rubén Flórez was named "Inspector de Conservación de esta zona" and declared a "war to the death" on her husband because of his political views.[127]

Other times Liberals subcontracted their repression of Gaitanistas to Conservatives. In Boyacá, Conservatives attacked Gaitanistas with Turbayista compliance. One victim wrote to explain why there was little voter turnout in his municipio on May 5th. There were only three policemen on hand, even though they had written to the government that for a month before the election the Conservatives had been stockpiling "arms of all kinds," including "rifles, carbines, revolvers, shotguns, machetes, clubs, lances," to use against Liberals. A week before the election the former impartial alcalde was replaced with a Turbayista. The local Gaitanista Liberals were poorly armed and scarcely able to defend themselves; they therefore largely abstained from voting. After the election the situation remained tense and dangerous given the "high passions and belligerent spirit" of the neighborhood. The Liberal campesinos were afraid of the Conservative campesinos (the majority?) who were being pushed toward violence by their leaders and by the local clerics. Their mood was one of "strong pessimism."[128] In another municipio the Turbayista faction of the Liberal party had "dedicated itself to hostility against Gaitanista *campesinos*." In fact, it was believed that the Turbayistas were in league with the local ecclesiastical authorities and Conservatives in attacking "the authentic Liberals."[129]

The situation only got worse after the election. Political violence intensified as soon as the Conservative party took over the presidency and began to appoint Conservatives as governors, mayors, and police chiefs. They immediately moved to enjoy the spoils of their victory, as on the city council in Chiquinquirá where Conservatives fired Liberal municipal employees.[130] This was repeated in municipios throughout Colombia. They also proceeded to apply official terror, as the Liberals had done sixteen years earlier. In 1930 the new Liberal administration "proceeded ruthlessly to purge the opposition from offices," and in the most heavily Conservative areas, violence was the result.[131] After 1930 the nationally directed police in the departments of Santander and Boyacá met resistance from Conservative guerrillas. Blood was spilled periodically until 1934 when the government sent in 1,800 troops to pacify the areas. Village burning, deportation, and voting fraud came to be called the "Liberal violence." The Conservatives, therefore, did not lack for models of behavior.

Conservatives overtly baited and threatened Liberals. In Boyacá they taunted Liberals with loud music and constant "vivas" for the Conservative party. They also shouted such offensive things as "abajo el liberalismo so [sic] hijueputa." The Conservatives believed, Liberals informed Gaitán, that they were "the owners of life." Bands of Conservatives and police harassed Liberals and held several in jail.[132] In particular, Conservatives utilized well-worn political dirty tricks aimed at the political rights of Liberals. In San Gil, Conservatives under Acevedo Diaz employed the "low electoral tactics" of "reevaluating the *cédulas*" of Liberal empleados and obreros with the obvious goal of "impeding their suffrage rights" before the October elections of 1947.[133] In particular, Conservatives took aim at Liberal workers (presumably the Gaitanista base), such as Conservative government attacks in Tuluá, in which "trabajadores honrados" were kicked out of their homes, which were then burned.[134]

Violence was carried out in Pasto to assure Liberal abstention. Liberals were pressed by an *alcalde militar* from Boyacá who represented "a grave danger to local elections." He was a Conservative "fanatic" who seemed intent on causing Liberal abstention from the ballot box.[135] Similar dynamics played out in the Santanderes and Caldas, where violence was used to disrupt elections and persecute Liberals.[136]

In fact, Gaitanistas were singled out among Liberals for attack. In Caldas "agents of the government" were daily threatening the members of "insurgent Liberalism" who lived in fear for their lives, "for the sole fact that they defended liberty and believed in the fundamental ideas and principles of democracy and equality for all Colombians" as defended by Gaitán, "the leader of the multitudes." They called on Gaitán to prepare the defense because in "the Santanders, Boyacá, and other departments" Gaitanistas were "victims of *bandolerismo* and official arms." Gaitán had to resist the "barbarism" and "reign of terror" with a repetition of his famous accusations against the government in the matter of "las bananeras."[137]

It was also clear that the situation was not just a struggle between Liberals and Conservatives. The considerable tension between Gaitanistas and the right of the Liberal party lived on even as they sought to retake power. Gaitanistas continued to feel persecuted by the Liberal authorities for the sole crime of supporting Gaitán. One equated "Santista" with "derechista" (right-winger), claiming that the Santos faction of the party never had any real political ideals to defend and "always moved in the shadows."[138] As the Liberal party went to the polls in October 1947, the defiant currents of left liberalism echoed the overtones of Gaitán's dichotomy. The Liberal majority went to vote "with discipline and faith in the future, without imagining the violence and heated atmosphere of insecurity that awaited them." Yet Liberals were still determined to vote "to win or die." Inspired by Uribe Uribe and following Gaitán, the "*masas obreras* of Colombia" would not leave the "reaction" to prosper.[139]

As the pages of *Jornada* testified throughout 1947 and into 1948, political violence was frightfully on the rise. In answer and lawful contrast to the official terror, as night fell on February 7, 1948, Gaitán summoned the Gaitanistas of Bogotá to the Plaza de Bolívar to mourn the victims of the expanding violence. Dubbed the "Manifestación del Silencio," Gaitán called for a "sacred silence," which over one hundred thousand Gaitanistas dressed in black respected. After speaking for only five minutes, during which he asked President Ospina Pérez to halt the killing, he sent the Gaitanistas home in uncanny quiet.[140] It was understood by all sides, however, that Gaitán would not call on the left Liberals to turn the other cheek indefinitely.

Intra-Liberal Conflict and the Death Throes of Radical Populist Politics

A central theme in the history of the Liberal Republic between 1930 and 1946 was intra-Liberal struggle over the nature of the party. Though all Liberals rejoiced in the Liberal presidential victory of 1930, establishment Liberals and left Liberals began to move slowly apart. Indeed, as noted at the beginning of this study, as early as 1928 the battle lines within the party were already being drawn, which in turn reflected a debate over the meaning, purpose, and nature of liberalism that stretched back to Uribe Uribe at the turn of the century and to the struggles of the nineteenth century.

The party enjoyed a few giddy years of peaceful coexistence. Between 1930 and 1934 Liberals were simply glad to be back in power. It was a time of hope and promise during which division remained largely below the surface. The years between 1934 and 1936, the early phase of the first López presidency and time of the Revolución en Marcha, represented the high-water mark of détente between the competing currents of Colombian liberalism. The cracks in the party, however, were all too evident by 1937 and 1938 as left Liberals unsuccessfully backed Darío Echandía as López's successor.

The Santos period between 1938 and 1942, the "pause" in López's controlled revolution, saw building tensions within the party as left Liberals became more and more frustrated with stymied reform and the party's retreat on social, political, and economic issues. And in 1941 and 1942, presidential politics once again precipitated a flare-up of dissension over the question of reelecting Alfonzo López Pumarejo. While many left Liberals, Gaitán included, saw his return as a step backwards, the PSD, organized labor, and a majority of the Liberal faithful rallied to his side and called on him to complete his "revolution." In this, of course, they were disappointed. After it became unmistakably clear that no efforts would be made to revive the left-Liberal agenda, the second half of López's second term brought an unmitigated collapse of Liberal party unity. The breakdown of establishment liberalism led to the crisis of open class warfare within the party and the rise of Gaitanismo between 1944 and 1946.

Gaitán was not the rainmaker who called up the storm of Gaitanismo. Rather, he was the lighting rod that directed its left-Liberal fury. By characterizing the struggle as a dichotomy between the pueblo and the oligarquía, he gave the movement coherence it might not otherwise have had. It was a dangerous strategy that would cause problems as soon as he took control of the party, though as an organizational tool it proved crucial to his success. Gaitán himself played a central role, yet the popular origins of the mobilization associated with his name cannot be denied. Gaitán was the unifying symbol, but the rank-and-file Gaitanistas made it happen. As Gaitán moved closer to real power he softened his position, but his behavior was dictated by political necessity. When he moved back into the Liberal political fold, both after UNIR and after the 1946 election, his primary concern was building a viable political movement, and he was willing to make compromises. Bowing to historical expediency, Gaitán's post-1946 "caudillismo" rose from the need for unity against the attacks of the traditional powers. Whatever Gaitán's personal motivations, however, his followers remembered the spirit of UNIR and stressed his critique of the existing political and economic order; the Gaitanistas never ceased applying pressure. These are the crucial elements for understanding Gaitanismo after May 1946.

The Gaitanistas strove to re-create the Colombian political system through democratic practice. Especially on the local level, Gaitanismo successfully challenged gamonal politics by mobilizing and voting. Though imperfectly melded with official liberalism, the movement held together after the presidential election of 1946; the Gaitanistas' victories of 1947 proved that. If only for a short time, liberalism had been forced to make space for Gaitanismo. Yet the old leadership ultimately found watching the different wings of liberalism go their separate ways preferable to allowing the total victory of the left-Liberal tradition. Humpty-Dumpty had fallen. The competing strains of popular left and elite liberalism had moved too far apart to be reunited.

Epilogue and Conclusion

Gaitanismo, *la Violencia,* and Colombia's Enduring Predicament

By early 1948 it was obvious that Gaitán would be the Liberal candidate in the 1950 presidential election, and therefore the next president. The big question remained: which Gaitán would rule, "the social agitator or the political conciliator"?[1] Many Colombians believe the oligarquía could not stand the suspense. Gaitán was assassinated on April 9, 1948.

On the night of April 8 Gaitán successfully wrapped up his defense of Jesús María Córtes Poveda, an army lieutenant who had killed Eudoro Galarza, a newspaper man, over a question of "honor."[2] Even though Gaitán had been out until 4:00 A.M. celebrating his victory, he was back at his law office soon after 8:00 A.M. on April 9. Gaitán was attending to his law practice and keeping a low profile while Bogotá hosted the IX Pan American Conference. Though the Ospina government had insultingly excluded him from the Colombian delegation, Gaitán restrained Liberals who wanted to boycott the conference and disrupt its proceedings. The atmosphere in the city was tense, given the increased security presence of army and police in place to watch over the large numbers of foreign dignitaries in town. There were also significant contingents of left-wing activists who came to Colombia to protest the signing of the anticommunist declaration brought by the U.S. secretary of state, George C. Marshall. Among their number was a young Cuban law student named Fidel Castro who had an afternoon appointment with Gaitán on the same day.

After addressing political questions during the morning hours, Gaitán accepted an invitation to lunch with Liberal politician Plinio Mendoza Niera. Accompanied by three of his most devoted cadres, Pedro Eliseo Cruz, Gaitán's personal physician and a senator from Cundinamarca; Alejandro Vallejo, co-director of *Jornada;* and Jorge Padilla, writer and treasurer of Bogotá, they set out. After descending in the elevator and crossing the narrow lobby, the group reached the curb a few minutes after

1:00 P.M. with Mendoza and Gaitán in front. Gaitán had just stepped into the street when Juan Roa Sierra (a marginal character with obscure political connections) stepped out from behind a pillar at the entrance of the building and fired three shots from a .38 caliber revolver at point-blank range into Gaitán's body, one piercing his lungs and another lodging at the base of his skull. Gaitán fell to the sidewalk never to regain consciousness. Rushed by taxis to the Clínica Central, he died at about 2:00 P.M. After firing a fourth shot into the air, Roa Sierra retreated towards the Avenida Jiménez a few yards away where he was immediately captured by a Bogotá policeman, Carlos Alberto Jiménez Díaz, who was walking up the avenue. (The municipal police were overwhelmingly Liberal.) Roa Sierra was pulled into a drugstore across the street. Herbert Braun recounted that "Jiménez pleaded with his captive. 'Tell me who ordered you to kill, for you are going to be lynched by the *pueblo.*' 'Oh, Señor,' the man answered . . . 'powerful things that I can't tell you, oh, Virgin of Carmen, save me!'" A few minutes later, the crowd that was gathering outside broke through the grating, seized Roa Sierra, and pummeled him to death. They then dragged his naked body down the Carrera Séptima toward the presidential palace, beginning one of Latin America's most notorious urban uprisings, and a good deal more.[3]

The question Colombians still ask is, who killed Gaitán? It is widely assumed that Roa Sierra was merely the tool of powerful anti-Gaitán interests, and there were many potential suspects. Herbert Braun did very little with this question, even though his book was about the effects of the assassination itself. Interestingly, its Spanish translation evoked intrigue and dark collusion with its title, *Mataron a Gaitán* (They killed Gaitán). This was the cry that went up throughout Colombia on the *nueve de abril* and the days thereafter. With some reservations, Braun generally accepted the notion that Gaitán's assassination was the work of a single man acting on personal motivations.[4] While this conclusion is debatable, Braun was undeniably wise to give the menacing bogs of conspiracy theory a respectfully wide berth. As much as the question continues to haunt Colombians, it is a fact that no smoking gun has yet to be uncovered that definitively connects Roa Sierra to any person or group. But whoever, if anyone, was behind the shooting, there is no question about its impact. It brought an end to Colombia's longest period of peaceful political development, swept away much of the legitimacy of its political class, and completely altered its political environment for decades to come.

Colombia is recognized as one of the most violent countries in Latin America. This reputation emerged during the period after Gaitán's death that Colombians call simply "la Violencia," the Violence. By the mid-1960s, Colombia had witnessed in excess of two hundred thousand politically motivated violent deaths. La Violencia, 1946–66, can be broken into five stages: it began in the revival of political violence before and after the presidential election of 1946; it blossomed in the popular urban upheavals generated by Gaitán's assassination; it transformed into open guerrilla war directed first against the Conservative government of Ospina Pérez and then against the even more repressive government of Laureano Gómez, which lasted from mid-1948 until June 1953; it continued amidst the incomplete attempts at pacification and negotiation resulting from the general amnesty offered by the military government of General Gustavo Rojas Pinilla (who had ousted Gómez), between 1953 and 1957; and lived on in the disjointed fighting under the Liberal/Conservative coalition of the "National Front," which came into power in 1958 and lasted until 1974. Easily one of the longest and most confusing chapters in all of Latin American history, the Violencia has been interpreted alternately as a continuation of the civil wars of the nineteenth century, as a failure of the national political system brought on by a long and bitter struggle for power between factions of the elite (resulting in an "institutional heart attack"),[5] and finally as a social revolution that failed to congeal. There is obviously some truth in each of these views, but none by itself is completely satisfactory. This is understandable considering the Violencia's duration, the ambiguity of its beginning, and the inconclusiveness of its ending. Add that the Violencia encompassed many regional variations and that its character demonstrated several marked changes over time, and it becomes clear that this phenomenon will always defy simple explanation.[6]

The spread of the Violencia did, however, play an indisputable role: it dealt a death blow to the democratically oriented political mobilizations of Gaitanismo. Indeed, the first wave of the Violencia came in the overt anti-Gaitanista campaign of the Liberal establishment before the election of 1946. Political violence intensified as soon as the Conservative president Ospina Pérez began to appoint Conservatives as governors, mayors, and police chiefs who proceeded to apply official terror. Gaitanistas lashed back in their reaction to Gaitán's assassination on April 9, known outside Colombia as the "Bogotazo." His death caused widespread urban uprisings, stretching from the capital (a large portion of which was destroyed) to Cali, Barranquilla, Cartagena, Ibagué, Barrancabermeja, and other cities. There is considerable evidence for the view that this insurrection was a beheaded left-Liberal social revolution. Gonzalo Sánchez pointed out that the "popular masses," supplemented by a large part of the national police force in Bogotá, attacked all the "symbols of oppression" such as the presidential palace, churches, jails, and oligarchic newspapers. It was overwhelmingly urban and considerably class-based.[7] The mortal weakness of this popular revolution, however, was that it never unified on the national level. Rather it became "a constellation of alternative local power centers with no connections between them." These pockets of revolution were put down once the insurrection in Bogotá collapsed. Not surprisingly, the radical Liberal pueblo was sold out by the elite Liberal "junta of notables" that negotiated with the government in the early hours of the crisis.[8]

Yet beyond the urban upheavals, early students of the Violencia refused to make the connection between the political mobilizations before 1948 and the violent conflicts in the years that came after. Relationships to the immediate past, the 1930s and 1940s, were typically skimmed over in deference to the Liberal and Conservative battles of the nineteenth century. The Violencia sprang forth fully clad in the colors of the traditional parties' seemingly eternal rivalry. The political origins of the Violencia were quickly subsumed into the "hereditary hatreds," thereby converting the struggle into a series of "irrational" or "apolitical" events unconnected to political struggles over real interests. Or they were interpreted as outgrowths of large, abstract structural processes regarding economic, judicial, and cultural questions.

Over the last two decades, however, students of the phenomenon have noted that Gaitanismo and the emergence of the Violencia were inextricably linked, even if on the surface many instances of violence followed the old patterns of the Liberal and Conservative division. Such scholars as Daniel Pécaut, Gonzalo Sánchez, Mary Roldán, and others, though offering different interpretations, have all pointed to the connections.[9]

The key, of course, was the strain generated by the Gaitanista left Liberals who demanded real change, and the increasing likelihood (before April 9, 1948) of their success in bringing it about. And after June 1949 it was clear that the more strident portions of the oligarquía had grown weary and impatient with attempting to control populist politics and opted for outright counter-revolutionary force. That month the Liberal elite pulled out (was largely pushed out) of the oligarchic coalition that formed in the wake of the urban uprisings. Laureano Gómez, soon to be installed as president in elections that Liberals either boycotted or were too afraid to participate in, believed that the only political solution was pure repression, an out-and-out campaign of terror against the chusma, carried out by the now Conservative-dominated National Police, the

Army, and bands of murderous thugs known as *pájaros* (the forerunners of the *sicarios* and *paramilitar* death squads of the 1980s, 1990s, and later). Such repression would become commonplace during the 1960s and 1970s as military governments throughout the region attempted to find authoritarian solutions to social problems earlier addressed by populist movements.

Gaitanismo threatened the old elite-dominated political structures of society. Yet many observers would still argue that Gaitán was an opportunist who used his movement as a vehicle for his own ambition, and that his personalistic style of populist leadership debilitated the popular mobilization. The focus of this study, therefore, has not been Gaitán, but rather what people did as Gaitanistas and how they revealed the currents of popular political mobilization emanating from the left-Liberal tradition that permeated Colombian society in these years.

As argued at the outset of this study, the hegemonic nature of Colombia's political system in the 1930s and 1940s is not in question. While the central government was (and remains to this day) relatively weak, Colombia's elite clearly dominated the nation's "oligarchic democracy." This political framework, however, had long been tempered by historically high degrees of popular political participation that both legitimized the hegemonic nature of the system and threatened it with destruction from within. State power was never particularly good at defining boundaries in Colombia, and left significant space for effective resistance. As an example of these trends, Gaitanismo offered a radical and popular threat to the economic and political status quo. In fact, when the Gaitanistas challenged the political mechanisms of oligarchic rule and it was clear that they might succeed, the oligarquía reverted (as they had at many points in Colombian history) to overt violence to maintain control.

While the Gaitanistas relied on a caudillo to focus their mobilization, this did not negate the power and character of the movement itself. The experience of Gaitanismo demonstrated that Colombia's popular classes were beginning to show signs of being able to look beyond the two-party system. The trend within the historiography is still to emphasize the hegemony of the traditional parties in the 1930s and 1940s, and there is ample justification for this view. Daniel Pécaut argued persuasively that the parties were "more subcultures than political organizations" and that, as a consequence, Gaitán was unable to create a movement outside the Liberal party.[10] But as Marx observed, while humans make their own history, they do not do so under conditions of their own choosing. In the 1940s, leftist currents of political mobilization could still not escape the massive attractive force of the Liberal party. Yet for the Gaitanistas, the left-Liberal tradition represented a vehicle for popular mobilization. Gaitanismo provided a real break with the past tradition of oligarchic political culture. It weakened the gamonal power system in cities throughout the country. Although the Liberal and Conservative parties continued as very important political players in Colombia, a breach was made in the vertically oriented political establishment, since Gaitán's attempt to bring members of the pueblo across party lines was not without some success.

Despite the presence of various social groups within the ranks, Gaitanismo was a "class" movement. "Middle-class" interests did not prove antithetical to "working-class" interests, as demonstrated by the cross-class alliance within the pueblo against the oligarquía. They did not share a clear relationship to the means of production. But Gaitanismo nevertheless found its inner drive in the struggle between the dark-skinned "productive masses" and the owners of political and economic power. This conflict reflected unmistakable popular interest in and agitation for increased democratic rights and more popularly controlled institutions, which in turn were closely related to widespread demands for social and economic justice. The ideas of democracia and justicia social, therefore, were intrinsically related in the minds of the pueblo. The popular Gaitanista ideology originated in popularly held notions of Colombian social reality. The Gaitanistas' shared moral sense of social justice and demands for more popularly based political representation unified their mobilization and drew them to Gaitán, the symbol of their aspirations. Gaitán served as a catalyst for the movement's ideological content but he did not create it. Ideas emerging from the left-Liberal tradition matured through an interactive relationship on the ideological level between Gaitanismo's leadership and its rank and file. Gaitán's influence, commonly attributed to his charisma, resulted from this intellectual heritage and from the hope he offered of completing and expanding the promise of the Revolución en Marcha. Gaitán himself played a central role, yet the popular origins of the mobilization associated with his name cannot be denied. Gaitán was the unifying symbol, but the Gaitanistas, especially on the local level, successfully challenged gamonal politics by mobilizing and voting. Integration with official liberalism proved painful for the movement but did not spell the end of the mobilization's popular character. And violent repression after May 1946 had the effect of solidifying Liberal support firmly under Gaitán. It also helped polarize the partisan struggle more directly along class lines than ever before.

Yet as Eric Hobsbawm pointed out long ago, there is still the nagging question of "why, having spontaneously flared up," did the revolution settle "back into a smoky mass showing only an occasional glimmer"?[11] Interpreting the Violencia as an unsuccessful "social revolution" is complicated by the fact that as the struggle moved out of the cities, where it was quickly smashed by the Army and by Conservative irregulars brought in to hunt down Liberals, it took on a decidedly partisan appearance in the countryside. And it has been argued that in spite of "innumerable socialist experiments" in the various enclaves of guerrilla control, the binder between leader and follower continued to be the gamonal system. The traditional political relationship dominated by the old parties persisted in the rural communities, "averting revolutionary violence which might have gradually developed."[12]

Partisan violence in the countryside was, nevertheless, connected to the struggles of Gaitanismo in two concrete ways. First, terror in the cities, towns, and Liberal regions generated a flood of refugees called "exilados" ("exiles"). *Pájaros,* in league with the Conservative partisan "police," dubbed "chulavitas" after the Chulavita district of Boyacá, were recruited to hunt Gaitanistas, crush Liberal resistance, and intimidate elections, before and after April 1948. (Boyacences, as the nickname chulavita suggests, and Antioqueños who were called *contrachusmas* served as enthusiastic storm troopers.) Sánchez noted that it "was from these zones that the Violence later advanced into Tolima, Valle de Cauca, and Viejo Caldas. In these regions peasants spoke not of 'when the violence started' but of 'when it arrived.'"[13] Exiles tended to be left Liberals, very likely Gaitanistas, and large numbers of them found their way to the various Liberal peasant guerrilla fronts, the largest being the ten thousand man (and woman) army in the Llanos Orientales. The second connection was that the Violencia proved fiercest and lasted the longest in the coffee regions, which were the scene of large-scale peasant mobilizations (and Unirista influence) during the 1930s.

The heavily Gaitanista Atlantic coast witnessed comparatively little violence. Fals Borda accounted for this situation by proposing a nonviolent ethos for costeño culture.[14] The obvious difficulty with this argument is its implication that in the highlands such a violent culture exists.[15] And there are less determinist reasons. Charles Bergquist, among others, linked continued violence to coffee cultivation and land tenure, a dynamic absent on the coast.[16] And Paul Oquist demonstrated that in areas heavily controlled by one party or the other, violence was less intense.[17] The Atlantic coast had long been such a formidable Liberal bastion that it proved difficult to repress. But both in the highlands and on the coast the result was the same. Gaitán's assassination and the flowering of the Violencia silenced the politically oriented strains of left liberalism that Gaitanismo represented and pushed them into new territory.

In 1952 the intra-Liberal division between the Liberal oligarquía and the armed pueblo was clear in the Llanos, a division that would soon become permanent. And in the Violencia's later phases, the leaders of the fighting bands were products of the lower classes themselves. Perhaps most importantly, it is obvious that the elites were terribly afraid of where the violence in the countryside might go. The leaders of both parties, therefore, welcomed Rojas Pinilla's coup against Gómez in 1953 and supported his efforts to pacify the countryside through amnesty (and selective repression). After 1957 the reunited elites mounted a concerted and bipartisan effort to put down the irregular forces, politically allied with the various organizations of opposition, and return control of the countryside to the united dominant classes.[18] In this they were simply repeating the actions of the unified elites at other points in Colombian history who faced class-based, popular challenges to their hegemony.

Gaitanismo was certainly a beheaded social movement. As it lost its focal point, the movement became engulfed in the regionalist and partisan struggles of Colombian history. The Violencia, nonetheless, embodied a disjointed process of desperate left-Liberal popular revolution that eventually was beaten back by a successful but ruinous counterattack of the Liberal and Conservative oligarquía. So not only was Gaitanismo beheaded, but its body was also hacked to pieces in the years after 1948, and along with it much of the legitimacy of Colombia's political system. The movement was ultimately defeated and the Gaitanistas' political victories were lost to violence, but only at great and enduring cost to Colombian society. Gaitanismo was hardly weak if to blunt its force as a popular mobilization required armed repression over two decades.

The victory of the oligarquía, however, remains incomplete. The spirit of left liberalism has proven to be a frustrating hydra, momentarily defeated only to spring back in new forms. Many left-Liberal currents of mobilization were ultimately pushed from the Liberal party in the 1950s and 1960s, creating new and often violent political entities that could trace their lineage directly to Gaitanismo and the left-Liberal tradition. This is important to note since much of the radicalism of Gaitanismo and its breaks with the past have been lost to view as the country reverted to its heritage of violent political struggles.

The National Front brought an end of sorts to the Violencia and endeavored to establish stable oligarchical control and allow capitalist development.[19] The parties' leaders won a partisan truce by alternating the presidency between them for sixteen years until 1974 and sharing positions in government. Yet in the process, they excluded other movements and organizations from formal participation in politics. This even more elite-controlled reordering of the Colombian state and the nation's capitalist system virtually insured the continuation of popular forms of mobilization, the coexistence of elite political, social, and economic hegemony and significant popular resistance.

The years since 1974 have encompassed organized protest, popularly oriented electoral drives, and armed movements. Working-class organizations with ties to leftist groups have paralleled a continuing wave of rural protest throughout Colombia. These efforts have coincided with calls in the principal urban areas for social justice that have resulted in impressive mobilization. Colombia can boast of human-rights, feminist, ecological, and Church social movements. In the late 1970s, 1980s, and 1990s however, electoral politics and legal popular organizations were paralleled by the continuing existence of revolutionary guerrilla movements. From the very ashes of the Violencia sprang the basic guerrilla groups that operate in Colombia today. The Ejército de Liberación Nacional (ELN) was founded in 1965 by middle-class Colombian students and radical petroleum workers in the Santanderes. While clearly influenced by the Cuban revolutionary "foco" model, it had strong roots in the Colombian tradition. In 1966 the Fuerzas Armadas Revolucionarias de Colombia (las FARC) emerged in the Communist (and Gaitanista) influenced large-hacienda regions southwest of Bogotá, areas of persistent peasant mobilization since at least the 1920s. And in 1970 the now defunct M-19 began urban guerrilla operations in Colombian cities.[20] These groups are the direct descendants of earlier mobilizations, demonstrating both generational and ideological continuities.

In general, Colombians are good Clausewitzians, always ready to pursue violence as politics by other means. Colombian politics in the first half of the twentieth century, after all, grew out of the nation's tradition of popular political mobilization, which had mutated back and forth between electoral politics and popular armed struggle throughout the nineteenth century. Popular mobilization and grassroots participation have been consistent elements in Colombia's political life since the late eighteenth century. Colombia is known, however, as an elite-dominated society, and perhaps the most notorious element of Colombian development has been the enduring hegemony of the elite-controlled Liberal and Conservative parties. Yet the paradox of Colombian political and social development remains that while the old regime survives, so does significant and determined resistance to its supremacy, especially at the local level. Social and political mobilization in twentieth-century Colombia has undoubtedly been overshadowed by the two-party system, but the dominion of the Liberal and Conservative parties has never been absolute. There have been many suggestive episodes of popular mobilization and ruptures in the uneasy elite hegemony.

A remarkable continuity exists among Colombian popular movements and social struggles. Popular mobilization and resistance have been expressed in different but interrelated ways over the last two centuries of Colombian history, and the experience of the twentieth century must be understood within this context. Born in the civil wars of the nineteenth century through which modern-day Colombia's tradition of armed struggle was forged, one can then follow it through the radical labor and political movements of the first thirty years of the twentieth century, the political mobilizations of the interrelated Socialist and Liberal left in the 1930s and 1940s, and the complicated encounters of the Violencia between 1946 and 1966. Finally, it is quite visible today in the leftist guerrilla movements, labor, and land struggles from the late 1960s to the 1990s. What all these currents of popular mobilization have in common is the left-Liberal tradition. Of course not all "mobilization" was derivative of the Liberal left (as Colombia's drug traffickers and right-wing *paramilitar autodefensa* groups demonstrate), but popular liberalism formed the heart of the legacy.

Though Colombia experienced no grand social revolution, significant popular resistance has persisted throughout Colombian history. Even if the popular classes made no single, great push against the status quo, the state has remained relatively weak and continues to suffer problems of legitimacy. The oligarquía's power has never gone unchallenged while the pueblo has consistently demonstrated a popular penchant for collective action. Despite elite repression, popular mobilization survives in local politics, guerrilla insurgencies, and land invasions. Though the Colombian ruling classes have repeatedly survived dangerous threats to their hegemony, the Colombian pueblo has historically demonstrated a seemingly inexhaustible capacity to form popular movements of mass mobilization, much of it since 1850 under the banner of left liberalism. This explains the tangible continuity of Colombia's many popular struggles and their unresolved natures.

Notes

Introduction: Populism, Popular Agency, Hegemony, and Gaitanismo

1. I use "Liberal" and "Liberals" when referring to the Colombian Liberal party, and "liberal" when referring to the broader political heritage. I employ the words "left Liberal," as opposed to "popular Liberal" (more in vogue with historians), because Colombians were more prone to use them. The phrase "liberal popular" was used, but not as much as "liberal de izquierda."

2. I have tried to balance the national context (Gaitanismo as left liberalism) and international context (Gaitanismo as populism), since both of these images are valid. I have sought to make the appropriate comparative parallels while still demonstrating Gaitanismo's embeddedness in Colombian history. In the work, therefore, there are necessary interpretive tensions between "splitting" and "lumping" regarding regional aspects on the one hand and my decision to do a broad study on the other, as well as the exigency of juxtaposing the Colombian case against several comparative examples. This introduction, therefore, briefly addresses the evolving theoretical context in which the study was conceived, researched, and written. I have synthesized many interpretive strains, practicing what Alan Knight has called "controlled . . . theoretical eclecticism," based on delicate but defendable "degrees of objectivity." I also agree with Florencia Mallon's suggestion that historians have no choice but to ride multiple theoretical steeds at once. Perhaps this image is not as problematic as she thought. She took it from Gyan Prakash's statement that we should "hang on to two horses, inconsistently," but which she lamented could be likened "to the physically impossible stunt of riding several steeds at all times!" Far from impossible, this is called tandem harnessing, and is generally done with two or three matched pairs. Rather than genteel equestrians, or even stunt riders, historians should be rough and ready teamsters. If different theories all pull in the same direction, by all means, let us hitch them together. Such eclecticism was necessary in making sense of Gaitanismo as a radical mobilization of popular agency in conflict with Colombia's hegemonic social and political system. See Alan Knight, *The Mexican Revolution,* 1:84 and note 54; Florencia Mallon, "The Promise and Dilemma of Subaltern Studies," 1491 and 1514–15.

3. Populists have, nevertheless, consistently been understood as the political descendants of the caudillos, because of their reputations for authoritarianism and because they were commonly called "caudillo," i.e., "leader." For the "mass"

aspects of caudillismo, and the caudillos' role as "cultural heros and symbols of collective identity," see John Chasteen, *Heroes on Horseback*, 5.

4. Although, as David Collier maintained, the link between industrialization and the rise of populism is a problematic one. See Collier, *The New Authoritarianism*, 371–77.

5. For detailed discussion and examination of the elements mentioned here, which are generally included in a definition of populism, see Michael Conniff, "Introduction," 3–30, and Paul W. Drake, "Conclusion: Requiem for Populism?" 217–45, in *Latin American Populism*.

6. Ernesto Laclau, "Towards a Theory of Populism," 147. For the early modernization approach, see Gino Germani, Torcuato Di Tella, and Octávio Ianni, *Populismo y contradicciones de clase*.

7. Torcuato Di Tella, "Populism and Reform in Latin America."

8. See Gino Germani, *Política y sociedad*. For the classic definition of social mobilization within a "modernizing" society, see Karl Deutsch, "Social Mobilization and Political Development."

9. See especially Francisco Weffort, *O populismo na política Brasileira*.

10. Steve Stein, *Populism in Peru*, 3–15.

11. James C. Scott, *The Moral Economy of the Peasant*.

12. James C. Scott, *Weapons of the Weak*, xv–xvi.

13. Daniel Nugent, "Introduction: Reasons to Be Cheerful," 14.

14. See Ranajit Guha and Gayatri Chakravorty Spivak, eds., *Selected Subaltern Studies*.

15. Antonio Gramsci, *Selections from the Prison Notebooks*. Gramsci's work on hegemony was paralleled by the increasingly pessimistic tone of Herbert Marcuse, Max Horkheimer, Theodor Adorno, and the other practitioners of "Critical Theory" within the "Frankfurt School" of social thought. See Martin Jay, *The Dialectical Imagination*.

16. Scott, *Weapons of the Weak*, 315–17.

17. James C. Scott, *Domination and the Arts of Resistance*.

18. James C. Scott, foreword to *Everyday Forms of State Formation*, vii and xi.

19. Alan Knight, "Weapons and Arches," 42–43, 46–47, 52, 55. Knight discussed Scott's work in juxtaposition to Philip Corrigan and Derek Sayer's *The Great Arch*.

20. William Roseberry, "Hegemony and the Language of Contention," 357–61.

21. Dealing with competing elite and popular notions of nationalism and liberalism in Mexico and Peru, Mallon argued that "political history from below" must move beyond "a simple celebration of subaltern agency" and "uncritical" commemoration of "popular resistance" (Mallon, *Peasant and Nation*, 5–9). Known for her work on resistance, *The Defense of Community*, Mallon has had to make peace with hegemony.

22. Scott, *Domination and the Arts of Resistance*, 18.

23. Paul Drake, "Conclusion: Requiem for Populism?" 234.

24. Such a statement is not completely opposed to the analysis of Di Tella or even Weffort, who recognized that the masses felt the first yearnings for authentic democracy. Drake suggested that in Chile, as in other parts of Latin America, "socialism and populism were not necessarily mutually exclusive forces" (Drake, *Socialism and Populism in Chile*, 1–13).

25. Laclau, "Towards a Theory of Populism," 173–74.

26. Robert Dix, "Populism: Authoritarian and Democratic."

27. Daniel James, *Resistance and Integration*. Traditionally the problem has been "approached from the perspective of more general notions concerning populism," which emphasized "the aberrant quality of working-class participation" and treated it "as something of an historical conundrum requiring explanation, most usually in terms of notions such as manipulation, passivity, cooptation, and not uncommonly, irrationality" (1–2).

28. John French, *The Brazilian Workers' abc*, 268. Though Brazilian populism blunted the radicalism of working-class mobilization, Getulismo was not a mere "capitalist tool." The political system that arose in Brazil in the 1940s "represented both a defeat and a victory for workers" (273). French pointed out the dual nature of populist mobilizations, arguing that "there was not one populism but many" (282).

29. Adrian A. Bantjes, *As If Jesus Walked on Earth*, 217–18.

30. The principal works on Gaitán and his movement include J. Cordell Robinson's *El movimiento gaitanista*, which provided a broad but rather superficial survey of the movement, focused especially on the years after 1944, and more involved with Gaitán than the Gaitanistas. Richard Sharpless's *Gaitán of Colombia* provided a succinct and well-documented biography that located Gaitán in his political context. While communicating the movement's popular character, Sharpless's subject was Gaitán himself. Gonzálo Sánchez G., in *Los días de la revolución*, pointed to Gaitanismo's radical nature as a mobilization, but was primarily concerned with the violent reactions to his assassination. Herbert Braun's *The Assassination of Gaitán* skillfully portrayed the interactions between Gaitán and the cozy and exclusive "convivialista" elites of the Liberal and Conservative parties, and examined their reactions to the movement before but especially after *el 9 de abril*. Daniel Pécaut, in *Orden y violencia*, took up the questions of "civilization" and "barbarism" in Colombia's political life, and their implications for Colombia's heritage of political violence. Pécaut ultimately concluded that Gaitanismo was not a truly popular movement because of the class confusion he believed that the movement generated. Though I have tried to move beyond these works, I owe them all a massive debt.

31. In this general category fall Charles Bergquist, *Labor in Latin America*; Christopher Abel, *Política, iglesia y partidos*; Mauricio Archila Neira, *Cultura e identidad obrera*; Mario Aguilera Peña and Renán Vega Cantor, *Ideal democrático y revuelta popular*; Christopher Abel and Marco Palacios, "Colombia, 1930–58";

David Bushnell, *The Making of Modern Colombia*; Marco Palacios, *Entre la legitimidad y la violencia*.

32. On the surface, Latin American populist mobilizations of the 1930s and 1940s greatly resemble contemporaneous social and political movements in other regions, movements generally regarded as "fascist." Both phenomena embody a personalistic and charismatic leader making highly emotional appeals based upon notions of the "national spirit" to a "mass" or multiclass following, which nevertheless is often solidly anchored in the petty bourgeoisie. Both populism and fascism arose during the world economic crises resulting from World War I and the Great Depression, and both frequently receive the contradictory labels of "revolutionary" and "counter-revolutionary." These similarities were reinforced by the common tendency of the organized left in Latin America to characterize populists as fascists.

33. Robert Dix, in *Colombia*, credited Miguel Antonio Caro with coining the phrase (211).

Chapter 1. Popular Mobilization and the Left-Liberal Tradition in Colombia

1. Daniel Pécaut, for example, argued somewhat reproachfully that Gaitán was unable to create a viable independent political movement. He believed that Gaitanismo's entanglement with liberalism doomed the popular mobilization to lose its soul in the endless struggles between the traditional parties (*Orden y violencia* 2:440).

2. The term "cachaco" refers most specifically to a resident of Bogotá, also called a *bogotano*, but is often heard used as a generic term for someone from the highlands.

3. For economic and political aspects of the divide, see Eduardo Posada-Carbó, "Notas para una historia de la costa atlántica," 4–13.

4. Yet it is also true that by the 1930s development was increasing on the Pacific coast, on the Orinoco plains, and in the Amazon region. See Jane Rausch, *Colombia: Territorial Rule*.

5. Abel and Palacios, "Colombia," 589.

6. Palacios, *Entre la legitimidad y la violencia*, 76. See also his *El café en Colombia*.

7. Bergquist, *Labor in Latin America*, 298–303.

8. Abel and Palacios, "Colombia," 589. Bergquist, for example, not only rejected the rosier aspects of the antioqueño myth but also identified widespread land ownership as the single most debilitating factor to popular labor struggles.

9. Abel and Palacios, "Colombia," 589.

10. See Keith Christie, "Antioqueño Colonization," 260–83; and his *Oligarcas*. See also Catherine LeGrand, *Frontier Expansion*.

11. Palacios, *Entre la legitimidad y la violencia*, 33. Mary Roldán pointed to an exception that demonstrated the rule. Though Antioquia for the most part conformed to the small-holder west, she argued that on its peripheries it demonstrated

the "economic pattern of declining wages, unemployment and land concentration typical of the decades of the 1930s and 1940s in Colombia." These areas were more prone to "the dangerous potential of popular dissatisfaction" (Mary Jean Roldán, "Genesis and Evolution of *La Violencia*," 58–59).

12. Palacios, *Entre la legitimidad y la violencia*, 19–24.

13. Eduardo Posada-Carbó, "La economía del Caribe," 69–71. In his more recent book, *El Caribe Colombiano*, Posada-Carbó was careful to emphasize the importance of small holders on the northern coast as well. But he still pointed out that despite their struggles to hold onto land, many colonos on the coast were pushed from their property (139–42).

14. In addition to being the nation's third largest city and principal port, Barranquilla had become a significant center of industry, commerce, and banking by the mid-1930s. See Gustavo Bell Lemus, "Barranquilla: 1920–1930"; and Posada Carbó, *Una invitación a la historia de Barranquilla*.

15. In the 1940s important river cities such as the oil center of Barrancabermeja were composed largely of costeños. In his interview with Mauricio Archila, Flavio Vasquez affirmed that after 1928, Barranca was home to more costeños than people from the interior.

16. For an idea of what river travel was like on the Magdalena, see Gabriel García Márquez, *Love in the Time of Cholera*, 140, from which this quote is taken.

17. Justo Ramón, "El río de la patria," 12.

18. Eduardo Acevedo Latorre, *El río grande de la Magdalena*, 50.

19. Nicholes, *Tres puertos*, 241. The heavily silted mouth of the Magdalena did not allow access to Barranquilla from the sea until the "Bocas de Ceniza" project began to clear it after 1936.

20. Abel and Palacios, "Colombia," 590.

21. See David Sowell, *The Early Colombian Labor Movement*; Archila, *Cultura e identidad obrera*; see also Gary Long, "The Dragon Finally Came."

22. Abel and Palacios, "Colombia," 588. Citing the census of 1938, they put the populations of Bogotá at 330,000; Medellín at 168,000; Barranquilla at 152,000; and Cali at 102,000. Another student gave slightly different numbers, putting the 1938 urban population at 2.7 million or 31 percent and the rural population at 6 million or 69 percent of the total; and the 1951 urban population at 4.5 million or 39 percent and the rural at 7 million or 61 percent of the total (Urbano Campo, *La urbanización en Colombia*, 15).

23. Palacios, *Entre la legitimidad y la violencia*, 84–86, 89.

24. See Frank Safford, "Social Aspects"; Dix, *Colombia*; Jaime Jaramillo Uribe, *La personalidad histórica*; Alvaro Tirado Mejia, *El Estado y la política* and *Aspectos sociales*; John Leddy Phelan, *The People and the King*; Gerardo Molina, *Las ideas liberales*; Charles Bergquist, *Coffee and Conflict*; Paul Oquist, *Violence*; Helen Delpar, *Red Against Blue*; David Church Johnson, *Santander*; Aguilera Peña and Vega Cantor, *Ideal democrático*; Sowell, *The Early Colombian Labor*

Movement; Richard Stoller, "Liberalism and Conflict"; Bushnell, *The Making of Modern Colombia*; Bushnell and Neill Macaulay, *The Emergence of Latin America*; Francisco Gutiérrez Sanín, *Curso y discurso*; Marco Palacios, *Entre la legitimidad y la violencia*; Gary Long, "Popular Liberalism" and "The Dragon Finally Came."

25. See, for example, Bushnell, *The Making of Modern Colombia*, 28.

26. Rebecca Earle has begun to address this imbalance with her *Spain and the Independence of Colombia, 1810–1825*.

27. Tirado Mejia, *Aspectos sociales*, 13. See also his *El estado y la política*, 85–101.

28. Abel and Palacios, "Colombia," 591–92.

29. Dix, *Colombia*, 231.

30. Gabriel García Márquez, *Cien años de soledad*, 148.

31. Safford, "Social Aspects," 351–52, 357, 360, 361–62.

32. Dix, *Colombia*, 233, 235.

33. Ibid., 216.

34. Fals Borda, *El presidente Nieto*, 73B–74B. See also Bergquist, *Labor in Latin America*.

35. See Pécaut, *Orden y violencia*, 1:16–17; and Malcolm Deas, "Algunas notas," 118–21.

36. Mallon, *Peasant and Nation*.

37. Tirado Mejia, *El estado y la política*, 87.

38. Gutiérrez Sanín, *Curso y discurso*, 132.

39. See Carlos Eduardo Jaramillo, *Los guerrilleros del novecientos*, for a general overview.

40. Bergquist, *Coffee and Conflict*, 131.

41. Ibid., 149.

42. Delpar, *Red Against Blue*, 188.

43. Bergquist, *Coffee and Conflict*, 157.

44. See Long, "The Dragon Finally Came."

45. Posada-Carbó, "Limits of Power," 249–50.

46. There were (and continue to be) breeds of popular conservatism as well, but they were of a different nature from currents on the Liberal left. In particular, they were not derivative of the Enlightenment tradition of 1776–1789–1848 but rather found their roots in Colombian Catholicism. The geographical distribution of such Conservative popular strains was more pronounced in Antioquia and its coffee country environs, in Boyacá, and, perhaps, in Nariño and Cauca. While relatively little research has been done on popular Conservative currents, César Ayala Diago addressed them seriously in his *Resistencia y oposición*. See also Mary Roldán, "Genesis and Evolution of *La Violencia*."

47. See Maurice Cranston, "Liberalism"; Pierre Manent, *An Intellectual History of Liberalism*; and John Gray, *Liberalism*.

48. Gray, *Liberalism*, x.

49. Ibid., x and 1.

50. Andrew Daitsman, "The People Shall Be All," 163.

51. Brian Hamnett, "Liberalism Divided," 662, 666. See also Guy Thomson, "Popular Aspects of Liberalism," 265–92; and Florencia Mallon, *Peasant and Nation.*

52. Daitsman, "The People Shall Be All," 161.

53. Bushnell, *The Making of Modern Colombia,* 117. Herbert Braun saw little ideological basis for nineteenth-century popular mobilization and civil war. In politics, "more than ideology, the life and livelihood of individuals was at stake" (*Assassination of Gaitán,* 13–14). Other historians have noted divisions among Liberals but have focused on divisions among the elite of the party; see Delpar, "Aspects of Liberal Factionalism."

54. Tirado Mejia, *El estado y la política,* 36.

55. Jaramillo Uribe, "La influencia de los románticos," in *La personalidad histórica de Colombia,* 162, 165–66.

56. Aguilera and Vega, *Ideal democrático,* 34, 42.

57. Bushnell, *The Making of Modern Colombia,* 102, 115.

58. Jaramillo Uribe, "Las sociedades democráticas," in *La personalidad histórica de Colombia,* 191.

59. Molina, *Las ideas liberales,* 1:62–63; Gutiérrez Sanín, *Curso y discurso,* 63–64.

60. Jaramillo Uribe, "Las sociedades democráticas," in *La personalidad histórica de Colombia,* 200–201.

61. Bushnell, *The Making of Modern Colombia,* 108

62. Ibid., 111–14.

63. Molina, *Las ideas liberales,* 1:64–65.

64. Jaramillo Uribe, "Las sociedades democráticas," in *La personalidad histórica de Colombia,* 208–10.

65. Tirado Mejia, *El estado y la política,* 91–92.

66. Sowell, *The Early Colombian Labor Movement,* 78, 52–53, 81.

67. Gutiérrez Sanín, *Curso y discurso,* 31–34, 79.

68. Ibid., 130, 155–58.

69. Stoller, "Liberalism and Conflict," 1–19. He focused on the case of Socorro, which was not well connected to the world market, and had "never had an important encounter with foreign capital." Consequently, "the economic prescriptions of liberal ideology were in constant danger of being overwhelmed by its subversive social possibilities" (19). See also the case of Bucaramanga in 1879 addressed by Thomas Fischer, "Craftsmen, Merchants, and Violence in Colombia."

70. Long, "Popular Liberalism," 18; see also Malcolm Deas, "Poverty, Civil War," 263–303.

71. Bergquist, *Coffee and Conflict,* 90–91.

72. Molina, *Las ideas Liberales,* 2:130.

73. *El Debate* (Cartagena), Dec. 13, 1935, p. 3, "La reforma liberal."

74. Two hundred Liberals to ALP, Toro, March, 1936; AP, v. 4, 1936.

75. Guillermo Cobanella, "Rafael Uribe Uribe," 21. Sharpless argued that, despite some radical ideas, for many young Liberals "theoretical knowledge and long-term commitment to Marxism were questionable" (*Gaitán of Colombia,* 44). Most radicals, therefore, paralleled Gaitán in maintaining their ties to Colombian liberalism.

76. Milton Puentes, *Historia del partido liberal,* 574.

77. Eduardo Santa, *El pensamiento político de Rafael Uribe Uribe,* 17.

78. Javier Henao Hidron quoted Uribe Uribe but did not give a source (*Uribe Uribe y Gaitán,* 140). Uribe Uribe's perspective reflected (and may have been influenced by) one of his British contemporaries, L. T. Hobhouse. Hobhouse also stressed the leftward drift of liberalism world-wide, remarking on the difference between the "old" liberalism and the "new," and also advocated a "Liberal Socialism" (see Hobhouse, *Liberalism*).

79. "El socialismo del estado," found in Uribe Uribe, *Escritos políticos,* 110–11, 116.

80. Molina, *Las ideas liberales,* 2:130.

81. Palacios, *Entre la legitimidad y la violencia,* 121, 131, 157–60; Stoller, "Alfonso López Pumarejo," 375; Robinson, *Movimiento gaitanista,* 25, 27–28.

82. Braun, *Assassination of Gaitán,* 20–28; Sharpless, *Gaitán of Colombia,* 22, 24.

83. Armando Solano, *Caudillos liberales,* v–vi.

84. Molina, *Las ideas socialistas,* 254–56.

85. Molina, *Las ideas socialistas,* as noted; Stoller, "Alfonso López Pumarejo," 381–82; Robinson, *Movimiento gaitanista,* 33.

86. Sharpless noted other wavering Liberals on the left, including Gabriel Turbay, Luís Tejada, José Mar, Moisés Prieto, Alejandro Vallejo, Roberto García Peña (and Gaitán), though the phenomenon was even more widespread (Sharpless, *Gaitán of Colombia,* 24).

87. *El Espectador* (Bogotá), April 20, 1928, p. 3, editorial "Un documento político."

88. *El Tiempo* (Bogotá), April 20, 1928, p. 1, editorial "Liberalismo y socialismo," commenting on a letter to *Diario Nacional* of the same date.

89. Posada-Carbó, "Limits of Power," 252; Oquist, *Violence,* 79; Deas, "Algunas notas," 223.

90. Molina, *Las ideas socialistas,* 244–45, and *Las ideas liberales,* 1:53.

91. Agustín Gusmán to JEG, Cúcuta, July 27, 1932; found in AICPG v.0044.

92. Eustorgio A. Sarria M. (lawyer) to JEG, Popayán, March 6, 1931; AICPG v.0090.

93. Nicolás Gutiérrez to JEG, Bucaramanga, Aug. 8, 1932; and Antonio Vicente Arenas and Nicolás Gutiérrez to JEG, Bucaramanga, Sept. 1, 1932; AICPG v.0089.

94. Antonio Vicente Arenas and Nicolás Gutiérrez (directors of *Santander Liberal*) to JEG, Bucaramanga, Nov. 7, 1932; AICPG v.0089.

95. Nicolás Gutiérrez to JEG, Bucaramanga, July 29, 1932; AICPG v.0089.

96. Joaquín Ardila Durán to JEG, Bucaramanga, July 25, 1932; AICPG v.0089.

97. Camilo Muñoz Obando to JEG, Popayán, May 25, 1932; AICPG v.0090.

98. *El Crisol* (Cali), April 23, 1933, p. 3, editorial "Huelgas justicieras y liberalismo."

99. *El Crisol* (Cali), April 2, 1933, p. 3, editorial "Ideas, disciplina y personalismo."

100. J. P. Rojas Gusmán to JEG, Neiva, Oct. 26, 1932; AICPG v.0044.

101. *Rumbos* (Plato), Jan. 7, 1937, p. 2, "Justicia Social" by Rogerio Gómez Suarez.

102. Félix Delgado Gómez to JEG, Pasto, May 9, 1939; AICPG v.0044.

103. Alonso García Bustamante to JEG, Pereira, Dec. 23, 1934; AICPG v.0092.

104. *El Crisol* (Cali), Aug. 31, 1933, p. 3, editorial "El Liberalismo frente a la revolución social."

105. *El Crisol* (Cali), Sept. 23, 1934, p. 3, editorial "El liberalismo conservador."

106. Daniel Gil Lemos to JEG, Popayán, July 12, 1932; AICPG v.0090.

107. *El Liberal* (Manizales), Feb. 8, 1937, p. 6, "Ideas de izquierda" by Marco Tulio S.

108. For the later years, see Green, "Sibling Rivalry on the Left," as well as chapters 6–9.

109. *Rumbos* (Plato), Jan. 7, 1937, p. 3, editorial "Izquierda."

110. Interview with Guillermo Hernández Rodríguez by Mauricio Archila.

111. Interview with Rafael Núñez by Mauricio Archila.

112. "Servidores y copartidarios" of Líbano to JEG and Carlos Arango Vélez, May 31, 1933; AICPG v.0052; *La Voz Liberal* (Cartago), Jan. 31, 1937, p. 3, editorial "La doctrina liberal."

113. *El Crisol* (Cali), April 9, 1933, p. 3, editorial "Liberalismo radical socialista."

114. *Rumbos* (Plato), Jan. 21, 1937, p. 4, "La Ideología Liberal" by Armando Solano.

115. *El Escándalo* (Santa Marta), June 14, 1936, p. 3, editorial "Frente Popular."

116. One who supported Gaitán and his candidacies in the paper *Santander Liberal* complained that some people "in their ignorance" called him "communist" (Joaquín Ardila Durán to JEG, Bucaramanga, July 25, 1932; AICPG v.0089).

117. Elías Castaño Henao to JEG, Montenegro, Nov. 29, 1933; AICPG v.0092.

118. Roberto Julio González to JEG, Pacho, Aug. 1, 1932; AICPG v.0086.

119. *Diario Nacional* (Bogotá), March 29, 1934, p. 3, editorial "La convención liberal."

120. *El Escándalo* (Santa Marta), July 19, 1936, p. 4, "¿Porqué somos de Izquierda?"

121. *El Crisol* (Cali), July 6, 1933, p. 3, editorial "La revolución integral."

122. *El Crisol* (Cali), July 9, 1933, p. 3, editorial "Pedimos justicia distribuitiva."

Chapter 2. Genesis of a Left-Liberal *Caudillo*

1. Information for the following paragraphs is taken from Sharpless, *Gaitán of Colombia*, 29–41; Braun, *Assassination of Gaitán*, 39–45; Robinson, *Movimiento gaitanista*, 47–66; and Gloria Gaitán, *Bolívar tuvo un caballo blanco, mi papá un Buick*, 36–78. These works provide detailed biographical sketches of Gaitán. Earlier works consulted include: Horacio Gómez Aristizábal, *Gaitán: enfoque histórico*; José Antonio Osorio, *Gaitán*; Luís David Peña, *Gaitán íntimo*; José María Córdoba, *Jorge Eliécer Gaitán*; Mauro Torres, *Gaitán*. Regarding Gaitán's birthdate, his daughter Gloria points out that some studies place it on January 26, 1898, because of an older brother who was born on that date, and also named Jorge Eliécer, but who died when he was a few months old. See Gloria Gaitán, *Bolívar tuvo un caballo blanco, mi papá un Buick*, 53–54.

2. Descriptions of Gaitán's time in Italy are found in Osorio Lisarazo, *Gaitán*; Sharpless, *Gaitán of Colombia*; Braun, *Assassination of Gaitán*; and Robinson, *Movimiento Gaitanista*.

3. *El Espectador* (Bogotá), Feb. 14, 1928, p. 1, "Un rato de charla con Jorge Eliécer Gaitán."

4. Braun, *Assassination of Gaitán*, 82, 117.

5. *El Tiempo* (Bogotá), March 7, 1928, p. 1, "Le fue concedido el Premio Ferri al Dr. J.E.G."

6. *El Espectador* (Bogotá), Feb. 14, 1928, p. 1, "Un rato de charla con Jorge Eliécer Gaitán."

7. Yet Hobsbawm sensed that there was a difference. Gaitán, "so far from choosing the political Right, captured the leadership of the Liberal Party and would certainly as president have led it in a radical direction, had he not been assassinated" (Hobsbawm, *The Age of Extremes*, 133–34).

8. For example, while I was doing research in the Biblioteca Nacional in Bogotá in 1996, a Colombian scholar saw the newspaper article on Gaitán that I was reading and said, "You know, he was a fascist."

9. Portions of this section appeared in Green, "Guilt by Association."

10. Moore, *The Social Origins of Dictatorship*, 436–37, 447.

11. Dulffer, "Bonapartism, Fascism and National Socialism," 112, 119.

12. Weber, "Revolution? Counterrevolution? What Revolution?" 441.

13. Kershaw, *The Nazi Dictatorship*, 131.

14. Weber, "Revolution? Counterrevolution? What Revolution?" 447, 446.

15. Kershaw, *The Nazi Dictatorship*, 147.

16. Francis L. Carsten quoted many writers—Paul Sering, Wolfgang Sauer, Gino Germani, Michael Hurst—ranging from contemporaries of fascism to later academics, who all agreed that the definition must go beyond the middle class to

include the uprooted and those assailed with the "loss of status" ("Interpretations of Fascism," in Walter Laqueur, ed., *Fascism, a Reader Guide*, 419).

17. Hobsbawm too recognized this point: "European fascist regimes destroyed labour movements, the Latin American leaders they inspired created them. Whatever the intellectual filiation, historically, we cannot speak of the same kind of movement" (*The Age of Extremes*, 135).

18. *El Espectador* (Bogotá), Feb. 14, 1928, p. 1, "Un rato de charla con Jorge Eliécer Gaitán."

19. *El Tiempo* (Bogotá) from early 1928, paraphrased by Sharpless, *Gaitán of Colombia*, 52.

20. See Gaitán's 1937 characterization of fascism in chapter 4.

21. Crassweller, *Perón and the Enigmas of Argentina*, 85–89.

22. It is also difficult to label Laureano Gómez, the most militant leader of Colombian conservatism, as fascist (though some of his followers certainly were—see chapter 6).

23. Osorio Lizarazo, *Gaitán*, 68–69

24. "Carta a Luís Tejada," in *Gaitán: Sus mejores escritos*, 13–17.

25. Molina, *Las ideas socialistas*, 245.

26. Gaitán, "Las ideas socialistas," in *Gaitán: Antología*, 49–213.

27. Sharpless, *Gaitán of Colombia*, 43–50; Braun, *Assassination of Gaitán*, 45–55; Molina, *Las ideas socialistas*, 245–48; *Las ideas liberales*, 2:139–45.

28. Sharpless, *Gaitán of Colombia*, 49, 50.

29. Molina, *Las ideas socialistas*, 245–48. Gaitán, after all, began his thesis by asking which system, individualist or socialist, best serves justice. For an even more insistent emphasis on Gaitán's "socialism," see Gloria Gaitán, *Bolívar tuvo un caballo blanco, mi papá un Buick*.

30. Braun, *Assassination of Gaitán*, 45, 47.

31. Gaitán, "Ideas socialistas," 68–69.

32. Braun, *Assassination of Gaitán*, 47; Gaitán, "Las ideas socialistas," 75.

33. Gaitán, "Las ideas socialistas," 89–90, 117.

34. Sharpless, *Gaitán of Colombia*, 48.

35. Braun, *Assassination of Gaitán*, 49.

36. Quoted by Sharpless, *Gaitán of Colombia*, 45.

37. Braun, *Assassination of Gaitán*, 60.

38. Gaitán, "El problema social," in *Mejores discursos*, 62.

39. Gaitán, "Función social de la propiedad," in *Mejores discursos*, 72–82.

40. Gaitán, "Las ideas socialistas," 85.

41. Molina, *Las ideas liberales*, 2:144–45.

42. See the "El Tolima" discussion in chapter 3.

43. Molina, *Las ideas liberales*, 2:145–46.

44. "Plataforma del Colón," *Gaitán: Antología*, esp. 329–47; see chapter 7.

45. Molina, *Las ideas liberales*, 2:139.

46. Maurice P. Brungardt has pointed out that historians have yet to sound the depths of the repressed strike's influence upon Colombians ("Mitos históricos y literarios," 63).

47. Posada-Carbó has debunked the alleged "conspiracy of silence" ("Fiction as History," 410).

48. The 1928 strike is the most investigated labor event in Colombian history. See Sharpless, *Gaitán of Colombia*, 56–61; Urrutia, *Colombian Labor*, 99–108; Judith White, *Historia*, 73–102; Herrera S. and Romero C., *La zona bananera*; and ongoing work by Catherine LeGrand.

49. Salvador Bronacelli, secretary general of the union during the strike, adds that land was also of primary concern (*Sobrevivientes de las Bananeras*, 35).

50. Estimates of the strikers killed still vary, from 80 to 100 in Sharpless, *Gaitán of Colombia*, 57; to 1,500 in Alberto Castrillón R., *120 Días bajo el terror*; to over 2,000 in White, *Historia*, 100.

51. *Diario de la Costa* (Cartagena), Jan. 17, 1929, p. 7.

52. *La Nación* (B/quilla), Jan. 8, 1929, p. 3.

53. Cortes Vargas, *Los sucesos de las Bananeras*, 85. Years later the events were still remembered as the work of "agitators" (Azula Barrera, *De la revolución*, 60).

54. Though originally organized by the PSR (the predecessor of the Communist party), it is widely recognized that Gaitán usurped the repressed strike and successfully used it as his vehicle into the Colombian collective consciousness. The Communists never forgave Gaitán this indignity.

55. Interview by Mauricio Archila with Erasmo Egea.

56. Sharpless, *Gaitán of Colombia*, 58–59.

57. Carmela Ramos P. to JEG, B/quilla, Sept. 27, 1929; AICPG v.0091; Juventud Izquierdista to JEG, Buga, Sept. 20, 1929, AICPG v.0013.

58. And no less true for being said sarcastically (Linares U., "Helius," *yo acuso*, 59); in his interview with the author, Heliodoro Cogua P. made a point confirmed repeatedly in the correspondence of the AICPG, that for all practical purposes "Gaitanismo began with the defense Dr. Gaitán made of the victims of the *zona bananera*."

59. *El Espectador* (Bogotá), June 13, 1928, p. 1, showcased Gaitán's defense of striking women telephone workers; see also *El Tiempo* (Bogotá), June 14 and 15, p. 1. Bavaria workers in Duitama remembered Gaitán as "the first lawyer that fought" for their interests before the bananeras; Luis A. Moreno, interview with Mauricio Archila.

60. Comité Nacional Liberal Obrero, Bogotá to JEG, March 27, 1932; Juan de Dios Romero of the Federación Sindical de Bogotá to JEG, Sept. 8, 1933; Confederación Nacional de Empleados to JEG, Bogotá, Nov. 9, 1933 (all in AICPG v.0014); *El Escándalo* (Santa Marta), June 21, 1936, p. 2, "Comentarios."

61. So notes Mauricio Archila, *Cultura e identidad obrera*, 285.

62. Ibid., 282.

63. See *El Estado* (Santa Marta), Aug. 3, on the strike in Medellín; Aug. 23, on the taxis strike; and Aug. 29 on the Cali strike.

64. Torres Giraldo, *Los inconformes*, 1105–12.

65. *El Crisol* (Cali), Sept. 9, 1934, p. 3, editorial "Jorge Eliécer Gaitán."

66. *Diario Nacional* (Bogotá), Sept. 9, 1934, p. 1, "Desacuerdo entre Gaitán y los ferroviarios."

67. *Diario Nacional* (Bogotá), May 18, 1934, p. 1, "J.E.G. es el conciliador."

Chapter 3. Early Mobilizations: Gaitán, the Liberal Party, and UNIR, 1928–1935

1. Sharpless, *Gaitán of Colombia*, 72; Braun, *Assassination of Gaitán*, 59.

2. Medina, "Terceros partidos," 13, 16–17; *Unirismo*, June 21, 1934; Medina drew the parallel to Lenin. Sharpless too noted Gaitán's lack of faith in mass consciousness (*Gaitán of Colombia*, 55).

3. Pécaut, *Política y sindicalismo*, 127; he made this argument particularly for the working class. Archila echoed his contention, asserting that in contrast to the Communist party, UNIR "reenforced" popular dependence on leaders and institutions (*Cultura e identidad obrera*, 293).

4. Bergquist, *Labor in Latin America*, 350; he also extended this judgement to the Communists.

5. Julio Ortíz to JEG, Medellín, July 13, 1932; AICPG v.0016.

6. Of course, they listed Gaitán first (*El Crisol* [Cali], Feb. 25, 1934, p. 3, editorial).

7. Braun, *Assassination of Gaitán*, 59, paraphrasing Samper's article in the first issue of *Acción Liberal*, May 1932, p. 36, dedicated to Gaitán. His piece on Gaitán also appeared in the first issue of *El Crisol* in Ibagué, also dedicated to Gaitán, April 9, 1932, p. 1. In it Samper says literally, "a socialist who wants [social] justice for Colombian proletarians."

8. *El Crisol* (Ibagué), April 9, 1932, p. 1.

9. Angel Maria López (sastre) to JEG, Pasto, April 19, 1932; AICPG v.0050.

10. "Carta abierta al doctor JEG" by Pedro N. Santamaría L., Medellín, June 4, 1932; AICPG v.0016.

11. Antonio Arenas, dir., *Santander Liberal*, to JEG, Bucaramanga, April 9, 1931; AICPG v.0089.

12. *El Crisol* (Cali), April 2, 1933, p. 3, editorial "Ideas, disciplina y personalismo."

13. Roberto Julio González to JEG, Pacho, June 20, 1932; AICPG v.0086.

14. (M?) Bolívar Mosquera to JEG, Popayán, Sept. 21, 1931; AICPG v.0090.

15. Rafael A. Grau to JEG, May 21, 1932; AICPG v.0086.

16. Eustorgio A. Sarria M. (abogado), to JEG, Popayán, March 6, 1931; AICPG v.0090.

17. Comité de la Juventud Lib., Univ. del Cauca, to JEG, Popayán, July 1, 1932; AICPG v.0090.

18. Comité Lib. Holayista de la Ave. Uribe Uribe del Piloto, Cali, to JEG, Jan. 17, 1930, AICPG v.0013.

19. Comité Liberal de Herveo, Tolima, to JEG, July 4, 1932; AICPG v.0052.

20. Pedro Rubiano V. (comerciante) to JEG, Mariquita, July 25, 1932; AICPG v.0052.

21. Plutarco Arévalo E. to JEG, Popayán, Aug. 2, 1932; AICPG v.0090.

22. H. Arturo to JEG, *La Unión* (Nariño), April 26, 1932; AICPG v.0044.

23. Centro Nacional Socialista, to JEG, Popayán, July 4, 1932; AICPG v.0090.

24. Eustorgio A. Sarria M. (abogado) to JEG, Popayán, April 19, 1930; AICPG v.0090.

25. Efraín Rojas Trujillo (abogado) to JEG, Neiva, Nov. 20, 1931; AICPG v.0044.

26. *El Mitín* (Cartagena), June 22, 1932, p. 3. He was the savior, the "defender of the proletariat" to whom beleaguered colonos turned in times of need, as politician and jurist ("Sociedad Agrícola de Riofrio" to JEG, Ciénaga, June 4, 1930; AICPG v.0017). Also colono Marco F. Vargas, dispossessed by United Fruit, June 20, 1932, same volume.

27. José M. Ortega N. to JEG, Montería, July 23, 1932; AICPG v.0053.

28. Saul Gaitán to JEG, Honda, Dec. 27, 1930; AICPG v.0052.

29. Guillermo Baena Torregroza to JEG, Aracataca, Aug. 10 1932; AICPG v.0017.

30. Miguel A. Logreira, pres., to JEG, B/quilla, May 29, 1931; AICPG v.0091.

31. Saluted by *La Tribuna*, July 8, 1933, p. 2.

32. Germán H. Hogos to JEG, Santa Marta, June 5, 1932; AICPG v.0011.

33. Cenovia Rangel to JEG, El Banco, Sept. 7, 1932; AICPG v.0011.

34. Rafael Redondo M. and five others to JEG; Cartagena, July 2, 1932; AICPG v.0053; J. M. Conde R. to JEG; Cartagena, June 27, 1932; AICPG v.0088; D. Rincones P. to JEG; Santa Marta, Aug. 6, 1932; AICPG v.0017.

35. E. Arango C., REC. LIB. IZQUIERDISTA to JEG, Colosó, Nov. 3, 1932; AICPG v.0088.

36. Fernando de Andreis to JEG, B/quilla, June 30, 1932; AICPG v.0091.

37. *La Tribuna*, July 1, 1933, issue no. 2; they were not "Manchesterian" Liberals.

38. Pécaut, *Política*, 117–20.

39. Braun, *Assassination of Gaitán*, 60.

40. Sharpless, *Gaitán of Colombia*, 63.

41. Both Sharpless and Braun ignored this aspect of Gaitán's career.

42. Sharpless, *Gaitán of Colombia*, 66.

43. E. Arango C. to JEG, Colosó, Nov. 23, 1932; AICPG v.0088.

44. J. M. Nieto Rojas, *La batalla contra el comunismo*, 15.

45. *El Tiempo*, June 29, 1932, p. 4.

46. Mario Fernández de S., Liberal senator mid-1930s; *Una revolución en Colombia*, 79.

47. Mauricio Torres, *La naturaleza de la revolución*, 48.

48. Raúl Eduardo Mahecha C. to JEG, Ciénaga, June 30, 1932; AICPG v.0011.

49. Gaitán kept the Communists at arm's length. Gaitán was also not alone in his move to the leftward side of official liberalism, as demonstrated by the case of Diego Luis Córdoba and his creation of a new party in Chocó called "Acción Democrática" (popularly known as Cordobismo) between 1933 and 1935. See Jane Rausch, "Diego Luis Córdoba," 56–57.

50. Sharpless, *Gaitán of Colombia*, 71, quoting Fermín López Giraldo, *El Apóstol Desnudo*, 44.

51. Sharpless, *Gaitán of Colombia*, 71–72; Braun, *Assassination of Gaitán*, 63. It was no accident that the acronym "UNIR" means "to unite" in Spanish.

52. Sharpless, *Gaitán of Colombia*, 80.

53. Some of the attention turned out to be unsympathetic. See *La Prensa* (Barranquilla), Feb. 5, 1934, p. 1, in which it was alleged that Gaitán himself shot at a Liberal; and *La Lucha* (Sincelejo), Feb. 10, 1934, claimed that Uniristas provoked the clash. *Relator* (Cali) published little on UNIR, just reporting on Fusagasugá; they were more establishment Liberal and strictly Lopista; see also *Vanguardia Liberal* (Bucaramanga) 1934. Yet by no means was all coverage antagonistic. *El Heraldo* (B/quilla), Feb. 5 and 6, 1934, was concerned for the safety of the "Tribune of the People"; *El Crisol* (Cali), Feb. 8, 1934, p. 3, published a very pro-Gaitán editorial, blaming the mayor; *Diario Nacional* (Bogotá), Feb. 22, 1934, pp. 1, 4, 5, published a long piece by Uniristas of the Fusagasugá concejo on the clash.

54. Sharpless, *Gaitán of Colombia*, 72, 75.

55. Ibid., 73.

56. Braun, *Assassination of Gaitán*, 64.

57. The first *Gaitán: Antología*, 220–51; the second in *Unirismo*, Aug. 23, 1934.

58. Sharpless, *Gaitán of Colombia*, 74; Medina, "Terceros partidos," 15; Pécaut, *Política*, 127; Braun, *Assassination of Colombia*, 63–66; Archila, *Cultura e identidad obrera*, 293.

59. Peña, *Gaitán íntimo*, 123.

60. *Unirismo* rose to a circulation of 15,000, making it Colombia's third widest-read paper.

61. *Diario Nacional* (Bogotá), March 21, 1934, p. 8, "Por qué fundó Gaitán nuevo partido"; March 28, 1934, p. 1, "Gaitán explicó . . . su misticismo," *Relator* (Cali), March 3, 1934, p. 1.

62. Constantino Reyes y León to JEG, Floresta, Sept. 30, 1933; AICPG v.0086.

63. Alonso García Bustamante to JEG, Pereira, Dec. 23, 1934; AICPG v.0092.

64. Efe Restrepo E. to JEG, Armenia, Sept. 30, 1933; AICPG v.0092.

65. Francisco Restrepo Suárez to JEG, Bogotá, July 15, 1934; AICPG v.0014.

66. *Unirismo*, "Plataforma de Acción de la UNIR," Aug. 23, 1934.

67. *Unirismo*, Aug. 23, 1934, p. 9.

68. César A. Cepeda A. to JEG, B/quilla, May 22, 1935; AICPG v.0091.

69. Julio Restrepo Toro (abogado) to JEG, Pereira, July 22, 1934; AICPG v.0092.

70. Adolfo Vergara, César Murillo, Pablo Chávez to JEG, Cartagena, Oct. 8, 1934; letter from the Consejo Municipal de Cartagena to JEG, Oct. 7, 1934; AICPG v.0088.

71. "Former Workers of the Santa Marta Railway" to JEG, Ciénaga, Jan. 10, 1934; AICPG v.0011; "Sociedad Obrera-Agrícola, Pabellón Gaitán" to JEG, Ovejas, May 17, 1933; AICPG v.0074.

72. JEG to G. Tulio Molina R., Margarita (Bol.), Aug. 4, 1934; AICPG v.0074.

73. *La Razón* (Aracataca), Jan. 29, 1934, p. 3, "La Ideología Liberal" by Dionisio Rincones P.

74. *La Tribuna* (B/quilla), Sept. 8, 1934, "El temor de los viejos partidos, Revolución!"

75. F. Peñaredonda Bolívar to JEG, Sucre, June 2, 1933; AICPG v.0074.

76. "Interpretación del UNIRISMO; Antítesis del Liberalismo: cooperacionismo, reformismo revolucionario, colectivismo," C. M. Céspedes Jiménez, Oct. 1934; AICPG v.0088.

77. "Resolución 11 de La UNIR de Cartagena," June 5, 1934; AICPG v.0053.

78. A. Amador y Cortes to JEG; Cartagena, Sept. 4, 1933, and July 29, 1934; AICPG v.0088.

79. Ramón Leon y B. to JEG, Cartagena, June 30, 1933; AICPG v.0074.

80. See Elsy Marulanda, *Colonización y conflicto,* 129–33, as well as Gloria Gaitán, *La lucha por la tierra,* and LeGrand, *Frontier Expansion.* See also Michael Jiménez, "The Limits of Export Capitalism," for the parallel mobilization dominated by UNIR's Communist competitors.

81. Federación de Dueños de Mejoras Ubicadas en Terrenos Hacienda de "El Chocho," Sociedad de Mutuo Apoyo de Agricultores to JEG, Los Puente-Fusagasugá, May 2, 1932; AICPG v.0086.

82. L. Gutiérrez F., Junta Municipal de Cafeteros, Gigante to JEG, July 10, 1932; AICPG v.0044.

83. Sharpless, *Gaitán of Colombia,* 79.

84. *Diario Nacional* (Bogotá), Aug. 17, 1934, pp. 1 and 8, "El debate . . . sobre lo del Tolima."

85. *Diario Nacional* (Bogotá), Aug. 17, 1934, p. 3, editorial "El Problema de la tierra."

86. *El Crisol* (Cali), Aug. 24, 1933, p. 1, "La UNIR se enfrenta resolutamente al individualismo."

87. Sharpless, *Gaitán of Colombia,* 73–74.

88. *Unirismo,* June 28, 1934, p. 6, "Exito en Santa Marta, Cartagena y Barranquilla"; July 12, p. 6, and July 19, p. 7, Santa Marta; July 26, p. 7, Puerto Colombia, Cartagena, Santa Marta; August 9, p. 7, Barranquilla; etc.

89. Pablo Balcázar of TODAMERICA to JEG, Medellín, June 9, 1934; AICPG v.0016.

90. "Afectísimos amigos y compañeros" to JEG, Cepitá, Aug. 27, 1934; AICPG v.0057.

91. *El Crisol* (Cali), March 1, 1934, p. 1, "Manifiesto del unirismo a las masas trabajadores."

92. Interview with Carlos Hernández by Mauricio Archila.

93. López Giraldo, *El Apóstol Desnudo* (The naked apostle).

94. Ermínsul Cortés Q. to JEG, Pasto, Sept. 3, 1933; AICPG v.0050.

95. A. Amador y Cortes to JEG, Cartagena, Oct. 27, 1933; AICPG v.0088.

96. *El Estado*, July 11, 1934, pp. 1 and 4. Their article, "La sensibilidad de la revolución," presented a panorama of different groups on the left as represented in the national press, ranging from *El Liberal* in Cali calling for defense of the "poorest classes" to *La Defensa* in Medellín advocating "catholic socialism." Of Gaitán they say, "In his speech at the Station of the Sabana [in Bogotá] he insisted that the country can only be saved through an integral revolution."

97. *La Razón* (Aracataca), Aug. 25, 1934, p. 3.

98. Armando Solano, "Liberalismo izquierda y derecha," *El Mitín* (Cartagena), Oct. 25, 1935, p. 1.

99. Medina, "Terceros partidos," 16.

100. *Pluma Libre,* Nov. 30, 1935, p. 3, editorial "The Significance of a Symbol."

101. *Pluma Libre* (Pereira), May 30, 1936, p. 3.

102. *Diario Nacional* (Bogotá), Feb. 5, 1934, pp. 1 and 3.

103. *Unirismo,* Aug. 16, 1934, p. 15, and Sept. 6, 1934, p. 10.

104. Efe Restrepo E. to JEG, Manizales, Feb. 4, 1935; AICPG v.0092.

105. *El Estado* (Santa Marta), Oct. 27, 1934, p. 1.

106. *La Lucha* (Sincelejo), Nov. 7, 1934, p. 1.

107. Joaquín Morillo C. writing in *La Razón,* Feb. 12 and 16, 1935, pp. 3–4.

108. *El Mitín* (Cartagena), Feb. 22, 1935, p. 3.

109. Efraín Rojas Trujillo (abogado) to JEG, Neiva, Sept. 12, 1932; AICPG v.0044.

110. Juan Julian Donneys to JEG, Cali (Puerto Mallarivo), Jan. 16, 1936, AICPG v.0013.

Chapter 4. The Lopista Interlude: *Revolución en Marcha,* Pause, and Crisis, 1934–1946

1. Mendoza Neira and Camacho Angarita, eds., *El liberalismo en el gobierno,* 2:241–42. See also *Diario Nacional* (Bogotá), Nov. 20, 1934, p. 1, "No gobernar con las oligarquías sino gobernar con el pueblo, es el programa del actual presidente Dr. López dijo Echandía."

2. See Pécaut, *Orden y violencia,* v. 1; Sharpless, *Gaitán of Colombia*; Archila, *Cultura e identidad obrera*; and Renán Vega Cantor, *Crisis y caída.*

3. See chapters 3, 4, and 5 of *Assassination of Gaitán.*

4. Eduardo Zuleta Angel, *El Presidente López Pumarejo*, 79–81.

5. Mendoza Neira and Camacho Angarita eds. *El liberalismo en el gobierno*, 1:72.

6. M. J. Serrano V. to ALP, Cúcuta, Feb. 28, 1935; AP, v. 22, 1935.

7. Ten doctors and lawyers to President ALP, Facatativa, Dec. 27, 1934; AP, v. 4, 1934.

8. Miguel E. Ahumada S. to ALP, Puerto Colombia (Atlántico), July 27, 1935; AP, v. 22, 1935.

9. Alejandro López, *Idearium Liberal*, 16 and 216–25.

10. José Antonio Osorio Lizarazo, *Ideas de Izquierda*, 3, 10.

11. Juan Ramón Lanao Loaiza, *Mirando las izquierdas*, 77.

12. *El Heraldo* (B/quilla), Oct. 30, 1933, p. 5; "Notas al margen—El concepto de revolución."

13. C. A. Tamara Manotas in *La Lucha* (Sincelejo), Feb. 10, 1934, p. 3.

14. *El Mitín* (Cartagena), March 13, 1935, p. 3.

15. *El Mitín* (Cartagena), May 2, 1936, p. 1, "Un fenómeno de las masas"; and May 8, 1936, p. 3, Armando Solano's "Una nueva política."

16. *La Razón* (Aracataca), Aug. 17, 1935, p. 3, and Sept. 10, 1935.

17. *Por la Unión* (Santa Marta), July 16, 1938, pp. 2 and 4.

18. *La Lucha* (Sincelejo), Feb. 3, 1934, p. 7; "Sin igualdad económica la democracia es un mito."

19. *El Heraldo* (B/quilla), Oct. 28, 1933, p. 1.

20. *El Estado* (Santa Marta), Nov. 3, 1934, p. 1; E. Conde Ribón to ALP, Cartagena, Aug. 2, 1934; AP, v. 5, 1934.

21. Alejandro Pavajeau to ALP, B/quilla, June 17, 1935; AP, v. 5 (handwritten number), 1935.

22. Ramón León y B. to ALP, Cartagena, Nov. 12, 1934; AP, v. 12, 1934.

23. Manuel Davila Pumarejo to Min. de gobierno, Santa Marta, Dec. 4, 1934; AP, v. 11, 1934.

24. Governor Andrés Rocha A. to ALP, Ibagué, Sept. 19, 1934; AP, v. 11, 1934.

25. ALP to Governor Andrés Rocha A., Bogotá, Sept. 27, 1934; AP, v. 11, 1934.

26. ALP to Governor of Caldas, Luís Jaramillo M., Bogotá, Nov. 12, 1934; AP, v. 11, 1934.

27. Tirado Mejía, *Aspectos políticos*, xi, 3–21.

28. Mauricio Torres, *La naturaleza de la revolución*, 50–51.

29. See Pécaut, *Orden y violencia* 2:212–84; and Archila, "Las ilusiones de reforma social," in *Cultura e identidad obrera*. Catherine LeGrand argued that the agrarian reform Law 200 of 1936 was an important legal gain for small holders without legal title, but that its effects were negligible in practical terms and hastened their transformation into rural wage laborers (*Frontier Expansion*, 149–62).

30. Rothlisberger, "Liberal Reform," 95; and Nieto Rojas, *La batalla contra comunismo*, 16.

31. Stoller, "Alfonso López Pumarejo," 370. Medina, *Historia del partido comunista,* 238; and Molina, *Las ideas liberales,* 3:91.

32. Interview by Mauricio Archila with Ramón de la Hoz.

33. Pacífico Almanza (Centro Obrero, Agraria, El Retén) to ALP, Feb. 22, 1935; AP, v. 14, 1935.

34. Federación Sindical del Magd. to ALP, Aracataca, March 1, 1937; AP, unnumbered vol., 1937.

35. Comité Liberal Municipal of Barrancabermeja to ALP, March 20, 1936; AP, v. 4, 1936.

36. Two hundred Liberals to ALP and the National Liberal Directorate, Toro, March 1936; AP, v. 4, 1936.

37. Diego Martínez C. and four others to ALP, Cartagena, Jan. 31, 1936; AP, v. 4, 1936.

38. *Por la Unión* (Santa Marta), March 6, 1937, p. 1, "Mueran los viejos prejuicios."

39. *Por la Unión* (Santa Marta), Feb. 19, 1938, p. 1, "Continúa la farsa."

40. *Por la Unión* (Santa Marta), March 27, 1937, p. 1.

41. For discussion of other movements in the early 1930s, see Pécaut, *Orden y violencia*; Bergquist, *Labor in Latin America*; Archila, *Cultura e identidad obrera*; Abel and Palacios, "Colombia, 1930–58"; Catherine LeGrand, *Frontier Expansion*; Medófilo Medina, *Historia del Partido Comunista* and *La protesta urbana*; Rausch, "Diego Luis Córdoba."

42. *El Soviet* (Cali), July 13, 1935, p. 1, "Organo Regional del Partido Comunista."

43. *El Obrero* (B/quilla), Nov. 16, 1935, p. 1. Throughout the 1930s the Communists continued to follow an inconsistent internationalism.

44. "Communist Activities in Colombia," June 16, 1943, SD 821.00B/92.

45. Memorandum, Feb. 1, 1938, attached to Despatch no. 1991, Jan. 8, 1938, SD 821.00B/67.

46. *La Tribuna* (B/quilla), May 27, 1934, p. 2.

47. *El Estado* (Santa Marta), May 2, 1944.

48. "Manifiesto: La misión . . ." in *El Estado* (Santa Marta), April 9, 10, 12, 16, 1945.

49. Palacios, *Entre la legitimidad y la violencia,* 158.

50. Concejo Municipal de B/quilla to ALP, Nov. 21, 1936; AP, v. 1, 1936.

51. "Communist Activities in Colombia," June 16, 1943, SD 821.00B/92.

52. See Archila Neira, *Barranquilla y el río*; and Green, "Sibling Rivalry on the Left."

53. See *Tierra*, an early organ of the Communist party, May 27, 1938, p. 9; and *Sentido y Realización de una Política Social,* 111–16, for the list of unions affiliated with the FEDENAL.

54. López's successor, Eduardo Santos, manifested his overt opposition to FEDENAL's closed shop from the outset. He gave a speech in Barranquilla in 1938

in which he said he would try to end the unions' ability to disrupt the companies' autonomy "in freely naming their employees" (*Diario Nacional* [Bogotá], April 11, 1938, p. 1). The transport companies, for their part, consistently attempted to ignore the collective bargaining pact negotiated in July of 1937.

55. The U.S. consulate in Barranquilla noted "a divergence of ideas" between Communist and non-Communist unions leading up to the strike in June 1937 (Vice Consul Raymond Phelan to the Embassy in Bogotá, June 23, 1937, SD, Consular Post File, Record Group 84). Another major split erupted between Liberals and Communists in 1939–1941 over how to renegotiate salaries in light of competition from the railroads (*El Liberal* [Bogotá], Nov. 26, 1940).

56. Pécaut, *Orden y violencia* 1:263.

57. Phelan to the Embassy in Bogotá, Sept. 20, 1936; SD Consular Post File, Record Group 84.

58. In fact, Gaitán was reelected president of the city council in May 1936 ("JEG fue reelegido presidente del concejo municipal," *Diario Nacional* [Bogotá], May 6, 1936, front-page headline).

59. *Diario Nacional* (Bogotá), May 16, 1936, p. 1, "Aceptada la renuncia de gobierno Tamayo."

60. See *Diario Nacional* (Bogotá), May 12, 1936, "¿Nombrado Alcalde de Bogotá JEG?"; May 13, 1936, "Gaitán, Alcalde de Bogotá."

61. *Diario Nacional* (Bogotá), May 15, 1936, p. 3, editorial "Gaitán en la Alcaldía."

62. *Diario Nacional* (Bogotá), May 23, 1936, headline "Con Emprestito o sin emprestito . . ."

63. Consul Harnden to Embassy in Bogotá, June 22, 1936; SD Consular Post File.

64. Sharpless, *Gaitán of Colombia*, 89–90.

65. *Diario Nacional* (Bogotá), June 8, 1936.

66. *Diario Nacional* (Bogotá), June 16, 1936, p. 3, "Ante el empuje del nuevo Alcalde."

67. See, for example, *Ahora* (Plato-Mag), May 21, 1936, p. 1, "Gaitán aceptó la alcaldía de Bogotá ayer en la noche." They noted "great enthusiasm" in the city "in general rallies for the new mayor." On June 4, 1936, p. 1, "El Dr. Jorge Eliécer Gaitán tomará posesión de la Alcaldía de Bogotá el día 8 de los corrientes." On June 11, 1936, p. 1, "Las actividades e iniciativas de Gaitán están mereciendo comentarios favorables y elogiosos."

68. See the detailed and specific plans outlined in the *Diario Nacional* (Bogotá), June 30, 1936.

69. Sharpless, *Gaitán of Colombia*, 91. A mason and inhabitant of the working-class (and radically Gaitanista) neighborhood of "la Perseverancia" in Bogotá spoke of Mayor Gaitán beautifying the city (Interview with Alfonso Garcia by Mauricio Archila).

70. Sharpless, *Gaitán of Colombia*, 90–91; see also Braun, *Assassination of Gaitán*, 68–73.

71. Sindicato de Empleados Municipales de Medellín to JEG, Jan. 28, 1937, found in AICPG v.0059; *La Tribuna* (B/quilla), Feb. 5, 1937, p. 2.

72. Braun, *The Assassination of Gaitán*, 72.

73. Sharpless, *Gaitán of Colombia*, 93. There was a great deal of irony in this confrontation, given that among the many groups of workers Gaitán represented were Bogotá's taxi drivers. In 1934 Gaitán represented the Sindicato de Choferes de Taxis Rojos (*Diario Nacional* [Bogotá], Aug. 25, 1934, p. 1). For more on the strike and its implications see Green, "Días de emoción espectacular."

74. *El Fígaro* (Cartagena), Feb. 8, 1937, p. 1; *Diario de la Costa* (Cartagena), Feb. 10, 1937, p. 3.

75. Braun, *Assassination of Gaitán*, 73; Archila, *Cultura e identidad obrera*, 303. Sharpless was more hesitant and noted that not all labor unions were against Gaitán during the crisis (*Gaitán of Colombia*, 94). Pécaut, *Política y sindicalismo*, 160, note 12, noted some union support, but stressed sympathy strikes in other cities and Gaitán's intransigence.

76. See *El Heraldo* (B/quilla), Feb. 2, p. 1; *El Fígaro* (Cartagena), Feb. 6, 1937, p. 1.

77. It is interesting to note that the first was reported in *El Liberal* (Manizales, a very left-Liberal paper), Feb. 12, 1937, p. 1, with the big headline, "Más de veinte mil personas aclamaron ayer en Bogotá al alcalde Doctor Gaitán"; and the second in the Conservative *Diario de la Costa* (Cartagena), Feb. 16, 1937, pp. 1, 8.

78. *Pluma Libre* (Pereira), Feb, 6, 1937, p. 1; Feb. 20, 1937, pp. 1 and 8, "Se impone el envío de protestas respetuosas al presidente López para que garantice la vida de los auténticos voceros de las masas laboriosas"; and p. 5, "JEG, bandera de las izquierdas."

79. *El Liberal* (Manizales), Feb. 17, 1937, pp. 4–5, "Conclusiones de la huelga" by Lozano y Lozano.

80. *El Heraldo* (B/quilla), Feb. 10, 1937, pp. 1 and 6; "Manifiesto . . ."

81. *Tipos* (Organo del sindicato de artes gráficas de Bogotá) noted "with great surprise" the profound division the drivers find themselves in (Feb. 1937, p. 2, "El conflicto de los choferes").

82. For the railroad workers see *El Heraldo* (B/quilla), Feb. 12, 1937, p. 1. For the drivers in Cali, see *La Prensa* (B/quilla), Feb. 11, 1937, p. 5.

83. Luis Ernesto Duque, Jesus Arana H., to JEG, Feb. 12, 1937, AICPG v.0020.

84. So noted *El Fígaro* (Cartagena), Feb. 12, 1937, p. 1.

85. *El Heraldo* (B/quilla), Feb. 13, 1937, p. 1; signed by the presidents of Asociación Electristas, Sindicato Empresa Colombiana Curtido, Sindicato Textiles Monserate, Sindicato Fábrica Fósforos "El Ruiz," Sindicato Paños Colombianos, Sindicato Central Nacional de Choferes, Federación Local de Trabajo,

Sindicato Fábrica Chocolates Santa Fe, Sindicato de Voceadores de Prensa, Confederación Sindical de Colombia, Sindicato Obrero Fábrica Calzado "Centaurio," Sindicato de Trabajadoras Domésticas, Sindicato de Bavaria, Federación Nacional de Transportes Marítimo, Unión Sindical Textiles, Sindicato de Trabajadores de Aseo.

86. *Relator* (Cali), Feb. 13, 1937, p. 5, "Los motoristas de Cali." The telegram from the workers' unions of Bogotá to Cali included all those organizations in the B/quilla message plus: Sindicato de Boleteros de la Ciudad; Sindicato de Artes Gráficos; Sindicato de Voceadores Ambulantes; Junta de Mejoras Barrio Providencia; Junta de Mejoras Barrio Gaitán; Junta de Mejoras Barrio González; Acción Nacional Democrática; Sindicato Sastres; Sindicato Nacional de Pintores; Sindicato de Ebanistas, Carpinteros y Similares; Sindicato Obreros Cajetilleras; Sindicato Construcciones.

87. *El Siglo* (Bogotá), Feb. 10, 1937, noted Communist support for Gaitán, and the equally Conservative paper *Oriente* of Bucaramanga noted that on the 15th in Girardot an "asamblea campesina comunista" protested to López and supported Gaitán (Feb. 16, 1937, p. 1, "Actividades comunistas"). And on the eve of the strike, Mayor Gaitán was praised by one of his longtime Communist rivals, Gilberto Vieira (Sharpless, *Gaitán of Colombia,* 92).

88. *La Defensa Social* (Bogotá), Feb. 16, 1937, p. 3, "El comunismo era la única fuerza que apoyaba a Gaitán."

89. Found in Ramón Manrique, *Bajo el signo de la hoz,* 60–61.

90. *Diario de la Costa* (Cartagena), Feb. 14, 1937, pp. 1, 8.

91. *Por la Unión* (Santa Marta), March 6, 1937, pp. 4, 5, and 6.

92. Manrique, *Bajo el signo de la hoz,* 60–61; *La Defensa Social* (Bogotá), Feb. 16, 1937, p. 3.

93. *Unión y Trabajo* of Medellín, Feb. 20, 1937, p. 3, editorial "La caída de Gaitán."

94. "Declaraciones . . . Confederación Sindical de Colombia," *Por la Unión* (Santa Marta), March 6, 1937, pp. 4–6. The Communist party central committee argued along similar lines—see Manrique, *Bajo el signo de la hoz,* 60–61.

95. Liga Venteros, Medellín, to JEG, Feb. 13, 1937; Sindicato Tranviario, Medellín, to JEG, Feb. 13, 1937; Federación Sindical, Medellín, to JEG, Feb. 13, 1937; Centro Obrero Juan Riveros, Socorro, to JEG, Feb. 13, 1937; all found in AICPG v.0020.

96. Pedro León Navarro, Bucaramanga, to JEG, Feb. 11, 1937; Gómez Parra, Garzón Rangel, Luis Eduardo Posada, Bucaramanga, to JEG, Feb. 12, 1937; Pios Santos R., Bogotá, to JEG, Feb. 13, 1937; all in AICPG v.0020.

97. Sindicato Choferes, Pasto, to JEG, Feb. 1937; Sindicato Lecheros, Pereira, to JEG, Feb. 12, 1937; José Eusebio Muñoz, Sesquile, to JEG, Feb. 11, 1937; Sindicato Pintores, Pereira, to JEG, Feb. 12, 1937; all in AICPG v.0020. Sindicato Independiente de Limpia-Botas de Bogotá, to JEG, Feb. 11, 1937, AICPG v.0059.

98. *El Espectador* (Bogotá), Feb. 11, 1937, p. 4, editorial "Reacción fascista";

Relator (Cali), Feb. 13, 1937, p. 3, editorial "La Huelga de Choferes de Bogotá"; *Orientación Liberal* (Popayán), Feb. 19, 1937, p. 5, editorial "La caída de Gaitán"; *Adelante* (Cali), Feb. 20, 1937, p. 1, "El movimiento de los motoristas bogotanos"; *Tribuna Libre* (Cali), Feb. 13, 1937, p. 1, "Estruendoso fracaso del disimulo conservador."

99. *La Prensa* (B/quilla), Feb. 13, 1937, p. 5, "Epílogo de sangre"; *El Siglo* (Bogotá), Feb. 10, 1937, p. 1, picture of Gaitán leaving work with the caption "El alcalde sin uniforme se prepara tomar y manejar su automóvil." Over the next few days they showed pictures of wounded drivers on the front page. On Feb. 15 they ran an interesting drawing of drivers running over Gaitán; Feb. 11, 1937, p. 4, editorial "El demagogo en el poder"; *El Fígaro* (Cartagena), Feb 10, 1937, p. 1; *El Bien Social* (Bogotá), Feb. 14, 1937, p. 3, editorial "Los falsos maestros"; *El Combate* (Neiva, Organo del Dir. Conservador Dep.), Feb. 14, 1937, p. 1, "Información general"; *Oriente* (Bucaramanga), Feb. 11, 1937, p. 1, headline "Gigantescas proporciones asume la huelga. . . La caída de Gaitán es inminente"; *La Prensa* (B/quilla), Feb. 12, 1937; *El Fígaro* (Cartagena), Feb. 15, 1937; *Correo del Cauca* (Cali), Feb. 14, 1937, p. 1, "Destuitido en forma violenta el alcalde de Bogotá," p. 5.

100. *Pluma Libre* (Pereira), Feb. 20, 1937, pp. 1 and 8, "Se impone el envío de protestas respetuosas al presidente López," and p. 5, "JEG, bandera de las izquierdas."

101. *Por la Unión* (Santa Marta), March 6, 1937, pp. 4, 5, and 6.

102. *El Liberal* (Manizales), Feb. 17, 1937, p. 4, editorial "La alegría derechista."

103. *El Espectador* (Bogotá), Feb. 15, 1937, p. 4., editorial "La destitución del doctor Gaitán."

104. *El Tiempo* (Bogotá), Calibán, "Danza de las horas," Feb. 11, 1937, p. 4; Feb. 12, 1937, p. 4.

105. *El Liberal* (Manizales), Feb. 17, 1937, pp. 4–5, "Conclusiones de la huelga" by Lozano y L.

106. *El Empleado* (Girardot), Feb. 19, 1937, p. 1, "El estropicio de los uniformes."

107. *Relator* (Cali), Feb. 13, 1937, p. 3, editorial "La Huelga de Choferes de Bogotá."

108. As an indication of how confused the episode was, during the strike Gaitán's opponents called him both a "communist" and a "fascist." The latter charge bothered him the most.

109. *El Fígaro* (Cartagena), Feb. 18, 1937, pp. 1, 4, and 6. See also *Relator* (Cali), Feb. 18, 1937, p. 8, "El magnífico discurso del Dr. Gaitán en la cámara."

110. *El Tiempo* (Bogotá), Feb. 14, 1937, p. 5, commentary "La Alcaldía de Jorge Eliécer Gaitán."

111. *El Crisol* (Cali), Feb. 18, 1937, p. 1, headline "Tumultuosas manifestaciones políticas."

112. *El Tiempo* (Bogotá), Feb. 14, 1937, "Danza de las horas."

113. Escipión Fernández to *Esfuerzo* (Honda), Feb. 25, 1937, p. 2, "La huelga de los choferes."

114. *El Empleado*, Feb. 19, 1937, p. 1, "El estropicio de los uniformes."

115. Tirado Mejía, *Aspectos políticos*, p. 15, quoting Alfonso López on December 20, 1936.

116. The official mobilization of the "oligarquía" to place Santos in the presidency, left Liberals claimed, represented a "falsification of the popular will" when Echandía was really the "candidate of the masses" (*El Mitín* [Cartagena], March 10, 1937, p. 3, "El querer popular").

117. *El Mitín* (Cartagena), April 1, 1937, p. 3, "La chusma y el liberalismo," reprint, *Diario Nacional*.

118. *El Mitín* (Cartagena), April 1, 1937, p. 3.

119. *El Mitín* (Cartagena), April 6, 1937, p. 3.

120. Eduardo Santos, "El partido liberal ante el frente popular y ante las derechas y las izquierdas" (in the Senate, Aug. 20, 1936), in *Una política liberal para Colombia*, 27–28.

121. Eduardo Santos, "La convivencia nacional, el régimen democrático y la política del gobierno" (Oct. 25, 1938), in *Las etapas de la vida colombiana*, 24.

122. *Vanguardia* (Santa Marta), May 26, 1943, p. 3.

123. *Vanguardia* (Santa Marta), Aug. 12, 1943, p. 1, "Las bases de una política social," reprinted from *El Liberal* (Bogotá).

124. López Pumarejo, "Manifiesto . . ." radio address, Sept. 17, 1941, *La reintegración*, 21–31.

125. *La Tribuna* (B/quilla), Jan. 18, 1943, p. 3.

126. *La Tribuna* (B/quilla), Aug. 11, 1943, p. 1; Oct. 6, 1943, p. 1.

127. Con. Daniel Anderson to Amb. Arthur Bliss Lane, Sept. 28, 1943 (SD, Consular Post File, Record Group 84).

128. Rodolfo Ponce (of *La Tribuna*) to JEG, B/quilla, Nov. 8 1944; AICPG v.0091.

129. *La Tribuna* (B/quilla), Nov. 3, 1943, p. 1, "La situación del Pres."

130. *El Estado* (Santa Marta), Jan. 12, 1945, p. 3.

131. *El Fígaro* (Cartagena), Feb. 25, 1944, p. 3.

132. Osorio Lizarazo in his novel, *El día del odio*, 222.

133. See Donald S. Barnhart, "Colombian Transport," 1–23.

134. Unionized railway workers outnumbered FEDENAL workers 15,000 to 10,000 (see *Tierra*, Oct. 14, 1938, p. 3). In 1945 FEDENAL could only count 8,000 members, and by 1947 the union census of that year showed only 5,000; see Pécaut, *Orden y violencia*, 2:421.

135. Medina, *Historia del Partido Comunista*, 492, 476.

136. Renan Vega C., *Crisis y caída*, 148–61; Pécaut, *Orden y violencia*, 2:416–23; Archila, *Cultura e identidad obrera*, 365–70.

137. Antonio Garcia, *Gaitán y el problema de la revolución colombiana*, 42.

138. Stoller equated Liberal radicalism exclusively with López Pumarejo and concluded that the "historical moment of Liberal radicalism was brief" ("Alfonso López Pumarejo," 394).

139. *Por la Unión* (Santa Marta), Feb. 13, 1937, p. 1, "Etica patronal."

140. *La Tribuna* (B/quilla), March 19, 1937, p. 3.

141. *La Tribuna* (B/quilla), April 4, 1938, p. 1, "La actitud del general Lázaro Cárdenas"; and *Por la Unión* (Santa Marta), April 2, 1938, p. 1, "El ejemplo mexicano."

142. *El Estado* (Santa Marta), Jan. 30, 1943, p. 3, reprint of "Manifiesto . . . doctrinario del Valle."

143. Sharpless, *Gaitán of Colombia*, 94.

144. Asamblea General de los vecinos . . . la Providencia, Bogotá, to JEG, Aug. 30, 1937; "Proposición . . . por la Asamblea . . . de los Barrios Unidos del Norte," Bogotá, to JEG, July 10, 1937; Barrio Libertador, Bogotá, to JEG, Dec. 2, 1937; Junta Pro-Defensa de los Barrios Altos, Bogotá, to JEG, Nov. 2, 1937; Barrio Gaitán, Bogotá, to JEG, Oct. 18, 1937; Juntas de Mejores Públicos de Barrio San Fernando, Bogotá, to JEG, Dec. 4, 1939; all in AICPG v.0021.

145. Organización Sindical de Tranviarios de Bogotá, to JEG, Sept. 23, 1937 (they wrote several letters in 1938); Asociación de Transportes Urbanos, Bogotá, to JEG, Sept. 29, 1937; Sindicato de Carteros de Correos y Telégrafos Nacionales, Bogotá, to JEG, March 31, 1938; Federación Sindical de las Empresas Unidas de Energía Eléctrica, Bogotá, to JEG, May 17, 1938; Sindicato de Limpia-Botas de Bogotá, to JEG, May 25, 1938; all in AICPG v.0059.

146. Asociación Nacional de Choferes, Bogotá, to JEG, June 28, 1938, AICPG v.0059.

147. Carlos Galvis Gómez, *Por qué cayó López*, 14.

148. *El Estado* (Santa Marta), Dec. 24, 1946, p. 1, "Lo que fue Gaitán como ministro de Ed."

149. Manuel Mosquera, "Sin. prensa/revista" to JEG, B/quilla, Feb. 11, 1943; AICPG v.0091.

150. JEG to Humberto López Gaviria, Bogotá, June 1, 1939; AICPG v.0065.

151. *El Liberal* (Bogotá), Nov. 6, 1943, pp. 1, 13, 16, "Nuevo plan social anuncia . . . Gaitán."

152. Juan de Dios Romero to JEG, B/quilla, Feb. 3, 1944; AICPG v.0021.

153. Antonio Ribera to JEG, Santa Marta, Sept. 22, 1937; AICPG v.0017.

154. *La Voz del Sinú* (Montería), Sept. 9, 1939, p. 3.

155. *Pluma Libre* (Pereira), Jan. 27, 1939, p. 5.

156. Antonio Caballero C. (Liberal Izq. Rev.) to JEG, Cartagena, Feb. 21, 1939; AICPG v.0053.

157. *Por la Unión* (Santa Marta), May 7, 1938, p. 1 (Luis Moreno, interview with Mauricio Archila).

158. Workers in Magdalena, remembering with gratitude his role after the massacre, pledged to always remain his followers (letter from Federación de

Trabajadores del Magd. [Aracataca] to JEG, July 6, 1938; AICPG v.0011). It is natural that banana workers and former banana workers would remember Gaitán (Manuel F. Robles to JEG, Santa Marta, Feb. 5, 1942; AICPG v.0011; Luis Sandoval P. to JEG, B/quilla, March 27, 1946; AICPG v.0043), but others did so as well. A mechanic in Barranquilla named his son Jorge Eliécer while a barber in Magdalena offered his "tears and blood" until the end of the struggle (Benigo Villa to JEG, B/quilla, Jan. 22, 1944; AICPG v.0026; Ignacio Salazar H. to JEG, Pato, Jan 31, 1946; AICPG v.0017).

159. *La Tribuna* (B/quilla), Dec. 23, 1944, p. 1; they refer to the politics of the Revolución en Marcha as "descabellada," pierced through the nape of the neck as a bull is when killed in the ring.

160. Gonzalo Sánchez "La violencia," 7.

Chapter 5. The *Pueblo*: Gender, Race, and Class in the Liberal Republic, 1930–1946

1. Eduardo Sáenz noted that industrialists in Medellín and Bogotá carried on a dogged struggle with Gaitán because of his campaign against protectionism in the name of the Colombian consumer, and even hinted that they had the most to gain from his assassination (*La Ofensiva Empresarial,* chapters 6, 7, and 8).

2. Friedrich Katz has noted that multiclass mobilizations, such as Villismo during the Mexican Revolution, are most successful when some political crisis unites the fractured subaltern classes. See Katz, *The Life and Times of Pancho Villa.*

3. Much of this discussion appeared in Green, "Mujeres radicales."

4. Ironically, Colombia was one of the first and one of the last countries in Latin America to extend voting rights to women. In 1853 the provincial legislature of the province of Vélez of Nueva Granada liberally interpreted the new constitution of that year and gave the vote to women, and even attempted to guarantee an equal role for women in political institutions. After this brief experiment, Colombian women would not have the vote again until 1957.

5. Magdala Velásquez T., "Condición jurídica y social de la mujer," 9, 13, 19–30.

6. Paulo Sandroni, "La proletarización de la mujer en Colombia después de 1945," in León, ed., *La realidad colombiana,* 74. He cites "El censo industrial de 1945."

7. Ibid., 74–75. For the case of Brazil see, Joel Wolfe, *Working Women, Working Men.*

8. The quote is from an interview López gave to Nelly Merino of *Hogar* magazine of Buenos Aires. *El Estado* (Santa Marta) reprinted part of the interview as part of "El Dr. López y la mujer Colombiana," by Gloria Dall (Feb. 16, 1934, pp. 1 and 4).

9. Prisco López C., Comité Gaitanista Univ., to JEG, Cartagena, June 14, 1946; AICPG v.0034.

10. Soledad Gómez Garzón, *Ciudadanía de la mujer colombiana*, 15, 46.

11. *Vanguardia* (Santa Marta), June 9, 1944, p. 3.

12. Luz Jaramillo, "Feminismo y luchas políticas: Anotaciones sobre la doble militancia," in León, ed., *La realidad colombiana*, 177.

13. Lola G. Luna, "Los movimientos de mujeres," 170.

14. *Agitación Femenina*, no. 4, Feb. 1945, p. 3.

15. *Agitación Femenina*, no. 1, Oct. 1944, p. 3, and no. 2, Nov. 1944, p. 16. In the early to mid-twentieth century, women's publications were generally dedicated to fashion and religious matters; see Patricia Londoño, "Las publicaciones periódicas dirigidas a la mujer," 3–23.

16. She gladly welcomed the assistance of such "valiant" men (both Liberals and Conservatives) as Luís López de Mesa, Jorge Soto del Corral, Augusto Ramírez Moreno, José Mar, Augusto Durán, and Jorge Eliécer Gaitán ("Una voz insurgente: entrevista . . . Ofelia Uribe de Acosta," 35).

17. Uribe wrote a letter of introduction for two men, "also Gaitanistas," to Gaitán; he responded with thanks for her services to "our cause" (June 24, 1946, and July 10, 1946; AICPG v.0019). Norma Villarreal has also noted the strong connections between the feminist activists of AF and Gaitanismo, and points out that Ofelia Uribe was a member of the Directorio Liberal Gaitanista de Boyacá (Lola Luna y Norma Villarreal, *Historia, género y política*, 98).

18. *Agitación Femenina*, no. 16, May 1946, p. 3.

19. *Agitación Femenina*, no. 2, Nov. 1944, p. 5.

20. *Agitación Femenina*, no. 1, Oct. 1944, pp. 14–15.

21. *Agitación Femenina*, no. 1, Oct. 1944, pp. 2 and 27.

22. Inés Gómez, Antilia Sánchez, Josefina de Calderón R., *Agitación Femenina*, no. 1, Oct. 1944.

23. Campaign Film, "Gaitán: Candidato del Pueblo," AFPF.

24. José María Córdoba to Centro Femenino Gaitanista of B/quilla, July 19, 1945; AICPG v.0069.

25. "La mujer y el liberalismo," *Jornada*, reprint *El Estado* (Santa Marta), Feb. 26, 1947, p. 3.

26. Alan Knight, "Populism and Neo-populism," 230.

27. And in Antioquia, Atlántico, Bolívar, and Magdalena the general rate of illiteracy among women was the lowest in the country in the 1940s. See the law thesis of Gabriela Pelaez Echeverri, *La condición social de la mujer*, 15, for statistics by department.

28. Carmelita Guerrero Mendoza, B/quilla, to *Agitación Femenina*, no. 15, April 1946, p. 23.

29. Tica A. Rubiano Rincón to JEG, B/quilla, March 28, 1946; AICPG v.0043.

30. Damas Liberales de Montería to JEG, Sept. 3, 1947; AICPG v.0053.

31. María Jaramillo, Elisa Navarro de Saavedra, Josefina S. de Vence, and Señora Rosa Rasas to JEG, B/quilla, Sept. 14, 1946; AICPG v.0012.

32. Speech by Gloria Girón in Guacamayal, published by *El Estado* (Santa

Marta), Feb. 21, 1947, pp. 2–4, "La Mujer Magdalenesa en el movimiento popular."

33. Mercedes Ortua, Santa Marta, Silvia Castro, B/quilla, to JEG, Aug. 13, 1946; AICPG v.0011.

34. See letters of allegiance from: Comités (femenino y masculino) Santa Marta, Sept. 11, 1945; María de la Cruz Viloria of the Comité del Bello Sexo, Santa Marta, Nov. 21, 1945; Comités Femeninos de los corregimientos Bonda and Gaira, spoken of by Rafael Davila, Santa Marta, Oct. 1, 1945; all in AICPG v.0011; Albertina María Cotes of the Sindicato Femenino, Santa Marta, Sept. 11, 1945; AICPG v.0017; Comité Femenino Porteño, Puerto Colombia, April 8, 1946; Comité Femenino Gaitanista, Chinú, March 6, 1946; AICPG v.0073; Comité Femenino Pro-Restauración Moral y Democrática, Mompós, March 15, 1947; AICPG v.0061.

35. Reported in El Estado (Santa Marta), April 29, 1946, p. 1, "Gran manifestación femenina en Bogotá" on the 27th. Gaitán's wife, Amparo Jaramillo de Gaitán, and the poet Laura Victoria y Anita de Díaz spoke, while his daughter Gloria shouted "¡Viva Colombia! ¡A La Carga!" into the microphone.

36. Córdoba, Tribuno Popular, 41–42.

37. Boletín de "Acción Femenista Nacional" (signed sec. Elisa Mújica, the writer) for a good example, probably 1947, AICPG.

38. Alan Knight, "Racism, Revolution, and Indigenismo," 72.

39. An expanded version of this discussion appeared in Green, "Left Liberalism and Race."

40. Jaramillo Uribe, "Mestizaje y diferenciación," in Ensayos sobre historia social de Colombia, 167.

41. Jaramillo Uribe, "La población indígena," in Ensayos sobre historia social de Colombia, 127–28.

42. Eduardo Santa, Sociología de Colombia, 69–70.

43. For an even more recent emphasis on the primacy of biology, albeit a "positive" interpretation, see Brazilian sociologist Darcy Ribeiro's The Americas and Civilization, 177.

44. Safford, "Race, Integration, and Progress," 1.

45. Knight, "Racism, Revolution, and Indigenismo," 82, 86.

46. See José Vasconcelos, La raza cósmica.

47. Safford, "Race, Integration, and Progress," 20–25.

48. Pan American Union, "Colombia in Brief," 10.

49. As does Juan Luís De Lannoy, Estructuras demográficas y sociales, p. 52.

50. Jaramillo Uribe, "Mestizaje," in Ensayos sobre historia social de Colombia, 167.

51. Luís López de Mesa, "El hombre," in Colombia en cifras, 66.

52. Javier Ocampo López, Historia básica de Colombia, 90–91.

53. W. O. Galbraith, Colombia: A General Survey, 19.

54. Orlando Fals Borda, Mompox y Loba, 150B.

55. Peter Wade, *Blackness and Race Mixture*, 56.

56. James Parsons, *Antioqueño Colonization*, 4. Colombia's racial composition in 1950: whites, 25 percent; Indians 5 percent; mestizos 42 percent; "Negroes and mulattoes," 28 percent (Lynn T. Smith, "The Racial Composition," 218).

57. Jaramillo Uribe, "Esclavos y señores," in *Ensayos sobre historia social de Colombia*, 10–12.

58. Ramón Franco R., *Colombia: geografía*, 142–43.

59. Miles Richardson, *San Pedro, Colombia*, 16.

60. Peter Wade, *Blackness and Race Mixture*, 3.

61. Richardson, *San Pedro*, 15–16.

62. "Carta abierta al Dr JEG" by Pedro Santamaría L., Medellín, June 4, 1932; AICPG v.0016.

63. Braun, *The Assassination of Gaitán*, 82–83.

64. David Bushnell, *The Making of Modern Colombia*, 107.

65. Gary Long, "Popular Liberalism," 6, 7; Rausch, "Diego Luis Córdoba," 57.

66. E. Puerta Toro (abogado) to JEG, Medellín, Oct. 26, 1945; AICPG v.0016.

67. Gonzalo Buenahora, *Biografía de una voluntad*, 104.

68. *República* (Cartagena), Aug. 5, 1945, "Gabriel Turbay no es Gabriel Turbay."

69. Comité Gaitanista de Manga, Cartagena, to JEG, Jan. 9, 1946; AICPG v.0074.

70. *El Estado* (Santa Marta), Feb. 11, 1946, p. 3.

71. Pedro J. Donado B. to JEG, Magangué, Bolívar, April 12, 1946; AICPG v.0011.

72. Letter from over one thousand adherents to JEG, Cartagena, April 3, 1946; AICPG v.0074.

73. Long, "The Dragon Finally Came," 252.

74. *El Estado* (Santa Marta), April 30, 1946, p. 1, "¡Gaitanistas: alerta, mucho alerta!"

75. José Domingo Goenaga to JEG, Santa Marta, March 15, 1944; AICPG v.0011.

76. Sixty-eight members, Acción Mun. Gaitanista, to JEG, Aracataca, April 11, 1946; AICPG v.0011.

77. Guillermo Núñez B., "Porque soy Gaitanista," *El Estado* (Santa Marta), April 29, 1946, p. 4.

78. Leonidas Vera Duran to JEG, Baranoa, Atl., May 24, 1946; AICPG v.0032.

79. Comité Liberal de la Clase Media de Atlántico "Antonio José Restrepo" to López, Santos, and Chaux, B/quilla, April 3, 1946; AICPG v.0043.

80. Interview with Luis A. Moreno by Mauricio Archila.

81. Mauricio Torres, *La naturaleza de la revolución*, 58–59.

82. Braun, *Assassination of Gaitán*, 8–9.

83. Alan Knight, *Mexican Revolution*, 1:312 and 100.

84. The phrase used by Alan Knight in his discussion of the petty bourgeoisie, peasants, and their intermediate brethren, *Mexican Revolution*, 2:228.

85. Pécaut, *Orden y violencia*, 2:447 (Pécaut asserts the "class synthesis" idea throughout vol. 2); Archila, *Cultura e identidad obrera*, 425; Bergquist, *Labor in Latin America*, 356.

86. One need look no further than the *Communist Manifesto* for Marx's view.

87. It is also interesting to note the differences between Colombia and other contemporary cases in Latin America. In Peru, the pueblo/oligarquía dualism was less likely in the case of the obreros and the white-collar empleados. There the pueblo suffered more serious cultural and racial divisions (see Parker, *The Idea of the Middle Class*). And in Brazil, Brian Owensby argued that the middle classes of São Paulo and Rio de Janeiro largely rejected populist political alliances, given their feelings of moral superiority to workers *(Intimate Ironies)*.

88. Hobsbawm, "The Aristocracy of Labour Reconsidered," in *Workers: Worlds of Labor*, 227.

89. Hobsbawm, "Lenin and the 'Aristocracy of Labour,'" in *Revolutionaries: Contemporary Essays*, 122.

90. Palacios, *Entre la legitimidad y la violencia*, 87–88, 114.

91. He argued that in nineteenth-century Britain, the "more riotous" lower-tiered workers were often led by the better-organized and more politically conscious aristocracy of labor (Hobsbawm, "Debating the Labour Aristocracy," 222–23, in *Workers: Worlds of Labor*).

92. Hobsbawm, "Aristocracy Reconsidered," in *Workers: Worlds of Labor*, 244.

93. From Thompson's essay "Eighteenth-Century English Society: Class Struggle Without Class?," quoted in William Roseberry, "Hegemony and the Language of Contention," 356.

94. Laclau, "Towards a Theory of Populism," 164–72.

95. James, *Resistance and Integration*, 261. Ultimately, he argued, "there was a tendency from the beginning of the Peronist experience for el pueblo to become transformed into el pueblo trabajador." Liberals in Boyacá proclaimed that "the victory of Gaitán embodied the victory of the *pueblo trabajador*" and "laborioso"; the pueblo was still "the owner of its own destiny" (Dir. Liberal Departamental de Boyacá to José María Córdoba, Duitama, Jan. 29, 1946; AICPG v.0019).

96. Knight, "Populism and Neo-populism," 232–39.

97. Michael Kazin, *The Populist Persuasion*, 1–2, 10.

98. Sharpless, *Gaitán of Colombia*, 30; Braun, *Assassination of Gaitán*, 40–41.

99. Bushnell, *Colombia*, 81.

100. Gutiérrez Sanín, *Curso y discurso*, 125, 173, 176.

101. Braun, *Assassination of Gaitán*, 39.

102. "Gaitán, hombre del pueblo," by Gerado Candamil Gómez, Pasto, no date; AICPG v.0050.

103. Junta Democrática Buenaventura, to JEG, July 25, 1931, AICPG v.0013;

Antonio José Forero to JEG, Tulsa (?), July 9, 1931; AICPG; *Diario Nacional* (Bogotá), Aug. 21, 1936, p. 3 editorial, "La clase media y la clase obrera."

104. *La voz del obrero* (Barrancabermeja), Oct. 30, 1937, p. 5.

105. Eduardo Saavedra G. to JEG, Santa Marta, March 14, 1944; AICPG v.0011.

106. José Bolano Avendaño to JEG, Ciénaga, July 2, 1945; AICPG v.0011.

107. Julian Melendez of "La Voz del Litoral" to JEG, B/quilla, May 10, 1945; AICPG v.0091.

108. José Díaz V., "Comité Def. Empl. Bol.," to JEG, Cartagena, March 24, 1944; AICPG v.0053.

109. Comité de Empleados y Obreros Jubilados to JEG, Mariquita, Oct., 1946; AICPG v.0052.

110. Juan Manuel Valdelamar to JEG, Cartagena, Feb. 4, 1944; AICPG v.0074.

111. Asdrubal Amarís to José María Córdoba, Santa Marta, July 16, 1945; AICPG v.0011.

112. To *El Estado* (Santa Marta) from twenty-six residents of El Banco, April 23, 1946, p. 1.

113. Noted by *El Fígaro* (Cartagena), July 2, 1945, p. 3, to name only one example.

114. JEG to José M. Blanco Núñez, B/quilla, Nov. 8, 1945; AICPG v.0065.

115. *La Tribuna* (B/quilla), Jan. 28, 1944, p. 1.

116. Juan de Dios Torres D. to JEG, B/quilla, Sept. 29, 1945; AICPG v.0091.

117. Thirty-four names to López, Turbay, Echandía, JEG, and Calibán, Cali, no date, AICPG v.0013.

118. As in Peru and Brazil, members of the Colombian middle classes felt cultural distance from the "lower" portions of the pueblo. For a discussion of how empleados in Bogotá defined their class status, see Abel Ricardo López P., "We Have Everything and We Have Nothing."

119. Sánchez, "The Violence: An Interpretative Synthesis," in Bergquist, Peñaranda, and Sánchez, eds., *Violence in Colombia*, 78.

120. *El Sindicalista* (Cartagena), Oct. 24, 1936, pp. 3 and 6.

121. Hobsbawm, "Aristocracy Reconsidered," in *Workers: Worlds of Labor,* 227.

122. Federación de Empleados del Valle, Cali, to JEG, Sept. 13, 1934; AICPG.

123. Sindicato de Empleados Municipales de Bogotá to JEG, Sept. 17, 1935; AICPG v.0059.

124. Unión Nacional de Empleados, Medellín, to JEG, July 25, 1934; AICPG v.0021.

125. *El Deber* (Bucaramanga), March 9, 1944, p. 1, "JEG será el candidato de los empleados."

126. Sociedad de Locatarios de la Plaza, Manizales, to JEG, April 20, 1944; AICPG v.0092.

127. José Domingo Isaza to JEG, B/quilla, June 24, 1947; AICPG v.0012.

128. José Domingo Arciniegas told of his efforts in organizing for Gaitán in river ports where the workers were too poor to create official unions (letter to JEG, B/quilla, June 12, 1945; AICPG v.0091).

129. Comité Liberal de la Clase Media de Atlántico "Antonio José Restrepo" to López, Santos, and Chaux, B/quilla, April 3, 1946; AICPG v.0043.

130. E. Puerta Toro (abogado) to JEG, Medellín, Oct. 26, 1945; AICPG v.0016.

131. Archila, *Cultura e identidad obrera*, 387–91.

132. Camilo Antonio de Guzmán to JEG, B/quilla, March 31, 1946; AICPG v.0091.

133. Abel Solano Rico to JEG, Calamar, April 1, 1947; AICPG v.0061.

134. Comité Mun. Lib. Gaitanista, Anapoima, to Dir. Nac. Lib., March 29, 1944; AICPG v.0086.

135. Letter, name missing, to JEG, Villa de Leiva, Dec. 10, 1946; AICPG v.0019.

136. Alfonso Alexander M. to JEG, Ipiales, Feb. 7, 1944; AICPG v.0050.

137. Braun, *Assassination of Gaitán*, 115.

138. Braun stated that his interpretation of Gaitán and Gaitanismo came from Gaitán's "writings and speeches, from his actions, and from what I learned of him in interviews with some of his closest followers" (*Assassination of Gaitán*, 6).

139. Mary Roldán made a similar case about the social makeup of Gaitanismo and drew a similar conclusion about the lack of radicalism in the upper reaches of the movement. She asserted, "The fact is that most of Gaitán's loyal associates were provincial, petit bourgeois or middle-class lawyers and professionals who were interested in expanding the political arena, but not in fundamentally altering the structure of Colombian society" (Roldán, "Genesis and Evolution of *La Violencia*," 44, note 68). She did, however, make the distinction between the goals of "Gaitán's lower-class followers" and the political professionals (ibid., 44).

140. Dir. Mun. Lib. Gaitanista, Baranoa, Atlántico, to JEG, March 25, 1946; AICPG. See also Sindicato de Empleados y Obreros de las Rentas del Tolima, Arnoldo Suarez D. to JEG, Ibagué, June 30, 1947; AICPG v.0051.

141. Ignacio Ordóñez H., Fed. de Trab. de Nariño to JEG, Pasto, Nov. 3, 1939; AICPG v.0050.

142. Gilberto Henriquez Gil to JEG, B/quilla, April 16, 1945; AICPG.

143. Braulio Henao Blanco in *Diario de la Costa* (Cartagena), Sept. 23, 1945, p. 3.

144. Sociedad de Agricultores J. E. Gaitán, Turbaco, Bolívar, to JEG, April 23, 1944; AICPG v.0026. Rural workers and small holders, not mutually exclusive on the coast, wrote to Gaitán for assistance in their struggles for land titles. Representative letters are from "twenty-one agricultural workers" to JEG, B/quilla, Sept. 29, 1947, AICPG v.0043; and from Eleuterio, Manuel, and Felipe Romero to JEG, Sincelejo, June 2, 1947, AICPG v.0060.

145. Gary Long, "The Dragon Finally Came."

146. Sin. Empl. y Obreros Fáb. "El Papagayo," Bogotá, to JEG, Nov. 20, 1935; AICPG v.0059.

147. Sin. Empl. y Obreros de Germania, Bogotá, to JEG, May 4, 1939; AICPG v.0059; Sin. de Obreros Jardineros de Bogotá to JEG, Aug. 29, 1946; AICPG v.0010.

148. Sin. Obrero de la Empresa Col. Curtidos, to JEG, Bogotá, Aug. 21, 1944; AICPG v.0014.

149. Forty Liberals proclaim for JEG, Tumaco, Nov. 26, 1945; AICPG v.0050.

150. Asamblea del Tolima to JEG, Ibagué, April 25, 1946; AICPG v.0052.

151. "Humildes compatriotas" to JEG, Armero, May 19, 1947; AICPG v.0051.

152. C.T.C. Comité Ejecutivo, Bogotá, to JEG, June 6, 1939; AICPG v.0059.

153. Comité Central Contra la Desocupación, Bogotá, to JEG, Feb. 1939; AICPG v.0021.

154. Sindicato de Zorreros y Carretilleros de Girardot to JEG, March 18, 1944.

155. Fed. de Choferes de Colombia, Consejo Directivo Federal, to JEG, Bogotá, Dec. 1, 1942; AICPG v.0010; Sin. de Trans. Urbanos de Bogotá to JEG, May 1, 1946; AICPG v.0054.

156. Gustavo Almario Salazar, *Historia de los trabajadores petroleros,* 120.

157. "Visitas indiscretas . . ." by Emilio Franco Franco, Medellín, April 1933; AICPG.

158. Centro Liberal JEG, Cali, to JEG, April 25, 1932; AICPG v.0013.

159. "Varias esposas de obreros" to JEG, Bogotá, Feb. 23, 1939; AICPG v.0014.

160. See Soc. Mutuario de Fogoneros y Freneros del Ferrocarril del Pacífico-Cali to JEG, April 3, 1934; AICPG v.0013; Comité Lib. del Barrio Acevedo Tejado, Bogotá, to JEG, April 6, 1938; Sin. Industrial de Revisadores Tranviarios, Medellín, to JEG, July 18 1934; Fed. Nac. de Comunicaciones (Eléctricas y Postales) Secc. Antioquia/Chocó, Medellín, to JEG, May 15, 1939; Secc. Valle, Cali, to JEG, March 14, 1938; Secc. Cauca, Popayán, to JEG, Sept. 15, 1939; Fed. de Trabajo de Nariño, Pasto, to JEG, July 3, 1938; Sindicatos: Motoristas Automotores de Nariño; Carpinteros "Pasto"; Albañiles de la Construcción y Anexos; Zapateros Nacionales; Industrias Textiles de Ipiales, all in AICPG v.0021.

161. Junta Pro-Intereses del Sec. del Guavio, Bogotá, to JEG, Sept. 8, 1941; Comité Pro-Defensa y Mejoras del Barrio de "La Providencia" de Bogotá to JEG, July 22, 1943; Asamblea General de los Barrios del Sur de Bogotá to JEG, Aug. 10, 1943; Junta de Mejoras Públicas del Barrio de Lourdes, Bogotá, to JEG, Sept. 8, 1941; see also the Centro Nacional de Acción Liberal de Bogotá to JEG, Sept. 13, 1941, all found in AICPG v.0014.

162. He received letters from many unions, for example, when he was made minister of education: Sin. de Empl. y Obreros del Ferrocarril de la Dorada y Cable Aéreo Mariquito, Manizales, April 26, 1940; Sin. Obrero Pereira, April 19, 1940; Sin. Obrero Armenia, no date, but probably early 1940; Sin. de la Construcción, Bucaramanga, Feb. 12, 1940; Sin. de Voc. de la Prensa, Bogotá, Feb. 2, 1940; Sin. Obrero Mun. de Bogotá, Secc. Obras Públicas, Feb. 5, 1940; all in AICPG v.0020; Fed. Local de Trabajo, Girardot, to JEG, April 13, 1940; AICPG v.0059.

163. Union Ferrocables de Caldas to JEG, Manizales, Feb. 11, 1943; Sin. de Oficios Domésticos de Pereira to JEG, Feb. 11, 1943; AICPG v.0092; Manuel

Mosquera, Sin. de voceadores de prensa y revista de B/quilla to JEG, B/quilla, Feb. 11, 1943; AICPG v.0091.

164. Centro Jorge Eliécer Gaitán Bogotá to JEG, Feb. 5, 1943; AICPG v.0014; La Sociedad de Auxilio Mútuo del Personal Obrero de la Estación Agrícola Experimental de Palmira-Valle, to JEG, Feb. 8, 1943; Centro Obrero de Cartago to JEG, Feb. 11, 1943; AICPG v.0013.

165. Samuel Guerrero to JEG, Cartagena, March 15, 1944; AICPG v.0053.

166. Adriano Rangel to JEG, B/quilla, Feb. 20, 1945; AICPG v.0091.

167. José María Córdoba to Pedro Romoña y demás firmantes, Quibdó, Chochó, Dec. 17, 1945; AICPG v.0070.

168. Letter from José María Córdoba to Abelardo Salgrad y demás firmantes, Mariquita, Dec. 5, 1945; v.0070.

169. Interview by Mauricio Archila with Cesar Ahumada.

170. Almario S. gives a detailed account in *Historia de los trabajadores petroleros*, 120–27.

171. See Apolinar Díaz C., *Diez días de poder popular*.

172. D. Aguirre González, dentista, to JEG, Medellín, April 12, 1946; AICPG v.0016

173. See Ann Farnsworth-Alvear, *Dulcinea in the Factory*; and Mary Roldán, "Genesis and Evolution of *La Violencia*," 211.

174. It is also clear that voter fraud on the part of the Liberal establishment obscured much of Gaitán's support (see chapter 6).

175. See Félix Millan L. to JEG, Guayabal, Sept. 18, 1945; AICPG v.0052.

176. Interview with José N. Torres by Mauricio Archila, Bogotá; "Los suscritos obreros, vecinos de Duitama, de profesión Sastres y Barberos" to JEG, Jan. 20, 1946; AICPG v.0019.

177. Agustín Novoa Pinzón to JEG, Ciénaga, April 1, 1946; AICPG v.0011.

178. Interview by Mauricio Archila with Roque Jiménez.

179. Victor Cuesta Fonseca to JEG, B/quilla, May 14, 1945; AICPG v.0091.

180. José María Blanco Núñez, *Memorias*, 76.

181. *Vanguardia* (Santa Marta), May 5, 1943, p. 4, identified 742 unions with 95,443 members.

182. *Vanguardia* (Santa Marta), Sept. 20, 1944, p. 1.

183. *Vanguardia* (Santa Marta), Jan. 8, 1945, "Plataforma . . ."

184. Sin. Lancheros Portuarios y Navegantes to JEG, B/quilla, March 15, 1944; AICPG v.0091.

185. *El Estado* (Santa Marta), Dec. 6, 1945.

186. Gustavo Pernett Miranda to JEG, B/quilla, June 11, 1945; AICPG v.0091.

187. Federación de Empleados de Bolívar to JEG, Cartagena, Sept. 7, 1944.

188. Gaitán received pledges of support from (among others): Comité de Barberos Gaitanistas, Bogotá, to Dir. Nac. Gaitanista, Jan. 16, 1946; Sin. Obrero de la fábrica de fósforos "El Ruiz," Bogotá, May 1, 1946; "Las suscritas empleadas de la Tipografía Prag," Bogotá, May 10, 1946; AICPG v.0054; Sastres

and Barberos of Duitama, Jan. 20, 1946; AICPG v.0019; Trabajadores de Antioquia Pro-Defensa Social y Económica, Sept. 15, 1945; AICPG v.0016; Sin. Ferrocarrileros de Nariño, March 31, 1944; AICPG v.0050; Sin. Obreros Sastres, Ibagué, Feb. 2, 1946; AICPG v.0052; Gremio de Choferes de B/quilla, June 12, 1945; Asociación de Fundidores Independentes del Atl., Sept. 22, 1945; Soc. de Barberos de B/quilla, March 31, 1946; Junta de Trabajadores de Panadería de B/quilla, April 23, 1946; Acción Dept. Obrera Sindical Independente, B/quilla, Sept. 27, 1945; Frente Obrera Gaitanista, B/quilla, Nov. 25, 1945; Obreros de la Fábrica de Tejidos "Filtta," B/quilla, May 30, 1945; all in AICPG v.0091; eight hundred workers in Curazao, Sept. 11, 1945; AICPG v.0074; Sociedad de Agricultores J. E. G. de Turbaco, Bol., April 23, 1944; AICPG v.0026; Enrique Cámpo, Compañía Colombiana de Electricidad, Santa Marta, Sept. 30, 1945; Trabajadores de la Compañía Shell, Fundación, Magd., Feb. 16, 1946; AICPG v.0011; Sin. Fluvial de Subsistancia, B/quilla, March 26, 1946; Comité Cen. Gaitanista de Montecristo, B/quilla, March 28, 1946; AICPG v.0043; Comité de Acción Política de Miembros del Sin. Fluvial de Subsistancia "Pro-Candidatura del Dr. JEG," Cartagena, March 10, 1944; AICPG v.0053; "Los empleados y obreros" of the Bavaria brewery in Santa Marta, *El Estado,* April 15, 1946.

189. Ailiados gremio de braceros, forty-five signatures, Gamarra, to JEG, Jan. 7, 1935; AICPG v.0059.

190. Carlos J. Moreno to JEG, B/quilla, March 11, 1944; AICPG v.0091.

191. Gilberto Henriquez Gil to JEG, B/quilla, Oct. 13, 1944; AICPG v.0091.

192. *Diario del Pacífico* (Cali), March 5, 1946, pp. 1 and 3.

193. Fidel Murillo to JEG, Honda, Aug. 3, 1945; AICPG v.0052.

Chapter 6. The Moral and Democratic Challenge: Oligarchic Political Practice and Gaitanismo, 1944–1946

1. The consensus position seems to be that in the 1930s and 1940s, the popular political challenge to Colombia's oligarchic democracy was "weak." See Abel and Palacios, "Colombia," 592.

2. There is some contention among historians over exactly what Gaitán expected to accomplish. Based on his interviews with Gaitán's widow, Sharpless argued that Gaitán never expected to win the election (*Gaitán of Colombia,* 103). Braun argued that he "campaigned as though there was never a doubt in his mind that he could win the election" (*Assassination of Gaitán,* 78). Certainly before the official Liberals rejected his bid for the nomination, he seemed like a strong candidate.

3. Pedro García B. to JEG, Rovira, Feb. 16, 1939; AICPG v.0052.

4. A. J. Ceron M., Fed. Nac. de Empl. de Com. to JEG, Ipiales, Aug. 10, 1939; AICPG v.0050.

5. Milton Puentes to JEG, Bogotá, Feb. 15, 1941; AICPG v.0014.

6. Luís Angel Jiménez J. and Urias Ardila B. to JEG, Puerto Carreño, Nov. 20, 1942; AICPG v.0057.

7. "Proclamación . . ." Jorge Nieto R., Bucaramanga, Dec. 1943, AICPG v.0089.

8. Abel Valencia L. (radio show "Bandera Lib.") to JEG, Calarcá, March 22, 1944; AICPG v.0092.

9. *La Opinión* (Ibagué) March 25, 1944, p. 3, editorial "A la carga!!" by "Ali Califa."

10. La Liga Nacional de Inquilinos, Bogotá, to JEG, May 9, 1944; AICPG v.0021.

11. Jorge Villaveces R. to JEG, Ibagué, March 21, 1944; AICPG v.0052.

12. José Loaiza to JEG, Marquetalia, March 13, 1944; AICPG v.0092.

13. *El Combate* (Cúcuta), April 18, 1944, p. 2, "Se instala el comité pro-candidatura JEG."

14. *El Combate* (Cúcuta), March 24, 1944, p. 2, "Examen de Candidatos" by Lozano y Lozano.

15. Alfonso Alexander M. to JEG, Ipiales, April 2, 1946; AICPG v.0050

16. *Unión Obrera* (Manizales), March 25, 1944, p. 1, "La susesión presidencial."

17. Quote from Richard Sharpless's paraphrase of Gaitán's speech (*Gaitán of Colombia*, 105).

18. Ibid., 105.

19. *El Estado* (Santa Marta), March 24, 1944.

20. *El Estado* (Santa Marta), Jan. 16, 1945, "Hacia la unión liberal."

21. *Vanguardia* (Santa Marta), March 5, 1945, p. 3, "Las candidaturas presidenciales."

22. Dionisio Rincones P. to JEG, Santa Marta, April 8, 1944; AICPG v.0011.

23. Julio Dangond Ovalle to José María Córdoba, Ciénaga, Sept. 8, 1945; AICPG v.0011.

24. Dionisio Rincones P. to José María Córdoba, Santa Marta, Dec. 14, 1945; AICPG v.0011.

25. Braun argued that Lleras and Echandía succumbed to Gaitanista harassment at their rallies (*Assassination of Gaitán*, 85–86). In B/quilla supporters of Echandía claimed up to 30,000 people attended one of his events in early 1945. Gaitanistas dismissed this estimate as grossly inflated, putting the number closer to 3,500 (Rodolfo Ponce to JEG, April 20, 1945). When Turbay visited B/quilla soon after, Carlos Moreno claimed that his rally drew as many curious Gaitanistas who went to heckle him as it did supporters (Moreno to JEG, B/quilla, May 16, 1945; AICPG v.0091).

26. José P. Esmeral, "Un paso en falso . . ." to Santos, B/quilla, May 8, 1944; AICPG v.0021.

27. Agustín Rodriquez Garavito, *Gabriel Turbay,* 61–63.

28. His quip was echoed by *El Fígaro* (Cartagena), Jan. 17, 1945, p. 4, "Turbay, candidato olig."

29. Sharpless, *Gaitán of Colombia,* 123–24.

30. *El Tiempo* (Bogotá), April 11, 1946, p. 4, editorial "Liberalismo, Conservatismo, Gaitanismo." See "Danza de las horas" throughout April 1946.

31. *La Razón* (Bogotá), Jan. 9, 1946, p. 4, editorial "La prueba final."

32. *El Nacional* (B/quilla), June 25, 1945, "La revolución Gaitán"; June 26, 1945, "El apóstol desnudo."

33. *El Nacional* (B/quilla), Sept. 24, 1945, p. 1, "Gaitán es Fascista."

34. *El Liberal* (Bogotá), Jan. 28, 1946, p. 4, editorial "Alternativas."

35. *El Espectador* (Bogotá), April 8, 1946, p. 1; April 9, 1946, p. 4, editorial "Culminación de la crisis."

36. As Sharpless discovered in his interview with Dr. Alberto Miramón, former director of the national library, Bogotá (*Gaitán of Colombia*, 124).

37. Juan Manuel Valdelamar to JEG, Cartagena, April 17, 1945; AICPG v.0053.

38. For Communists' disadvantages, see Pécaut, *Orden y violencia*, 2:400–401.

39. For a good example, see Manrique, *Bajo el signo de la hoz*, 66–68.

40. Ibid., 16–17. Manrique called himself a friend of many Communists, a Liberal "of the blood," and a "child of the *Revolución en Marcha*," 141–43.

41. *La Tribuna* (B/quilla), March 7, 1938, p. 1, "La propaganda comunista."

42. *El Mitín* (Cartagena), Jan. 28, 1936.

43. *El Estado* (Santa Marta), April 26, 1946, p. 3.

44. While the PCC has long since publicly declared mea culpa concerning its opposition to Gaitanismo, some Communists remained unrepentant. Torres Giraldo always maintained that Gaitán was a "candidate of Conservative manipulation" (*Los inconformes*, vol. 5, 1396, 1401). In the same vein, a director of FEDETRAL denied that there was any rebellion of the rank and file. Those who voted for Gaitán were not organized workers but the pueblo "in its common denominator." Gaitán was simply a "fascist" (interview by Mauricio Archila with Roberto Insignares).

45. FBI report "Summary of Communist Activities . . ." Feb. 5, 1947, SD 821.00B/3–1047.

46. *Diario Popular,* July 31, 1945, p. 3.

47. *Diario Popular,* Aug. 28, 1945, p. 2, "El Apóstol Desnudo."

48. *Diario Popular,* Sept. 5, 1945, p. 2, "Gaitán, mampara de la reacción."

49. *Diario Popular,* Jan. 23, 1946, p. 3, "Contra los obreros . . . se unen godos y gaitanistas."

50. *Diario Popular,* Sept. 28, 1945; *El Nacional* (B/quilla), Sept. 28, 1945.

51. Information for this description was taken from Sharpless, *Gaitán of Colombia,* 112–13.

52. The text of the "Discurso-Programa" is preserved in *Los mejores discursos,* 391–406.

53. For an extended discussion of these questions, see Green, "Sibling Rivalry on the Left."

54. The Gaitanistas even attempted to set up a rival labor confederation, the Confederación Nacional de Trabajadores, though it rapidly imploded. But with

the failure of the broken FEDENAL strike, the Communist victory in the CTC proved hollow.

55. This discrepancy has endured in the historiography. Pécaut generally recognized Gaitanismo and the union movement as separate entities. Medófilo Medina contended that Gaitán disregarded "the necessity of union organization" in preference for mass "spontaneity" that he could control with his "charisma" (*Historia del Partido Comunista,* 509). Yet as Juan Manuel Valdelamar put it, the Communists' "nightmare" turned reality was the existence of a huge, militant, and independently Gaitanista sector of the working class (Cartagena, Aug. 14, 1944; AICPG v.0053).

56. As Ramón de la Hoz remembered in his interview with Mauricio Archila.

57. Córdoba, *Tribuno popular,* 43.

58. Juan Manuel Valdelamar to JEG, March 29, 1944; AICPG v.0074.

59. Sindicato de Obreros Sastres de Ibagué to JEG, Feb. 2, 1946; AICPG v.0052.

60. F. Ortiz B., Sin. Ferrocarrileros de Nariño, Tumaco, to JEG, March 31, 1944; AICPG v.0050.

61. Dionisio Rincones Ponce to JEG, Santa Marta, Nov. 19, 1945; AICPG v.0011.

62. Horiberto Rodelo V., Magdalena, to José María Córdoba, July 25, 1946; AICPG v.0051.

63. Interview with Eugenio Colorado by Mauricio Archila.

64. *El Deber* (Bucaramanga), March 16, 1944, p. 3, editorial "El festín es interrumpido."

65. *Diario del Pacífico* (Cali), Feb. 21, 1946, p. 4, editorial "La realidad político."

66. Abel, *Política,* 143. Abel argued that Gaitán himself "presented a favorable contrast between the combative qualities of Gómez and the weakness of López and the *oligarquía*" (see Pécaut, *Orden y violencia,* 2:463; Henderson, *Conservative Thought,* 24–27).

67. Henderson has argued that Gómez was not an admirer of Hitler or Mussolini and pointed to various instances in which Gómez denounced the Nazi leader (*Conservative Thought,* 110). It is true that Gómez, like Gaitán, suffered from guilt by association since he had served as Colombian ambassador to Germany in 1930–32. This no more made him a Nazi than Gaitán's time in Italy made him a fascist. But while Gómez was certainly closer to the tradition of corporativist conservatism than to fascism, he was undeniably reactionary against the entire left-Liberal, Enlightenment-inspired heritage. He was also a political extremist, and one need look no further than the pages of *El Siglo* to see the deep hatreds expressed in his rhetoric.

68. Peña, *Gaitán íntimo,* 160–62.

69. Sharpless, *Gaitán of Colombia,* 127. *El Radio* (Pasto) a very Turbayista paper, even jumped the gun on April 6, 1946, with a huge headline declaring Liberal union.

70. Sharpless, *Gaitán of Colombia*, 127.

71. *El Demócrata* (Bucaramanga), April 12, 1946, p. 3, editorial "Tres candidatos y un presidente."

72. *El Demócrata* (Bucaramanga), April 21, 1946, p. 3, editorial "Los traidores."

73. *Relator* (Cali), March 9, 1946, p. 1, "Grato huésped de Cali."

74. Colombia, "Tendencias electorales, 1935–1968," 111–13.

75. Election returns are not the only indicator of the depth of Gaitán's support. There is also no doubt that electoral fraud severely affected Gaitán's showing in Antioquia. See below.

76. Anita Weiss, *Tendencias de la participación electoral*, 90.

77. Ortíz Márquez, *El hombre que fue un pueblo*, 131.

78. For a more detailed discussion of these structures, see Roldán, "Genesis and Evolution of *La Violencia*," 354–61. Since "the number of votes needed to elect an individual was calculated on a proportional basis determined by the total number of votes cast," the system encouraged minority party representation and ensured that local elections could be "hotly contested" (359–60).

79. Fals Borda, *El presidente Nieto*, 150B, 157B–158B, 147B.

80. And such leaders were quite successful in passing on their power to successors of their choosing (ibid., 159B). Gamonal power has been on the wane since the 1930s but is still significant in districts of less than 5,000 voters (Christie, *Oligarcas*, 159).

81. Dent, "Oligarchy and Power Structure," 113.

82. Christie, *Oligarcas*, 132–33.

83. Bergquist, *Labor in Latin America*, 292.

84. Ortiz Sarmiento, *Estado y subversión*, 51–52.

85. Kaufman, "The Patron-Client Concept," 285.

86. Deas, "Algunas notas, 122.

87. Roldán, "Genesis and Evolution of *La Violencia*," 362–68 and 367–79.

88. Deas, "Algunas notas," 125.

89. Ortiz Sarmiento, *Estado y subversión*, 52–53.

90. Christie, *Oligarcas*, 159.

91. Ibid., 158.

92. Luís F. Gómez M. to JEG, B/quilla, June 22, 1945; AICPG v.0091.

93. Ortiz Sarmiento, *Estado y subversión*, 54–55.

94. Dent, "Oligarchy," 132.

95. Deas, "Algunas notas," 119, 127.

96. Posada-Carbó, "Limits of Power," 265, 258.

97. Deas, "Algunas notas," 118–19.

98. Posada-Carbó, introduction to *Elections Before Democracy*, 2.

99. Christie, *Oligarcas*, 157–58. The Conservative constitution had long been hated and resisted. A left-Liberal assured Gaitán in 1932 that the pueblo was

aware of the "great lies that exist in this catalogue of ignominy, index of malediction that is the Constitution of 1886" ("Carta abierta al doctor JEG" by Pedro N. Santamaría López, Medellín, June 4, 1932; AICPG v.0016).

100. Posada-Carbó, "Limits of Power," 260, 258.

101. Deas, "The Role of the Church," 169.

102. Graham, *Patronage and Politics*, 86.

103. Deas, "The Role of the Church," 168.

104. "El caciquismo, gangrena de la patria," *El Cenit* (Sincelejo), April 7, 1945, pp. 1 and 3.

105. J. P. Rojas Gusmán to JEG, Neiva, Oct. 26, 1932; AICPG v.0044.

106. H.S. (signature unintelligible) to JEG, Ciénaga, Sept. 13, 1932; AICPG v.0017.

107. Posada-Carbó, "Limits of Power," 266–67.

108. Ortiz Sarmiento, *Estado y subversión*, 56. For Ortiz, fraud and controlling "electoral clients," both aimed at augmenting "the quantity of votes," were the "strong point of the *gamonal*."

109. Posada-Carbó, "Limits of Power," 262–63, 266–67.

110. Deas, "The Role of the Church," 169.

111. Mary Roldán noted Gaitán's strength in other urban areas but was undisturbed by his "failure to capture the urban vote of Antioquia" and accepted, as have most other historians, the official tally which gave him the votes of "less than 5 percent of Antioquia's eligible electorate" ("Genesis and Evolution of *La Violencia*," 257).

112. Froilán Montoya Mazo to JEG, Medellín, Jan. 10, 1946; AICPG v.0016.

113. Froilán Montoya Mazo to JEG, Medellín, Feb. 14, 1946; AICPG v.0016.

114. R. Castro G. to JEG, B/quilla, April 5, 1937; AICPG v.0091.

115. Hoberto Velandía to JEG, San Bernardo, March 19, 1944; AICPG v.0052.

116. Eustorgio A. Sarria M. (abogado) to JEG, Popayán, March 13, 1931; AICPG v.0090.

117. Edmundo Delgado to JEG, Tumaco, March 18, 1944; AICPG v.0050.

118. Samuel Guerrero to JEG, Cartagena, Oct. 6, 1947; AICPG v.0053.

119. Luís Gómez R. and Gabriel Castro M. to JEG, Corozal, April 3 and 25, 1946; AICPG v.0011.

120. *El Estado* (Santa Marta), April 25, 1946, p. 4.

121. *El Estado* (Santa Marta), April 29, 1946, p. 3, "El arma con que se piensa vencer a Gaitán."

122. Samuel Guerrero to JEG, B/quilla, April 30, 1946; AICPG v.0043.

123. Dir. Lib. Gaitanista, Coromoro to Lleras C., April 28, 1946; AP, v. without no., April, 1946.

124. Unión Juvenil Colombiana de Cartagena to JEG, Cartagena, Nov. 10, 1945; AICPG v.0074.

125. Manuel Hernándes R., Sociedad JEG de B/quilla, March 11, 1944; AICPG v.0091.

126. Miguel P. García to José María Córdoba, Riohacha, Oct. 2, 1945; AICPG v.0011.

127. Frente Obrero Gaitanista to Dir. Nac. Gaitanista, B/quilla, Jan. 15, 1946; AICPG v.0012.

128. Eloy Olaya Villareal to JEG, B/quilla, Oct. 5, 1945; AICPG v.0091.

129. Comité Liberal JEG #10 to JEG, B/quilla, May 30, 1945; AICPG v.0091.

130. *El Demócrata* (Bucaramanga), Jan. 4, 1946, p. 1, "Antes con Turbay . . ."

131. Justo Ortiz, Comité Gaitanista Barrio Manga, to José María Córdoba, Cartagena, mid-1947; AICPG v.0060.

132. "Asamblea Par. de Juventudes Lib." to JEG, B/quilla, March 8, 1946; AICPG v.0043.

133. Nicandor de Avila to JEG, B/quilla, June 5, 1947; AICPG v.0012.

134. Luís Emilio Plata to José María Córdoba, Riohacha, Sept. 25, 1945; AICPG v.0011.

135. Bernardo Betancourt to JEG, Medellín, Sept. 15, 1945; AICPG v.0016.

136. Comité Gaitanista Universitaria to José María Córdoba, Cartagena, Sept. 7, 1945; AICPG v.0074.

137. *El Estado* (Santa Marta), Aug. 3, 1945, reprint of "Pánico de las camarillas" from *Jornada*.

138. *El Estado* (Santa Marta), Sept. 27, 1945, "Los jefes liberales y el gaitanismo."

139. Joaquín Madariaga Vidal to JEG, B/quilla, March 20, 1946; AICPG v.0043.

140. Comité Lib. Gaitanista El Carmen to Dir. Nac. Gaitanista, May 15, 1946; AICPG v.0051.

141. Mario E. Baños C. to JEG, Ibagué, Aug. 6, 1945; AICPG v.0052.

142. Bernardo Angel to JEG, Medellín, Jan. 15, 1945; AICPG v.0016.

143. *El Fígaro* (Cartagena), Jan. 4, 1946, p. 3, "Dos políticas."

144. *La Tribuna* (B/quilla), April 26 and Nov. 8, 1944.

145. *El Fígaro* (Cartagena), Feb. 12, 1946, p. 3.

146. Sharpless, *Gaitán of Colombia*, 122.

147. Centro Jorge Eliécer Gaitán, *Gaitán y la constituyente*, 3.

148. The caudillo often "came to embody" political symbolism. Fals Borda, *El Presidente Nieto*, 157B (see chapter 7).

149. Nestor Madrid-Malo (abogado) to JEG, B/quilla, Nov. 8, 1944; AICPG v.0091.

150. Antonio López to JEG, Majagual, Bolívar, Nov. 22, 1946; AICPG v.0034.

151. Juan Manuel Valdelamar to JEG, Cartagena, Sept. 14, 1944; AICPG v.0074.

152. *El Estado* (Santa Marta), March 21, 1944.

153. Lázaro F. Soto to JEG, Bucaramanga, April 11, 1946; AICPG v.0089.

154. Evelio González B., Leonidas Escobar to JEG, Líbano, April 10, 1946; AICPG v.0052.

155. *El Nacional* (B/quilla), June 21, 1945, p. 3.

156. Con. Dawson to Amb. Wiley, Oct. 10, 1945; SD, Consular Post file,

Record Group 84. But in towns outside Barranquilla, Malambo, Santo Tomás, and Polonuevo, the Gaitanistas got the highest number of votes and "polled a considerable number" in three other towns.

157. Con. Dawson to Amb. Wiley, Oct. 1, 1945; SD, Consular Post File, Record Group 84. He made these comments concerning the small turnout for a pro-Gaitán torchlight procession in B/quilla, qualifying his opinion that "the failure to the Gaitanistas to turn out in large numbers on this occasion is not to be taken as a lack of interest."

158. JEG to Jorge Ospina Londoño, May 22, 1945; AICPG v.0068.

159. Braun, *Assassination of Gaitán*, 72.

160. José María Córdoba, instructions to various people, 1945; AICPG v.0069.

161. José María Córdoba to Marco A. Hormiga and others in Popayán, March 8, 1946; AICPG v.0071.

162. Adictos . . . GRANDIOSO MOVIMIENTO to José María Córdoba, Mariquita, Nov. 25, 1945; AICPG v.0052.

163. Carlos E. Fajardo Palacio to JEG, B/quilla, March 7, 1944; AICPG v.0091.

164. Luís A. Ortega to JEG, Montería, Sept. 5, 1947; AICPG v.0053.

165. Carlos J. Moreno to JEG, B/quilla, April 4, 1945; AICPG v.0091.

166. Juan Manuel Valdelamar to JEG, Cartagena, March 29, 1944; AICPG v.0074.

167. Jorge Parra, Dir. Lib. Dep. G., Tolima, to Dir. Lib. Nac. G., Oct. 26, 1945; AICPG v.0052.

168. JEG to Jorge Ospina Londoño in Medellín, May 22, 1945; AICPG v.0068.

169. José María Córdoba to Augusto Esparza Gómez in Pasto, June 11, 1945; AICPG v.0069.

170. Sánchez, "The Violence: An Interpretative Synthesis," 80–81.

171. José María Córdoba to Darío G. Perdomo D., Melgar, Nov. 14, 1945; AICPG v.0070.

172. Sánchez noted that reliance on popular committees "had advantages, but also important limitations. It permitted broad diversification as the movement expanded and incorporated the masses . . . but it was an obstacle to ideological unity and disciplinary cohesion in moments of crisis" ("The Violence: An Interpretative Synthesis," 80).

173. Theme of 1945, repeated many times in different variations, AICPG v.0069.

174. José María Córdoba to Eduardo Octavio O., Santa Marta, April 18, 1945; AICPG v.0069.

175. José María Córdoba to Luís Heli Tovar, Florencia, Magdalena, March 20, 1946; AICPG v.0081.

176. Posada-Carbó, "Limits of Power," 275–76.

177. Dir. Liberal Gaitanista de Nariño to JEG, Pasto, Nov. 15, 1945; AICPG v.0050.

178. Jorge E. Parra to José María Córdoba, Ibagué, Sept. 12, 1945; AICPG v.0052.

179. Eduardo Tribiño Sáenz to JEG, Valle de Risaralda, April 24, 1946; AICPG v.0092.

180. Manuel Cárdenas to JEG, Bogotá, March 14, 1934; AICPG v.0014.

181. *El Mitín* (Cartagena), 1935.

182. Junta Liberal de Tierralta, Montería, to JEG, Aug. 14, 1946; AICPG v.0088. They spoke of the corregimientos of Tierralta, Tucurá, Tres Piedras, Río Negro, and Tres Palmas.

183. Camilo Falla to JEG, Neiva, Jan. 9, 1946; AICPG v.0044.

184. Dir. de Cedulación, Bogotá, to JEG, Oct. 25, 1947; AICPG v.0022.

185. Leonardo Villamizar R. to JEG, Arboldas Norte de S/der, Sept. 19, 1946; AICPG v.0051.

186. *El Estado* (Santa Marta), July 11, 1947, p. 3, "La cedulación, sillar de la reconquista."

187. The letter writer had his miracles mixed up. He combined the miracle where Jesus turned water into wine with the miracle of the loaves and fishes.

188. Dir. Liberal Municipal Chinchiná to JEG, May 6, 1946; AICPG v.0092.

189. Alfonso Alexander Montcayo to JEG, May 2, 1946; AICPG v.0044.

190. *El Fígaro* (Cartagena), March 15, 1944, p. 3, "Frente Antioligárquica."

191. Carlos Támara L. and Henrique Verbel P. to JEG, Sincelejo, Feb. 15, 1946; AICPG v.0050.

192. Augusto Esparza G. to JEG, Pasto, Feb. 17, 1946; AICPG v.0050.

193. Julio Ortega Amarís to JEG, Santa Marta, Aug. 9, 1945; AICPG v.0011.

194. Samuel Guerrero to JEG, Cartagena, March 23, 1946; AICPG v.0088.

195. *El Fígaro* (Cartagena), March 30, 1944, p. 3.

196. *El Mitín* (Cartagena), May 3, 1935, p. 1, "El varguismo como partido social."

197. *El Debate* (Cartagena), July 20, 1935, pp. 1–3.

198. *El Mitín* (Cartagena), April 6, 1937, p. 1.

199. Pécaut, *Orden y violencia*, 2:392; and Braun, *Assassination of Gaitán*, 115.

200. Blanco Núñez, *Memorias*, 69.

201. Camilo Falla to JEG, Neiva, Jan. 9, 1946; AICPG v.0044.

202. Gaitán himself had not supported the FEDENAL strike, largely because of his Communist rivals' influence. He did, nevertheless, artfully hold the Liberal reaction at arms length. After the election, river workers reaffirmed their status as Gaitanistas (Dago Barbaza, Sin. de Trabajadores de la Regularización . . . del Río Magdalena to JEG, B/quilla, June 5, 1946; AICPG v.0012).

203. Pedro A. Gómez Cera (diputado) to JEG, B/quilla, Feb. 25, 1945; AICPG v.0091.

204. Tomás Villanueva O. to the Lib. G. Dir., Mun. and Dep., B/quilla, April 23, 1946; AICPG v.0012. He noticed six men from Piojó, the two from Usiacurí he

himself had brought, one from Alarcón, several from Polonuevo, two from Suan, two from Tubará, two from Santo Tomás, two from Palmar, two from Repelón, two from Manatí, and two from Luruace. Most included the mayor.

205. Ibid. While standing outside the door, Villanueva's co-worker Ligie Tatis drove by. A letter he sent testifies to Villanueva's presence there.

206. Blanco Núñez, *Memorias*, 76.

207. Medófilo Medina has produced a fascinating and in-depth study of Charris de la Hoz as an example of the regional political elite, *Juegos de rebeldía*.

208. Ibid., 57–58, 69, and 80.

209. Ibid., 90–93 and 95–96; and interview by the author with Saúl Charris de la Hoz.

210. Though a minority, Gaitanista concejales attacked oligarchic corruption and advocated spending on a school, a park, and a "popular neighborhood" (Medina, *Juegos de rebeldía*, 98–99).

211. Ibid., 96.

212. Concejo Municipal de B/quilla to JEG, March 30, 1946; AICPG v.0043.

213. Medina, *Juegos de rebeldía*, 101.

214. Camilo Falla to JEG, Neiva, Jan. 9, 1946; AICPG v.0044.

215. La Asamblea Popular Gaitanista de Girardot, March 26, 1946; AICPG v.0086.

216. The worst case of leadership struggles, one that paralyzed the movement, was in Antioquia. Bernardo Betancourt described the political situation in Medellín in Sept. 1945 of a "directorate without a head or hands," and from which squabbling leaders were "even trying to cut the legs." Gaitanismo there lacked three things: "unity of action, organized masses, and money" (letter to JEG, Medellín, Sept. 15, 1945). He was allied with Bernardo Angel against Jorge Ospina Londoño. To make matters worse, Froilán Montoya Mazo believed that the absence of one Dr. Restrepo Botero in Bogotá was hampering the movement because he was the principal intermediary between the Gaitanista factions in Antioquia. Montoya Mazo pointed to "considerable Gaitanista fervor" in Medellín and the towns of Antioquia, but in addition to organizational problems, they had little money to organize this support (letter to JEG, Medellín, Jan. 24, 1946). Ultimately, Montoya Mazo laid the blame for Gaitanismo's weakness in Antioquia on betrayals and a very late start that arose from internal Gaitanista bickering. He told of one Hernando Rojas Ospina, elected concejal in Rionegro by the Liga Obrero-Campesina. This group's leadership had proclaimed itself as Gaitanista, and many of them formed that city's Comité Gaitanista. Rojas Ospina had cut a deal with the Turbayistas on filling official positions. The Liga felt that he had betrayed the movement and wanted help. Montoya Mazo complained that leaders like Ospina Londoño and Rojas Ospina had wasted the last two years "without developing any initiatives worthy of the movement." If they had, the department would be "inundated with Gaitanista *mística*." Only in the first few months of 1946 had they led the movement "down different paths, which is to say, com-

ported in the way a political campaign should be run." They had finally opened a Casa Gaitanista, distributed literature, sent commissions to different municipios in the department, all of which was beginning to have an effect. Yet they were still hampered by "loafers" who did their politics "from behind a desk" and whose only objective was to posture (Froilán Montoya Mazo to JEG, Medellín, Feb. 22, 1946; all in AICPG v.0016).

217. Hipolito Hernández M. to JEG, B/quilla, April 15, 1945; AICPG v.0091.

218. José María Córdoba to Carlos J. Moreno, B/quilla, March 23, 1945; AICPG v.0069.

219. Gerardo Certain E. to JEG, B/quilla, April 21, 1945; AICPG v.0091.

220. Santander León y B. to JEG, B/quilla, April 21, 1945; AICPG v.0091.

221. Calixto Villa to JEG, B/quilla, Jan. 24, 1946; AICPG v.0012.

222. H. Pérez to JEG, B/quilla, Oct. 12, 1946; AICPG v.0012.

223. Francisco Castro Vargas to JEG, B/quilla, Oct. 28, 1946; AICPG v.0012.

224. Elías Moisés to JEG, B/quilla, Sept. 27, 1946; AICPG v.0012.

225. JEG to Elías Moisés in B/quilla, Oct. 4, 1946; AICPG v.0012.

226. "Political Report . . ." Feb. 6, 1947, S. William Clark, Vice Con., to Thomas Lockett, Chargé d'Affaires; SD, Consular Post File, Record Group 84.

227. Vice Con. Clark to Lockett, Chargé d'Affaires, Feb. 15, 1947; SD, Consular Post File, Record Group 84.

228. "Report on Political Conditions in B/quilla . . ." Con. George Graves to Amb. Wiley, March 7, 1947; SD, Consular Post File, Record Group 84.

229. Ramón Castro G. to JEG, B/quilla, Sept. 18, 1947; AICPG v.0043.

230. Pablo Vergara Barrios to José María Córdoba, El Guamo, Aug. 11, 1946; AICPG v.0034.

231. Luis Mario Rivadeneira to JEG, Tunja, June 28, 1946; AICPG v.0019.

Chapter 7. Collective Vibrations: The Ideologies of Gaitanismo

1. Valdelamar to JEG, March 22, 1947; AICPG v.0061. Much of this chapter appeared in Green, "Vibrations of the Collective."

2. They also felt a sense of urgency. The "golpe de Pasto," as the coup attempt against López in 1944 was known, warned left Liberals about the dangers of the rising tide of reaction.

3. Interview by the author with Heliodoro Cogua P.

4. Comité Gaitanista of Segovia-Sincelejo, Bolívar, to JEG, Sept. 9, 1946; AICPG v.0034.

5. Excellent recordings can be heard on *Caudillos y muchedumbres,* vols. 1, 2, and 6.

6. The process that other historians have called the resurrection/reconstruction of subaltern voices or, in James Scott's phrase, of the "hidden transcripts," is not difficult in the case of the Gaitanistas. Their transcripts of resistance were never well hidden.

7. One is reminded of George Orwell's comment on the questionable ortho-

doxy of most of the working class concerning the definition of "socialism." As in the case of Catholicism, only the "educated" can boast ideological purity (*The Road to Wigan Pier*, 177).

8. Interview by the author with Heliodoro Cogua P.; "Una voz insurgente: Entrevista con Ofelia Uribe de Acosta," 29; *El Estado* (Santa Marta), April 29, 1946, p. 4, "Porque soy gaitanista" by Guillermo Núñez B.; Graciela M. de Morkin to JEG, B/quilla, July 20, 1946; AICPG v.0012.

9. Comité Lib. Pro Mov. Popular, Morales, Bolívar, to JEG, Feb. 12, 1947; AICPG.

10. *El Estado* (Santa Marta), Oct. 14, 1947, p. 1.

11. *Pluma Libre* (Pereira), Aug. 4 and Aug. 20; Aug. 13, 1939.

12. *El Estado* (Santa Marta), Feb. 29, 1944; "Benjamín Herrera," Oct. 15, 1945.

13. Osorio Lizarazo, *Ideas de izquierda*, 13–14; Córdoba, *Tribuno popular*, 82; Gonzalo Buenahora, *Los orígenes del gaitanismo*, 23.

14. Manuel Márquez R. to JEG, B/quilla, April 22, 1945; AICPG v.0091; see the poem by Dolores Prieto de Silva to JEG, B/quilla, Feb. 21, 1946; AICPG v.0043; Alejandro Lozano Ricaurte to JEG, Cunday, June 26, 1944; AICPG v.0052.

15. Lib. Gaitanista Command Mompós to JEG, June 17, 1947; AICPG v.0060; *Vanguardia* (Santa Marta), Feb. 28, 1945, p. 1, "En Orihueca proclaman a Gaitán"; Santiago Cárdenas G. to JEG, Los Palmitos, April 10, 1946; AICPG v.0088; Alfonso Romero A., Carlos Esquivia, and Samuel Guerrero to JEG, Cartagena, Sept. 7, 1946; AICPG v.0034 ; Comité Lib. de La Jagua de Ibirico to JEG, Sept. 20, 1946; AICPG v.0011; José Blas Vergara B. to JEG, Cartagena, April 7, 1947; AICPG v.0061.

16. Bergquist, *Labor in Latin America*, 311–12. But one is compelled to ask, were the 1940s as devoid of radicalism as Bergquist suggested? If one defines the left in Colombia only in terms of the Communists, then it does seem to have been weak in the 1930s and 1940s. But if the definition is broadened to include Gaitanismo and the left-Liberal tradition it represented, then the picture changes considerably (see Green, "Sibling Rivalry on the Left").

17. Palacios, *Entre la legitimidad y la violencia*, 196.

18. Bergquist, *Labor in Latin America*, 12–13.

19. Archila, *Cultura e identidad*, 406.

20. Palacios, *Entre la legitimidad y la violencia*, 122.

21. Michael Jiménez noted the connections between "Liberal leftists" and Communists around Viotá in the late 1920s and early 1930s ("The Limits of Export Capitalism").

22. Braun too was skeptical about radicalism in Gaitanismo. He argued that Gaitán was closer to Proudhon than to Marx, and that Marx called Proudhon a petty bourgeois, therefore Gaitán was petty bourgeois and not socialist (*Assassination of Gaitán*, 48, and note 49, same page). But as Stephen Bronner has asked, "What is socialism? The question marks the crisis" (*Socialism Unbound*, xi).

Bronner identified a socialist core, however, centered on social justice and democracy. These concepts were at the very heart of Gaitanista ideology.

23. *El Estado* (Santa Marta), April 9, 1946, p. 3, "El Capitán del pueblo."

24. Buenahora, *Los orígenes del gaitanismo,* 21; Córdoba, *Tribuno Popular,* 1; Osorio Lizarazo, *Ideas de izquierda,* 41; Nieto Rojas, *La batalla contra el comunismo,* 38.

25. "Por una Colombia Justa," manifesto with twenty signatories, AICPG v.0057.

26. Speech by Fran. J. Chaux to the Liberals of Antioquia, reprinted by *El Estado,* April 12, 1946, p. 4; *El Estado* (Santa Marta), Feb. 12, 1947, p. 3; poster entitled "Decididamente hacia la izquierda," from Honda, Oct. 10, 1946; AICPG v.0063.

27. *El Estado* (Santa Marta), Feb. 12, 1947, p. 3.

28. "Jorge Eliécer Gaitán," by Gilberto Henriquez Gil, B/quilla, early 1948; AICPG v.0091.

29. Partido Liberal Izquierdista to JEG, Cartagena, Sept. 22, 1947; AICPG v.0053.

30. He went on to say that the "slogan seemed to take Gaitán back to the egalitarian spirit that was at the heart of *Las ideas socialistas* but did not fit comfortably with his more recent emphasis on the meritocratic ideal" (Braun, *Assassination of Gaitán,* 101). Braun stated that "the slogan hardly ever came up in the interviews with Gaitán's followers" (note 94, same page). This was probably due to the social makeup of his interviewees, as earlier noted.

31. *El Estado* (Santa Marta), March 16, 1944, "Liberalismo es democracia"; Edmundo Delgado to JEG, Tumaco, March 18, 1944; AICPG v.0050.

32. Julio Vélez Micola, Dir. Lib. Dep., Cartagena, Bolívar, to JEG, April 10, 1946; AICPG v.0053; Samuel Guerrero to JEG, B/quilla, April 30, 1946; AICPG v.0043; Manifiesto Cívico de las Comités Municipales, August 1947; AICPG v.0060.

33. As did Pascual Del Vecchio R. in his interview with the author.

34. JEG to Roberto Castañeda, Santa Marta, Jan. 8, 1946; AICPG v.0068.

35. Manifiesto del Comité Liberal de la Clase Media del Atlántico, B/quilla, Dec. 12, 1945, and the letter from Antonio José Restrepo to JEG, Feb. 23, 1946; AICPG v.0091.

36. *El Estado* (Santa Marta), March 20, 1945.

37. Pedro Osorio C., "Comité JEG No. 2," to JEG, B/quilla, May 16, 1945; AICPG v.0091.

38. Comité Lib. Gaitanista del barrio Manga de Cartagena to JEG, July 11, 1947; AICPG v.0060.

39. Alvaro García D. and Alonso Mazo M. to JEG, Nov. 11, 1945; AICPG v.0016.

40. Arturo Besada to JEG, Cartagena, Dec. 9, 1944, Jan. 24, 1945; AICPG v.0074.

41. Eduardo A. Price O. to Dir. Nac. Gaitanista, B/quilla, Jan. 28, 1946; AICPG v.0012.

42. Alfonso Alexander M. to JEG, Ipiales, April 2, 1946; AICPG v.0050.

43. The popular ideology of populism is often skimmed over since most studies approach from the top. Michael Kazin, for example, placed his emphasis on "movements and prominent figures who sought to speak *for* the people instead of to attempt what, by necessity, would have been an anecdotal, scattershot presentation of what ordinary, nonactivist Americans were saying" (*The Populist Persuasion*, 6). Does its "anecdotal" and "scattershot" nature make it irrelevant?

44. Interview by Mauricio Archila with Gonzalo Buenahora.

45. He wrote of simultaneous demonstrations in favor of Gaitán in Bogotá and B/quilla; Con. Dawson to Amb. Wiley, B/quilla, Oct. 1, 1945; SD, Consular Post File, Record Group 84.

46. Arturo Quintero P. to JEG, B/quilla, May 28, 1945; AICPG v.0091.

47. Rafael Arévalo Arenas to JEG, B/quilla, June 12, 1946; AICPG v.0012.

48. Manuel Hernández R., Arcadio de la Torre to JEG, B/quilla, April 24, 1945; AICPG v.0091.

49. Esaú Conde Ribón to JEG, Cartagena, Dec. 1, 1945; AICPG v.0053.

50. Juan Manuel Valdelamar to JEG, Cartagena, April 25, 1944; AICPG v.0053. Yet even the press of the oligarquía could not completely ignore his efforts on the coast.

51. Fidel Murillo to JEG, Honda, Dec. 28, 1946; AICPG v.0052.

52. *El Estado* (Santa Marta), July 25, 1947, pp. 3 and 6, "La prensa oligárquica y Gaitán."

53. Estheiman Amaya Solano, "*Jornada:* El periódico del Pueblo," 51–55.

54. José María Córdoba to Jorge Ospina in Medellín, July 1945; AICPG v.0069; Arturo Besada to JEG, Cartagena, Dec. 9, 1944; AICPG v.0074.

55. Augusto Esparza G. to JEG, Pasto, April 17, 1945; AICPG v.0050.

56. Con. Dawson to Amb. Wiley, B/quilla, Oct. 1, 1945; SD, Consular Post File, Record Group 84.

57. C. J. Moreno to JEG, B/quilla, May 16, 1945; AICPG v.0091.

58. Rodolfo Ponce reported on their activities to JEG, B/quilla, March 7 1945; AICPG v.0091.

59. Asdrubal Amarís to José María Córdoba, Santa Marta, Oct. 23, 1945; AICPG v.0011. In April 1946 they called his movement "the most transcendental event in the country's recent political history" ("Una atenta carta del director de *Vanguardia*" to *El Estado*, April 11, 1946). See also the way *El Estado*, Santa Marta's leading daily, got behind Gaitán (after some hedging) between the latter half of 1945 and April 1946.

60. Aureliano Gómez Olaciregui, *Prensa y periodismo en Barranquilla*, 209.

61. For many of these I know only a name, place, perhaps publisher, and sympathy for Gaitanismo. *Estrella Roja* and *Antorcha,* reported as Gaitanista semanarios in Medellín in 1945 by E. Puerta Toro; *República* of Cartagena

"semanario Liberal" had a "Gaitanista page"; Juan Manuel Valdelamar's *El Frente Obrero* in Cartagena, probably very small; *El Sesquiplano* of Santa Marta, weekly, director Juan del Villar, supported Gaitán; *Voz Nacional,* Carlos J. Moreno's paper after 1946 in Barranquilla; *Mundo Nuevo* in Cartagena, owner/publisher Esaú Conde Ribón; *El Pueblo,* perhaps founded in Ciénaga in October 1946; *La Razón* of Santa Marta; *La Voz Liberal* of Santa Marta, director Aquileo Lanao Loaiza, declared for Gaitán; *Correo de Sabanas* of Sincelejo, "semanario Liberal independente," director Juan Jaraba, supported Gaitán; *La Voz del Pueblo* of Sincelejo, Gaitanista and associated with Carlos Támara L. and Edmundo Pizarro after June 1946; *La Suegra* and *Liga Comerical,* both of Barranquilla and both called Gaitanista in 1945; *La Región,* Gaitanista weekly in Bolívar, first issue Feb. 5, 1948; *Ahora* in Chinú Bolívar, Gaitanista weekly, first issue July 1947; *La Bandera Liberal* of Cartagena, Gaitanista paper founded on July 25, 1947; *Rojo y Blanco* in Ciénaga, new Gaitanista paper noted by *El Estado* in October 1946; *El Trópico* of Barrancabermeja, Gaitanista paper in 1946; *Restauración* (Buga); *La Voz del Obrero,* semanario; *Atalaya* (Cereté—órgano al servicio de la causa democrática del liberalismo), Jorge Franco Múnera, dir., Sept. 17, 1947; *Izquierdas* (Bogotá), dir. Germán Arango Escobar (former gerente de *Jornada*), 1946; *Batalla* (Ibagué), dir. Luís A. Ramirez C., Gaitanista semanario, Aug. 1945; *Opinión Pública* (Pasto), April 1946; *La Voz del Líbano* (semanario), April 1946; *Guerra* (Tumaco), March 1944; *Ecos del Tetoná* (Yalí—Futuro Municipio de Antioquia), Feb. 17, 1946, very humble sort of publication, but ardently Gaitanista; *Fray-Trabuco* (Pasto—Periódico crítico y de variedades), Feb. 1948.

62. Aline Helg, *La educación en Colombia,* 197–98.

63. An ideological tension apparent in Peronism; see James, *Resistance and Integration,* 33–37.

64. Braun noted that while José María Córdoba claimed membership in the "JEGA," the band of supporters who looked after Gaitán's interests and identified themselves collectively with Gaitán's initials, he "also tried to establish his distance from it" (*Assassination of Gaitán,* 88, note 52).

65. José María Córdoba to Sergio Gómez, Tamalameque, Magdalena, Oct. 31, 1945; AICPG v.0070.

66. Córdoba, *Tribuno Popular,* 41.

67. Sharpless, *Gaitán of Colombia,* 115.

68. Medina, *La protesta urbana,* 73.

69. Sharpless, *Gaitán of Colombia,* 151.

70. Antolín Díaz, *Los verdugos del caudillo,* 58.

71. *El Fígaro* (Cartagena), Aug. 25, 1945, p. 3, "El hijo del pueblo"; April 10, 1946, p. 4, "Demagogía Gaitanista."

72. Interview by Mauricio Archila with Bernardo Medina; J. Carrillo P. to JEG, Cartagena, Dec. 17, 1947; AICPG v.0053.

73. Julio Ricardo Garcia B. to JEG, Moniquirá, July 5, 1946; AICPG v.0019.

74. A Gaitanista missionary reported how the residents of San Marcos, Bolívar,

had no understanding of the "healthy ideas of Gaitanismo." When made aware of the "future salvation of their interests" these ideas represented, however, they reportedly joined the movement (*El Fígaro* [Cartagena], Sept. 15, 1945, p. 5, "El gaitanismo de San Marcos y la mansa ovejita").

75. Díaz, *Los verdugos del caudillo*, 84–87.

76. Chaux, *Homenaje a Gaitán*, 9, 11.

77. Bergquist, *Labor in Latin America*, 356.

78. Diogenes Guerra to JEG, Cartagena, Aug. 30, 1943; AICPG v.0074.

79. *El Estado* (Santa Marta), April 30, 1946, p. 3.

80. Lorenzo Ortega to JEG, Sept. 5, 1946; AICPG v.0012.

81. Sharpless, *Gaitán of Colombia*, 116.

82. Found in *Gaitán: Antología*, "Plataforma del Colón," esp. 329–47; "Plan Gaitán," esp. 258–95. Citations from this edition will be given in the text. These texts were clearly the direct decedents of Gaitán's *Ideas socialistas en Colombia* and the *Manifiesto de unir*.

83. See the similarities with a letter from fifteen citizens to JEG, B/quilla, Oct. 9, 1931; AICPG v.0091 (Gaitán, answering in his typical fashion, assured them that he was working on this problem in the Congress); and the letter from Gilberto Castillo and eighty others to JEG, Morroa, Nov. 20, 1946; AICPG v.0034.

84. "Manifiesto: La misión de avanzada del Liberalismo," *El Estado*, April 9, 10, 12, 16 of 1945.

85. Marco T. Lerraniaga to JEG, Cunday, July 19, 1947; AICPG v.0051.

86. *La Tribuna* (B/quilla), March 10, 1943, p. 3.

87. Franco Ezenarro to JEG, B/quilla, March 6, 1944; AICPG v.0091.

88. *El Estado* (Santa Marta), March 15, 1945.

89. *Vanguardia* (Santa Marta), Dec. 6, 1943, p. 3.

90. Fermín Linares G. and twenty-two others to JEG, B/quilla, May 14, 1947; AICPG v.0012.

91. "Manifiesto Cívico . . ." copy sent to JEG, August, 1947; AICPG v.0060.

92. *El Estado* (Santa Marta), Jan. 21, 1947, pp. 1, 6, "Gaitán . . . jefe único del Lib. popular."

93. "Un Barranquillero Gaitanista" to JEG, B/quilla, July 16, 1947; AICPG v.0012.

94. Fifteen citizens to JEG, B/quilla, Oct. 9, 1931; AICPG v.0091.

95. *El Estado* (Santa Marta), March 15, 1945.

96. Gilberto Castillo and eighty others to JEG, Morroa, Nov. 20, 1946; AICPG v.0034.

97. *Jornada*, May 1, 1947, p. 4.

98. Social justice and "popular" power were general concerns among Colombian working class in the 1940s (not just the left and Liberal left). See the radical-sounding names of Catholic workers' papers in the late 1930s and 1940s. *Justicia Social* (Bogotá) 1945, generally anti-Communist, anti-womens' suffrage yet pro-union (just not CTC); *El Amigo del Pueblo* (Bogotá); *El Bien Social* (Bogotá); *La*

Defensa Social (Bogotá); *Semanario Popular* (Cartagena); *Labor Social* (Sogamosa).

99. *La Tribuna* (B/quilla), Aug. 18, 1943, p. 3; Feb. 24, 1943, p. 1; Jan. 21, 1944, p. 3.

100. *Agitación Femenina*, Inés Gómez, no. 1, Oct. 1944; Mariana de Pinzón S., no. 3, Dec. 1944.

101. Carolina and Teresita Barrera to JEG, Cartagena, April 8, 1947; AICPG v.0061.

102. Alfonso Romero A., Carlos M. Esquivia C., and Samuel Guerrero to JEG, Cartagena, Sept. 7, 1946; AICPG v.0034.

103. J. Antonio Cianci to JEG, El Banco, May 10, 1946; AICPG v.0017.

104. José Francisco Gómez Negrett to JEG, Magangué, Feb. 1, 1947; AICPG v.0061.

105. Azula Barrera, *De la revolución*, 60.

106. Luís Arenas Serrano to JEG, Bucaramanga, Aug. 2, 1932; AICPG v.0089; "Junta Pro-rebaja de pena" to JEG, Manizales, July 27, 1939; AICPG v.0092; Edmundo Delgado to JEG, Tumaco, Dec. 10, 1940; AICPG v.0044; José Loaiza to JEG, Marquetalia, May 6, 1944; AICPG v.0092.

107. Thirty-one Liberals to Dir. Liberal Gaitanista, Pedregoza, Guamul-Magdalena, Dec. 25, 1945; AICPG v.0011; *Agitación Femenina*, no. 3, Dec. 1944, p. 13 ("Calibán" called them, disparagingly, "leftist feminists"); *Vanguardia* (Santa Marta), April 5, 1943, p. 3; May 19, 1943.

108. Alfonso Alexander to JEG, Bogotá, Aug. 29, 1942, AICPG v.0021; Concejales Liberales del Municipio de Buenosaires Cauca, Nov. 2, 1947; AICPG v.0090; "Manifiesto a los habitantes del Municipio de Turbo!" AICPG v.0016; Julián Meléndez, owner-operator of the radio station "La Voz del Litoral," to JEG, B/quilla, May 7, 1946; AICPG v.0012.

109. Córdoba, *Tribuno popular*, 82.

110. Peña, *Gaitán íntimo*, 97.

111. Antonio García, *Gaitán y el problema de la revolución colombiana*, 14–15, 146–49.

112. *El Estado* (Santa Marta), Feb. 4, 1947, pp. 2 and 4, "Plataforma ideológica del liberalismo."

113. Miguel P. García to JEG, Riohacha, Dec. 2, 1946; AICPG v.0011.

114. Pablo M. Matos to JEG, B/quilla, May 10, 1947; AICPG v.0012.

115. J. Carrillo P. to JEG, Cartagena, Dec. 17, 1947; AICPG v.0053. And years later the idea of "real democracy," understood as "a degree of economic equality and social justice," would seem tame as mainstream Liberal dogma (see Carlos Lleras Restrepo, *El liberalismo colombiano*, 14).

116. See Miguel P. Garcia to JEG, Riohacha, Dec. 2, 1946; AICPG v.0011; J. Carrillo P. to JEG, Cartagena, Dec. 17, 1947; AICPG v.0053; Julio Flórez R. to JEG, Tibacuy, Aug. 12, 1945; AICPG v.0073; Comité Gaitanista de Manga, Cartagena, to JEG, Jan. 9, 1946; AICPG v.0074.

117. Roberto Barrero V. to JEG, Girardot, March 28, 1944; AICPG v.0086.

118. Gabriel Vélez and Antonio Valencia P. to JEG, Líbano, June 16, 1947; AICPG v.0051.

119. Hernando Pastor G. to Dir. Nac. Gaitanista, Santa Isabel, Dec. 10, 1945; AICPG v.0052.

120. Daniel James's work on Argentina leaves a feeling of déjà-vu in relation to the case of Colombia. While elements of Peronist ideology did indeed "help ensure the reproduction of the dominant capitalist social relations," these elements could explicitly deny "capitalist values and needs, posing an alternative reading of reality" (*Resistance and Integration,* 260–61).

121. Julio Flórez R. to JEG, Tibacuy, Aug. 12, 1945; AICPG v.0073.

122. Comité Gaitanista de Manga, Cartagena, to JEG, Jan. 9, 1946; AICPG v.0074.

123. Julio Dangond Ovalle to JEG, Ciénaga, June 6, 1945; AICPG v.0011.

124. Rafael Alvear Terán to JEG March, 1946; AICPG v.0053.

125. Julio Vélez Micolao to JEG, Cartagena, March 18, 1944; AICPG v.0053.

126. *El Estado* (Santa Marta), Dec. 13, 1945.

127. Julián Meléndez to JEG, B/quilla, May 7, 1946; AICPG v.0012.

128. Pablo Cardozo to JEG, Honda, Nov. 5, 1946; AICPG v.0052.

129. José Blas Vergara B. to JEG, Cartagena, April 7, 1947; AICPG v.0061.

130. Milton Puentes, *Gaitán,* 44; *El Fígaro* (Cartagena), July 2, 1945, p. 3. In Barranquilla, *El Nacional,* though fiercely anti-Gaitán, noted that Gaitanismo was "a natural reaction against the atmosphere of corruption" (*El Nacional,* Oct. 3, 1945, p. 1).

131. See *La Tribuna* (B/quilla), Aug. 18, 1943, p. 3; Pedro J. Duran to JEG, B/quilla, May 6, 1945; AICPG v.0091; interview with Andrés Barandica Troya by Mauricio Archila.

132. *La Opinión* (Ibagué), March 18, 1944.

133. "Gaitán, hombre del pueblo," by Geraldo Candamil Gómez, Pasto, no date; AICPG v.0050.

134. José Domingo Arciniegas A. to JEG, B/quilla, May 5, 1945; AICPG v.0091; Carlos M. Luna M. to JEG, San Bernardo, Magd., Jan. 15, 1946; AICPG v.0011; Julio Vélez Micolao to JEG, Cartagena, March 18, 1944; AICPG v.0053; Dago Barboza to JEG, B/quilla, June 5, 1946; AICPG v.0012; Buenaventura Campo to JEG, Santa Marta, Sept. 26, 1946; AICPG v.0017.

135. Renulfo A. Navarro and 199 others to JEG, Sucre, April, 1946; AICPG v.0053; Julio Barrios C. to JEG, Montelibano, March 17, 1947; AICPG v.0061; Comando Liberal Gaitanista de Mompós to JEG, June 17, 1947; AICPG v.0060.

136. Manifiesto a los liberales . . . Atlántico, Comité "JEG," to JEG, late 1945; AICPG v.0043.

137. Poem by Delores Prieto de Silva, Sept. 23, 1945, B/quilla; AICPG v.0043.

138. *La Tribuna* (B/quilla), April 5, 1944, p. 1, "A la carga contra la oligarquía."

139. Pablo Vergara B., Sin. Vaqueros . . . de El Guamo, to JEG, March 21, 1945; AICPG v.0074.

140. Dir. Liberal Departamental Gaitanista to JEG, Aug. 2, 1945; AICPG v.0052.

141. Constitución del Comité Pro-Candidatura Gaitán, March 18, 1944; AICPG v.0052.

142. Enrique Arbeláez to JEG, Frias, April 12, 1946; AICPG v.0052.

143. Comité Liberal Gaitanista de Tumaco to JEG, Jan. 7, 1946; AICPG v.0050.

144. (Over) 234 "Ciudadanos Liberales . . . del Fresno," Nov. 5, 1946; AICPG v.0052.

145. See Gilberto Henriquez Gil to JEG, B/quilla, Jan. 9, 1945; fifty "jóvenes" to JEG, B/quilla, June 21, 1945, AICPG v.0091; El Comité Gaitanista de Calle Nueva del Espinal, Cartagena, to JEG, June 6, 1945, AICPG v.0074; Sociedad Pro-Vivienda del Barrio Sur, B/quilla, Jan. 1946, Rafael Reales A., B/quilla, Sept. 26, 1947, AICPG v.0043.

146. El Estado (Santa Marta), April 12, 1946, p. 1, "El movimiento de la restoración no es electoral sino revolucionario, dice Rincones P."

147. "Una Figura Simbólica," from Orientación Liberal (Popayán), reprinted by El Estado (Santa Marta), Feb. 24, 1947, pp. 1 and 6.

Chapter 8. The Dilemmas of Liberal Integration in the Twilight of Politics, 1946–1948

1. El Tiempo, May 6, 1946, "Danza de las horas," p. 4.

2. Mendoza P. and Camacho A., eds., El liberalismo en el gobierno.

3. Efraim de J. Castillo G. to Dir. Nac. Liberal, Pajarito, July 26, 1946; AICPG v.0019.

4. Manuel Robles piled scorn on such fantasies in El Estado (Santa Marta), Dec. 24, 1946, p. 3.

5. Rafael Cortés Vargas to JEG, Pasto, March 29, 1948; AICPG v.0044.

6. Carlos Rafael Villamizar V. to JEG, Cúcuta (Hacienda "Moros"), July 20, 1946.

7. Letter from over fifty "hombres de la costa Atl." to JEG, B/quilla, Dec. 19, 1947; AICPG v.0043. In May 1947 the departmental assembly of Magdalena protested against El Espectador, La Razón, and, of course, El Tiempo for their statements denigrating Gaitán's person and their attempts to split the movement (El Estado (Santa Marta), May 22, 1947, p. 1, "La asamblea protesta contra los insultos de la prensa oligárquica a Gaitán"). Jornada later called them, including El Liberal, "traitor publications" (Jornada, Dec. 23, 1947, p. 1, "Contra la prensa oligárca").

8. Reconquista (Bogotá), no. 2, July 1947, p. 3.

9. Dir. Liberal de Saboyá to JEG, Sept. 8, 1946; AICPG v.0019.

10. Eustasio Sánchez M. to JEG, Paz de Río, June 13, 1946; AICPG v.0019.

11. Pécaut's subtle argument unfolds in Orden y violencia, 2:439–85.

12. As Roberto Insignares claimed in his interview with Mauricio Archila.

13. Sánchez, *Los días de la revolución*, 12.

14. Sharpless, *Gaitán of Colombia*, 107.

15. Interview by Mauricio Archila with Alfredo de la Espriella.

16. In 1944, for example, Magdalena Liberals clamored for new party organization (*Vanguardia* [Santa Marta], Sept. 6, 1944, p. 3, "Política Liberal" by "Un Liberal de Santa Marta").

17. *Vanguardia* (Santa Marta), April 21, 1944, p. 3.

18. Francisco José Chaux, *Homenaje a Gaitán*, 10.

19. *El Estado* (Santa Marta), April 9, 1946, p. 3, "El capitán del pueblo."

20. Tito de Santal to JEG, Santa Lucia, Atlántico, March 20, 1946; AICPG v.0091.

21. Centro Liberal Pro-Suan to JEG, Suan, July 27, 1946; AICPG v.0012.

22. Centro de Accíon Gaitanista, Ciénaga, to José María Córdoba, May 20, 1946; AICPG v.0051.

23. *El Estado* (Santa Marta), Sept. 16, 1946, p. 3, "Dos frentes de lucha."

24. Aquileo Lanao Loaiza to José María Córdoba, Santa Marta, Dec. 26, 1946; AICPG v.0011.

25. Julio Ortega Amarís to Francisco José Chaux, Santa Marta, Dec. 27, 1946; AICPG v.0011.

26. Asdrúbal Amarís, "El liberalismo se robustecerá con JEG," to JEG in *El Estado* (Santa Marta), May 10, 1946, pp. 1, 3. The situation was similar all over the coast. In Bolívar "everyone, from the humble peasant to the most illustrious political chief," worked from morning until night (C. A. Doval to JEG, Montería, Sept. 1, 1947; AICPG v.0053). In Atlántico, though the Conservatives had taken the presidency, the pueblo of Atlántico was "blind to any other possibility" than that the next governor of the department would be Blanco Núñez, a Gaitanista (Zolio Ruíz to JEG, B/quilla, July 25, 1946; AICPG v.0012).

27. *Jornada*, Feb. 5, 1947, p. 5, "Gaitán en Santa Marta," reprint from *Vanguardia*.

28. Carlos Luis García F. to JEG, Cúcuta, Oct. 22, 1946; AICPG v.0051.

29. Sin. Prof. Varios to JEG, Heriberto Rodelo to José María Córdoba, Sevilla, Sept. 6, 1946; AICPG v.0011.

30. Sin. Unificado de Empleados y Obreros de la Compañía Colombiana de Electricidad, División del Atl., to Doña Amparo Jarramillo de Gaitán, B/quilla, Dec. 31, 1946; AICPG v.0012.

31. Concejo Mun. de Yaguará to JEG, Nov. 1, 1946; AICPG v.0044; Sindicato de Mineros de Valle, Cali, to JEG, Sept. 3, 1947; AICPG v.0013.

32. *El Estado* (Santa Marta), April 22, 1947, p. 1.

33. Asociación de Motoristas Mecánicos Navales, Oct. 16, 1947, Sin. de Trabajadores de la Renta de Licores del Atl., Oct. 18, 1947, B/quilla; both in AICPG v.0043.

34. Angel Rafael Blanco to JEG, Santa Marta, July 28, 1947; AICPG v.0017.

35. Unión Obrero de Colombia, Bogotá, to JEG, Sept. 19, 1947; AICPG v.0022.

Their candidates were José A. Sabogal and Esteban Vesga. See also the Comité Liberal Gaitanista de los Barrios Altos de Bogotá (La Peña; Los Laches; El Charrerón; Samper; la parte alta de Egipto) to JEG, Sept. 5, 1947, and the Comité Liberal Gaitanista del Barrio Doce de Octubre, Bogotá, to JEG, Sept. 16, 1947, both in AICPG v.0022, who insisted that Efrain Cañavera Romero was their man for the city council (as a "defender of the worker neighborhoods and of the middle classes"). The Comité Liberal "Uribe Uribe" del Barrio "La Providencia," Bogotá, to JEG, Sept. 10, 1947; AICPG v.0022, proclaimed Dr. Joaquín Viloria as their candidate.

36. Lots and lots of lists of candidates for 1947 in AICPG v.0022, from barrios, cab drivers, university professors, etc., from every part of Colombia.

37. Letter, name missing, to JEG, Villa de Leiva, Dec. 10, 1946; AICPG v.0019.

38. José C. Briñez to JEG, Ibagué, May 23, 1947; AICPG v.0051.

39. Carlos Luis García F. to JEG, Cúcuta, Oct. 22, 1946; AICPG v.0051.

40. *El Estado* (Santa Marta), May 30, 1946, p. 4, "La convención de Gaitán."

41. See Sharpless, *Gaitán of Colombia*, 148–50; and Braun, *Assassination of Gaitán*, 116–18. Braun pointed out that the second convention was more formal in appearance and structure. The irony of Gaitán's use of the elite Teatro Colón, where the oligarquía had so often mobilized against him, was not missed. Yet Gaitán might also have been making a subtle point about how he had defeated the Liberal notables on the field of political battle and entered their stronghold.

42. *El Estado* (Santa Marta), Jan. 16, 1947, p. 3, "La convención del pueblo."

43. Proposición No. II, Bogotá, Jan. 20, 1947; AICPG v.0062.

44. Braun, *Assassination of Gaitán*, 118. He noted that the Conservatives increased their support to 653,987 votes, which was not surprising given their emerging control of the government.

45. *El Estado*, July 7, 1947, p. 3.

46. Centro de Orientación y Organización Lib. to JEG, B/quilla, Sept. 6, 1947; AICPG v.0043.

47. Braun, *Assassination of Gaitán*, 118.

48. For a more detailed discussion of the process, see Green, "Sibling Rivalry on the Left."

49. Milton Puentes, *Gaitán*, 37.

50. Embassy Circular no. 21, Feb. 15, 1944, "Report on the Communist Party," SD, Record Group 84.

51. Interview with Alfonso García by Mauricio Archila, Bogotá.

52. Blanco Núñez recalled that in April 1945, his friend Gustavo Solano said, "If this is not the last straw . . . that you too have become a Communist and support Gaitán" (*Memorias*, 69).

53. *El Mitín* (Cartagena), June 27, 1936, p. 1, "La manifestación comunista."

54. "Membership, Activities, and Designs of the Communist Party in Colombia," Hernan C. Vogenitz, American Consul in Cartagena, April 11, 1947, SD 821.00B/4–1147.

55. *Diario Popular,* March 6, 7, and 9, 1942.

56. Samuel Guerrero to JEG, Cartagena, March 27, 1944; AICPG v.0053.

57. Eduardo Octavio Cotes to JEG, Santa Marta, April 8, 1945; AICPG v.0017.

58. Interview by Mauricio Archila with Jorge Mateus.

59. *El Liberal* (Bogotá), April 12, 1946, p. 1.

60. Interview by Mauricio Archila with Ramón de la Hoz.

61. See the interviews by Mauricio Archila with Bernardo Medina and Andrés Barandica Troya.

62. He welcomed López to Santa Marta in 1944 (*Vanguardia* [Santa Marta], Feb. 14, 1944, p. 1).

63. Carlos Giacometto del Real to JEG, Santa Marta, July 31, 1947; AICPG v.0017. Gaitán answered his letter, welcoming him to the Liberal party.

64. Durán, however, was not alone among the Communist leadership in this regard. In his interview with the author, Hector Molina Rojas remembered that many in the party simply could not get beyond their personal distaste for Gaitán's "demagoguery." He noted also their tendency to dismiss the Gaitanistas with humor. One old-time Communist made a vulgar play on the words of Gaitán's rallying call "a la carga," substituting "a cagarla," literally, to make it all shitty.

65. FBI report "Summary of Communist Activities . . ." Feb. 5, 1947, SD 821.00B/3–1047.

66. FBI Report on Communist Activity in Colombia to the Division of Foreign Activity Correlation, concerning PSD member Alvaro Pio Valencia, Bogotá, Nov. 12, 1946; SD 821.00B/12–2746.

67. FBI report "Summary of Communist Activities . . ." Feb. 5, 1947, SD 821.00B/3–1047.

68. Juan Manuel Valdelamar to JEG, Cartagena, Feb. 20, 1947; AICPG v.0061.

69. FBI report "Summary of Communist Activities . . ." Feb. 5, 1947, SD 821.00B/3–1047.

70. From Dispatch no. 2551, "Colombian Communist Party," July 1, 1947; SD 821.00B/7–147. Pécaut concludes that the PSD (and the CTC) were too close to the Liberal establishment and lost contact with the base (*Orden y violencia,* 2:406–7).

71. See *Jornada,* March 28 and 29, 1947.

72. "Carta Política" by Carlos Giacometto del Real to JEG, July 26, 1947; AICPG v.0017.

73. *El Estado* (Santa Marta), Aug. 18, 1947, p. 3.

74. Carlos Giacometto del Real to the editor of *El Estado* (Santa Marta), Feb. 19, 1948, p. 5.

75. Luís E. Prias B. to JEG, Tunja, July 6, 1946; AICPG v.0019.

76. Miguel Parra to JEG, Ibagué, Nov. 3, 1946; AICPG v.0052.

77. N. Emilio Prince Lobo to JEG, Ocaña, Sept. 16, 1946; AICPG v.0051.

78. Antonio Morales "y demás firmantes" to JEG, B/quilla, Oct. 21, 1946; AICPG v.0012.

79. Sánchez, "The Violence: An Interpretative Synthesis," 77.

80. Pécaut, *Orden y violencia*, 2:439–85. But it should be remembered that many important middle-class politicians were present within the movement before.

81. Interview by Mauricio Archila with Roberto Insignares, June 14, 1986.

82. Dionisio Rincones Ponce to JEG, Santa Marta, Sept. 23, 1946; AICPG v.0011.

83. Jorge Tobón Restrepo (Diputado) to JEG, Medellín, May 8, 1946; AICPG v.0016.

84. Rafael Tirana O. to JEG, Yopal (Cunday), June 30, 1947; AICPG v.0051. And not everyone who returned to the party was "false." Left Liberals reentered the party in October 1947, calling liberalism now "the party of the Colombian revolution" (Maximiliano Santacruz and thirty-six others to JEG, Caloto, Oct. 25, 1947; AICPG v.0090).

85. Carlos Stacey Insignares to JEG, B/quilla, January 1945; AICPG v.0091.

86. Carlos J. Moreno to JEG, B/quilla, March 31, 1945; AICPG v.0091.

87. Carlos J. Moreno to JEG, B/quilla, Nov. 2, 1945; AICPG v.0091.

88. Santander Leon y B. to JEG, B/quilla, May 31, 1945; AICPG v.0091.

89. César Roncallo Llinás to JEG, B/quilla, April 13, 1946; AICPG v.0091.

90. Santos Valencia Asprilla to JEG, Puerto Colombia, Nov. 12, 1946; AICPG v.0012.

91. Pablo M. Matos to JEG, B/quilla, May 10, 1947; AICPG v.0012.

92. Acción Liberal Municipal Gaitanista de Aracataca to JEG, Oct. 4, 1946; AICPG v.0011.

93. Carlos Tamara L. to JEG, Sincelejo, Sept. 19, 1946; AICPG v.0034.

94. Julio Vélez Micolao to JEG, Cartagena, Oct. 25, 1947; AICPG v.0053.

95. *El Estado* (Santa Marta), Aug. 20, 1946, p. 2.

96. *El Estado* (Santa Marta), Jan. 6, 1947, p. 3, "El grito no debe ser de unión . . ."

97. Justino Navarro M. to JEG, Suárez, July 7, 1947; AICPG v.0051.

98. Ismael Santofimio, Alejandro Alcazar Varón to JEG, Ibagué, July 29, 1947; AICPG v.0051.

99. Carlos Luis García F. to JEG, Cúcuta, Oct. 22, 1946; AICPG v.0051.

100. Dir. Lib. Gaitanista Municipal de Mompós to José María Córdoba, May 15, 1946; AICPG v.0034.

101. Antonio Zapata Olivella to JEG, Cartagena, May 24, 1947; AICPG v.0060.

102. Victor Benito and eighty others to JEG, San Bernardo del Viento, May 29, 1947; AICPG v.0060.

103. Julio Dangond Ovalle to JEG, Ciénaga, Oct. 8, 1946; AICPG v.0011.

104. Mario Charrís Cabana and twenty-three others to JEG, Ciénaga, Jan. 11, 1947; AICPG v.0062.

105. Juan N. Payares to JEG, Ciénaga, Jan. 27, 1947; AICPG v.0062.

106. Dionisio Rincones Ponce to JEG, Santa Marta, June 26, 1946; AICPG v.0051.

107. Luís A. Ortega, Comité Central Lib. Pop. to JEG, Montería, Nov. 6, 1947; AICPG v.0053.

108. JEG to Luís A. Ortega, Nov. 29, 1947; AICPG v.0053.

109. Ortíz Márquez, *El hombre que fue un pueblo*, 131–32.

110. José María Córdoba to Carlos Rendón and others, Fundación, Magdalena, May 31, 1946; AICPG v.0071.

111. Enrique (?) to JEG, Tunja, June 23, 1946; AICPG v.0019.

112. Gabriel Vélez and Antonio J. Valencia P. to JEG, Líbano, June 16, 1947; AICPG v.0051.

113. Januario Yate B. to JEG, San Juan y Chaparre-Coyaima, May 28, 1947; AICPG v.0051.

114. Pécaut, *Orden y violencia*, 2:439–40.

115. Ibid., 2:443.

116. Many of Gaitán's lieutenants even urged what amounted to a coup. Gaitanistas smashed the windows of the Liberal party's headquarters in Bogotá and telegraphs poured in asking Gaitán to "save our families from Conservative persecution" (Sharpless, *Gaitán of Colombia*, 139–42).

117. Pécaut, *Orden y violencia*, 2:448–55.

118. *El Estado* (Santa Marta), July 17, 1947, p. 3, "Dos posiciones, dos criterios."

119. Pedro Antonio Durán Solano to JEG, Ibagué, July 15, 1947; AICPG v.0051.

120. *Reconquista* (Bogotá), June 1947, pp. 10–11, 19, "Interpretaciones del liberalismo moderno."

121. Medina, *Juegos de rebeldía*, 113 and 117.

122. Posada-Carbó, "Limits of Power," 268.

123. It is clear, however, that despite their shared hatred of Gaitanismo, the Liberal and Conservative elites were also moving toward violent conflict. See Darío Acevedo Carmona, *La mentalidad de las élites sobre la violencia*.

124. Enrique Alvarez, Charala, Santander, to Dir. Nac. Lib. G., April 20, 1946; AICPG v.0089.

125. Comando Municipal Gaitanista Quimbaya to JEG, May 6, 1946; AICPG v.0092.

126. See, for example, Roberto A. Calderón to JEG, Guateque, April 30, 1946; AICPG v.0086.

127. Carmen de Vidal to JEG, Tumaco, June 3, 1946; AICPG v.0044.

128. Jorge D. Galindo to Dir. Nac. Liberal, Campohermoso, June 10, 1946; AICPG v.0019.

129. Comité Liberal Gaitanista, Tibana, to Dir. Nac. Liberal, June 12, 1946; AICPG v.0019.

130. Sociedad Obrera de Mutuo Apoyo, Chiquinquirá, to JEG, July 21, 1946; AICPG v.0019.

131. Schmidt, "La Violencia Revisited," 101.

132. Six "servidores y copartidarios" to JEG, Belén, Dec. 15, 1946; AICPG v.0019.

133. Camilo Gómez Serrano to JEG, Bogotá, Sept. 12, 1947; AICPG v.0022.

134. See letters and *informes*, Oct. 1947; AICPG v.0022.

135. Colón Pérez Montenegro to JEG, Pasto, Sept. 5, 1947; AICPG.

136. See Saúl Moreno Gutiérrez to JEG, Guavatá, Sept. 17, 1947; AICPG v.0089; Eduardo Tribiño Sáenz to JEG, Manizales, Nov. 18, 1947; AICPG v.0092; F. Mejía Trujillo to JEG, Manizales, Sept. 15, 1947; AICPG v.0092.

137. Comité de Defensa Liberal de Génova to JEG, Jan. 19, 1948; AICPG v.0092.

138. Enrique Cuero O. to JEG, Rovira, July 31, 1947; AICPG v.0051.

139. Aristídes Bolaños Muñoz to JEG, La Cruz, Oct. 9, 1947; AICPG v.0050.

140. See Herbert Braun's description, *Assassination of Gaitán*, 127–28.

Epilogue and Conclusion: Gaitanismo, *la Violencia*, and Colombia's Enduring Predicament

1. Gonzalo Sánchez and Donny Meertens, *Bandoleros, gamonales y campesinos*, 33.

2. Gaitán was not unaware of the potential political importance of the largely Conservative Colombian army to his prospective presidency. In his closing arguments, Gaitán "included a ringing eulogy for the Colombian Army and its performance of duty" (Secret Intelligence Report of the U.S. Naval Attaché, "Summary of Events in Colombia During Rioting and Abortive Revolution Period of 9 April, 1948, to 20 April, 1948," May 18, 1948; File no. AA 74179, U.S. National Archives, p. 2).

3. See Braun, *Assassination of Gaitán*, 132–36; Sharpless, *Gaitán of Colombia*, 171–73; Intelligence Report of the U.S. Naval Attaché, "Summary of Events," File no. AA 74179, U.S. National Archives, pp. 2–3.

4. Braun worked extensively with the Proceso Gaitán, the official investigation into Gaitán's assassination, housed at the AICPG. The investigation went on for twenty-five years and was only made public in 1978. Reminiscent of the Warren Commission investigation of the assassination of John F. Kennedy, its conclusions are considered suspect by large numbers of Colombians, though as Braun pointed out, while it "never fully established a motive for the crime, few convincing alternative leads were uncovered." He allowed, however, that Roa Sierra may have been egged on by some of Gaitán's enemies (Braun, *Assassination of Gaitán*, 186, note 57).

5. Oquist, *Violence*, 111. His analysis largely excludes the lower classes.

6. The literature on the Violencia has become truly enormous, as studies at the local level are growing exponentially. While this is a welcome trend, it does mean that anything even approaching a rudimentary bibliography would be out of place in this context. A basic picture of the state of the art is provided in Bergquist, Peñaranda, and Sánchez's *Violence in Colombia*.

7. Sánchez, "La Violencia y sus efectos," 10. See also his *Los días de la revolución*.

8. Sánchez, "The Violence," 83.

9. In the introduction to "Genesis and Evolution of *La Violencia*," 1–66, Roldán offered a useful survey of the literature and its evolution.

10. Pécaut, *Orden y violencia*, 1:208.

11. Hobsbawm, "The Revolutionary Situation in Colombia," 249.

12. Schmidt, "La Violencia Revisited," 102–3.

13. Sánchez, "The Violence," 5. For eyewitness testimony, see Arturo Alape, *El Bogotazo*, as well as his *La paz, la violencia*. For a chulavita participant, see Alfonso Hilarión, *Balas de la ley*.

14. This is one of the major themes of Fals Borda, *El presidente Nieto*.

15. And there was some evidence of violent mobilization among costeños. After Bogotá, two of the most significant urban uprisings took place in Barranquilla and in Barrancabermeja, whose population was largely composed of costeños. See Diaz Callejas, *Diez días del poder popular*.

16. Bergquist, *Labor in Latin America*, 359–68; Ortiz Sarmiento, *Estado y subversion*, and "'The Business of the Violence': The Quindío in the 1950s and 1960s," in Bergquist, Peñaranda, and Sánchez, eds., *Violence in Colombia*.

17. Oquist, *Violence*, 237.

18. Pécaut, "Reflexiones sobre el fenómeno de la Violencia," 72.

19. Many students of the Colombian Violencia, however, now tend to see it as merely the first phase of an ongoing, fifty-five year (and counting) process.

20. See Eduardo Pizarro Leongómez, *Las Farc*; Chernick and Jiménez, "Popular Liberalism, Radical Democracy, and Marxism," 61–81.

Bibliography

Archives

Archivo del Centro de Investigación y Educación Popular (CINEP), Bogotá.

Archivo Histórico de Cartagena.

Archivo Histórico de la Fundación Patrimonio Fílmico Colombiano (AFPF), Bogotá.

Archivo del Instituto Colombiano de la Participación "Jorge Eliécer Gaitán" (AICPG), Bogotá. Also known as COLPARTICIPAR (formally Centro Gaitán). Volumes cited: v.0010 "Cartas Bogotá, 1946." v.0011 "Cartas Magdalena." v.0012 "Cartas Atlántico (1946) 1947." v.0013 "Adhesiones Valle." v.0014 "Adhesiones Bogotá." v.0016 "Adhesiones y quejas Antioquia." v.0017 "Adhesiones Magdalena." v.0019 "Adhesiones Boyacá." v.0020 "Cartas Adhesión." v.0021 "Cartas Adhesión." v.0022 "Cartas Adhesión." v.0026 "Cartas Adhesión." v.0032 "Cartas Adhesión." v.0034 "Cartas Bolívar 1946." v.0043 "Cartas Atlántico." v.0044 "Adhesiones y quejas Chocó y Huila." v.0050 "Cartas Nariño." v.0051 "Cartas Tolima-Santander/47." v.0052 "Cartas Tolima." v.0053 "Cartas Bolívar." v.0054 "Cartas Bogotá, 1946." v.0057 "Cartas Santander." v.0059 "Cartas Cundinamarca." v.0060 "Cartas Bolívar." v.0061 "Cartas Bolívar y Nariño." v.0062 "Cartas convención liberal/47." v.0063 "Cartas convención liberal/46." v.0065 "Correspondencia enviada." v.0068 "Correspondencia enviada." v.0069 "Cartas despachadas, tomo I." v.0070 "Cartas despachadas, tomo II." v.0071 "Cartas enviadas." v.0073 "Cartas políticas." v.0074 "Cartas políticas." v.0081 "Cartas dirigidas, 1946." v.0086 "Adhesiones Cundinamarca." v.0088 "Adhesiones y quejas Bolívar." v.0089 "Adhesiones y quejas Sur de Santander." v.0090 "Adhesiones y quejas Cauca." v.0091 "Adhesiones y quejas Atlántico." v.0092 "Adhesiones y quejas Caldas."

Archivo Presidencial de Colombia, General Correspondence 1930–1946, (AP), Bogotá.

Biblioteca Departamental del Atlántico.

Biblioteca Luis-Angel Arango, Bogotá.

Biblioteca Nacional, Bogotá.

National Archives of the United States, Department of State (SD), Records of the Embassy in Bogotá, Barranquilla consular reports (1928–1948), Intelligence reports of the Naval Attaché, and FBI reports on communist activity in Colombia, Washington D.C.

Official Documents

Colombia. Departamento Administrativo Nacional de Estadistica. "Tendencias Electorales, 1935–1968." *Boletín Mensual de Estadistica* 221 (December 1969).

———. Ministerio de Trabajo, Higiene y Previsión Social. *Sentido y Realización de una Política Social: Informe del Jefe de Departamento Nacional del Trabajo, Francisco Posada Zarate.* Bogotá: Imprenta Nacional, 1939.

Interviews

Published

Alape, Arturo. *El Bogotazo: Memorias del olvido.* Bogotá: Editorial Planeta Colombiana, 1983.

———. *La paz, la violencia: Testigos de excepción.* Bogotá: Editorial Planeta Colombiana, 1985.

Arango Z., Carlos. *Forjadores de la revolución colombiana.* Bogotá: Editorial Colombia, 1983.

———. *Sobrevivientes de las Bananeras.* Bogotá: Ecoe Ediciones, (1981) 1985.

"Una voz insurgente: entrevista con Ofelia Uribe de Acosta," by Anabel Torres in *Voces Insurgentes,* ed. Maria Cristina Laverde Toscano and Luz Helena Sánchez Gómez (Bogotá: Editorial Guadalupe, 1986), 23–45.

By the Author

Charris de la Hoz, Saul. Lawyer, B/quilla city councilman, Gaitanista senator from Atlántico in 1947, and later senator for Rojas Penilla's ANAPO party. B/quilla, June 14, 1990.

Cogua Pulido, Helidorio. Small holder in Valle, Gaitanista, and former guide at the Casa Museo Gaitán. Bogotá, May 17, 1990.

Del Vecchio R., Pascual. Organizer in B/quilla, financial consultant to the movement. Bogotá, April 2, 1992.

Molina Rojas, Hector. Worker, PSD member in the 1940s, Gaitanista, and union leader in the 1950s and 1960s. Bogotá, Sept. 20, 1994.

By Mauricio Archila Neira (transcriptions at CINEP)

Ahumada, Cesar. Union leader at Bavaria in Barranquilla, 1936–1938, and later of FEDEPUERTOS and FEDETRAL. Barranquilla, May 19, 1986.

Barandica Troya, Andres. Leader of the Antiqua Federación Textil and of FEDETRAL, Communist party militant until 1947. Barranquilla, April 15, 1986.

Buenahora, Gonzalo. Medical doctor, writer, and Liberal politician in Barrancabermeja until the 1950s. Bogotá, August 31, 1985.

Colorado, Eugenio. Shoemaker, Catholic union member, once director of FANAL and the UTC, president for ten years of "Juventud Obrera Católica." Bogotá, May 6, 1988.

De la Espriella, Alfredo. Director of the Museo Romántico. Barranquilla, June 13, 1986.

De la Hoz, Ramón. Union leader and Liberal. Barranquilla, April 14, 1986.

Egea, Erasmo. Worked for Topical Oil Co. from 1924 to 1935, first president of the USO, Liberal. Barrancabermeja, May 19, 1985.

Galindo, Pedro. Arrived in Barrancabermeja from Cundinamarca in 1927; oil worker, journalist, and Liberal politician. Barrancabermeja, May 18, 1985.

Garcia, Alfonso. Mason and inhabitant of the working-class (and radically Gaitanista) neighborhood of "La Perseverancia" in Bogotá. Bogotá, May 20, 1988.

Hernández, Carlos. Construction worker and municipal employee; Communist militant; Liberal family background, his father idolized Uribe Uribe and Herrera. Bogotá, June 16, 1988.

Hernández Rodríguez, Guillermo. Lawyer; leftist activist; among the founders of the PSR, serving as secretary general; a friend and lifelong admirer of Gaitán. Bogotá, June 22, 1988.

Insignares, Roberto. Worked in construction, director of FEDETRAL. B/quilla, June 14, 1986.

Jiménez, Roque. White-collar employee of Tropical Oil Co. Barrancabermeja, January 15, 1985.

Mateus, Jorge. Oil worker and Communist party militant. Barrancabermeja, September 5, 1985.

Medina, Bernardo. Tailor and Communist party militant. Barranquilla, June 13, 1986.

Moreno, Luis A. Bavaria worker in Duitama, Boyacá, and union leader. Bogotá, March 5, 1988.

Morón, Julio. Bracero, leader of FEDENAL, and Communist party militant until 1947. Barranquilla, October 11, 1986.

Núñez, Rafael. Born in Barrancabermeja in 1912; historian. Barrancabermeja, April 20, 1985.

Torres, José N. Worker for "Cementos Samper," worked in construction and hotels in the Santanders, Boyacá, Tolima, and Valle. Bogotá, June 1, 1988.

Vásquez, Flavio. Liberal merchant. Barrancabermeja, April 22, 1985.

Newspapers and Periodicals

Adelante (Cali), 1937

Ahora (Plato), 1936

Agitación Femenina (Tunja), 1944–46

El Bien Social (Bogotá), 1937

El Combate (Cúcuta), 1944

El Combate (Neiva), 1937
El Correo (Medellín), 1946
Correo del Cauca (Cali), 1937
El Crisol (Cali), 1933–34
El Crisol (Ibagué), 1932
El Debate (Cartagena), 1935
El Deber (Bucaramanga), 1944
La Defensa Social (Bogotá), 1937
El Demócrata (Bucaramanga), 1946
El Diario (Medellín), 1946
Diario de la Costa (Cartagena), 1929, 1937, 1944–45
Diario del Pacífico (Cali), 1946
Diario Nacional (Bogotá), 1929–38
Diario Popular (Bogotá), 1942–46
Ecos del Tetoná (Yalí), 1946
El Empleado (Girardot), 1937
El Escándalo (Santa Marta), 1936
Esfuerzo (Honda), 1937
El Espectador (Bogotá), 1928–48
El Estado (Santa Marta), 1934–48
El Fígaro (Cartagena), 1937–46
El Heraldo (Barranquilla), 1933–48
Jornada (Bogotá), 1944–48
El Liberal (Bogotá), 1940, 1943, 1946
El Liberal (Manizales), 1937
La Lucha (Sincelejo), 1934
El Mitín (Cartagena), 1932, 1935–37
La Nación (Barranquilla), 1929
El Nacional (Barranquilla), 1945
Nosotros (Bogotá), 1937
El Obrero (Barranquilla), 1933, 1935
La Opinión (Ibagué), 1937–46
Orientación Liberal (Popayán), 1937
Oriente (Bucaramanga), 1937
Pluma Libre (Pereira), 1935–39
Por la Unión (Santa Marta), 1937–38
La Prensa (Barranquilla), 1929–48
El Radio (Pasto), 1937, 1946
La Razón (Aracataca), 1933–36
La Razón (Bogotá), 1946
Reconquista (Bogotá), 1947
Relator (Cali), 1934–48
República (Cartagena), 1945

Rumbos (Plato), 1937
El Siglo (1937–48)
El Sindicalista (Cartagena), 1936
El Soviet (Cali), 1935
El Tiempo (Bogotá) 1928–48
Tierra (Bogotá), 1938
Tipos (Bogotá), 1937
La Tribuna (Barranquilla), 1933–38, 1943–44
La Tribuna (Cúcuta), 1944
Tribuna Libre (Cali), 1937
Unión Obrera (Manizales), 1944
Unión y Trabajo (Medellín), 1937
Unirismo (Bogotá), 1934
Vanguardia (Santa Marta), 1943–45
Vanguardia Liberal (Bucaramanga), 1934, 1937, 1946
La Voz del Obrero (Barrancabermeja), 1937
La Voz del Sinú (Montería), 1938–39
La Voz Liberal (Cartago), 1937

Books, Articles, and Unpublished Papers and Theses

Abel, Christopher. *Política, iglesia y partidos en Colombia, 1886–1953*. Bogotá: Universidad Nacional de Colombia, 1987.

Abel, Christopher, and Marco Palacios. "Colombia, 1930–1958." In *The Cambridge History of Latin America*. Ed. Leslie Bethell. Vol. 8. Cambridge: Cambridge University Press, 1991. 587–667.

Acevedo Carmona, Darío. *La mentalidad de las élites sobre la violencia en Colombia: 1936–1949*. Bogotá: El Ancora Editores, 1995.

Acevedo Latorre, Eduardo. *El río grande de la Magdalena*. Bogotá: Banco de la República, 1981.

Aguilera P., Mario, and Renan Vega C. *Ideal democrático y revuelta popular: bosquejo histórico de la mentalidad política popular en Colombia, 1781–1948*. Bogotá: Inst. Maria Cano, 1991.

Almario S., Gustavo. *Historia de los trabajadores petroleros*. Bogotá: CEDETRABAJO, 1984.

Amaya Solano, Estheiman, "*Jornada*: El periódico del pueblo." Thesis, Fundación Escuela Superior Profesional-INPAHU, Bogotá, 1989.

Archila Neira, Mauricio. *Barranquilla y el río*. Bogotá: Ediciones CINEP, 1987.

———. *Cultura e identidad obrera: Colombia 1910–1945*. Bogotá: Ediciones CINEP, 1991.

Arciniegas, Germán. *Entre la libertad y el miedo*. Buenos Aires: Editorial Sudamérica, 1957.

Ayala Diago, César. *Resistencia y oposición al establecimiento del Frente Na-*

cional: Los orígenes de la Alianza Nacional Popular, Colombia 1953–1964. Bogotá: COLCIENCIAS, 1996.

Azula Barrera, Rafael. *De la revolución al orden nuevo: proceso y drama de un pueblo.* Bogotá: Editorial Kelly, 1956.

Bantjes, Adrian A. *As If Jesus Walked on Earth: Cardenismo, Sonora, and the Mexican Revolution.* Wilmington, Delaware: Scholarly Resources, 1998.

Barnhart, Donald S. "Colombian Transport and the Reforms of 1931: An Evaluation." *Hispanic American Historical Review* 38 (1958): 1–23.

Bell Lemus, Gustavo. "Barranquilla 1920–1930." *Huellas* 11 (April 1984): 13–23.

———, ed. *El caribe colombiano: selección de textos históricos.* B/quilla: Uninorte, 1988.

Bergquist, Charles W. *Coffee and Conflict in Colombia, 1886–1910.* Durham: Duke University Press, 1978.

———. "En nombre de la historia: una crítica disciplinaria de *Historia doble de la Costa* de Orlando Fals Borda." *Huellas* 26 (Aug. 1989): 40–56.

———. *Labor in Latin America.* Stanford: Stanford University Press, 1986.

Bergquist, Charles, Ricardo Peñaranda, and Gonzalo Sánchez, eds. *Violencia in Colombia: The Contemporary Crisis in Historical Perspective.* Wilmington, Del.: Scholarly Resources, 1992.

Blanco Núñez, José Maria. *Memorias de un gobernador: El Nueve de Abril de 1948, antes, durante y después.* Barranquilla: n.p., 1968.

Braun, Herbert. *The Assassination of Gaitán: Public Life and Urban Violence in Colombia.* Madison: University of Wisconsin Press, 1985.

Bronner, Stephen Eric. *Socialism Unbound.* New York: Routledge, 1990.

Brungardt, Maurice P. "Mitos históricos y literarios: *La Casa Grande.*" In *De ficciones y realidades: perspectivas sobre literatura e historia colombiana.* Ed. Alvaro Pineda Botero and Raymond Williams. Bogotá: Tercer Mundo Editores, 1989. 63–72.

Buenahora, Gonzalo. *Biografía de una voluntad.* Bogotá: Editorial Minerva, 1948.

———. *Los origenes del gaitanismo.* Bogotá: n.p.

Bushnell, David. *The Making of Modern Colombia: A Nation in Spite of Itself.* Berkeley: University of California Press, 1993.

Bushnell, David, and Neill Macaulay. *The Emergence of Latin America in the Nineteenth Century.* 2nd ed. Oxford: Oxford University Press, 1994.

Campo, Urbano. *La urbanización en Colombia.* Bogotá: Ediciones Suramérica, n.d.

Castrillón R., Alberto. *120 días bajo del terror: la huelga de las bananeras.* 1929. Reprint, Bogotá: Editorial Tupac Amaru, 1974.

Centro Jorge Eliécer Gaitán. *Gaitán y la constituyente del Liberalismo de 1947: Un ejemplo de democracia participativa.* Bogotá: Centro Gaitán, 1984.

Cepeda Samudio, Alvaro. *La casa grande.* Bogotá: El Ancora Editores, 1962.

Chasteen, John Charles. *Heroes on Horseback: A Life and Times of the Last Gaucho Caudillos.* Albuquerque: University of New Mexico Press, 1995.

Chaux, Francisco José. *Homenaje a Gaitán.* Bogotá: Minerva, 1949.

Chernick, Marc W., and Michael F. Jiménez. "Popular Liberalism, Radical Democracy, and Marxism: Leftist Politics in Contemporary Colombia, 1974–1991." In *The Latin American Left: From the Fall of Allende to Perestroika.* Ed. Barry Carr and Steve Ellner. Boulder, Colo.: Westview Press, 1993. 61–81.

Christie, Keith H. "Antioqueño Colonization in Western Colombia: A Reappraisal." *Hispanic American Historical Review* 58:2 (1978): 260–283.

———. *Oligarcas, campesinos y política en Colombia: Aspectos de la historia sociopolítica de la frontera antioqueña.* Bogotá: Universidad Nacional de Colombia, 1986.

Collier, David, ed. *The New Authoritarianism in Latin America.* Princeton: Princeton University Press, 1979.

Conniff, Michael, ed. *Latin American Populism in Comparative Perspective.* Albuquerque: University of New Mexico Press, 1982.

Córdoba, José Maria. *Jorge Eliécer Gaitán: Tribuno popular de Colombia.* Bogotá: n.p.

Corrigan, Philip, and Derek Sayer. *The Great Arch: English State Formation as Cultural Revolution.* Cambridge, Mass.: Basil Blackwell, 1985.

Cortes Vargas, Carlos. *Los sucesos de las bananeras.* 1929. Reprint, Bogotá: Ed. Desarrollo, 1979.

Cranston, Maurice. "Liberalism." In *The Encyclopedia of Philosophy.* Vol. 4. New York: Macmillan, 1967. 458–61.

Crassweller, Robert D. *Perón and the Enigmas of Argentina.* New York: W. W. Norton, 1987.

Daitsman, Andrew L. "The People Shall Be All: Liberal Rebellion and Popular Mobilization in Chile, 1850–1860." Ph.D. diss., University of Wisconsin, Madison, 1995.

Deas, Malcolm. "Algunas notas sobre la historia del caciquismo en Colombia." *Revista de Occidente* 127 (Oct. 1973): 118–40.

———. "Poverty, Civil War and Politics: Ricardo Gaitán Obeso and His Magdalena River Campaign in Colombia, 1885," *Nova Americana* 2 (1979): 263–303.

———. "The Role of the Church, the Army and the Police in Colombian Elections, c. 1850–1930." In *Elections Before Democracy: The History of Elections in Europe and Latin America.* Ed. Eduardo Posada-Carbó. London: Institute of Latin American Studies, University of London, 1996. 163–80.

De Lannoy, Juan Luís. *Estructuras demográficas y sociales de Colombia.* Bogotá: Centro de Investigaciones Sociales, 1961.

Delpar, Helen. "Aspects of Liberal Factionalism in Colombia, 1875–1885," *Hispanic American Historical Review* 51:2 (1971): 250–74.

———. *Red Against Blue: The Liberal Party in Colombian Politics, 1863–1899.* Tuscaloosa: University of Alabama Press, 1981.

Dent, David W. "Oligarchy and Power Structure in Urban Colombia: The Case of Cali." *Journal of Latin American Studies* 6:1 (May 1974): 113–33.

Deutsch, Karl. "Social Mobilization and Political Development." In *Comparative Politics: A Reader.* Ed. Harry Eckstein and David E. Apter. New York: Free Press of Glencoe, 1963. 582–603.

Diaz, Antolin. *Los verdugos del caudillo y de su pueblo.* Bogotá: Editorial ABC, 1948.

Diaz Callejas, Apolinar. *Diez días de poder popular: el 9 de abril 1948 en Barrancabermeja.* Bogotá: Editorial El Labrador, 1988.

Di Tella, Torcuato. "Populism and Reformism in Latin America." In *Obstacles to Change in Latin America.* Ed. Claudio Veliz. Oxford: Oxford University Press, 1965. 40–74.

Dix, Robert H. *The Political Dimensions of Change.* New Haven: Yale University Press, 1967.

———. "Populism: Authoritarian and Democratic." *Latin American Research Review* 20:2 (1985).

Drake, Paul W. *Socialism and Populism in Chile, 1932–1952.* Urbana: University of Illinois Press, 1978.

Dulffer, Jost. "Bonapartism, Fascism and National Socialism." *Journal of Contemporary History* 11 (1976).

Earle, Rebecca A. *Spain and the Independence of Colombia, 1810–1825.* Exeter: University of Exeter Press, 2000.

Fals Borda, Orlando. *Historia doble de la costa: vol. 1, Mompox y Loba.* Bogotá: Carlos Valencia Editores, 1979.

———. *Historia doble de la costa: vol. 2, El presidente Nieto.* Bogotá: Carlos Valencia Editores, 1981.

———. *Historia doble de la costa: vol. 3, Resistencia en el San Jorge.* Bogotá: Carlos Valencia Editores, 1984.

———. *Historia doble de la costa: vol. 4, Retorno a la tierra.* Bogotá: Carlos Valencia Editores, 1986.

Farnsworth-Alvear, Ann. *Dulcinea in the Factory: Myths, Morals, Men, and Women in Colombia's Industrial Experiment, 1905–1960.* Durham: Duke University Press, 2000.

Fernández de Soto, Mario. *Una revolución en Colombia: Jorge Eliécer Gaitán y Mariano Ospina Perez.* Madrid: Ediciones Cultura Hispánica, 1951.

Fischer, Thomas. "Craftsmen, Merchants, and Violence in Colombia: The *Sucesos de Bucaramanga* of 1879." *Itinerario* 20, no. 1 (1996): 79–99.

Franco R., Ramón. *Colombia: geografía superior económica y humana.* Bogotá: Imprenta del Banco de la República, 1952.

French, John D. *The Brazilian Workers' abc: Class Conflict and Alliances in Modern São Paulo.* Chapel Hill: University of North Carolina Press, 1992.

Galbraith, W. O. *Colombia: A General Survey*. London: Oxford University Press, 1966.

Gaitán, Gloria. *Bolívar tuvo un caballo blanco, mi papá un Buick*. Bogotá: Colparticipar, 1998.

———. *La lucha por la tierra en la década del 30*. Bogotá: El Ancora Editores, 1976.

Gaitán, Jorge Eliécer. *Escritos Políticos*. Bogotá: El Ancora Editores, 1985.

———. *Jorge Eliécer Gaitán: Sus mejores escritos*. Bogotá: Círculo de Lectores, 1987.

Galvis Gómez, Carlos. *Porque cayó López*. Bogotá: Editorial ABC, 1946.

García, Antonio. *Gaitán y el problema de la revolución colombiana*. Bogotá: M.S.C., 1955.

García Márquez, Gabriel. *Cien años de soledad*. Madrid: Espasa-Calpe, 1985.

———. *Love in the Time of Cholera*. Trans. Edith Grossman. New York: Penguin Books, 1989.

Germani, Gino. *Política y sociedad en una época de transición*. Buenos Aires: n.p., 1965.

Germani, Gino, Torcuato Di Tella, and Octávio Ianni, eds. *Populismo y contradicciones de clase en Latinoamérica*. México: Ediciones Era, 1973.

Girón Barrios, Jorge Eduardo, ed. *Caudillos y muchedumbres*. Medellín: Discos Fuentes, 1975.

Gómez Aristizábal, Horacio. *Gaitán: enfoque histórico*. Bogotá: Editorial Cosmos, 1975.

Gómez G., Soledad. *Ciudadanía de la mujer colombiana*. Bogotá: Univ. Católica Javeriana, 1946.

Gómez Olaciregui, Aureliano. *Prensa y periodismo en Barranquilla, Siglo XX*. Barranquilla: Ediciones Lallemand Abramuck, 1979.

Graham, Richard. *Patronage and Politics in Nineteenth-Century Brazil*. Stanford: Stanford University Press, 1990.

Gramsci, Antonio. *Selections from the Prison Notebooks*. Ed. and trans. Quinten Hoare and Geoffrey Nowell Smith. London: Lawrence and Wishart, 1971.

Gray, John. *Liberalism*. Concepts of Social Thought Series. Minneapolis: University of Minnesota Press, 1986.

Green, W. John. "'Días de emoción espectacular:' Choque cultural, intriga política y la huelga de choferes de Bogotá en 1937." *Historia Crítica* no. 24 (July–Dec. 2002): 27–47.

———. "Guilt by Association: Jorge Eliécer Gaitán and the Legacy of his Studies in 'Fascist' Italy." In *Strange Pilgrimages: Travel, Exile, and National Identity in Latin America, 1800–1990s*. Ed. Ingrid Fey and Karen Racine. Wilmington: Scholarly Resources, 2000. 179–92.

———. "Left Liberalism and Race in the Evolution of Colombian Popular National Identity." *The Americas* 57:1 (July 2000): 95–124.

———. "Mujeres radicales, el voto y la participación femenina en la política gaitanista." *Anuario Colombiano de la Historia Social y de la Cultura* (1996): 161–70.

———. "Popular Mobilization in Colombia: The Social Composition, Ideology, and Political Practice of Gaitanismo on the Atlantic Coast and Magdalena River, 1928–1948." Ph.D. diss., University of Texas at Austin, 1994.

———. "Sibling Rivalry on the Left and Labor Struggles in Colombia during the 1940s." *Latin American Research Review* 35:1 (2000): 85–117.

———. "'Vibrations of the Collective': The Popular Ideology of Gaitanismo on Colombia's Atlantic Coast, 1944–1948." *Hispanic American Historical Review* 76:2 (1996): 283–311.

Guha, Ranajit, and Gayatri Chakravorty Spivak, eds. *Selected Subaltern Studies.* New York: Oxford University Press, 1988.

Gutiérrez, José. *La rebeldía colombiana.* Bogotá: Ediciones Tercer Mundo, 1962.

Gutiérrez Sanín, Francisco. *Curso y discurso del movimiento plebeyo: 1849–1854.* Bogotá: Instituto de Estudios Políticos y Relaciones Internacionales—El Ancora Editores, 1995.

Hamnett, Brain R. "Liberalism Divided: Regional Politics and the National Project During the Mexican Restored Republic, 1867–1876." *Hispanic American Historical Review* 76:4 (1996): 659–89.

Helg, Aline. *La educación en Colombia, 1918–1957: Una historia social, económica y política.* Bogotá: Fondo Editorial CEREC, 1987.

Helguera, J. Leon. "The Problem of Liberalism versus Conservatism in Colombia: 1849–1885." In *Latin American History: Select Problems.* Ed. Frederick B. Pike. New York: Harcourt, Brace and World, 1969. 223–58.

Henao H., Javier. *Uribe Uribe y Gaitán: caudillos del pueblo.* Medellín: Editorial Bedout, 1986.

Henderson, James D. *Conservative Thought in Twentieth-Century Latin America: The Ideas of Laureano Gómez.* Latin America Series, no. 13. Athens: Ohio University Monographs in International Studies, 1988.

———. *When Colombia Bled: A History of the Violencia in Tolima.* Tuscaloosa: University of Alabama Press, 1985.

Herrera Soto, Roberto, and Rafael Romero Castañeda. *La zona bananera del Magdalena: Historia y lexico.* Bogota: Caro y Cuervo, 1979.

Hilarión, Alfonso. *Balas de la ley.* Bogotá: Editorial Santafé, 1953.

Hobhouse, Leonard T. *Liberalism.* New York: Oxford University Press, 1964.

Hobsbawm, Eric. *The Age of Extremes: A History of the World, 1914–1991.* New York: Pantheon Books, 1994.

———. *Revolutionaries: Contemporary Essays.* New York: Pantheon Books, 1973.

———. "The Revolutionary Situation in Colombia." *The World Today* 19 (1963): 248–58.

———. *Workers: Worlds of Labor.* New York: Pantheon Books, 1984.

James, Daniel. *Resistance and Integration*. Cambridge: Cambridge University Press, 1988.

Jaramillo, Carlos Eduardo. *Los guerrilleros del novecientos*. Bogotá: Editorial CEREC, 1991.

Jaramillo Uribe, Jaime. *Ensayos sobre historia social de Colombia*. Bogotá: Universidad Nacional de Colombia, 1968.

——. *La personalidad histórica de Colombia y otros ensayos*. Bogotá: El Ancora Editores, [1977] 1994.

Jay, Martin. *The Dialectical Imagination: A History of the Frankfurt School and the Institute of Social Research, 1923–1950*. Boston: Little, Brown, 1973.

Jiménez, Michael F. "The Limits of Export Capitalism: Economic Structure, Class, and Politics in a Colombian Coffee Municipality, 1900–1930," Ph.D. diss., Harvard University, 1985.

Johnson, David Church. *Santander, siglo XIX: Cambios socioeconómicos*. Bogotá: Carlos Valencia Editores, 1984.

Joseph, Gilbert M., and Daniel Nugent, eds. *Everyday Forms of State Formation: Revolution and the Negotiation of Rule in Modern Mexico*. Durham: Duke University Press, 1994.

Katz, Friedrich. *The Life and Times of Pancho Villa*. Stanford: Stanford University Press, 1998.

Kaufman, Robert R. "The Patron-Client Concept in Macro-Politics: Prospects and Problems." *Comparative Studies in Society and History* 16:3 (June 1974): 285–308.

Kazin, Michael. *The Populist Persuasion: An American History*. New York: BasicBooks, 1995.

Kershaw, Ian. *The Nazi Dictatorship: Problems and Perspectives of Interpretation*. London: Edward Arnold, [1985] 1989.

Knight, Alan. *The Mexican Revolution: Counter-Revolution and Reconstruction*. Cambridge: Cambridge University Press, 1986.

——. *The Mexican Revolution: Porfirians, Liberals, and Peasants*. Cambridge: Cambridge University Press, 1986.

——. "Populism and Neo-populism in Latin America, especially Mexico." *Journal of Latin American Studies* 30:2 (1998): 223–48.

——. "Racism, Revolution, and *Indigenismo*: Mexico, 1910–1940." In *The Idea of Race in Latin America, 1870–1940*. Ed. Richard Graham. Austin: University of Texas Press, 1990. 71–113.

——. "Weapons and Arches in the Mexican Revolutionary Landscape." In *Everyday Forms of State Formation: Revolution and the Negotiation of Rule in Modern Mexico*. Ed. Gilbert M. Joseph and Daniel Nugent. Durham: Duke University Press, 1994. 24–66.

Laclau, Ernesto. *Politics and Ideology in Marxist Theory*. London: Verso, 1977.

Lanao Loaiza, Juan Ramón. *Mirando las izquierdas*. Manizales: Editorial Arturo Zapata, 1935.

Laqueur, Walter, ed. *Fascism, A Reader's Guide: Analyses, Interpretations, Bibliography.* Berkeley: University of California Press, 1976.

LeGrand, Catherine. *Frontier Expansion and Peasant Protest in Colombia, 1830–1936.* Albuquerque: University of New Mexico Press, 1986.

León, Magdalena, ed. *La realidad colombiana, vol. 1: Debate sobre la mujer en América Latina y el Caribe.* Bogotá: ACEP, 1982.

Linares U., Heliodorio. "Helius." In *Yo ACUSO: biografía de Gaitán y Fajardo. Diez años después 1948–9 de Abril 1959.* Bogotá: Editorial Iqueima, 1959.

Lleras Restrepo, Carlos. *El liberalismo colombiano.* Bogotá: Tercer Mundo, 1972.

Londoño, Patricia. "Las publicaciones periódicas dirigidas a la mujer, 1858–1930." *Boletín Cultural y Bibliográfico* 27:23 (1990): 3–23.

Long, Gary. "The Dragon Finally Came: Industrial Capitalism, Radical Artisans and the Liberal Party in Colombia, 1910–1948." Ph.D. diss., University of Pittsburgh, 1995.

———. "Popular Liberalism and Civil War in Nineteenth-Century Colombia: Historical Roots of Labor's Radical Ideology in the Twentieth Century." Paper presented at the XIV Latin American Labor History Conference, Duke University, May 3, 1997.

López, Alejandro. *Idearium liberal.* París: Ediciones La Antorcha, 1931.

López Giraldo, Fermín. *El Apóstol Desnudo, o dos años al lado de un mito.* Manizales: Editorial Arturo Zapata, 1936.

López de Mesa, Luís. "El hombre." In *Colombia en cifras.* Bogotá: Imprenta Nacional, 1945–46.

López P., Abel Ricardo. "We Have Everything and We Have Nothing: Empleados and Middle-Class Identities in Bogotá, Colombia, 1930–1955," M.A. thesis, Virginia Tech University, 2001.

López Pumarejo, Alfonso. *La reintegración liberal.* Bogotá: Editorial Cromos, 1941.

Lozano y Lozano, Carlos. *Ideario del liberalismo actual.* Bogotá: Imprenta Nacional, 1939.

Luna, Lola, and Norma Villarreal. *Historia, género y política—Movimientos de mujeres y participación política en Colombia, 1930–1991.* Barcelona: CICYT, 1994.

Mallon, Florencia E. *The Defense of Community in Peru's Central Highlands: Peasant Struggle and Capitalist Transition, 1860–1940.* Princeton: Princeton University Press, 1983.

———. *Peasant and Nation: The Making of Postcolonial Mexico and Peru.* Berkeley: University of California Press, 1995.

———. "The Promise and Dilemma of Subaltern Studies: Perspectives from Latin American History," *American Historical Review* 99:5 (1994): 1491–1515.

Manent, Pierre. *An Intellectual History of Liberalism.* Trans. Rebecca Balinski. Princeton: Princeton University Press, 1995.

Manrique, Ramón. *Bajo el signo de la hoz.* Bogotá: Editorial ABC, 1937.

———. *A sangre y fuego: un dramático reportaje del 9 de abril en todo Colombia.* Barranquilla: Librería Nacional, 1948.

Marulanda, Elsy. *Colonización y conflicto: las lecciones del Sumapaz.* Bogotá: Ediciones CINEP, 1990.

Medina, Medófilo. *Historia del Partido Comunista.* Bogotá: Ediciones CEIS, 1980.

———. *Juegos de rebeldía: La trayectoría política de Saúl Charrís de la Hoz (1914–).* Bogotá: CINDEC, Universidad Nacional, 1997.

———. *La protesta urbana en Colombia en el siglo XX.* Bogotá: Ediciones Aurora, 1984.

———. "Los terceros partidos en Colombia." *Estudios Marxistas* 18 (Sept.–Dec. 1979): 3–31.

Mendoza Neira, Pulinio, and Alberto Camacho Angarita, eds. *El Liberalismo en el gobierno, 1930–1946: tomo 1, sus hombres, sus ideas, su obra.* Bogotá: Editorial Minerva, 1946.

———. *El Liberalismo en el gobierno, 1930–1946: tomo 2, sus realizaciones.* Bogotá: Editorial Minerva, 1946.

Molina, Gerardo. *Las ideas liberales en Colombia, tomo 1, 1849–1914.* Bogotá: Tercer Mundo, 1988.

———. *Las ideas liberales en Colombia, tomo 2, 1915–1934.* Bogotá: Tercer Mundo, 1989.

———. *Las ideas liberales en Colombia, tomo 3, 1935 al Frente Nacional.* Bogotá: Tercer Mundo, 1989.

———. *Las ideas socialistas en Colombia.* 3rd ed. Bogotá: Tercer Mundo Editores, 1988.

Moore, Barrington. *The Social Origins of Dictatorship and Democracy: Lord and Peasant in the Making of the Modern World.* Boston: Beacon Press, 1966.

Morales Benítez, Otto. *El pensamiento social de Uribe Uribe.* Medellín: Ediciones Especiales Sec. de Educación y Cultura de Antioquia, 1988.

Moreno, David. *Trayectoría del pensamiento político de Gaitán.* Bogotá: Centro Gaitán, 1983.

Nicholes, Theodore E. *Tres puertos de Colombia: Estudio sobre el desarrollo de Cartagena, Santa Marta y Barranquilla.* Bogotá: Banco Popular, 1973.

Nieto Rojas, J. M. *La batalla contra el comunismo en Colombia.* Bogotá: Empresa Nacional, 1956.

Nugent, Daniel, ed. *Rural Revolt in Mexico: U.S. Intervention and the Domain of Subaltern Politics.* 2nd ed. Durham: Duke University Press, 1998.

Ocampo López, Javier. *Historia básica de Colombia.* Bogotá: Plaza and Janes, Editores Colombia Ltd., 1984.

Oquist, Paul. *Violence, Conflict, and Politics in Colombia.* New York: Academic Press, 1980.

Ortíz Márquez, Julio. *El hombre que fue un pueblo.* Bogotá: Carlos Valencia Editores, 1978.

Ortiz Sarmiento, Carlos Miguel. *Estado y subversión en Colombia: La violencia en el Quindío años 50*. Bogotá: Editorial CEREC, 1985.

Orwell, George. *The Road to Wigan Pier*. London: Left Book Club, 1937.

Osorio Lizarazo, José Antonio. *El día del odio*. 1959. Reprint, Bogotá: Carlos Valencia Editores, 1979.

———. *Gaitán: vida, muerte y permanente presencia*. 1952. Reprint, Bogotá: Carlos Valencia Editor, 1982.

———. *Ideas de izquierda: liberalismo, partido revolucionario*. n.p., 1935.

Owensby, Brian. *Intimate Ironies: Modernity and the Making of Middle-Class Lives in Brazil*. Stanford: Stanford University Press, 1999.

Pacheco G., Margarita. *La fiesta liberal en Cali*. Cali: Ediciones Universidad del Valle, 1992.

Palacios, Marco. *El café en Colombia, 1850–1970: Una historia económica, social y política*. Mexico City: El Ancora Editores, 1979.

———. *Entre la legitimidad y la violencia: Colombia, 1875–1994*. Bogotá: Editorial Norma, 1995.

Pan American Union. "Colombia in Brief." Washington D.C.: Pan American Union, 1945.

Parker, D. S. *The Idea of the Middle Class: White-Collar Workers and Peruvian Society, 1900–1950*. University Park: Pennsylvania State University Press, 1998.

Parsons, James. *Antioqueño Colonization in Western Colombia*. Berkeley: University of California Press, 1949.

Pécaut, Daniel. *Orden y violencia: Colombia 1930–1954*. 2 vols. Bogotá: Ediciones Tercer Mundo, 1987.

———. *Política y sindicalismo en Colombia*. Bogotá: Editorial "La Carreta," 1973.

———. "Reflexiones sobre el fenómeno de la Violencia." *Ideología y Sociedad* 19 (1976): 71–79.

Pelaez, Gabriela. *La condición social de la mujer en Colombia*. Bogotá: Editorial Cromos, 1944.

Peña, Luís David. *Gaitán íntimo*. Bogotá: Editorial Iqueima, 1948.

Phelan, John Leddy. *The People and the King: The Comunero Revolution in Colombia, 1781*. Madison: University of Wisconsin Press, 1978.

Pizarro Leongómez, Eduardo. *Las Farc: De la autodefensa a la combinación de todas las formas de lucha*. Bogotá: Tercer Mundo Editores, 1991.

Posada-Carbó, Eduardo. *El Caribe Colombiano: Una historia regional, 1870–1950*. Bogotá: Banco de la República/El Ancora Editores, 1998.

———. "La economía del caribe colombiano a comienzos del siglo: 1900–1930." *Estudios Sociales* 2 (May 1988): 69–104.

———. "Fiction as History: The *bananeras* and Gabriel García Márquez's *One Hundred Years of Solitude*." *Journal of Latin American Studies* 30:2 (1998): 395–414.

———. "Identidad y conflicto en la formación de la regionalidad, 1900–1930." *Huellas* 3 (Sept. 1982): 4–13.

———. *Una invitación a la historia de Barranquilla.* Bogotá: Editorial CEREC, 1987.

———. "Limits of Power: Elections Under the Conservative Hegemony in Colombia, 1886–1930." *Hispanic American Historical Review* 77:2 (1997): 245–79.

———. "Notas para una historia de la costa atlántica: Identidad y conflicto en la formación de la regionalidad, 1900–1930," *Huellas* 3:7 (September 1982): 4–13.

Posada-Carbó, Eduardo, ed. *Elections Before Democracy: The History of Elections in Europe and Latin America.* London: Institute of Latin American Studies, University of London, 1996.

Puentes, Milton. *Gaitán.* Bogotá: Editorial ABC, 1945.

———. *Historia del partido liberal colombiano.* 2nd ed. Bogotá: Editorial Prag, 1961.

Ramón, Justo. "El río de la patria," *Organo de la Contraloría de la República* 6, 7 (1944).

Rausch, Jane M. *Colombia: Territorial Rule and the Llanos Frontier.* Gainesville: University Press of Florida, 1999.

———. "Diego Luis Córdoba and the Emergence of Afro-Colombian Identity in the Mid-Twentieth Century." *Journal of the Southeastern Council on Latin American Studies* 32 (November 2000): 51–65.

Ribeiro, Darcy. *The Americas and Civilization.* New York: E. P. Dutton, 1971.

Richardson, Miles. *San Pedro, Colombia: Small Town in a Developing Society.* New York: Holt, Rinehart and Winston, 1970.

Robinson, J. Cordell. *El movimiento gaitanista en Colombia.* Bogotá: Ediciones Tercer Mundo, 1976.

de Rodriquez, Cecilia. *La costa atlántica: algunos aspectos socio-económicos de su desarrollo.* Bogotá: Fundación para la Educación Superior y el Desarrollo, 1973.

Rodríguez, Gustavo H. *Benjamín Herrera en la guerra y en la paz.* Bogotá: Universidad Libre, 1973.

Rodríguez Garavito, Agustín. *Gabriel Turbay: un solitario de la grandeza.* Bogotá: Ediciones Tercer Mundo, 1977.

Roldán, Mary Jean. "Genesis and Evolution of *La Violencia* in Antioquia, Colombia (1900–1953)." Ph.D. diss., Harvard University, 1992.

Roseberry, William. "Hegemony and the Language of Contention." In *Everyday Forms of State Formation: Revolution and the Negotiation of Rule in Modern Mexico.* Ed. Gilbert M. Joseph and Daniel Nugent. Durham: Duke University Press, 1994. 355–66.

Rothlisberger, Dora F. "Liberal Reform in Colombia: Alfonso López Pumarejo, 1934–1938," M.A. thesis, Columbia College, George Washington University, 1967.

Sáenz Rovner, Eduardo. *La Ofensiva Empresarial: Industriales, políticos y violencia en los años 40 en Colombia*. Bogotá: Tercer Mundo Editores, 1992.

Safford, Frank. "Race, Integration, and Progress: Elite Attitudes and the Indian in Colombia, 1750–1870." *Hispanic American Historical Review* 71:1 (1991): 1–33.

———. "Social Aspects of Politics in Nineteenth-Century Spanish America: New Granada, 1825–1850." *Journal of Social History* 5 (1972): 344–70.

Sánchez, Gonzalo. *Los días de la revolución: Gaitanismo y 9 de abril en provincia*. Bogotá: Centro Gaitán, 1983.

———. "The Violence: An Interpretive Synthesis." In *Violence in Colombia: The Contemporary Crisis in Historical Perspective*. Ed. Charles Bergquist, Ricardo Peñaranda, and Gonzalo Sánchez. Wilmington, Del.: Scholarly Resources, 1992. 75–124.

———. "La Violencia y sus efectos en el sistema político colombiano." *Cuadernos Colombianos* 9 (Jan.–April 1976): 1–44.

Sánchez, Gonzalo, and Donny Meertens. *Bandoleros, Gamonales y Campesinos*. Bogotá: El Ancora Editores, 1983.

———. "La Violencia, el estado y las clases sociales." *Anuario de Historia Social y de la Cultura* 10 (1982), 253–58.

Santa, Eduardo. *El pensamiento político de Rafael Uribe Uribe*. Bogotá: Tercer Mundo, 1980.

———. *Rafael Uribe Uribe: El caudillo de la esperanza*. Bogotá: Editorial Iqueima, 1962.

———. *Sociología de Colombia*. Bogotá: Editorial Iqueima, 1955.

Santos, Eduardo. *Las etapas de la vida colombiana: discursos y mensajes, 1938–1942*. Bogotá: Imprenta Nacional, 1946.

———. *Una política liberal para Colombia*. Bogotá: Editorial Minerva, 1937.

Schmidt, Steffen W. "La Violencia Revisited: The Clientelist Bases of Political Violence in Colombia." *Journal of Latin American Studies* 6 (1974): 97–111.

Scott, James C. *Domination and the Arts of Resistance: Hidden Transcripts*. New Haven: Yale University Press, 1990.

———. Foreword to *Everyday Forms of State Formation: Revolution and the Negotiation of Rule in Modern Mexico*. Ed. Gilbert M. Joseph and Daniel Nugent. Durham: Duke University Press, 1994. vii–xii.

———. *The Moral Economy of the Peasant: Rebellion and Subsistence in Southeast Asia*. New Haven: Yale University Press, 1976.

———. *Weapons of the Weak: Everyday Forms of Peasant Resistance*. New Haven: Yale University Press, 1985.

Sharpless, Richard. *Gaitán of Colombia: A Political Biography*. Pittsburgh: University of Pittsburgh Press, 1978.

Smith, T. Lynn. "The Racial Composition of the Population of Colombia." *Journal of Inter-American Studies* 8:2 (1966): 213–35.

Solano, Armando. Prologue to *Caudillos liberales*. Bogotá: Ediciones Antena, 1936.

Sowell, David. *The Early Colombian Labor Movement: Artisans and Politics in Bogotá, 1832–1919.* Philadelphia: Temple University Press, 1992.

Stein, Steve. *Populism in Peru: The Emergence of the Masses and the Politics of Social Control.* Madison: University of Wisconsin Press, 1980.

Stoller, Richard. "Alfonso López Pumarejo and Liberal Radicalism in 1930s Colombia." *Journal of Latin American Studies* 27 (1995): 367–97.

———. "Liberalism and Conflict in Socorro, Colombia, 1830–1870." Ph.D. diss., Duke University, 1991.

Tirado, Thomas C. *Alfonso López Pumarejo el conciliador: su contribución a la paz política en Colombia.* Bogotá: Editorial Planeta Colombiana, 1986.

Tirado Mejía, Alvaro. *Aspectos políticos del primer gobierno de Alfonso López Pumarejo, 1934–1938.* Bogotá: Instituto Colombiano de Cultura, 1981.

———. *Aspectos sociales de las guerras civiles en Colombia.* Bogotá: Biblioteca Básica Colombia, 1976.

———. *El Estado y la política en el siglo XIX.* Bogotá: El Ancora Editores, [1978] 1983.

———, ed. *Estado y Economía: 50 años de la reforma del 36.* Bogotá: Contraloría General de la República, 1986.

Thomson, Guy P. C. "Popular Aspects of Liberalism in Mexico, 1848–1888." *Bulletin of Latin American Research* 10:3 (1991): 265–92.

Torres, Mauricio. *La naturaleza de la revolución colombiana.* Bogotá: Editorial Iqueima, 1959.

Torres, Mauro. *Gaitán: grandeza y limitaciones psicológicas.* Bogotá: Ediciones Tercer Mundo, 1976.

Torres Giraldo, Ignacio. *Los inconformes: historia de la rebeldía de las masas en Colombia.* Vols. 4 and 5. Bogotá: Editorial Latina, 1967.

Urrutia, Miguel. *The Development of the Colombian Labor Movement.* New Haven: Yale University Press, 1969.

Valencia, Luís Emiro, ed. *Gaitán: Antología de su pensamiento social y económico.* Bogotá: Ediciones Suramérica, 1968.

Vasconcelos, José. *La raza cósmica, misión de la raza iberoamericana.* Paris: Agencia Mundial de Librería, 1925.

Vega Cantor, Renan. *Crisis y caída de la República Liberal.* Ibagué: Editorial Mohan, 1988.

Velásquez Toro, Magdala. "Condición jurídica y social de la mujer." In *Nueva historia de Colombia, Vol. 4: Educación y ciencia, luchas de la mujer, vida diaria.* Dir. Alvaro Tirado Mejía. Bogotá: Planeta Colombiana Editorial, 1989.

Verdugo y Oquendo, Andrés. "Informe sobre el estado social y económico de la población indígena, blanca y mestiza de las provincias de Tunja y Vélez a mediados del siglo XVIII." *Anuario Colombiano de Historia Social y de la Cultura* 1, no. 1 (1963).

Vergara y Velasco, F. J. *Nueva geografía de Colombia.* Vol. 3. Bogotá: Publicaciones del Banco de la República, 1974.

Villaveces, Jorge, ed. *Los mejores discursos de Gaitán*. Bogotá: Editorial Jorvi, 1968.

Wade, Peter. *Blackness and Race Mixture: The Dynamics of Racial Identity in Colombia*. Baltimore: Johns Hopkins University Press, 1993.

Weffort, Francisco Correa. *O populismo na politica brasileira*. Rio de Janeiro: Paz e Terra, 1978.

Weiss, Anita. *Tendencias de la participación electoral en Colombia, 1935–1966*. Bogotá: Universidad Nacional, 1968.

White, Judith. *Historia de una ignominia: la United Fruit Co. en Colombia*. Bogotá: Editorial Presencia, 1978.

Wolfe, Joel. *Working Women, Working Men: São Paulo and the Rise of Brazil's Industrial Working Class, 1900–1955*. Durham: Duke University Press, 1993.

Yúnis, José, and Carlos Nicolas Hernández. *Barrancabermeja: nacimiento de la clase obrera*. Bogotá: Editores Tres Culturas, 1986.

Zuleta Angel, Eduardo. *El presidente López Pumarejo*. Bogotá: Ediciones Gamma, 1966.

Index

Note: *Italicized page numbers indicate photos and illustrations.*

Abel, Christopher, 171, 273n.31, 308n.66
Acción Colombianista, 244–45
Acción Democrática (of Chocó). *See* Córdoba, Diego Luís
Acción Democrática (of Venezuela), 11
Acción Liberal, 283n.7
Adorno, Theodor, 272n.15
Africa, 119
agency (and resistance), 4–5, 15, 32–33, 204, 272n.21. *See also* Gaitanismo; hegemony; liberalism; popular mobilization
Agitación Femenina (Tunja), 114–16, 225–26; cover illustration of, *146*
Aguilera Peña, Mario, 273–74n.31
Alarcón, 314–15n.204
Alarcón, Agustín, 198
Amador, Heriberto, 79
Amarís, Asdrubal, 130, 216, 238
Amarís, Julio, 216
Anapoima, 134
anarchism, 28
Andean Colombia (highlands), 16, 18
Andrés, 182
Angel, Bernardo, 186, 314–15n.216
antioqueño colonization, 16–17, 119
Antioquia, department of, 16, 19, 80,120, 139, 172, 174, 176, 181–82, 186, 212, 246, 276n.46, 297n.27, 310n.111, 314–15n.216
El Apóstol Desnudo, 83. *See also* López Giraldo, Fermín
Aracataca, 68, 88
Arango Vélez, Carlos, 49, 72
Araújo, Alfonso, *158*

Araújo, Simón, 47
Archila, Mauricio, 25, 133–34, 142, 208, 273n.31, 283n.3, 288n.29, 289n.41; *Cultura e identidad obrera*, 134
Argentina, 7–8, 54, 71, 135, 322n.120
Arias, Carlos, 242
Armenia, 75, 89, 104
Arnold, Matthew, 28
artisans, 19, 24–25, 29–33, 123–24, 126, 128–29, 133–36, 142, 179, 217
Asociación Nacional de Choferes, 98, 108
Atlantic coast, 16–19, 27, 80, 96, 105, 116, 120, 141, 165, 185, 195, 216, 231, 235–36, 266
Atlántico, department of, 19, 95, 107, 123, 133, 140, 165–66, 174, 183, 186, 188, 194–97, 199–200, 214, 217, 223–24, 237, 245, 247, 297n.27, 324n.26
Austria, 126
Avanti, 49
Avenida Jiménez, 261
Ayala Diago, César, 276n.46
Azuero, Vicente, 161
Azula Barrera, Rafael, 226

Balcázar, Pablo, 80
banana workers' strike of 1928, 72, 79–80, 130; compared to the banana workers' strike of 1934, 88–89; Gaitán's role in the aftermath of, 60–62; Gaitán's role remembered, 65, 110, 124, 133, 141; strike and massacre described, 26. *See also* Gaitán, Jorge Eliécer
las bananeras. *See* banana workers' strike of 1928

Bantjes, Adrian, 7
Barrancabermeja, 42, 61, 91, 122, 130,
    139–40, 208, 242, 262, 275n.15,
    292n.87, 330n.15
Barranquilla, 18–19, 62–63, 69–70, 76,
    80, 83, 87, 89, 93–95, 97, 99, 103,
    105–9, 116, 130–31, 134, 138–40, 168,
    170, 173, 185–89, 193, 195–201, 205,
    210–13, 216–17, 219–20, 223–24, 227,
    229–31, 238–39, 242, 246, 262,
    275nn.14, 19, 22, 289n.54, 290n.55,
    296n.158, 311–12n.156, 330n.15
Barrios, Juan, 249
Bavaria Brewery, 99
Bentham, Jeremy, 40
Bergquist, Charles, 16–17, 33, 66, 125,
    135, 176, 207, 213, 266, 273–74n.31,
    274n.8, 283n.4, 289n.41, 316n.16; La-
    bor in Latin America, 134, 208
Betancourt, Bernardo, 314–15n.216
Bismarck, Otto von, 53
Blanc, Louis, 30
Blanco de la Rosa, Rafael, 195–96
Blanco Núñez, José María, 140, 194, 197,
    200, 246, 324n.26, 325n.52
Bocas de Ceniza, 275n.19
Bogotá, 1, 16, 18–20, 22, 24, 30, 35–38,
    40, 44, 46–48, 61–64, 70–71, 75, 79–
    81, 83, 93, 96–97, 99–102, 107–9, 116,
    124, 131–34, 136–39, 163, 169, 173,
    176, 180, 185, 188–90, 195, 197, 214–
    16, 235, 239–40, 257, 260, 262,
    275n.22, 290n.69, 291n.73, 296n.1,
    301n.118, 314–15n.216, 328n.116,
    330n.15
Bogotazo, 262
Bolívar, department of, 19, 69, 122, 174,
    183–84, 187, 189, 192, 194, 203, 207,
    224–25, 228, 230–31, 242, 247,
    297n.27, 319–20n.74, 324n.26
Bolívar, Simón, 21, 161, 207
Bolsheviks, 38
Bonaparte, Napoleon, 34
boss politics. See electoral politics;
    gamonalismo
Boyacá, department of, 19, 48, 114, 134,
    140, 219, 234, 255–56, 266, 276n.46,
    300n.95
Braun, Herbert (Tico), 36, 50, 56–58, 65,
    86, 121, 124, 128–29, 133, 135, 188,
    211, 240, 261, 273n.30, 277n.53,
    302n.138, 305n.2, 306n.25, 316–
    17nn.22, 30, 319n.64, 325n.41, 329n.4
Brazil, 7–8, 16, 135, 178, 273n.28,
    296n.7, 300n.87, 301n.118
Britain, 28, 41, 107, 126, 300n.91
British Liberal party: Manchester School
    of, 28. See also liberalism
Bronacelli, Slavador, 282n.49
Bronner, Stephen, 316–17n.22
Brungardt, Maurice, 282n.46
Bucaramanga, 39, 67, 162, 166, 170–71,
    185, 187, 223, 277n.69
Buenahora, Gonzalo, 122, 206, 209, 214
Buenaventura, 129
Buendía, (Colonel) Aureliano, 22
Buenos Aires, 296n.8
Buga, 30
Bushnell, David, 26, 128, 273–74n.31

cachacos, 16, 121, 274n.2
cacique. See gamonalismo
caciquismo. See gamonalismo
Caldas, department of, 16, 19, 48, 80, 89,
    162, 163, 191–92, 254, 256, 266
Cali, 16, 19, 30, 40, 43–44, 63, 67–68, 81,
    93, 99, 119–21, 131, 133, 137, 139,
    173, 193, 262, 275n.22
Calibán (Enrique Santos), 101–2, 115,
    129, 131, 166, 234, 240
Cano, María, 61, 114
capitalism, 10, 38, 41, 52, 57–59, 221–24,
    229, 267, 322n.120
Caquetá, 208
Cárdenas, Lázaro, 7, 46, 107
Cardenismo, 7, 11
Caribbean coast. See Atlantic coast
El Carmen, 186
Caro, Miguel Antonio, 274n.32
Carrasquilla, Bernardo, 254
Carrera Séptima, 261
Carsten, Francis L., 280–81n.16

Cartagena, 16, 22, 30, 34, 68–69, 77, 80, 91, 105, 109, 114, 116, 120–23, 130–32, 134, 138, 170, 185–86, 189, 193–94, 207, 211–15, 219–20, 224, 226–29, 241–42, 262
Cartago, 41, 138
Castrillón, Alberto, 61
Castro, Fidel, 260
Castro Monsalvo, Pedro, 249–50
Catholic Church, 22–23, 28, 91, 94, 113, 139–40, 172, 177, 179, 315–16n.7
Cauca, department of, 67, 120–21, 174, 226, 276n.46
Cauca Valley, 16, 18, 27; called the Gran Cauca, 17
caudillo. See caudillismo
caudillismo: in Colombian political development, 175; and relationship to populists (as leaders), 2, 271n.3; and Simón Bolívar as the quintessential caudillo, 21. See also Gaitán, Jorge Eliécer; Gaitanismo; gamonalismo; populism
center-east (also called the Upper Magdalena), 16–17, 27
Cepeda Samudio, Álvaro: La casa grande, 60
Certain, Gerardo, 198–99
Cervantes Núñez, Carlos, 198
Charris de la Hoz, Saúl, 197, 314n.207
Chasteen, John, 271–72n.3
Chaux, Francisco, 220
Chile, 29, 71, 126
Chinchiná, 83, 192
Chiquinquirá, 179, 255
El Chocó, department of, 120–21, 238
Christ, Jesus, 31, 38, 231, 313n.187
Christe, Keith, 17, 176
chulavitas, 266
Churchill, Winston Leonard Spencer, 93
Ciénaga, 26, 72, 110, 140, 184, 228, 249
Circo de Santamaría, 169, 240
civil wars, 2, 14, 21–24, 33, 41, 237, 262–63, 269
coffee, 16–17, 24–25, 66, 72–73, 78, 81, 86, 94, 135, 266
Cogua Pulido, Heliodoro, 204–5, 282n.58

Colegio Araúo, 47
Colegio Martín Restrepo Mejía, 47
collectivist liberalism. See liberalism
Collier, David, 272n.4
Colombian Communists: activities of, covered in the left-Liberal press, 216; agenda of, highjacked by the Liberal party, 85, 92; alliances of, with UNIR, 83; characterization by, of Gaitán as a fascist and Gaitanismo as fascism, 167–68, 173, 241; on the city council of B/quilla, 188, 197; close ties of, to the Liberal establishment, 163, 167, 326n.70; compared to UNIR, 71, 283n.3; co-opted by López Pumarejo and the Revolución en Marcha, 85, 92, 95, 107; continued loathing of Gaitán after 1946 by the leadership of, 241, 243–45; and disintegration of the PSD in 1946–47, 241–45; and the election of 1946, 173; and the FEDENAL strike of 1945, 106; and fight with Gaitanistas for control of the CTC, 169–70, 307–8n.54; and frictions with Gaitán expressed by Torres Giraldo, 63; and the Gaitanista base of many labor unions, 170; as Gaitanistas, 72, 219, 241–445; Gaitán's legal expertise called on by, 136; organizing in the coffee country, 72; as the Partido Comunista, 60–61; as the Partido Socialista Democrático (PSD), 95; and the problem of seeing them as the extent of the left, 316n.16; and the reforms of 1936, 91; relations of, with the Comintern, 93; relations of, with López Pumarejo and the Revolución en Marcha, 91–95, 106–7, 258; and unimpressive results of mobilization, 283n.4; and rivalry with Gaitán, 208; as the rivals of UNIR, 65, 72; spawned by the left-Liberal tradition, 51; successes of, in union organization, 94–95, 107, 290n.55; support of, for Gaitán in 1937, 99–100; and women, 114, 117. See also Gaitanismo; liberalism; socialism; UNIR

Colombian left, interconnectedness of, 41, 43, 82, 93, 209, 236, 241, 243, 316n.16. *See also* Colombian Communists; Gaitanismo; liberalism; socialism; UNIR

colonos, 16, 25, 71, 140

Comintern (Third Communist International): characterization by, of fascism as agent of capitalism, 52; popular fronts of, 53, 93, 104. *See also* Colombian Communists

Comité Gaitanista de Atlántico, 165

Comité Liberal de la Clase Media del Atlántico, 212

Comité Nacional Liberal Obrero, 62

Comité Pro-Candidatura Gaitán, 170

Committee of Middle-Class Action, 132

communism, 28; and liberals labeled communist, 39, 43, 69, 71, 92, 209, 241. *See also* Comintern; Colombian Communists; liberalism; Gaitanismo

Communist Party. *See* Colombian Communists; communism

Comunero rebellion, 20–21, 25

Conde Ribón, J. M., 69

Confederación de Trabajadores Colombianos (CTC—Confederation of Colombian Workers), 94, 106, 136, 140, 169–70, 241–42, 244, 251–52, 326n.70

Confederación Nacional de Empleados, 62

Confederación Nacional de Trabajadores, 307–8n.54

Confederación Sindical de Colombia, 100–101

congressional elections of March 1947. *See* Gaitanismo

Conniff, Michael, 272n.5

Conservative Hegemony, 26, 62, 86, 177–78, 180, 191

Conservative party, 2, 8, 11, 20–21, 24, 27, 32–33, 36–38, 44, 47, 61, 70–71, 83, 86–87, 92–94, 96–97, 99–102, 104, 114, 123, 139, 160–61, 168, 171–74, 176, 178, 185, 188, 192, 197, 203–4, 212–13, 226, 233–35, 237, 239, 243–45, 250, 252, 254–57, 263, 265, 268–69

Constant, Benjamin, 28–29

Constitution: of 1853, 31, 178; of 1886, 22, 26, 90, 178, 309–10n.99; of 1936, 90, 159, 174, 178, 201

Consuegra, Néstor Carlos, 198–200, 247

contrachusmas, 266

Córdoba, Diego Luís, 121, 285n.49

Córdoba, José María, 115, 117, 139, 170, 188, 190–91, 198, 206, 209, 215, 217–18, 227, 250, 319n.64

Cordobismo. *See* Córdoba, Diego Luís

Coromoro, 184

Corozal, 184

El Correo (Medellín), 166

Corrigan, Philip, 272n.19

Córtes Poveda, Jesús María, 260

Cortés Vargas, Carlos, 61, 79–80

costeños, 16, 122

Coyaima, 251

El Crisol (Cali), 40, 44, 285n.53

El Crisol (Ibagué), 283n.7

Critical Theory: as understood by the "Frankfurt School," 272n.15

Las Cruces, 46

Cruz, Pedro Elieso, *157*, 260

Cúcuta, 39, 163, 174, 235, 238–39, 248

Cundinamarca, department of, 16, 19, 48, 66–67, 72–73, 78–81, 96–98, 129, 134–35, 141, 174, 208, 260

Daitsman, Andrew, 29

Darrow, Clarence, 80

Davila Pumarejo, Manuel, 89

Dawson, Leonard, 188

Deas, Malcolm, 26, 38, 178

El Deber (Bucaramanga), 171

Declaration of the Rights of Man. *See* France

La Defensa (Medellín), 287n.96

Delpar, Helen, 277n.53

democracy, 1–2, 8, 10–12, 21, 23, 29–33, 37–38, 41–42, 67–68, 70, 73, 75, 87–88; 90–91, 104, 107, 111, 113, 116, 120, 129, 134, 136–37, 140, 159–63, 167, 173, 178–79, 181, 191, 194, 196–97, 200, 205–6, 209–10,

213, 215, 219, 221, 225–30, 236, 238, 240, 258, 265. *See also* liberalism; oligarchic democracy; *sociedades democráticas*
El Demócrata (Bucaramanga), 173
Deutsch, Karl, 272n.8
El Diario (Medellín), 166
Diario Nacional (Bogotá), 37, 44, 63, 80, 96–97, 129, 132, 215, 285n.53
El Diario del Pacífico (Cali), 171
Diario Popular, 107, 168, 170
Díaz, Antolín, 219–20
Díaz, Laura Victoria y Anita de, 298n.35
distributive justice. *See* social justice
Di Tella, Torcuato, 3, 273n.24
Dix, Robert, 7
Donado, José A., 198
Draconianos, 31–32. *See also* liberalism
Drake, Paul, 6, 273n.24
Duitama, 124, 140, 282n.59
Durán, Augusto, 93, 95, 168, 297n.16, 326n.64

Earle, Rebecca, 276n.26
Echandía, Darío, 103–4, 107, 131, *158*, 165, 241, 257, 294n.116, 306n.25
economic justice. *See* social justice
El Egipto, 46
Ejército de Liberación Nacional (ELN—Army of National Liberation), 268
electoral fraud. *See* gamonalismo
electoral politics, 2, 14, 20, 25–26, 42, 159, 173–74, 178–95, 197, 209, 234, 237–40, 243, 249–50, 253, 258, 268
El Empleado (Girardot), 101, 103
Engels, Friedrich, 52, 129
Enlightenment, 172, 276n.46, 308n.67
Escuela Normal, 47
Esparza G., Augusto, 193, 216
El Espectador (Bogotá), 37–38, 51, 101–2, 167, 235, 323n.7
Espinosa, Betsabé, 114
El Estado (Santa Marta), 61, 115, 122, 165, 206, 209, 211–12, 224, 227, 228, 244, 247
Europe, 27, 29, 35, 48–49, 53, 117–18, 121

false consciousness, 5
Fals Borda, Orlando, 23, 119, 175, 187, 266, 330n.14
Farnsworth-Alvear, Ann, 304n.173
fascism: characterizations of populism as, 11, 274n.32; compared and contrasted to populism, 51–54; Gaitán's attitudes toward, 53–54, 102, 169; Gaitán called a fascist, 167–68, 241, 245, 293n.108; Gaitán's supposed connections to, 51–54, 122; Laureano Gómez associated with, 172, 308n.67. *See also* Colombian Communists; Gaitán, Jorge Eliécer; Gaitanismo; populism
FEDENAL (National Federation of Maritime, River, and Port Transportation Workers), 94–95, 141–42, 242, 289n.53, 289–90n.54, 294n.134; and the strike of 1945, 106–7, 167, 307–8n.54, 313n.202
Federación de Choferes, 137
Federación Nacional de Comunicaciones, 109
Federación Sindical de Bogotá, 62
Federación Sindical del Magdalena, 91
Federation of Empleados of Valle, 133
Federation of Workers of Magdalena, 140
Feminist Union of Colombia, 115
Ferri, Enrico, 48–50, 54, 57, 72
Ferrocarril de Nariño, 255
feudalism, 52
El Fígaro (Cartagena), 194, 219
fincas, 16
Fischer, Thomas, 277n.69
Flórez, Rubén, 255
France: constitutionalism of, 43; Declaration of the Rights of Man in, 41; liberal tradition in, 28–29, 41; Revolution of 1789 in, 29–30, 43, 52, 77, 254, 276n.46; counter-revolution of 1848 in, 31, 126
French, John, 7, 273n.28
French Revolution. *See* France
Frente Nacional, 247
Fresno, 231
Fuenmayor, Raúl, 196

Fuerzas Armadas Revolucionarias de Co-
lombia (las FARC—Revolutionary
Armed Forces of Colombia), 268
Fusagasugá, 72, 79, 83, 285n.53

Gaitán, Amparo Jaramillo de, 298n.35,
305n.2
Gaitán, Eliécer, 46–47, 128
Gaitán, Gloria, 280n.1, 281n.29, 286n.80,
298n.35
Gaitán, Jorge Eliécer, 149, 151, 153, 154,
156, 157; against López's reelection,
104; almost killed in Fusagasugá, 73;
and the Army, 329n.2; assassination of,
1, 14, 188, 237, 260–62, 267; association of, with socialism, 55–60, 66, 68,
72–73, 83, 129, 168, 208, 241; association of, with Uribe Uribe and Herrera,
161, 213, 231, 257; attendance of, at
Fascist rallies, 50; attitudes of, toward
fascism, 53–54, 102, 169; authoritarian
nature of, 65–66, 73–74, 98–99, 102–3;
awarded Ferri prize, 50; and the Bogotá
drivers' strike of 1937, 97–103; and
break with liberalism, 72–81; called
both communist and fascist, 293n.108;
called a fascist by the PSD, 167–68, 241,
245; in the Cámara de Representantes,
48, 66, 68, 71, 77–78; career of, remembered and summarized, 133, 162; as a
caudillo, 76, 103, 160, 171, 177, 186–
88, 201, 230, 232, 234, 236, 251, 258,
264; as champion of the ideas of Enrico
Ferri, 48–49; charisma of, 204, 218–19,
223; as city councilman of Bogotá, 96,
108, 290n.58; clashes of, with his father,
47; Communist support in 1937 for, 99–
100; compared to former Liberal heroes,
161; compared to Gómez, 252–53; on
the connections between liberalism and
socialism, 55–56, 60; detractors on the
left of, 8, 63; divergences from and af-
finities with Marx of, 58–59, 209; dual
personality of, 55, 103; election of (to
the assembly of C/marca, 48; as president of the Liberal National Directorate,
66); and the FEDENAL strike of 1945,
313n.202; and frictions with the Communists, 63, 79, 208, 241–45, 282n.54,
285n.49; ideas about property of, 58–
59, 78–80, 71, 224–25; and impact of
his skin color ("raza"), 47, 49–50, 120–
24; as jefe único of the Liberal party, 1,
162, 233, 241; and the "JEGA,"
319n.64; as a labor lawyer, 62–64, 71,
124, 136–37, 162; and Laureano
Gómez, 168, 171–72, 308n.66; and the
left Liberals, 66–70; and the left-Liberal
tradition, 9, 46, 55, 107, 134, 230; and
the Manifestación del Silencio, 257; as
mayor of Bogotá, 95–103; and meeting
with Turbay, López, and Santos in 1946,
172; memorial service for, 158; as a
messianic figure, 230–31; as minister of
education, 108–9, 133; as minister of
Labor, 108–9, 131, 133, 137; mística of,
203; morality of, 116, 205, 225, 229–
30; movement of, compared to Revolución en Marcha, 164; obsession with
justice of, 55–59; and offer of votes for
trucks, 177; origins of, 46–48; as part of
the left-Liberal vanguard, 55, 61; and
the Plataforma del Colón, 59, 221–23;
and the political bosses (país político, la
oligarquía, the gamonales), 164–65,
169; political speaking tours of, as a
student, 48; position of, on left of mainstream liberalism, 65–66, 70, 95–96,
278n.86; public positions and offices of,
1; return(s) by, to the Liberal party, 81–
84, 246, 258; role of, in the banana
workers' strike of 1928 and its recollec-
tion, 60–62, 65, 110, 124, 133, 141,
189, 256, 295–96n.158; in the Senate,
138; split in Liberal party in 1946
caused by, 161; as a student in Colombia, 47–48; as a student in Italy, 48–50;
supposed connections of, to fascism, 51–
54, 122; as a symbol, 10, 83, 109, 210,
230–32, 258, 265; tension of, with capitalism, 10, 57–59, 221–23; ties of, to
liberalism over Marxism, 278n.75; as
"Tribune of the People," 1, 55, 73, 76,
171, 285n.53; understanding of Colom-

bian history and left-Liberal tradition of, 47; and UNIR, 65–66, 72–84; and view of thought as revealed in *Las ideas socialistas*, 56–60; and vision of the Liberal party as an interventionist party of the masses, 221–23; women and, 114–17; and his viernes culturales, 137, 214; win by, of urban vote in the election of 1946, 173. *See also* banana workers' strike of 1928; Gaitanismo; liberalism; populism; socialism; UNIR

Gaitán, Manuel, 48

Gaitán, Manuela Ayala de, 47–48, 128

Gaitanismo: and autonomous popular mobilization, 185–86; campaign posters, *149, 150*; and challenge to PSD for dominance of the CTC, 169–70; and characterization as fascism by the PSD, 167–68; charisma of, versus program in the Plataforma del Colón, 218–25, 240; class struggle in, 111–12, 229, 237, 258, 265; as a combination of resistance and hegemony, 8; and Communists as Gaitanistas, 72, 219, 241–445; compared to fascism, 11; compared to other populist movements, 8; compared unfavorably to pure working-class movements, 111; and congressional elections of March 1947, 234, 240; Conservative repression of, 252–57; and creation of openings in the oligarchic political structure, 193–97; disputed interpretations of, 8, 273–74nn.30, 31; and disrespect for elite Liberals after 1946, 237–38; and elements of controlled mobilization, 185; and endorsement of campaign by the concejo of B/quilla, 198; and Gaitanista rally at the start of the presidential campaign, *148*; and Gaitanista rally where Gaitán is pictured with Rafael Uribe Uribe and Benjamín Herrera, *151*; geographic extent of, 2, 63; as heir to the Revolución en Marcha, 232; ideology of, 9–10, 12, 111, 203–32; and infighting on the local level, 198–201, 314–15n.216; interactive development of the ideology of, 204, 213–18, 223–30; *Jornada*,

newpaper of, 215–16; and Liberal/Conservative division aspects of the pueblo/oligarquía conflict after 1946, 252, 257; as left liberalism, 2, 9, 204–5, 217, 258, 265–67, 271n.2; and Lopistas becoming Gaitanistas, 183; and mass media, 214–17; middle class in, 111–12, 124–34, 222, 230; multiclass social composition of, 9–10, 12, 75–76, 111–12, 124–34, 143, 265; nationalistic character of, 167–68; and official liberalism's resilience, 197–98; and Plataforma del Colón and Uribe Uribe, 222; and Popular Convention of 1945, 168–69; and Popular Convention of 1947, 221, 239–40; as popular mobilization, 8, 220, 233–34, 238, 251; and the presidential election of 1946, 159–202; problem of dependence on the leader within, 12, 46, 65–66, 72–75, 98, 103, 160, 185, 187–89, 195, 198–202, 218–19, 264; and problem of false Gaitanistas, 195, 234, 245–50, 253; and problems of mobilization, 187–92; and race, 10, 12, 30, 112, 117–24, 126, 142–43, 265; as radical mobilization, 124, 164, 203, 205–13, 217–18, 221, 224, 229, 264; and radio, 137, 214; and the reconquista of presidential power, 233, 240, 248, 250–53; in relation to political structures, 9, 11–12; 191–92; and state intervention, 73–74, 221–23; social justice and democracy in, 205–6, 209–10, 221–30, 236, 265; UNIR as early version of, 65–66; as an urban movement, 2, 160, 178–79, 185; violent suppression of, 2, 14, 261–63, 267; women in, 69, 74, 112–17, 223, 225–26; working class in, 111–12, 124–42, 169–70, 222, 230. *See also* democracy; Gaitán, Jorge Eliécer; liberalism; populism; popular mobilization; socialism; social justice; UNIR

Gaitanista Workers' Front, 185

Galarza, Eudoro, 260

Gamarra, 141

gamonal, synonyms for, 175

gamonalismo (boss politics), 31, 165, 169; and the case of B/quilla, 195–201; and false Gaitanistas, 245–50; and fraud, 174, 177–84, 186, 192, 225; and Gaitán defied by Santos to survive without the bosses after March 1947, 240; as a mechanism of hegemonic control, 11, 159–60, 174–84, 192–93, 195, 209, 225, 233; and the patron-client relationship, 175–80; in urban settings, 178–83. *See also* Gaitanismo; hegemony

García, Antonio, 58, 107, 227
García Caratt, Miguel, 197
García Márquez, Gabriel, 22; *Cien años de soledad (One Hundred Years of Solitude)* 33, 60
García Peña, Roberto, *156*, 278n.86
Germani, Gino, 3, 280–81n.16
Germania Brewery, 63
Germany, 28, 126, 308n.67
Getulismo, 273n.28. *See also* Vargas, Getúlio
Giacometto del Real, Carlos, 242–45
Girardot, 18, 48, 99, 101, 103, 136, 198, 227, 292n.87
Gladstone, William Ewart, 40
godo, 87, 140, 204
gold, 15, 19
Gólgotas, 31–32. *See also* liberalism
Golpe de Pasto, 315n.2
Gómez, Laureano: 100, *154*, 168, 171–72, 252, 262–63, 267, 281n.22, 308nn.66, 67
Gómez Suarez, Rogerio, 40
Gomezlandia, 177
Gracchi: Gaius Sempronius Gracchus, Tiberius Sempronius Gracchus, 55
Gramsci, Antonio, 5–6
Great Depression, 44, 51, 90
Green, T. H., 28
Guavio, 138
Guerrero, Samuel, 138, 183–84, 193–94, 211, 242
guerrilla movements, 13, 24, 255, 262, 266, 268–69

Guha, Ranajit, 5
Gusmán, Agustín, 39
Gutiérrez Sanín, Francisco, 23, 32, 128–29

Hamiltonians, 128
Hamnett, Brian, 29
hegemony, 5–6, 8, 11, 15, 20, 23, 32–33, 159–60, 174–84, 195, 203–4, 221, 229, 264, 267–69, 272nn.15, 21
Helg, Aline, 319n.62
Henderson, James, 172, 308n.67
El Heraldo (B/quilla), 83, 200, 285n.53
hereditary hatreds, 11, 20, 27, 87, 101–2, 223, 233, 252, 263, 274n.32. *See also* civil wars; Conservative party; liberalism; Liberal party
Hitler, Adolf, 168, 308n.67
Hernández Barreto, Alfonso, 198–99, 247
Hernández Rodríguez, Guillermo, 41
Herrera, Benjamín, 122, *151*; fight of, for principles and ideas, 205; Gaitán accompanied by the spirit of, 207; Gaitán a symbol of justice like, 231; idolized by liberals, 81; invoked at the popular Gaitanista convention of 1945, 169; as Liberal general in the War of a Thousand Days, 34; as Liberal presidential candidate of 1922, 34, 48; remembered as a defender of the working class, 206; on workers and liberalism, 104. *See also* liberalism
Hitler, Adolf, 168, 308n.67
Hobhouse, L. T., 278n.78
Hobsbawm, Eric, 51, 126, 132, 265, 280n.7, 281n.17
Hogar (Buenos Aires), 296n.8
Honda, 68, 142, 210, 215, 229
Horkheimer, Max, 272n.15
de la Hoz, Ramón, 242
Hugo, Victor, 30
Huila, department of, 19, 68, 80, 174, 192, 194–95
Hurst, Michael, 280–81n.16

Ibagué, 79, 139, 162–63, 170, 173, 186, 191, 193, 239, 245, 248, 253, 262

Las ideas socialistas en Colombia, 56–59, 74. *See also* Gaitán, Jorge Eliécer
import substitution industrialization, 2
industrialization, 19
Ipiales, 134, 164, 213
Italy, 48–51, 54, 308n.67

Jacobin(s), 27, 125
La Jagua de Ibirico, 207
James, Daniel, 7, 127, 273n.27, 300n.95, 322n.120
Jaramillo, Carlos Eduardo, 276n.39
Jaramillo, Hernando, 79
Jaramillo, Samuel, 254
Jaramillo Uribe, Jaime, 32, 117, 119–20
Javeriana University, 114
jefe político. See gamonalismo
Jeffersonians, 128
Jerusalem, 97
Jiménez, Michel, 286n.80, 316n.21
Jiménez Díaz, Carlos Alberto, 261
Jimeno Collante, Roberto, 247
Job, 68
Jockey Club, 121
Jornada, 115, 139, 186, 189, 191, 215–16, 225, 242, 244, 257, 260, 323n.7;
Gaitanistas in Barranquilla in, *152*; Liberal and Conservative parties as boxers in, *146*; oligarchic elections in, *154*. *See also* Gaitanismo

Katz, Friederich, 296n.2
Kazin, Michael, 128, 318n.43
Kennedy, John F., 329n.4
Kershaw, Ian, 52
King David, 75
Knight, Alan, 5–6, 116–17, 124–25, 127–28, 271n.2, 300n.84

Laclau, Ernesto, 7, 127, 221
Lamartine, Alphonse de, 30
Lanao Loaiza, Juan, 87
Latin America, 2–6, 10–11, 13, 15, 20–21, 28–29, 35, 46, 50–53, 117–18, 175, 205, 261–62
Law 200 of 1936, 90

Lebanon, 122
Lébolo de la Espriella, Emilio, 198
left liberalism. *See* liberalism; left-Liberal tradition
left Liberals, 39–40, 42, *144*, 271n.1; called communists, 39, 43, 69, 71, 92, 209, 241; and socialists, 25, 41, 68, 238
left-Liberal tradition, 2, 10–11, 12, 14–15, 27–45, 46–47, 51, 55, 66, 84, 162–63, 201, 204–7, 217, 230, 232, 264–65, 267, 269
legitimacy of the political system, 6, 8, 10, 159–60, 229, 261, 267. *See also* hegemony
LeGrand, Catherine, 286n.80, 288n.29, 289n.41
Lenin, Vladimir Ilyich, 72, 125–26, 283n.2
Leticia, 71
Leyes, Martín, 246
Líbano, 42, 188, 251
El Liberal (Bogotá), 167, 215, 235
El Liberal (Cali), 287n.96
liberalism: classical and laissez-faire, 10, 23, 27–28, 35–36, 57, 223; connections of, to the Communists, 93; conservative and/or bourgeois, 29, 38–40, 43; defined, 27; effects of, in slave holding areas, 22, 27; elite v. popular, 14, 29–33, 38; geography of left, 2, 27, 30, 33, 48, 63, 93, 121, 140; Gólgotas and Dracionianos, 31–32; individualist v. collectivist (dos corrientes), 10, 14–15, 27–28, 35, 39–40, 43–45, 55–56, 69, 76–77, 82, 88, 104, 163, 203, 207, 210, 221, 223, 229; influences of, after the wars of independence, 30; and intra-Liberal struggle, 15, 29, 32–45, 66–72, 101–2, 107, 110, 159, 172–74, 253–54, 257–59, 267; and Liberal factionalism, 38–39; and socialism, 15, 25, 34–35, 37–38, 41–43, 55–56, 60, 209, 287n.78; and Liberal regime's policies of free trade, 24, 31; Liberals v. Conservatives, 11, 20–24, 33, 36, 38, 274n.1; liberal v. Liberal, 271n.1; Lockean ideas of, 28–29; and Manchesterian Liberals

liberalism—*continued*
  (manchesterianos), 39–40, 44; modern,
  39–41, 43; patricians v. plebeians, 32–
  33; race, left liberalism, and national
  identity, 117–24; and radical and subversive potential of liberal ideas, 9–10,
  14, 32–36, 37, 41–45, 206, 277n.69;
  red Liberals (liberales rojos), 32; and the
  revolutions of 1848, 30; struggles of
  right and left Liberals, 86; war Liberals
  v. peace Liberals, 33; women and the
  Liberal left, 112–17; young Liberals and
  Marxism, 278n.75, 278n.86. *See also*
  British Liberal party; Colombian Communists; democracy; France; Gaitanismo; Liberal party
Liberal party, 2, 8, 11, 20–21, 24, 26–27,
  29–45, 47, 51, 61, 65–67, 70–72, 81–
  83, 87–88, 92–93, 96, 98, 100–102,
  104, 114, 121, 159–62, 165–66, 168–
  69, 174, 176, 178, 182–85, 192–93,
  196, 198, 203–7, 212, 219–21, 225–26,
  228, 229–31, 233–37, 240, 243–59,
  263–65, 267–69
Liberal Republic, 10, 26, 62, 85, 87–88,
  94, 180, 234, 252, 257
Lleras Camargo, Alberto, 106, *153*, 167,
  231, 240
Lleras Restrepo, Carlos, *158*, 163–65, 240,
  306n.25
Long, Gary, 121, 123, 136
López, Alejandro, 87
López, José Hilario, 30–31
López de Mesa, Luís, 297n.16, 119
López Gaviria, Humberto, 108–9
López Giraldo, Fermín, 81, 83, 168, 246
López P., Abel Ricardo, 301n.118
López Pumarejo, Alfonso, 34–36, 131,
  135, *145*, *147*, 170, 172, 188–89, 194,
  255, 257–58, 292n.87, 308n.66; after
  March 1947, 240; associated with
  Gaitán, 84; and the banana workers,
  89; and the Communists, 91–95, 163,
  243, 258; compared to Gaitán regarding
  charisma, 218; constitutional reform
  under, 90, 159, 174, 178; coup attempt
  against, 105–6, 315n.2; declared a pause
  in his revolution, 103; expectations focused on, 88; follower of (Lopista), 41,
  85; foresaw the end of the Conservative
  Hegemony, 86; and Gaitán as mayor of
  Bogotá, 96, 98; idealized by popular
  Liberals, 105; identified as the high-
  water mark of Liberal radicalism,
  295n.138; interpretations of his Revolución, 90–92; new popular Liberal attitudes of, 89; popular disillusion over,
  105–6, 110, 162, 187, 296n.159; reelection in 1942, 104–5; reform movement
  of, 2, 85; relationship between Lopistas
  and Gaitanistas, 85–86; withdrawal
  from the presidency, 106; and women,
  113, 115, 117, 296n.8; and the working
  class, 91–92, 94–95; revolution of, compared to revolution of Gaitán, 164. *See
  also* Revolución en Marcha
Lopismo. *See* López Pumarejo, Alfonso
Louis XIV, 248
Lourdes, 138
Lozano y Lozano, Carlos, *147*
Lozano y Lozano, Juan, 99, 101, 163–64,
  166
La Lucha (Sincelejo), 285n.53
Luna, Lola, 114
Luruace, 313–14n.204

M-19, 268
Maceo, 182
Magdalena, department of, 18–19, 26, 41,
  60, 89, 93, 123, 130, 140, 165, 170,
  174, 180, 187, 205, 207–8, 212, 223,
  226, 231, 237–38, 241–42, 247–49,
  295–96n.158, 297n.27, 323n.7,
  324n.16
Magdalena River, 2, 18–19, 27, 61, 63,
  93–95, 133, 137, 141–42, 195, 208,
  243
Mahecha C., Raúl Eduardo, 72
Malambo, 311–12n.156
Mallon, Florencia, 6, 23, 271n.2, 272n.21
Manatí, 313–14n.204
manchesterianos. *See* liberalism

Manchester School. *See* British Liberal party; liberalism

Manifestación del Silencio, *155*, 257. *See also* Gaitán, Jorge Eliécer

Manifiesto of Unirismo, 74. *See also* UNIR

Manizales, 101, 133, 138, 164, 226

Manotas, Roberto, 196

Mar, José, 220, 278n.86, 297n.16

Marcuse, Herbert, 272n.15

Marshall, George C., 260

Martín Blanco, Claudio, 200

Marulanda, Elsy, 286n.80

Marx, Karl: compared to Uribe Uribe, 34; and the fixed ideas of the past, 203; and interpretation of Bonapartism, 52; and interpretations of class, 9, 126; Marxist phrases, 44; on material and class bases of domination in *The German Ideology*, 5; and observation about humans making history, 264; and Proudhon, 316–17n.22; and view of the middle class vis-à-vis the working class, 125, 300n.86; young Liberals and Marxism, 278n.75

Medellín, 16, 18–19, 38, 63, 67, 78–80, 97, 100, 104, 133–34, 137, 139, 174, 181–82, 186, 246, 275n.22, 296n.1, 314–15n.216

Medina, Medófilo, 65, 219, 283n.2, 289n.41, 308n.55, 314n.207

Melo, José María, 24, 31

Mendoza Neira, Plinio, *156*, 240, 260–61

Merchán, Víctor J., *158*

Merino, Nelly, 296n.8

mestizaje, 117–20

Meta, intendancy of, 174

Mexican Revolution, 296n.2

Mexico, 7–8, 21, 23, 29, 71, 107, 117–18, 135

Mill, John Stuart, 35, 40

Ministry of Education, 48

Miramón, Alberto, 307n.36

El Mitín (Cartagena), 192, 241

Moisés, Elías, 197–200, 246

Molina, Gerardo, 30–31, 35, 38, 56–57, 59–60, 96

Molina Rojas, Hector, 326n.64

Molinares, Rafael U., 198

Mompós, 30, 207, 231, 248

Monatas Wilches, Edgardo, 200

Montaña Cuéllar, Diego, 243–44

Montería, 116, 250

Montoya Mazo, Froilán, 181–83, 314–15n.216

Moore, Barrington, 52

Moreno, Carlos J., 246, 306n.25

Morroa, 224

Moscow, 61, 72, 168

Municipal Theater. *See* Teatro Municipal

Mussolini, Benito, 50, 54, 73, 168, 308n.67

El Nacional (B/quilla), 166–67, 188, 322n.130

Nariño, department of, 68, 134, 137, 170, 191, 211, 226, 231, 255, 276n.46

National Federation of Empleados, 133

National Front, 262, 267

nationalism: Liberal/Conservative v. Communist/Fascist, 167–68; and national character of Gaitanismo, 167–68; and national identity and race, 117–24. *See also* Colombian Communists; Gaitanismo; liberalism

Navarro, Antonio, 250

Nazism (German National Socialism): fear of Nazi submarines, 242; Laureano Gómez associated with, 172, 308n.67; in relation to fascism, 52–53

Nehemiah, 97

Neiva, 18, 30, 40, 68, 83–84, 173, 180, 192, 198

New Deal, 90

New Granada (Nueva Granada), 20–21, 119, 296n.4

New York, 240

Norte de Santander, department of, 16, 19, 80, 186

nueve de abril, 1

Nugent, Daniel, 4

Núñez, Rafael (historian), 42

Obando, José María, 161

Octavio C., Eduardo, 242

Olaya Herrera, Enrique, 66, 70, 86, 207
oligarchic democracy, 1, 8, 11, 21–22, 90,
    111, 159, 174–84, 233–41, 245–53,
    264–65, 267, 325n.41. *See also* democ-
    racy; gamonalismo
oligarquía, 8, 10, 11–12, 21, 50, 76, 90–
    91, 111–12, 122–23, 130–31, 162–65,
    167–69, 175, 177–78, 181, 186, 189,
    191, 193–94, 199, 208, 210, 212–15,
    221, 225, 227, 230–31, 234, 236–37,
    240, 242, 245–46, 252–53, 263, 265,
    267–69, 294n.116
La Opinión (Ibagué), 230
Oquist, Paul, 38, 266
Oriente (Bucaramanga), 292n.87
Ortega Amarís, Julio, 193, 238
Ortiz Sarmiento, Carlos Miguel, 176–77,
    180
Orwell, George, 315–16n.7
Osorio Lizarazo, José Antonio, 55, 87,
    206, 209
Ospina Londoño, Jorge, 314–15n.216
Ospina Pérez, Mariano, *152*, 172, 174,
    209, 223, 257, 260, 262; as winner of
    the election of 1946, 173
Ottoman Turkish empire, 122
Owensby, Brian, 300n.87

Pacific coast, 27, 121
Padilla, Jorge, 260
páis político/páis nacional, 10, 112, 125,
    164–65, 186, 194, 218, 220, 225, 247
pájaros, 264, 266
Palacios, Marco, 17, 35, 93, 126, 207–8,
    273–74n.31
Palestina, 83, 192
Palmar, 313–14n.204
Palmira, 138
Palonegro, Battle of, 24
Pan American Conference (IX), 260
Panamá, 25
Paris, 50, 240
Parker, D. S., 300n.87
Parra S., Efraín, 254
Parsons, James, 119
Partido Liberal Izquierdista, 211

Partido Socialista Democrático (PSD—
    Democratic Socialist Party). *See* Colom-
    bian Communists
Partido Socialista Revolucionario (PSR—
    Revolutionary Socialist Party), 25–26,
    60, 282n.54
Pasto, 67, 129, 191, 193, 216, 230, 235,
    256
Paz de Río, 140, 236
Pécaut, Daniel, 125, 171–72, 236, 245,
    251–52, 263–64, 273n.30, 274n.1,
    283n.3, 288n.29, 289n.41, 291n.75,
    308n.55, 326n.70; *Política y sindi-
    calismo en Colombia*, 134; *Orden y
    violencia*, 134
Peña, Luís David, 227
Pereira, 75–76, 80, 83, 99, 138–39
Perón, Juan Domingo, 46, 51, 54
Peronism, 7, 127, 273n.27, 300n.95,
    322n.120
Peru, 20, 23, 71, 117, 300n.87, 301n.118
Pinochet, Augusto, 126
Piojó, 313–14n.204
Plan Gaitán, 221
Plataforma del Colón, 59, 221. *See also*
    Gaitán, Jorge Eliécer; Gaitanismo; liber-
    alism
Platform of Action for UNIR, 65, 74. *See
    also* UNIR
Plaza de Bolívar, 100, 109, 257
Pluma Libre (Pereira), 83, 99, 101, 109, 206
political violence. *See* civil wars; Gaitán,
    Jorge Eliécer; Gaitanismo; gamonalismo;
    liberalism; UNIR; La Violencia
Polonuevo, 311–12n.156, 313–14n.204
Ponce, Rodolfo, 216
Popayán, 22, 39, 41, 67–68, 119, 137,
    174, 183, 232
popular conservatism, 276n.46
Popular Liberal Conventions of 1945 and
    1947. *See* Gaitanismo
popular liberalism, 29, 271n.1. *See also*
    liberalism
popular mobilization, 23, 26–27, 32, 42,
    45–46, 68, 72, 74, 177–79, 185–87,
    190, 201, 238, 264, 268–69

populism: as agency and resistance, 4–5, 6–7; dual nature of, 6–7, 185, 204, 221, 273n.27, 273n.28; charismatic personalism in, 46, 21–19; compared to caudillismo, 2, 271–72n.3; compared to fascism, 51–54, 167; in connection to import-substitution industrialization, 2; as co-optation or demobilization, 3–4, 6–7, 13, 208, 273n.27; interpretations of, 2–4; interpretive conundrum of the multiclass social composition of, 127–28; as leadership, 3, 8, 218–19; programs of, 220–21; relation to hegemony, 6–8; relation to modernization theory, 3, 272n.6; as social control, 3–4, 7; unfavorable comparisons of, to pure working-class movements, 111. *See also* Gaitanismo; hegemony

Posada, Jaime, *158*

Posada-Carbó, Eduardo, 26, 38, 177–78, 180–81, 191, 253, 275n.13, 282n.47

Prakash, Gyan, 271n.2

La Prensa (B/quilla), 83, 285n.53

presidential election of 1946. *See* Gaitanismo

Prieto, Moisés, 278n.86

Proceso Gaitán, 329n.4

Protesta Liberal (B/quilla), 216

Proudhon, Pierre Joseph, 316–17n.22

La Perseverancia, 290n.69

La Providencia, 108, 138

el pueblo, 1, 10, 12

Puentes, Milton, 161, 229

Puerto Berrío, 142

Puerto Colombia, 19

Puerto Wilches, 61

Pumarejo, Alberto, 196–97, 200, 246

Quibdó, 173

Quimbaya, 254

Quindío region, 16

quinine, 15

El Radio (Pasto), 308n.69

Radio Barranquilla, 214

Ramírez Moreno, Augusto, 297n.16

Rangel, Adriano, 139, 198, 246–47

Rausch, Jane, 274n.4, 289n.41

La Razón (Bogotá), 115, 166, 235, 323n.7

Reagan Democrats, 126

Rebolo, 212, 216

reconquista. *See* Gaitanismo

Red Taxis, 63

regions of Colombia, 2, 15–19, 48, 274n.4; early geography of Liberal and Conservative tendencies, 22; elite distance from the pueblo, 134; geography of race, 119; regionalism, 19; of La Violencia, 266; variations of Gaitanista influence in conservative regions, 140. *See also* Gaitanismo; liberalism

Relator (Cali), 101–3, 173, 285n.53

Repelón, 313–14n.204

resistance. *See* agency

Restrepo, Martín, 79

Restrepo Botero, Dr., 314–15n.216

Revolución en Marcha: as both social change through reform, and as co-optation and subversion of popular mobilization, 85–86, 221; constitutional reform during, 90, 159, 174, 178; interpretations of, 90–92, 257; and the Communists, 91–95; compared to Gaitanismo, 165; as controlled mobilization, 185; heightened expectations created by, 86, 110, 193; Gaitán as the hope of fulling the promise of, 142, 265; pause in, declared by López, 103; in the popular imagination, 105; and Uribe Uribe, 221; and the working class, 91–92. *See also* López Pumarejo, Alfonso; liberalism; Gaitán, Jorge Eliécer; Gaitanismo

Revolution of 1776, 29, 276n.46

Revolutions of 1848, 29–31, 276n.46

Rey, Carlos V., 104

Ribeiro, Darcy, 298n.43

Ribeiro de Andrada, Antonio Carlos, 4

Rincones Ponce, Dionisio, 69, 165, 170, 231, 246, 249

Rio de Janeiro, 300n.87

Riohacha, 227

Rionegro (Antioquia), 314–15n.216

Rionegro (Santander), 67
Roa Sierra, Juan, 261, 329n.4
Robinson, J. Cordell, 36, 273n.30
Rojas Ospina, Hernando, 314–15n.216
Rojas Pinilla, Gustavo, 262, 267
Roldán, Mary Jean, 176, 263, 274–75n.11, 302n.139, 304n.173, 309n.78, 310n.111, 330n.9
Rome, 49, 51, 54, 78; the Republic v. the Empire, 55
Romero Aguirre, Alfonso, 121
Roosevelt, Franklin Delano, 93
Roseberry, William, 6
Rousseau, Jean-Jacques, 27–29
Royal University, 49
Russia, 100
Russo, José G., 216, 242

Sábado (Bogotá), 115
Saboyá, 235
Sáenz, Eduardo, 296n.1
Safford, Frank, 22, 118
Salazar Campuzano, Arturo, 192
Salcedo, Ernesto, 198
Samper, Darío, 66–67, 96, 283n.7
San Bernardo, 183
San Bernardo del Viento, 248
Sánchez, Gonzalo, 110, 132, 190, 236, 245, 262–63, 266, 273n.30, 312n.172
San Gil, 254, 256
San José, 191
San Marcos, 319–20n.74
Santa Marta, 26, 30, 43, 61–62, 69, 80, 82–83, 89, 92, 105, 107, 109, 114, 116, 122, 130, 165, 170, 173, 189, 193, 210–11, 215–16, 223–24, 228, 234, 238, 242
Santa Rosa de Caldas, 83
Santander, department of, 16, 19, 39, 80, 184, 209, 254–56
Santander, Francisco de Paula, 21, 70, 207
Santander León y B., 198–99, 247
Santos, Eduardo, 101, 103–4, 165–66, 172, 189, 231, 238, 240, 257, 289–90n.54, 294n.116
Santos, Enrique. See Calibán

Santos Cabrera, José, 248
Santo Tomás, 197, 311–12n.156, 313–14n.204
São Paulo, 300n.87
Satan, 38
Sauer, Wolfgang, 280–81n.16
Sayer, Derek, 272n.19
Scott, James, 4–6, 315n.6
Sering, Paul, 280–81n.16
Sevilla, 170
Sharpless, Richard, 36, 56, 62, 65, 74, 128, 187, 218–20, 236, 273n.30, 278nn.75, 86, 283n.2, 303n.75, 305n.2, 307n.36
sicarios, 264
El Siglo (Bogotá), 100, 168, 171, 308n.67
Sincelejo, 87, 193
El Sindicalista (Cartagena), 132
Sindicato Central Nacional de Choferes, 99
Sindicato de Choferes de Taxis Rojos, 291n.73
Smith, Adam, 35
Smith, Lynn T., 119
socialism, 15, 25, 28, 31–32, 34–35, 37–38, 41, 43, 55–60, 65, 68, 205–6, 225, 229, 287n.96, 316–17n.22. See also liberalism; Gaitanismo; UNIR
social justice, 7, 10, 12, 30, 34, 40–43, 55–59, 67, 72–73, 75, 88, 92, 107, 205, 220–30, 235–36; as distributive justice, 44–45, 80, 82, 104, 111, 161, 226–28, 265. See also liberalism
sociedades democráticas, 30, 32, 179. See also artisans
Socorro, 20, 33n.69
Socotá, 140
Solano, Armando, 37–38, 43, 82
Solano, Gustavo, 325n.52
Sonora (Mexican state of), 7
Soto del Corral, Jorge, 297n.16
Soviets, 167
Sowell, David, 32
Spain, 28, 122
Spencer, Herbert, 35
Stalin, Joseph, 93

Station of the Sabana, 287n.96
Stein, Steve, 4
Stoller, Richard, 33, 35, 91, 277n.69, 295n.138
Suan, 237, 313–14n.204
subaltern: concepts of class, 9–10; classes, 30, 112; joining in the struggles of their leaders, 23; studies, 5, 9; syndicalism, 28
Sue, Eugène, 30

Tamara, Carlos, 247
Tammany Hall, 179
Tasca, 140
Tasco, 140
Tatis, Ligie, 314n.205
Teatro Colón (Bogotá), 165, 221, 237, 240, 325n.41
Teatro Municipal (Bogotá), 34–35, 164, 172, 230
Tejada, Luís, 55–56, 278n.86
Téllez, Hernando, 235
Thatcherite workers, 126
Third Communist International (Third International). See Comintern
Third National Congress of Workers, 92
Thompson, E. P., 127
Thomson, Guy, 29
El Tiempo (Bogotá), 37–38, 70–72, 101, 108, 115, 129, 140, 166, 183, 215, 235, 323n.7
Tirado Mejía, Alvaro, 23, 32, 90
Tiriribí, 182
tobacco, 15, 20, 113
Todamerica, 80
Tolima, department of, 19, 48, 66, 68, 78, 80–81, 88, 130, 135–36, 163, 170, 183, 186, 189, 208, 227, 231, 248, 266
El Tolima, 78–80, 83, 89
Toro, 34, 91
Torres Barreto, Germán, 248
Torres Giraldo, Ignacio, 61, 63–64, 307n.44. See also Colombian Communists
Tribiño Sáenz, Eduardo, 191
La Tribuna (B/quilla), 93, 131, 216, 225, 229, 231

Tubará, 313–14n.204
Tulio Salgado, Marco, 41
Tuluá, 256
Tumaco, 136, 183, 226, 231
Tunja, 114, 245, 250
Túpac Amaru, 20
Turbay, Gabriel, 131, 147, 163, 173, 193, 196, 198, 209, 237, 242, 245, 249, 254, 278n.86, 306n.25; background of, 166; meetings with Gaitán in 1946, 172; and the question of race, 122–23; rude plays on the name of, 186; selected as the official candidate of the Liberal party in 1945, 165
Tweed, Boss, 179

La Unión, 68
Union of Industrials and Workers, 25
Union of Pilots and Navigators of Barranquilla, 140
Union of Various Professions, 170
UNIR, Unión Nacional Izquierdista Revolucionaria (Revolutionary Leftist National Union), also called Unirismo, 87, 98, 102, 104, 162, 191, 209, 222, 234, 246, 258, 285n.51; agenda of, highjacked by the Liberal party, 82, 85, 92; compared to, or contrasted with, communism, 71, 75, 79; connections to the Violencia of, 266; emblem of, 145; founded, 72–73; interpretations of, 65–66, 73–74, 283n.3; as leftist pressure on liberalism, 75; as left liberalism, 66; and questions of land and property, 78–80; as rural movement compared to more urban Gaitanismo, 160; and state intervention, 73–74; social composition of, 75–76; as socialism, 65, 73, 77; and struggles with Communists, 81; urban, 80–81; and violent clashes, 73, 78–80, 83, 285n.53; women in, 74, 115. See also Gaitán, Jorge Eliécer; Gaitanismo; liberalism; populism; socialism
Unirismo, 66, 74, 76, 80, 285n.60. See also UNIR

United Fruit Company, 26, 60, 89. *See also* banana workers' strike of 1928

United States of America, 41, 89, 93–94, 96, 105, 107, 126, 128, 188, 200, 214, 216, 241, 243, 290n.55

Universidad Nacional, 47

University Center for Cultural Propaganda, 48

urbanization, 19, 275n.22

Uribe de Acosta, Ofelia, 114, 205

Uribe Márquez, Jorge, 251

Uribe Uribe, Rafael, *144, 151*; compared to Marx, 34; concept of "socialism of the state," 10, 34–35; contrasted with Napoleon, 34; fight of, for principles and ideas, 205; Gaitán accompanied by the spirit of, 207; Gaitán a symbol of justice like, 231; and idea of liberalism drinking at the fount of socialism, 34, 206–7, 228; ideas alluded to, 38, 40–41, 44, 55–57, 69–71, 82, 133, 206–7, 222, 228, 230, 257; idolized by Liberals, 81; invoked at the popular Gaitanista convention of 1945, 169; left interpretation of liberalism, 14, 37, 257; as Liberal general in the War of a Thousand Days, 34, 213; Liberals marked the anniversary of the assassination of, 206; parallels to L. T. Hobhouse of, 278n.78; remembered as a defender of the working class, 206; veterans of army of, salute Gaitán, 133. *See also* Gaitán, Jorge Eliécer; liberalism; socialism

Urdaneta, Roberto, *154*

Usiacurí, 186, 196, 313–14n.204

Valdelamar, Juan Manuel, 130, 167, 170, 187, 189, 203, 241–43, 308n.55

Valencia, Guillermo, 47

del Valle, Agustín, 198

Valle de Cauca, department of, 19, 21, 48, 62–63, 80, 121, 135, 174, 208, 238, 266

Vallejo, Alejandro, 260, 278n.86

Vanguardia, 165, 216, 226

Vanguardia Liberal (Bucaramanga), 166, 285n.53

Vanguardia Obrera, 72

Vargas, Antonio, 183

Vargas, Francisco de Paula (Pacho), 194, 248

Vargas, Getúlio, 7, 46, 51

Vasconcelos, José, 118

Del Vecchio R., Pascual, *151, 153*, 317n.33

Vega Cantor, Renán, 273–74n.31

Velasco Ibarra, José María, 46

Velásquez Toro, Magdala, 113

Vélez (of Nueva Granada), 296n.4

Vélez Micola, Julio, 211

Venecia, 182

Venezuela, 11, 21, 93

del Vidal, Carmen, 254

Vieira, Gilberto, 243–44, 292n.87

viernes culturales. *See* Gaitán, Jorge Eliécer

Villa de Leiva, 134, 239

Villanueva Ortega, Tomás, 196

Villarreal, Norma, 297n.17

Villismo, 296n.2

La Violencia: Colombia known as a violent country because of, 261–62; connections to recent violence of, 267–69; degree of allegiance to the traditional parties during, 11, 266; and Gaitanismo, 261–67; interpretations of, 262–63; as a period of armed struggle, 8, 262; Gaitanistas on the nueve de abril, *156, 157, 158*; political context at the beginning of, 213; political origins of, 261–66; precursor of (known as the "Liberal Violencia"), 255–56; rising level of, before and after the presidential election of 1946, 250, 252–57, 328n.116

Viotá, 208, 316n.21

Victor Emanuel, King of Italy, 50

Virgin of Carmen, 261

Vives, José B., 249

Wade, Peter, 120

War of a Thousand Days (1899–1902), 24–26, 34, 213
War of 1853, 24
Warren Commission, 329n.4
wars for independence, 20–21, 30
Washington, D.C., 240
Weber, Eugen, 52–53

Weffort, Francisco, 3, 273n.24
western cordillera, 16
Wolfe, Joel, 296n.7
Worker Union of Colombia, 25
World War I, 25, 51, 54, 274n.32

Zapata Olivella, Antonio, 248

W. John Green has published widely on twentieth-century Colombian history in *Hispanic American Historical Review*, *Latin American Research Review*, *The Americas*, *Historia Critica*, and the *Anuario Colombiano de la Historia Social y de la Cultura*, as well as other journals and collections in Colombia, the United States, and Germany.

www.ingramcontent.com/pod-product-compliance
Lightning Source LLC
Chambersburg PA
CBHW020602270326
41927CB00005B/136